The Standard Cata
Hard Times Tokens

The most complete catalog ever assembled of the coin
substitutes, merchant counterstamps and satirical scrip of
the Jacksonian Period, 1832-1844

Includes all Slave Tags of the South 1800-1865

Special Consultants

Q. David Bowers
Wesley S. Cox
Charles E. Kirtley
Stephen L. Tanenbaum
Steve Hayden

Gregory G. Brunk
Larry Johnson
Robert J. Merchant
Alan York
H. Joseph Levine

Published by

krause
publications

700 E. State Street • Iola, WI 54990-0001
Telephone: 715/445-2214

Library of Congress Catalog Number: 2001097898
ISBN: 0-87341-0-87349-265-X

Printed in the United States of America

PREFACE

About this Ninth Edition, now called the *Standard Catalog of Hard Times Tokens*....

The last edition of *Hard Times Tokens* as a separate volume was the Sixth, in 1996.

A Fifth edition was included in the 1st edition of the *Standard Catalog of United States Tokens 1700-1900,* released in 1994. Seventh and Eighth editions were part of the *Standard Catalog's* 2nd edition (1997) and 3rd edition (1999).

Hard Times tokens continue to be a sought-after segment of America's unofficial coinage, and demand from collectors, dealers, librarians and historians for another separate edition of their standard guide to the series has continued unabated. So this author and the publishers decided upon a sort of "super catalog," greatly expanding the coverage in ways to which the larger volume could not devote space.

In nine unpublished notebooks containing detailed photo enlargements and die-evidence studies, as well as copies of many pieces of correspondence from the 1830's and 1840's, our colleague Wesley S. Cox has kindly supplied enough evidence to decide who made many of these tokens. The notebooks are far too extensive to publish themselves, so we have extracted useful materials to exhibit to users of this reference just how decisions were made.

The information contained herein has been revised in all aspects. Each line listing has been examined and new data or corrections have been entered. All prices have been revised to reflect 2002 reality, and many new items are being published for the first time. Hard Times tokens are far from a static collecting reality; every day we learn more.

The user may feel confident that this latest version of *HTT* can be relied upon to contain all new discoveries and interpretations of data published elsewhere in the numismatic world, as well as reflecting the author's continuous monitoring of this subject.

In 1899 Lyman H. Low cataloged less than 200 varieties of Hard Times tokens, numbered from 1 through 183. Beginning in 1961 and through 1964, your author added about 100 items which Low had either overlooked or chosen to ignore because of the relatively poor state of token research at that time. Thus pseudo-Low numbers 190 upward were assigned by me in the *TAMS Journal* and in *Coin World* starting some 41 years ago.

In 1980 the First edition of *Hard Times Tokens* by your author made its appearance, and it quickly sold out, necessitating a second printing of that 1980 edition. Here is a brief history of *Hard Times Tokens* in the modern era:

First edition – 1980 (2 printings)
Second edition – 1981
Third edition – 1987
Fourth edition – 1992
Fifth edition – 1994 (bound as part of the SCUST 1700-1900)
Sixth edition – 1996
Seventh edition – 1997 (bound as part of 2nd edition of SCUST 1700-1900)
Eighth edition – 1999 (bound as part of 3rd edition of SCUST 1700-1900)
Ninth edition – 2002, now called the SCHTT

Use of the Low (1 to 183) and pseudo-Low (190 to 418) numbers had become cumbersome and illogical by the late 1980's, as all these numbers had been assigned in sequential order as new discoveries were made. Like Topsy, they just "grow'd." A complete renumbering of all Hard Times items in a logical order followed and new HT numbers alongside the Low numbers appeared in 1992 in the Fourth edition. After a century of use of Low numbering, there was some natural resistance to any change, but collectors and dealers soon began to realize the advantages of the logical numbering system and in the Fifth edition the Low numbers were simply dropped (but with a chart to convert Low numbers to HT numbers for veteran collectors whose records were kept that way).

Lyman Haynes Low listed only metallic tokens, mostly bearing dates, and only one counterstamp, the PB Nouvelle Orleans punch on cut Spanish silver. When my own cataloging of this series started in 1961, counterstamps and undated store cards which could logically be assigned to the 1832-1844 period were consistently added.

Starting with the Third edition in 1987, I also began adding bank notes with direct ties to the token issuers, as well as Hard Times satirical notes. The latter series had been almost totally ignored by the numismatic fraternity until that time, and the few specimens which had escaped the destruction of the years were invariably scarce to rare. The satirical notes assist the scholar and researcher to understand the full panoply of that remarkable period in American economic history, our first "Great Depression."

A very early discussion in Europe of the Hard Times tokens was written by Alexandre Vattemare in the 1864 volume of *Revue Numismatique* in Paris, pages 59-68 with two plates. Titled "Numismatique des Etats-Unis d'Amerique, Pieces Taractiques," it compares them to the 18th century halfpenny tokens of England, and the Revolutionary France Monneron tokens as circulating emergency money with political characteristics. Vattemare was "on target" in many of his conclusions. In the mid-19th century, numismatics was much more developed in Europe than in America.

Interest in collecting Hard Times tokens has not waned with the years. It continues to grow and prices continue to rise, especially in the higher grades of preservation.

Since 1997 *A Guide Book of United States Coins*, the annual Red Book, added a 6-page illustrated, priced section on Hard Times satirical tokens, which is introducing the series to even more collectors. Both HT and Low numbers are given, and each of the 32 basic types is valued in VF, EF and AU grades. Editor Kenneth Bressett and valuer Larry Johnson are responsible; the pricing closely mirrors our own VF and EF assessments (we do not use the AU grade, but do provide VG and Unc-MS 63 grades generally).

Red Book exposure also provides a degree of collector legitimacy to the series, such as has long been enjoyed by Colonial and Early Republic tokens.

In some ways, this Ninth edition sums up a lifetime of numismatic study for your author, a love for coins that began in the summer of 1939 and has never stopped during a military career, marriage, fatherhood, journalistic adventures and active retirement. We hope you will enjoy the end result.

Russell Rulau
Iola, Wisconsin
December, 2001

"Hard Times in 1837" (From the Library of Congress)

LOW NUMBER INDEX

This ready-finding index enables collectors who keep their holdings by Low numbers to determine its new Hard Times (HT) number.

Low No.	HT No.
1	1
1A	2
1B	3
2	4
3	5
3A	5A
4	6
4A	6A
5	7
5A	8
6	14
6A	14A
6B	14B
6C	14C
7	15
7B	15B
7C	15C
7D	15D
8	9
9	10
9B	10A
10	11
11	12
11A	12A
12	25
12A	25A
13	26
13A	26A
14	27
14A	27A
15	28
15A	28A
16	30
16A	30A
16B	30B
17	31
17B	31B
18	32
19	33
19A	33A
20	34
21	35
22	36
23	37
24	38
25	39
26	40
26A	40A
26B	40B
27	41
27A	41A
28	42
29	44
30	45
31	46
32	47
33	48
33A	48A
34	49
35	50
36	51
37	61
38	62
39	52
40	65
41	53
41A	53A
42	54
42A	54A
43	55
43A	55A
44	69
45	56
46	57
47	66
47A	66A
48	67
49	73
50	74
51	70
52	71
53	72
54	81
54A	82
54B	81A
55	63
56	75
57	76
58	16
59	17
60	18
61	19
62	20
62A	20A
62C	20B
63	21
64	22
64A	22A
65	23
66	24
67	68
68	64
69	58
70	59
70A	59A
71	60
71A	60A
72	175
72A	175A
73	176
73A	176A
74	428
74A	428A
75	152
76	153
77	348
78	427
79	361
80	157
81	200
82	123
82A	124
82B	125
82C	126
83	150
84	158
85	121
85A	121A
86	174
87	347
87A	347A
88	350
89	349
90	351
91	352
92	353
92A	354
93	355
94	425
95	291
96	292
97	293
98	294
99	216
100	217
101	218
102	187
102A	188
102B	188A
103	154
104	155
105	156
106	129
106A	129A
107	219
108	430
109	104
110	239
111	240
111A	240A
112	243
113	244
114	249
115	250
116	172
116A	172A
117	262
117A	262A
118	263
119	265
119B	266
120 vars	268
121	117
122	283
123	284
124	194
125	289
126	290
127	304
128	309
129	169
129A	169A
130	105
130A	107
130R	106
131	192-193
132	195
133	311
133B	312
134	313
135	314
136	315
137	316
138	317
139	464
140	334
141	335
142	205
143	206
144	206A
145 vars	356-358
146	359
147	360
148	204
149	413
150	202
151	272
152	412
153	305
154	306
155	204B
156	366
157	367
158	377
158A	377A
159	378
160 vars	379 vars
161	211
162	77
163	201
163A	201A
164	151-159
165	2A
166	1A
167	3A
168	13
168R	13R
169	29
169A	29A
170	43
171	70A
172	75A
172A	75B
173	139
174	347B
175	433
176	434
176A	434A
177	187A
178	187B
179A	267
180	205
180A	205A
181	399
182	399A
182A	389
183	77A
190	78
191	78A
192	79
193	79A
194	83
194A	83A
198	85
199	86
200	220
201	221
202	222
203	223
204	224
205	224A
206	226
206A	226A
207	227
208	227A
209	228
210	228A
210A	229
211	386
212	387
212A	388
213	390
214	391
215	392
216	393
217	394
218	395
219	396
220	235
221	335A
222	236
223	236A
224	237
225	237A
226	238
227	403
227A	404
228	405
229	405A
230	406
230A	406A
231	406B
232	407
233	241
234	182
235	182A
236	115
236A	115A
237	116
238A	245
238B	246
239	247
240	247A
241	248
242	255
243	256
244	257
245 vars	258-259
246	408
247	260
248	261
249	269
250	270
251	275
252	276
253	277
254	120
254A	119
254B	119A
255	278
256	279
257	282
258	282A
259	285
260	285A
261	286
262	287
262A	287A
263	288
264	122
265	163
266	164
267	165
267A	166
268	302
269	303
270	303A
271	363
272	364
272A	365
273	307
273A	307A
274	308
274A	308A
275	441
276	441A
277	441B
278	234
279	318
279A	318A
279B	319
280	320
280A	320A
281	321
282	322
282A	323
283 vars	324-325
284 vars	368-371
285	332
286	333
287	336
288	128
289	M26
290	M27
291	102
292	242
293	440
294	440A
295	273
296	273A
297	273B
298	274
300	181
301	181A
301A	181B
302	207
303	207A
304	207B
305	101
306	900
307	901A
308	902
309	902A
309A	902B
310	253
311	254
312	375
312A	375A
313 vars	376
314	162
315	110
316	110A
317	344
318	345
318A	346
319	380
320 vars	381
321	295
322	296
323	297
324	212
324A	212A
325	167
326	160 & 168
326A	161
327	170
328	171
328A	171A
329	340
330	340A
331	341
332	342
335	251
336	252
338	230
340	135
341	135A
342	136
343	137
344	118
348	210
349	210A
350 vars	231
351 vars	435
352	456
353	420
356	419
357	419A
358	418
359	418A
360	280
361	280A
362	280B
363	281
364	M17
365	339
366	M19
367 vars	M20-M22
368	M23
368A	M24
369	372
370	298
371	299
372	300
374	203
375	M9
378	132
379	133
379A	134
380	457
382	84
383	410
383A	410A
384 vars	421
385	411
386	417
386A	417A
387	215
388	215A
389	215B
392 vars	337
395 vars	327-328
396 vars	329
398	385
400 vars	140-144
403 vars	147-148
404	402
415	M1
417	271
418	416

INTRODUCTION

The series known as Hard Times tokens comprises tokens issued privately in the United States from 1832 to 1844. The pieces, mostly made of copper and the size of a United States cent of the period, can be divided into several categories:

(1) Pieces referring to the Bank of the United States and the controversy surrounding it.

(2) Those with inscriptions relating to political and satirical situations of the era.

(3) Tokens with inscriptions and designs closely resembling the regular cent coinage, but with some differences in order to evade the counterfeiting laws.

(4) Examples bearing the advertisements of private merchants - ''Store cards.''

(5) Die mulings: Combinations with the obverses or reverses of any of the preceding.

The Hard Times tokens with political motifs center on issues of the Andrew Jackson and Martin Van Buren Administrations (1829-1841).

Andrew Jackson, military hero of the Battle of New Orleans in 1815, defeated President John Quincy Adams' reelection bid in 1828. Jackson, not an educated man, was the subject of much ridicule. His ''Roman firmness'' was mentioned on tokens, as was his statement made at a Democratic banquet in April 1839: ''Our federal union must be preserved,'' or as it was sometimes quoted, ''Our federal union, it must and shall be preserved.''

In 1832 Harvard College conferred upon Jackson an honorary Doctorate of laws. This LLD degree caused much amusement. As Lyman H. Low has written, ''The judicious grieved, and his enemies rejoiced at the absurdity of the title; and it was not long before the honorary degree appeared upon a token which ridiculed him.''

On one of the most widely circulated tokens of the era, Jackson is depicted emerging from a chest of money holding a purse in one hand and a sword in the other. This was a reference to the fear, subsequently reported in the *Albany Argus* on Oct. 1, 1842, that the liberties of the Union were threatened ''by union of the purse and the sword in the same hands,'' a reference in this in-

stance to the following administration of Martin Van Buren. Presidential power over the nation's money and military has been the subject for concern at intermittent intervals since that time.

In 1832 Jackson campaigned against Henry Clay. The president's stand against the Second Bank of the United States struck a popular chord and resulted in an overwhelming victory for him. In order to lessen the effectiveness of the Bank, which was chartered to continue until 1836, Jackson removed federal deposits from it and placed them in state banks. This and his July 1836 Specie Circular were among the causes of the nationwide financial panic of 1837 and the consequent depression.

In May 1836 Martin Van Buren, Jackson's vice president, was nominated for the presidency. His platform included opposition to rechartering the Bank of the United States. During his administration the main problem concerned the nation's depressed economy. Van Buren urged that an independent Treasury be established apart from the United States government and that the Treasury surplus not be distributed to the states.

His stand on this and other issues alienated many conservative Democrats and at the same time caused him to be denounced by the Whigs.

In his inaugural address Van Buren declared, ''I follow in the steps of my illustrious predecessor,'' a reference to Jackson. Caricaturists of the time represented the newly-elected president carefully stepping in the footprints of a jackass, a sentiment which extended itself to certain tokens of the time. Seeking reelection, he was defeated overwhelmingly by William Henry Harrison in the 1840 election campaign.

Damaged by the wild issue of bank paper money in the West, and excessive speculation in the public lands, President Jackson put a stop to it - so drastically that the country plunged from inflation into disaster just weeks after Van Buren's inauguration.

On July 11, 1836 Jackson issued the Specie Circular, declaring that deposit banks and receivers of public money could accept nothing but gold or silver coin for the sale of public lands after Aug. 15. Jackson hoped this move would halt the ruinous

Whig political satire note of 1837 for 6 cents depicts six Jackson ''cents'' and a number of other symbols associated with his presidency - donkey, hickory leaf, tall hat and spectacles, and peace pipe. It was supposedly issued by the Humbug Glory Bank. Hundreds of parody bank notes were printed with quotes from Benton and Van Buren, this one borrowing from Daniel Webster's plaint, ''The gold humbug exploded.''

speculation in public lands and curb the rampant inflation. The results proved destructive in practice, and in timing.

The result was to drain much of the gold westward. Consternation reigned in the East. Loans were called. In March 1837 a panic in England caused American shock waves - three great cotton firms in New Orleans went bankrupt; 128 companies in New York went under by April, including 100 banks!

In May a run on the nation's banks started and they suspended specie (coin) payments on May 10. By that summer, 90 percent of Eastern factories had shut down. Many people starved and froze in the winter of 1837-1838.

The Panic of 1837 resulted in hoarding of coins in circulation. This period is generally referred to as the Era of Hard Times, the title of which was later adapted to include tokens of the wider 1832-1844 period.

To fill the need for small change in circulation, a wide variety of copper tokens appeared in 1837. One issue bore the legend SUBSTITUTE FOR SHIN PLASTERS, a reference to the flood of often worthless paper money issues distributed by banks, merchants, canals, turnpikes and others, which were called Shinplasters and which had backing no stronger than the financial credit of the issuer, which was sometimes nil.

Important among the minters of Hard Times tokens was the firm of J.(ames) M.(itchell) L.(amson) & W.(illiam) H.(enry) Scovill, of Waterbury, Connecticut, claiming beginnings in 1802. This firm and its successors have a rich numismatic history. In 1862 Scovill produced encased postage stamps. Later the firm supplied planchets to the United States Mint for the production of nickel alloy coins, and it made Depression scrip in 1933. The Scovill Manufacturing Company is still in business today, though it sold off its brass works in the late 1970's.

Our friend and contributor H. Joseph Levine has come into Scovill Mfg. Co. correspondence which shows conclusively that certain tokens can be dated back to 1835, as that is when Scovill struck them for the merchants involved.

These are: James Watson, Philadelphia, HT 422; Stickney & Wilson, Montgomery, Ala., and Kohn Daron & Co., New Orleans. These valuable records enable us to confirm what research had begun to indicate - that all three issuers were Hard Times era people.

In Attleboro, Massachusetts, the firm of H.M. & E.I. Richards, controlled by two cousins, Herve Manning Richards and Edmund Ira Richards, spurred a wide variety of Hard Times tokens. Another Attleboro firm built around the Robinson Brothers and Jones struck many of them.

A succession of firms built around James Bale operated to produce Hard Times merchant cards from 1829 through 1838 or later. Charles Cushing Wright, the great early American medalist, and Bale were in partnership in New York City from May 1829 to late 1833. Bale then was in business alone 1833-1835, and Bale and F.B. Smith were in business as Bale & Smith 1835-1838. The signatures of these combinations - W & B NY, BALE, B & S NY, etc. - are found on cards of Atwood's Railroad Hotel, Bale & Smith, J. & L. Brewster, Doremus Suydam & Nixon, P. Evens, Nathan C. Folger, Hiram Judson, and others.

In Belleville, New Jersey, John Gibbs was a senior partner of Gibbs, Gardner & Co. His business was located in a building on the same premises as Stevens, Thomas & Fuller, a company which produced dies or struck minor coins for Brazil, Liberia, Santo Domingo and various private merchants. Stevens had earlier obtained his training in Birmingham, England. The combined coining facility became known as the Belleville Mint.

Many different pieces associated with the Hard Times token series, including some bearing the NOT ONE CENT reverse, were made there. Similar sized copper tokens known as Bou-

quet Sous were made at Belleville for circulation in Canada. The floral bouquet design was used in one instance as reverse for a token issued by William Gibbs, father of John Gibbs, who proclaimed himself an "agriculturist."

In one sense, the production of Hard Times tokens and store cards was an expansion of the aggressive button-making trade in Attleborough, Mass. and Waterbury, Conn. The Attleborough (now Attleboro) firms of Robinsons, Jones & Co. and its successor, R. & W. Robinson, struck many of the pieces. The Waterbury firm of Benedict & Burnham also made some tokens.

In New York City, James G. Moffet, Robert B. Ruggles and Robert Lovett Sr. also competed for token business.

Low described 183 different types of tokens from the 1832-1844 period. These tokens, mostly the size of the contemporary U.S. large cent, circulated freely at the value of one cent. A profit was shown by the issuers who paid less than face value for them.

Eugene H. Richards, a descendant of one of the founders of H.M. & E.I. Richards, informed Low that the token distribution firm shipped pieces by the thousands in kegs to customers at 60 to 75 cents per hundred.

A token issued by Clark & Anthony (HT 425) was struck to the number of 36,000 pieces, for which the jewelry firm paid Richards $270.

The number of well worn Hard Times tokens in existence today is abundant proof of the status which these pieces once enjoyed as a circulating medium of exchange. By 1857, when the Large cents were replaced by small Flying Eagle cents, scattered examples were still to be seen in commercial channels.

SECOND BANK OF THE UNITED STATES

Alexander Hamilton's creation, the (First) Bank of the United States, was chartered in 1792 and expired in 1812. The Second Bank was chartered in April 1816 for 20 years. The federal government had a large interest in it as a shareholder and as a director. Both these measures were opposed by the Democratic Republican Party, which dropped the "Republican" part of their title a few years later and called themselves Democrats, but were stigmatized by their opponents as "Loco-Focos" - a name given them in consequence of an occurrence at an 1835 political gathering of Democrats in New York, when their adversaries attempted to break up the meeting by extinguishing the gas lights.

Some of the company present came prepared with "Locofoco matches" and candles in their pockets and they relighted the room, and continued the meeting.

In 1834 the National Republicans began to call themselves Whigs, because they considered Jackson as a kind of tyrant whom they opposed just as Whigs of an earlier time had opposed King George III, and the new party name will be found on some of the tokens.

Jackson believed the Bank operated to benefit the rich, and that it used public funds deposited with it to benefit special interest groups. Jackson's men charged that in the election of 1828 several branches used their funds to defeat Jackson.

Nicholas Biddle, the Bank's elegant president, denied the charges and they were never proved. When Congress voted to recharter the Bank in 1832, Jackson vetoed the measure and his veto was sustained. The Bank itself became the issue in the 1832 elections, in which Jackson defeated Henry Clay. Jackson gradually pulled all the government deposits out of the Bank, placing them in certain state banks, the so-called "pet banks."

The Bank of the United States and its 29 branches, facing liquidation as a government institution with the expiration of its federal charter in March 1836, obtained a charter in Feb. 1836 from the state of Pennsylvania. After the March expiration, it continued to do business as the Bank of the United States of Pennsylvania (though its later bank notes, drafts, bills of exchange, etc., seldom made any distinction from its old, familiar name).

During 1838 most of the nation's banks resumed the specie payments they had suspended in May 1837, and the banking system appeared to be returning to normal, when suddenly in Oct. 1839 the Hard Times returned. The Bank of the U.S. of Pennsylvania, then the nation's largest state bank, suspended operations. It had overextended itself trying to help out the Southern cotton banks, which started crashing with a roar.

The Southern banks and most Pennsylvania banks suspended specie payments again and more than 100 small banks failed. Biddle resigned, but in Feb. 1841 his bank failed outright, owing other banks over $7.5 million. Its collapse shook the country and Southern banks suspended specie payments a third time. Some 91 more banks failed in 1841.

"King Andrew the First" tramples the Constitution in this contemporary Whig satirical cartoon.

TOKEN DESIGNS

Various influences made up the political issues of that period. Many of these pieces carried utterances of the statesmen of the time on two great issues - Jackson's hostility to the Bank, and Daniel Webster's defense of the Constitution - issues which extended into the presidency of Van Buren, whose declaration in his Inaugural, "I follow in the steps of my illustrious predecessor" was seized by the caricaturists of the day, who represented him as carefully stepping in the footprints of a jackass marching solemnly along the highway, which suggested a device found on one of the types.

Even the humourous legend, "A friend to the Constitution" with the figure of a steer, on the Gibbs tokens, doubtless refers to the speeches of Webster, the great expounder of the Constitution (as opposed to the Nullification theories of John C. Calhoun), and the defender of the Bank.

Many devices allude to the firmness of character justly attributed to Jackson, which his enemies chose to call stubborness, and the "jack" was the favorite symbol of this quality. Others refer to the burden laid upon the people by the refusal to grant a

new charter to the Bank; to the destruction which seemed to one party to be the inevitable consequence of the acts of the other; to the ship of state, in danger of wreck, to indicate the ruin which would follow, or sailing proudly on with prospering gales to symbolize the prosperity which the nation would enjoy if the plans of friends of a high tariff and the Bank failed or succeeded; and to the Sub-treasury system of Van Buren stigmatized as an "Executive Experiment" and "Financiering" by his opponents.

The balky mule was probably suggested in a letter from Senator Thomas Hart Benton, written Aug. 11, 1837, and printed in the *New Yorker* on Sept. 2 that year, in which, praising Jackson, he said, "His policy has balked this system, etc," referring to a movement to issue paper money. To this letter he added a toast using the same words. From this opposition to the Bank, as announced by Jackson, came also the mottoes "My policy," "Veto" and similar catchwords.

The tortoise and safe are believed to allude to the slow and insecure method of moving the government deposits from the Bank to the state banks, or to the proposed Sub-treasuries. The phoenix probably alludes to the resumption of specie payment.

Of the legends, "The Constitution as I understand it" is quoted from Jackson's second Inaugural. "Executive Experiment" is a sneer at what one party judged as the stupidity of its opponent in employing banks as "Fiscal Agents." Jackson's policy, says Benton, in the letter cited above, had "fortified the country with 80 millions of hard money," and was a plan to require all payments to be made to or by the government in specie. It was really a "sound money" policy; as we look back on it we wonder that it aroused such bitter opposition from financiers of acknowledged ability, and that the Democrat Party which claims to be the legitimate successor of "Jacksonian Democracy," should have wandered since so far from the hard money precepts of its founder.

Advocates of the "State Bank Deposit System" - seemingly advanced as a compromise between friends of the U.S. Bank and its opponents - proposed that instead of requiring all payments to and from the government to pass directly through the national Treasury or its branches called Sub-treasuries, Congress should select some of the strongest banks throughout the country as depositories or "fiscal agents." This expression will be found on some tokens.

In an 1837 message to Congress, Van Buren advocated establishment of a Sub-treasury, with enactment of a law for the exaction of specie or Treasury paper for all payments due to government, and also requiring all demands against it to be paid, inflexibly, in coin. This scheme was called "most extraordinary" by opponents, but was advocated by Benton, Calhoun, Wright and others. We find references on the tokens to these schemes.

The phrase "Substitute for shinplasters" alludes to a folly of the time, the establishment of irresponsible state and private banks over which the government had no control. These banks issued notes of nominal value, ranging from 6-1/4 cents (half bit) upward, during the dearth of currency. Even the New York Joint Stock Exchange Company put out a bill of 12-1/2 cents printed from a copper plate engraved by Charles C. Wright, which was made payable "at one day sight to J. Smith or bearer, in current Bank Bills," duly signed by its officers, and embellished with a vignette of its fine building.

The country was overwhelmed with worthless fractional notes, which for a few months in 1837 seem to have driven out all coin from circulation. This miserable currency was popularly and contemptuously called "Shinplasters," "Red Dog" (perhaps from bills with red edges put out by one Jacob Barker of New York, who, when asked to redeem his pledges replied with much indifference that as soon as he could make arrangements to do so he would publish an advertisement to this effect), "Wildcat Money," "White Dog," "Blue Pup" and many other opprobrious names varying in different localities, but all satirical.

In the summer of 1837, "John Neale of 6 John Street, near Broadway, New York," and Valentine, at 50 John Street in the same city, advertised their readiness to "supply the present scarcity of specie." The plates were neatly engraved, the printed notes were kept on sale, and all that was necessary was to add a signature or two, with the location where they should be redeemed, and pay them out as money! These burlesques on a legitimate currency were forbidden in New York by a resolution of the Legislature which took effect May 7, 1839; their value vanished in a single night, and innocent holders all over the country were obliged to pocket their losses - which were enormous.

Gresham's Law - "Bad money drives the good from circulation" - had abundant proof.

The phrase "Millions for defense, but not one cent for tribute," is carried on many pieces. Charles Cotesworth Pinckney of South Carolina, U.S. minister to France in 1796, was declined reception by the French Directory, which hoped to force the U.S. to side with France against England. War was imminent and Talleyrand secretly sent word to Pinckney that it could be averted by the payment of large bribes to certain officials. This led to the sententious remark which at once raised its author to the highest point in American public esteem.

The cry was taken up again at the outbreak of the War against the Barbary Pirates, previous to which our government, in its days of weakness, had paid an annual tribute, as did most of the European powers, to the semi-barbarous rulers of North Africa. When its strength increased, and it was realized the tribute far exceeded the cost of maintaining a navy, the young Republic threw off the Barbary yoke; acting on the patriotic spirit embodied in the maxim, the frigates *Constitution, Congress, United States, Constellation,* and others, built to oppose French arrogance, settled the tribute forever with their guns at Tripoli.

It was still a phrase to conjure with when placed on these tokens, where it served as a protection for the coppers issued during the suspension of specie payments in Van Buren's new administration, so that they might truly be said to declare their character as a nonlegal coinage. The NOT ONE CENT of the Pinckney cry is always stressed on the tokens.

THE STORE CARDS

The Store Cards supplemented newspaper advertising in many cases. Most were placed in circulation in large cities where many other forms of advertising were also available. A few pieces, such as those of Walsh's General Store in Lansingburgh, N.Y., may have represented a primary advertising medium for their issuers.

Store Cards first appeared in New York in 1794, but between 1820 and 1825 they were introduced in a more widespread manner, and they held a place of utility until about 1860. While the original intent of these pieces was probably to advertise the wares, services or persons of the tradesmen, during the stringency of a circulating medium in the Hard Times, they were for a time accepted readily as currency - not alone by the customers of the issuers, but by the general public.

During the years 1828-1841 there were an estimated 10 to 20 million private tokens struck in the United States. In the same period the U.S. Mint struck only about 29 million copper cents. Thus the tokens represented a substantial portion of the cent pieces circulating in the Jacksonian era.

New theories were advanced in 1981 to explain why there were so many merchant cards issued from about 1828 through about

1841. These theories were embodied in Thomas Schweich's penetrating analysis, "Hard Times Tokens, Relics of Jacksonian America" (see Bibliography).

These studies advance the theory that the merchant tokens were *status symbols* for the wealthy merchant class in a very inegalitarian America - much as the British tokens of the 1789-1796 period were to *that* industrialized, unequal society. Schweich's theories deserve study by serious collectors of the HTT series.

New York City's wealthy families of the HT period were concentrated in the southern tip of Manhattan, near the Battery and along Broadway. Both the token issuers and the token engravers and manufacturers were located conveniently in their midst.

FIRE AND RIOT IN MANHATTAN

The Hard Times period in New York City was disturbed by more than just the financial panic which began in earnest in 1837. The Great Fire of 1835 was partially a result of the city's lack of an adequate water supply. After 1798 Aaron Burr's Manhattan Company was chartered to supply the city with water and engage in banking.

The new company used Colles' reservoir (built 1774) between Pearl and White Streets, but the wooden pipes leaked badly and the firm paid far more attention to banking and its 1822 note issues than to the water supply.

The Great Fire of 1835, mentioned on HT 291 to 293, the Merchants Exchange coppers, destroyed 648 houses and cost the city $18 million, then an enormous sum.

Water from the Croton reservoir was supplied to the city beginning July 4, 1842 and the event was celebrated on Oct. 14 that year with the most imposing celebration the 200-plus year old city had ever seen, eclipsing even the celebration of British troop withdrawals in Nov., 1783.

Abolition of slavery took a strong hold on the city about 1834-35, but that cause was overlooked when the financial panic precipitated by Pres. Jackson's July, 1836 "specie circular" created real hardship. In February, 1837, before Jackson could leave office, a huge riot took place which history books seem to have overlooked, or downplayed. This notice appeared in newspapers and flyers around the city on Feb. 10, 1837:

BREAD, MEAT, RENT, FUEL!
THEIR PRICES MUST COME DOWN!

The voice of the People will be heard, and must prevail. The People will meet in the Park, rain or shine, at 4 o'clock Monday afternoon,

To inquire into the cause of the present unexampled distress and to devise a suitable remedy. All friends of humanity, determined to resist monopolists and extortionists, are invited to attend.

Moses Jacques	Daniel Gorham
Paulus Heddle	John Windy
Daniel A. Robinson	Alexander Ming Jr.
Warden Hayward	Elijah F. Crane

Fully 6,000 persons assembled in front of City Hall Feb. 15 and Moses Jacques was chosen chairman. The multitude was divided up into groups and each was harangued by different orators. The chief theme was a denunciation of the rich, of landlords, and of dealers in provisions – especially flour, which cost $12 per barrel. In the eyes of the mob the principal offender was Eli Hart & Co. One speaker aroused his crowd with this cry:

"Fellow citizens, Eli Hart & Co. have now 53,000 barrels of flour in their store; let us go and offer them $8 a barrel for it, and if they do not accept it - - -" here he paused, considering the penalty for inciting to loot. "If they will not accept it, we will depart in peace." The hint was sufficient; the crowd heard what it wanted to hear.

The great crowd, swelling in numbers as they rushed down Broadway toward Dey Street, became a roaring, unstoppable mob as they reached Washington Street. Hart's store was attacked and 400 barrels of flour were rolled into the street and broken open, until police began arriving on the scene. The police were overwhelmed by the surging mobs and the work of destruction continued until the city militia arrived. At this point, the mob dispersed.

During the height of the looting, a literal army of women and boys gathered up the spilled flour in pails, bags and whatever other vessels came to hand. Several other provisions stores in the area of Hart's establishment were also sacked at the height of the excitement, and it is estimated that 1,000 bushels of wheat and 600 barrels of flour were emptied into the streets.

The results of this February looting were these: The price of flour became much more expensive than earlier, and none of the ringleaders and local politicians and demagogs who joined in the incitement to riot were punished, but some 40 of their dupes who were arrested went to prison.

(Much of the above is extracted from "The Greatest Street in the World, Broadway" by Stephen Jenkins, New York, 1911. Jenkins used daily and weekly newspaper files of the era for his source material.)

PRICES IN SHILLINGS AND PENCE IN NEW YORK CITY

Beginning about 1834, worn Spanish-American silver coins, especially in the 2-reales, 1-real and 1/2-real denominations, began flooding American cities to take advantage of the price differential between the more generous U.S. valuation and the tightly-controlled British and European rates of exchange.

At various times from 1790 through 1820 in England, the Spanish dollar was worth 4 shillings sixpence, four shillings ninepence and five shillings. In the same period in the new American republic the rate of exchange was a much more favorable eight shillings in the ports and sometimes more in the interior.

In 1831 the United States quarter dollar was reduced in size from 27mm, the same size as the Spanish 2-reales, to 24.3mm, while retaining its full measure of silver, 6.74 grams of .8924 fine metal. But in 1838 the silver content of the 24.3mm quarter was reduced to 6.68 grams of .900 fine metal.

New York journalists of the 1840 period often quoted the prices of meals and lodgings in shillings and pence, just as the establishments all over the lower end of Manhattan did on their menus. These were "New York shillings" and not British shillings; the shilling in New York being in reality the Spanish real, or one-eighth of a Spanish dollar. The "pence" were actually U.S. cents and half cents, about equal in size to a British halfpenny and farthing but double their worth in New York money.

A rather interesting account of this system was recalled in "Writing New York" published by Library of America, which was pursued by ANS associates John Kleeberg and Michael Bates in connection with the 2001 exhibit "Money in Old New York" mounted at the New York Federal Reserve Bank. All daily transactions at that time (1840) were in dollars, shillings and pence, but not in pounds sterling.

"Fast food" establishments in the Wall Street area charged one shilling (or 12 1/2 cents) for a typical lunch of "rosebeef and taters." The bill would run up quickly if extras were ordered, bread and a pat of butter were sixpence each, doubling the luncheon price. Some restaurants mentioned in "Writing New

Broadway in Manhattan in 1831, from a drawing by A. Dick. Trinity Church (with tall spire) is at left, with Grace Church (with rounded dome) beyond it. The large building at center is the four-story City Hotel. The four-story building at right houses R. & W. Nenns' pianoforte warehouse above and J. J. Hewitt & Co. on the ground floor (No. 137 Broadway). A typical 4-horse drawn omnibus stands before the hotel. City Hotel was erected 1792 by the Tontine Association.

York" were Sweeny's, Brown's and Delmonico's – respectively lower, middle and upper-class eateries.

Thus, in 1840 New York, one shilling equaled 12 1/2 cents and the half-real was 6 1/4 cents, exactly twice the value they were soon to become nationwide. Apparently it wasn't until 1854 that U.S. currency came into regular use in New York City, except for the cent and half cent.

This local value-system should be kept in mind when thinking about the purchasing power of Hard Times tokens and the multiplicity of counterstamped Spanish silver in this period.

THE STRANGE POLITICAL CAMPAIGN OF 1840

Both Martin Van Buren and William Henry Harrison were aristocrats, but a fatal Democrat political blunder as the campaign of 1840 began gave the Whigs a motto, symbolism and slogans which were to overwhelm Van Buren's reelection bid even though the Whigs had little if any domestic political agenda to announce.

Harrison was a genuine war hero of the War of 1812. As military governor of Indiana Territory in 1811, his regulars and militia put down a Shawnee Indian uprising led by "The Prophet" at Tippecanoe. In 1813 his victory over Gen. Proctor and Chief Tecumseh at the Thames in Canada assured control over the old Northwest.

Only 27 years old, Harrison was appointed military governor of Indiana in 1800 due in part to the great wealth and influence of his father, Governor Benjamin Harrison of Virginia. His military and administrative talents were considered limited. After the war, he was an Ohio state senator, U.S. congressman and in 1828 ambassador to Colombia. President John Quincy Adams had a low regard for Harrison's abilities, and this seemed shared by most Washington insiders.

In the Whig nominating process in 1836 Harrison was an also-ran, but the nation remembered his military exploits. His Whig managers artfully designed an 1840 campaign to exploit the Democrats while revealing few of Harrison's ideas for the nation.

The Democrats assailed Harrison's "western" roots (Indiana and Ohio were still then considered the rum-bucket West) by proclaiming him a simple man used to living in a log cabin and drinking hard cider. The log cabin and cider barrel were turned into Whig rallying symbols for their "peoples choice". Meanwhile the Whig platform consisted solely of blaming Van Buren for the Panic in 1837 and the failure of major banks in 1839, while keeping their man silent.

It has been said that "Harrison rode to glory by saying nothing." His critics called him "General Mum." While Harrison was silent, the Whig managers devised a rallying cry, "Tippecanoe and Tyler too." They had recruited a states' rights southern Democrat, John Tyler, as his running mate. Then they derided "Van" for his aristocratic manners and set up another cry, "Van is a Used-up Man."

The Whig propaganda transformed the Virginia aristocrat into a poor backwoods pioneer. Seldom has demagoguery paid off so well, and seldom has the Democratic party blundered so badly in an unfounded personal attack (it is not known whether Harrison ever actually lived in a log cabin, or whether he preferred hard cider to fine wine).

Harrison overwhelmed Van Buren, capturing 234 electoral votes to the Democrat's 60.

The campaign tokens of the 1840 Harrison run for the presidency are alive with sly Whig assaults on Van Buren ("up Salt River" for example) and relentless reminders of the Battles of Tippecanoe and the Thames. The Whigs were exacting vengeance for General Andrew Jackson's constant reminders of his great military exploits, defeat of the Creeks at Horseshoe Bend and the British at New Orleans during the same War of 1812.

THE ELECTIONS OF 1824 THROUGH 1844

It may be interesting to recall the election results (electoral votes only) of the period history has dubbed the Jacksonian Era. (Winner in bold face)

1824. (No parties involved). Andrew Jackson 99; John Quincy Adams 84; William H. Crawford 41; Henry Clay 37. Since no candidate had an electoral majority, the House of Representatives, with one vote per state, chose the president from among the top three vote-getters. Odd-man-out Clay threw his support to Adams. The final tally: **Adams** 13 states; Jackson 7 states; Crawford 4 states.

1828. Andrew Jackson, Democrat, 178; John Quincy Adams, National Republican, 83.

1832. Andrew Jackson, Democrat; 218; Henry Clay, National Republican, 49; John Floyd, Independent, 11; William Wirt, Antimasonic, 7; votes not cast, 2.

1836. Martin Van Buren, Democrat, 170; William H. Harrison, Whig, 73; Hugh L. White, Whig, 26; Daniel Webster, Whig, 14; W. P. Mangum, Independent, 11.

1840. William H. Harrison, Whig, 234; Martin Van Buren, Democrat, 60.

1844. James K. Polk, Democrat, 170; Henry Clay, Whig, 105.

The vice presidents elected in this same period, with their respective electoral votes, were: John C. Calhoun, 1824, 182. John C. Calhoun, 1828, 171. Martin Van Buren, 1832, 189. Richard M. Johnson, 1836, 147. John Tyler, 1840, 234. George M. Dallas, 1844, 170.

THE LAND LIMITATION SCHEME

A totally new element in the political maneuverings of the Hard Times era was introduced by our colleague Q. David Bowers of Wolfeboro, New Hampshire in mid-2001, just in time for inclusion in this catalog.

Agitation for land, really for *free land* from the government as well as the breakup of large landed estates, entered into the political arena about March, 1844 at almost the end of the Hard Times period. According to Bowers' research, this led to the counterstamping of coins as a cheap, effective method of broadcasting the proposals of the "land limitation" scheme.

These counterstamps include the almost unknown LAND / LIMITATION logotype and one of the best-known pre-Civil War stamps, VOTE THE LAND / FREE. The latter stamp has been considered for at least 125 years the political statement of the 1848 Free Soil Party which nominated Martin Van Buren for the presidency.

The words and research which follow are primarily those of Bowers, who is publishing a major work on this subject. We use them with permission, but supplement them with our own interpretations.

George Henry Evans (1805-1855) was born in England and emigrated to America as a teenager, settling in upstate New York. He became an apprentice printer and came to know the duty and drudgery of the common working man, while at the same time gathering an awareness of agriculture and farming practices in the area. In 1826 he moved to New York City to become editor of *The Correspondant* which advocated the rights of the common man and emulated the quixotic utopian community-founders of the era, such as Robert Owen (founder of New Harmony, Indiana).

The Workingmen's Party was founded by Evans and others in 1829 as Andrew Jackson was new in the White House, and

Evans published the *Working Man's Advocate*. In 1837, feeling repercussions from the financial panic of that year which placed the interests of workingmen far below the collapsing interests of business people, Evans moved to a farm in northern New Jersey, where he remained until early 1844.

Evans returned to New York as 1844 dawned, and many commentaries and essays on the subject of land were being published. Frederick W. Evans of Mount Lebanon, N.Y. published *A Shaker's View on the Land Limitation Scheme and Land Monopoly, and Mormon Persecution*, a treatise brought to your author's attention by collector Robert Merchant. In 1845 Lewis Masquerier of New York wrote *Monopoly of Land the Great Evil*, located by Bowers. In these and other tracts, the word "land" is used over and over, but "soil" (as in Free Soil Party in 1848) is not stressed; "free soil" referred to territory free of slavery, not free government land for the common man.

George H. Evans united the Workingmen's Party of 1829, then somewhat moribund; the National Trades Union; the Locofoco faction of the Democratic Party, and other disaffected men into the National Reform Association (NRA), in a mass meeting on March 13, 1844 at Chatham and Mulberry Streets. A committee was formed "to investigate a depression of labor, and a social degradation of the laborer."

Q. David Bowers now advances the theory that all the "Vote the Land Free" counterstamps which numismatics has accepted as Free Soil Party issues of 1848 are in fact NRA issues of early 1844. Examination of the host coin dates bears out his contention, as almost all the 60 or more known pieces are dated 1843 or earlier, only three dated 1844, and the one each reportedly bearing dates 1845, 1846, 1847 and 1848 have not actually been examined by the author or his contributors. (Even should post-1844 stamped coins appear, they could be merely reissues by whoever possessed the dies.)

In 1845 the NRA joined with the Fourierist movement to schedule the first of a series of national industrial congresses. The NRA achieved no real objectives, though both Henry Clay (Whig) and James K. Polk (Democrat) adopted the disposition and proceeds of public land in their 1844 campaign platforms.

NEW TYPE TOKENS ADDED TO THIS CATALOG

A large number of additional types and varieties of Hard times period satirical and store card tokens have been added to this HT "super catalog." Wherever a die variety could be fitted into the basic HT numbering system by use of prefix or suffix letters, this has been done.

In the satirical token segment, never-before-listed types of tokens – especially from the presidential campaign of 1840 – have been added, and these are distinguished by use of catalog numbers from the 800 block. Thus no doubt will be left in the minds of users; if the satirical token is numbered between 800 and 899 it is completely new to all previous Hard Times coverage.

It is doubtful whether many of the Martin Van Buren tokens listed for years by Lyman H. Low or this author (HT 75 through 78A) actually saw currency use. Only HT 75 to 75B are of correct cent size, yet all these pieces have been accepted by collectors for more than a century and in fact are among the most expensive Hard Times tokens.

Medalets of the Harrison campaign of 1840 have been mentioned in notes in previous editions of my catalogs, and there have been so many requests for their cataloging that we are including some of them for the first time. The selection is representative, but "Tippecanoe and Tyler too" and the log cabins and cider barrels will have their day before the numismatic court.

Likewise we are adding a few of the smaller Van Buren and Henry Clay pieces from the 1836-1844 period.

Anticipating that opening this floodgate door to political campaign medalets will lead to demands for information on the larger politicals of the Hard Times era, we have also added a special appendix to the back of the catalog, and are assigning HT "K" numbers to pieces cataloged there. Again, the selection is representative, but may well add an appreciation for the political slugfests each election in the Jacksonian era became. (Political campaigns from 1968 through 2000 have been relatively tame compared to those from 1824 through 1844.)

In the much larger store card segment, a number of Early American tokens with Rulau-E numbers have been moved to this catalog. These are pieces whose probable date of issuance brackets the 1832-1833 period. Some of these have already been assigned pseudo-Low numbers by me in the early 1960's.

The argument has been put forth that, because Lyman H. Low included Jackson-supporter issues of 1832, that we should also include store cards of that year. The argument is somewhat specious – the reason such issues as "The Bank Must Perish" pieces (HT 1 through 3A) are included is because these are ingrained in the consciousness of HT collectors influenced by Low's writing efforts dating back to the 1880's. We have always hesitated to rock the collecting boat in our own cataloging activities.

The actual first Hard Times satirical piece was struck in the autumn of 1833, HT 70, a Hulseman-designed Jackson-in-safe token. Our late contributor and friend Bob Lindesmith, who died in 1999, discovered this in 1967.

However, this catalog and all other book products by this author are aimed at inclusiveness and thus – for the 9th edition – these "twilight crossover" issues are included. All store cards of this type are given HT numbers in the 900 block, that is, 900 through 999, for distinctiveness.

Of course, newly-discovered store cards are also included, and these are enumerated from the 500 block we began using for the South Carolina slave tags in previous editions.

Several tokens listed in the Merchant Token era (1845-1860) have been shown by Wesley Cox' die-link studies to actually emanate from the Hard Times period. These include Ettenheimer's, Chamberlain-Woodruff-Scranton and others.

Lyman Haynes Low gave the name "Hard Times Tokens" to his listings which spanned the period 1832 through 1844. The name has stuck very well and is accepted without question by collectors today. Yet the real "hard times" began only when specie payments were suspended in May, 1837 and ended with the bank failures of 1841. We point this out only to show that numismatic monickers, once entered into our lexicon of terms, have a lasting significance whether factually accurate or not.

SOME NON-TRADITIONAL HTT USES

Plentiful contemporary circulation evidence exists to show that the U.S. Mint Bureau and U.S. Justice Department did a great deal of public posturing about the illegality of Hard Times tokens passing as money, but that this availed little in reality.

Hard Times tokens remained in circulation in the United States as long as the government's Large cent did, though in severely decreased numbers after the 1837-1841 period. The last Large cents were struck in 1857, but they did not disappear from circulation until the 1862 Civil War change shortage.

The famous Civil War coin hoarder Aaron White had a fair number of HTT's mixed with the Large cents and Small cents he had hoarded from the change in circulation.

The tokens found at least three other uses their creators never envisioned: (1) Circulation as halfpennies in Canada. (2) Host coins for the activities of counterstampers. (3) Blanks for making tokens of South America.

Almost any copper or brass disc from 27.5 to 29.5mm found acceptance in change-short Canada before the first national cents were struck in 1858. Some Bouquet sous were specially struck for use in Canada at the Belleville Mint, but other HTT's also saw use there. Hard Times tokens and U.S. Large cents circulated side by side in Canada with both English-produced and locally-struck tokens (many American cents and tokens were later counterstamped by such Canadian firms as Devins & Bolton and Rouleau).

U.S. counterstamps do not appear on HTT's with the frequency that they do on regular Large cents, but they occur frequently enough to define patterns. Some counterstamped HTT's appear in this reference when the time of their use is proper, but more appear in our catalogs covering the 1845-1860 and 1866-1889 periods (*U.S. Merchant Tokens* and *U.S. Trade Tokens*), respectively.

Hard Times tokens were overstruck by an American firm for use in Colombia, South America. Some of the 1838 tokens of Manuel Maria Pla of Cartagena, 1835-40 Velez Matos pieces, 1839-40 Manuel Angulo tokens of Barranquilla and 1840's Espinosa-Olier pieces are known on HTT's. Some 1844 Jose M. Ruiz tokens of Mompos also may have been struck this way.

Other tokens of the same design of the five issuers named were coined on fresh copper blanks.

Valez Matos token of Colombia, circa 1837-40, overstruck on HT 34, an 1837 Executive Financiering/Illustrious Predecessor satirical piece.

Enlargement of part of the Valez Matos overstrike on HT 34. I FOL / IN TH and the forepart of the donkey are clearly visible in the undertype.

Examination of the undertypes reveals that these HTT's were used for Colombian tokens: HT 16, 1841 Webster Credit Current; HT 34, 1837 Executive Financiering; HT 53, 1837-dated Bushnell restrike; HT 69, 1837 Shipwreck; HT 154, 1836 R. & W. Robinson of Attleboro, Mass.; HT 239, 1837 Centre Market; HT 291 and HT 293 and 294, 1837 Merchants Exchange of New York. The HT 53 report has not yet been verified.

Our new catalog, *Latin American Tokens*, details the Colombian connection.

BUSHNELL FANTASIES

Collector Charles Ira Bushnell (1826-1880), a New York City attorney, commissioned Scovill Mfg. Co. of Waterbury, Conn. to make Hard Times token fantasies in the 1850's, all similar to genuine pieces Scovill had struck 20 years or so earlier.

These fantasies were of types HT 38, 39, 40, 41, 53, 54, 55, 59 and 60 — the first seven types dated 1837 and the last two dated 1841.

Mintages were very small, and occurred in both copper and silver.

Bushnell originally did not attempt to deceive, but closer to 1860 it is reported he "aged" some of them by oxidizing and slightly corroding. Bushnell died in 1880 and his collection, auctioned in 1882 by his nephews, Philadelphia coin dealers S. Hudson and Henry Chapman, helped begin the fantasies' gradual acceptance as part of the Hard Times series. Lyman H. Low in his 1886, 1899 and 1906 monographs completed the "acceptance" movement and today the Bushnell pieces bring prices higher than many of the original tokens.

Nicholas Biddle signed this 1837 $10 note of the Bank of the United States, drawn on the Philadelphia main branch.

HARD TIMES DIE VARIATIONS

Our collaborator Wesley S. Cox Sr. has produced an unpublished series of detailed die studies, reinforced by photographs, for many of the Scovill, Wright-Bale and other producers' struck Hard Times tokens.

Some of his excellent monographs which have been submitted to your author for publication, are included in this edition, but most of the work has not. A general reference such as this catalog must concentrate on listing important new discoveries, rather than becoming laden with minor differences in die deterioration, die linkages and other small variations.

However, we do present a good number of the Cox photographs, sketches and conclusions for the benefit of dedicated Hard Times token enthusiasts. The valuable studies merit such special attention.

Gratefully we acknowledge his work in this public manner. His generosity will benefit the Hard Times literature.

ARRANGEMENT

The store cards are arranged both on a geographic and alphabetical basis. Thus all the store cards of New York, Boston, Philadelphia, etc. may be found together.

Some rearrangement of the political cards has been effected. To make hunting for ''Low numbers'' easier, a special up-front Index tells the reader what each Low number is now numbered.

The new "HT" numbers are assigned along logical lines. A complete renumbering of all Hard Times tokens was long overdue, and this was accomplished in the Third edition of our catalog, and expanded in this largest edition.

Appendices cover quasi-HTT's, satirical notes, etc.

VALUATIONS

The 1980 Garrett II sale of Hard Times tokens produced such record high prices in what had been a long-dormant facet of the hobby that most experts assumed the Garrett prices were an aberration. People simply wanted an ex-Garrett specimen in their holdings.

Garrett II proved not to have been an aberration, but rather a harbinger of things to come. In quick order came the Garrett IV, Harte, Chesterfield, NASCA HTT, Kessler-Spangenberger and Levine and other sales - plus the Hartzog and smaller groupings and - lo and behold - the Garrett II prices seem modest indeed from hindsight advantage!

Bidders found the only way they could purchase the truly rare, choice HTT's at public auction was by continuing their floor bidding beyond all their own pre-sale estimates of "top dollar." Mail bidders were mostly frozen out in the process. Far from discouraging new collectors, the constantly higher prices seemed to be spurring them to vigorous pursuit of elusive specimens.

The first three editions of this catalog arrived at a fortuitous upswing in American appreciation for the token. They benefited from - but also helped expand - that movement.

Valuations included herein reflect the actual record prices paid at auction recently for rarities, as well as dealers' retail prices on the more available items. A panel of top professional exonumists has arrived at the published valuations, and an especial debt is owed to Robert A. Vlack, H. Joseph Levine, Steve Hayden and George J. Fuld, who determined Rarity ratings for this edition.

IMPORTANT: Uncirculated HTT's.

A special note about the Uncirculated prices in this catalog: Our Unc. prices are given for attractive, part red, no problem pieces that are unquestionably uncirculated - roughly equivalent to the MS 63 grading standard of United States coins. Many pieces sold at auction which bring low prices though described as Unc. are not choice and in some cases are not even technically "uncirculated."

Thus the Unc. prices in this catalog reflect the desire of collectors to own the finest tokens and may seem high at first glance. A special pricing panel has extensively overhauled all Unc. prices for this new edition.

A fine run of choice Uncirculated HTT's appeared in Stack's Jan. 2001 Americana sale, lots 427-470, which confirmed the continuing desire of collectors to seek out the finest Unc. pieces with traces of mint red luster, regardless of cost. Other recent auctions in the 1999-2001 period have also been monitored for this same trend.

AUCTION RESULTS AFFECT PRICES:

A spate of very important sales in the 1995-2001 period once again has raised overall Hard Times token prices except in the lowest grades. These include the magnificent Steinberg, Schenkel, Middendorf, Gold Medal, Ganter, Sebring, McSorley, Fred, Lindesmith, Stack's Americana and Vlack auction sales.

BRASS VERSUS COPPER

In this section we have removed a number of the Hard Times tokens formerly listed by Low, Vlack and others as Brass strikes of Copper pieces. Our panel of contributors is now in agreement that the best evidence of recent study through specific gravity analysis and spectro-analysis indicates that little real differences (if any) exist in the metallic composition of such pieces.

Alloying procedures in the 1830's and 1840's were indifferent. Pure copper often was copper with more than just traces of impurities present. The tokenmakers of that day were held to no standards, except the generalized standard of imitation of the legal U.S. cent.

It is now known that Scovill's used brass flans which were copper or bronze coated in many instances.

If specimens are known which are provably Brass, and are colored much as a brass doorknob is colored, the listing has been retained. If there is genuine doubt, the listing also has been retained in this Edition.

There are certain to be differences of opinion on this subject. We recognize this, and will restore in future editions any listings which require restoration.

The grace and dignity of the Pantheon were invested in the Grecian-columned second Bank of the United States in Philadelphia by architect William Strickland. The facade of the bank building appeared on several bank notes issued from 1816 to 1840.

JUST WHO WAS LYMAN HAYNES LOW?

Lyman Haynes Low will always be best remembered as the "father" of Hard Times token collecting, though he was much more than that in life. Expert general numismatist, coin dealer, soldier, stamp dealer, numismatic cataloger, auctioneer, and co-editor (with William T. R. Marvin) of the erudite *American Journal of Numismatics.*

Low was born 1845 in Boston, a descendant of an old New England family. He was a direct descendant of Vice Admiral John Low, deputy to Admiral Winthrop on the ship which carried Governor Bradford to England in 1632. Low's parents were Captain Francis Low and Reliance Cobb Burrill Low. He married Ella Mordaunt Peshine, who preceded him in death by five years.

Lyman Low died at age 78 on Feb. 10, 1924 at his home in New Rochelle, N.Y. When the American Numismatic Association was organized in 1891, he was a founding member. Prior to that he had been a member of the American Numismatic Society (New York) and co-editor of its journal for a 15-year span.

He began collecting coins as a boy in 1856. He frequented the tollhouse of the Chelsea Ferry every Saturday to look over the box of odd pieces collected by the ferry company. He stated in 1908: "It was the custom of the tollman to accept anything having the semblance of a coin. If it proved other than a U.S. coin it was thrown into this box. Connecticut cents, Hard Times tokens and an occasional store card composed the bulk of my treasures. I never found a half cent . . . at that period none were in circulation in Massachusetts."

He added, "When the Civil War broke out I took my collection to a State Street broker and sold it for $5."

Coin collecting had to wait during Low's enlistment as a soldier. He volunteered for Company B, 13th Massachusetts Volunteers. In 1865 he returned to Boston, but moved to New York in 1870. In 1878 he was hired by Scott Stamp & Coin Co. as manager at its 178 Fulton Street outlet. He stayed with the John W. Scott organization until 1896.

In 1896 Low opened his own coin dealership and auction house, holding in all 211 public sales in New York until 1911 and then from his new locale in New Rochelle until his death. His last auciton was the collection of J. Coolidge Hills on Dec. 1, 1923.

His research on Hard Times tokens began in the 1880's and culminated in his 1899 opus *Hard Times Tokens,* which he supplemented in 1906. This work, reprinted a number of times, remained the gospel for collectors of the 1832-1844 tokens until 1980, when the first edition of the Russell Rulau catalog of the same title replaced it as the standard work on the series. Together with William Marvin, Low also completed the manuscript and published C. Wyllys Betts' memorable *American Colonial History Illustrated by Contemporary Medals* in 1894.

The year of his matriculation from semi-dormant coin collector to manager at Scott's, then a leading American coin and stamp firm, 1878, was explained by Low himself in his 1908 address before the A.N.A. Philadelphia convention that year: "In that year, while a commercial traveler, I was in the West on the Mississippi River just below St. Paul. Many foreign copper and silver coins were in circulation in that community and I soon made a collection of the various kinds I met with. My ardor was thoroughly aroused."

Low added that his first public auction on his own, while still employed by Scott, was the Alexander Balmanno collection of Brooklyn, sold sometime soon after 1883. Low made a special-ty of copper coins, offering his own accumulation of 15,000 pieces in 1883 at a sale at 838 Broadway in New York City. Low was a man of enormous energy and imagination, self-taught and self-motivated.

Low was inducted into the Numismatic Hall of Fame in Colorado Springs in 1972.

RARITY SCALE

R1	Common
R2	Less Common
R3	Scarce
R4	Estimated 76-200 specimens survive
R5	Estimated 31-75 specimens survive
R6	Estimated 13-30 specimens survive
R7	Estimated 4-12 specimens survive
R8	Estimated 2 or 3 specimens survive
R9	Unique (only one known)

DIESINKERS AND TOKEN MAKERS ACTIVE IN THE HARD TIMES TOKEN PERIOD

** Indicates individual is known to have prepared HTT's

Name	City	Years	Mark
John F. Bartholdt	Baltimore	1841-60	
Z. Bisbee Co.	Cincinnati	1835-51	
James Bale **	New York	1833-35	BALE
Bale & Smith **	New York	1835-48	B&S NY
Belleville Mint **	Belleville, NJ	1833-41	
(Gibbs Gardner & Co. and Stevens Thomas & Fuller)			
Benedict & Burnham **	Waterbury, CT	1834-57	
W. H. Bridgens	New York	1840-63	
W. Cammeyer	Philadelphia	1832	
Shubael D. Childs	Chicago	1837-1900	CHILDS
Godfrey Conradt **	Philadelphia	1828-48	CONRADT
(worked for Scovills 1828 & later?)			
Joseph Conradt	Philadelphia	1805-32	CONRADT
William Eaves **	Waterbury, CT	1829-41	
William Eaves	Wolcottville, CT	1842-48	
Joseph B. Gardner	Belleville, NJ	1833-41	
John B. Gardiner **		1840	I.B.G.
W. L. German	Philadelphia	1844	
John Gibbs **	Belleville, NJ	1833-41	
Hiram W. Hayden **	Waterbury, CT	1841-52	
Edward Hulseman **	Attleboro, MA	1833-36	H
Edward Hulseman **	New York	1837-41	
William H. Jones & Co. **	Waterbury, CT	1835-40	
Louisa Lander	New York	1847	LANDER
Joseph Lewis	Philadelphia	1824-	
Robert Lovett Sr. **	New York	1806-60's	
Francis Napoleon Mitchell **	Boston	1838-95	MITCHELL
James G. Moffet **	New York	1802-37	
Alexander C. Morin	Philadelphia	1821-60	A.C. MORIN
E. E. Pritchard **	Waterbury, CT	1840	
H. M. & E. I. Richards	Attleboro, MA	1833-	
R. & W. Robinson **	Attleboro, MA	1834-48	
Robinson's Jones & Co. **	Attleboro, MA	1828-34	
Scovill Mfg. Co. **	Waterbury, CT	1820-1905	
Frederick B. Smith **	New York	1835-64	
Stimpson		1840	
Joseph F. Thomas **	Newark, NJ	1840-52	JF THOMAS I. F. T.
Robert Tiller Jr.	Philadelphia	1835	
Benjamin C. True **	Albany, NY	1832-48	* T TRUE ALB TRUE F.
Daniel True	Albany, NY	1837-79	
James Turpin	New York	1840	TURPIN
William M. Wagner **	Pennsylvania	1844-48	WAGNER
John S. Warner	Philadelphia	1823-68	
Charles Cushing Wright **	New York	1824-57	CCW
Thomas Wyatt	New York	1840-60	

CONTRIBUTORS TO THE EXPANDED NINTH EDITION OF HTT

It would be impossible to name all the persons upon whose research this catalog was constructed. Virtually everyone who wrote on the subject of Hard Times tokens over the years would need to be thanked. The Bibliography mentions some of the more prominent of these sources.

Many of those named below provided direct assistance on this Hard Times "super catalog" project. Others, who contributed to past editions or who – long before the First Edition of this reference (in 1980) – toiled the gardens of this estate are named in a special section below.

Pricing input is due almost entirely to these collectors and dealers, and to the recorded prices realized of public auctions and private treaty sales which took place from 1999 through 2001.

James K. Allen
Ralph Angeletti
Herman M. Aqua
William Aquilino
Warren Baker
Michael L. Bates
R. K. "Ken" Bauer
Paul J. Bosco
Q. David Bowers
Kenneth E. Bressett
Gregory G. Brunk
Catherine E. Bullowa-Moore
Jane E. Campbell
John A. Cheramy
Elvira Clain-Stefanelli
Donald K. Clifford
Wesley S. Cox Sr.
Paul A. Cunningham
Denton V. Curtis
Dwight B. Demeritt
Rocco A. DiGiacomo

Richard T. Doty
Lawrence C. Dziubek
L. B. "Benj" Fauver
John J. Ford Jr.
Bob Forrest
George J. Fuld
David M. Gale
Jeffrey Gardiner
Gary E. Glise
Jim Hartman
Rich A. Hartzog
Steve Hayden
James Henderson
Michael J. Hodder
Arvid O. Johnson
Larry A. Johnson
Robert W. Julian
Charles E. Kirtley
John Kleeberg
Paul L. Koppenhaver
Chester L. Krause

Robert D. Leonard Jr.
H. Joseph Levine
Charles Litman
Albert Marecki
Gary L. Mauer
Robert J. Merchant Jr.
Clifford L. Mishler
Eric P. Newman
Arthur Newmark
Donald Partrick
Paul G. Pettazoni
Robert M. Ramsay
Fred L. Reed III
Jeff Rock
Richard A. Rossa
David E. Schenkman
Robert A. Schuman
Russell W. Sears
Neil Shafer
Arlie R. Slabaugh
Robert F. Slawsky

Les LeRoy Smith
Robert M. Stark
Stanley L. Steinberg
Henry C. Stouffer
Edmund Sullivan
William B. Swoger
Stephen L. Tanenbaum
Sol Taylor
Henry C. Thoele
Warren K. Tice
Alan V. Weinberg
Louis T. Wells
Joseph Whipple
Dennis P. Wierzba
John W. Wilson
Alan York
Joseph H. Zaffern
Alexander Zaika
Michael Brand Zeddies

American Antiquarian Society
American Numismatic Association
American Numismatic Society
Amos Press
Bank of Canada

Charleston (S.C.) Museum
"Grouseland," W. H. Harrison Mansion
Maryland Token and Medal Society
Mormon Genealogical Library
Quarterman Publications Inc.

Smithsonian Institution
Stack's Inc.
Token and Medal Society
Winterthur Museum
Wisconsin Historical Society

AND TO THOSE WHO PRECEDED US ....

Edgar H. Adams
David T. Alexander
Roland Atwood
Bangs Merwin & Co.
Louise Conway Belden
Morris Bram
Walter H. Breen
Charles Ira Bushnell
Raymond Byrne
Carl W. A. Carlson
Alva Christensen
Grover C. Criswell
James J. Curto
Jack R. Detwiler
J. Doyle Dewitt
Frank G. Duffield
William Forrester Dunham
Thomas L. Elder
Jules Fonrobert
Sarah Elizabeth Freeman
Melvin Fuld
George R. Ganter

John Work Garrett
T. Harrison Garrett
Maurice M. Gould
Cynthia W. "Cindy" Grellman
Julius Guttag
Kenneth L. Hallenbeck
Lee F. Hewitt
J. Coolidge Hills
Edward Janis
Byron F. Johnson
Donald Kagin
Charles V. Kappen
James H. Keller
Frank Kovacs
Julian M. Leidman
Joseph N. T. Levick
Robert J. Lindesmith
Gaylor D. Lipscomb
Lyman Haynes Low
Theodore Francis Marburg
William T. R. Marvin
Donald M. Miller

Ralph A. "Curly" Mitchell
Waldo C. Moore
Al Oravec
Wayte Raymond
Alfred Z. Reed
Kenneth W. Rendell
Alfred H. Satterlee
John W. Scott
C. P. Serrure
Elizabeth C. Steinle
Ethel R. Stone
Malcolm Storer
Georg F. Ulex-Hamburg
Roy H. Van Ormer
Alexandre Vattemare
Robert A. Vlack
Adolf Weyl
R. Byron White
Stewart P. Witham
P. H. Wittlin
Howland Wood
Benjamin P. Wright

Table of Contents

ANDREW JACKSON

Small Head

HT #	Rarity	Year	Metal	Size	VG	F	VF	EF
1	R6	(1832)	Copper	27mm	1500.	3650.	5750.	9000.
1A	R8	(1832)	Brass	—	—	7000.	11,000.	14,000.

Scowling Head

2	R8	(1832)	Copper	27mm	2000.	4500.	6500.	10,000.

2A	R8	(1832)	White Metal	29mm		5000.	7000.	10,000.

Aged Head

3	R7	(1832)	Copper	27mm	2000.	4500.	6500.	16,500.
3A	R8	(1832)	Silver	27mm				May not exist

This 1832 token was supposedly issued by Daniel Jackson of the firm of Suydam and Jackson, Indian contractors, Pearl St., New York. Jackson (no relation to the president) was an arch-foe of the U.S. Bank.

Die varieties of the obverse of Low 1 (see Carl Wurtzbach's article in March 1910 *The Numismatist*) are called Small Head, Aged Head and Scowling Head.

Wesley S. Cox has shown by die-link evidence that HT 1, 2 and 3 and their variations are the work of the firm of Wright & Bale, not of Robert Lovett Sr. An appendix to this volume shows photo-evidence of Cox' conclusions.

The firm of Suydam and Jackson was founded originally by Richard Suydam in 1811, at 140 Pearl Street. In 1824 Richard Suydam took in two partners, Daniel Jackson and Allen Peck, and the firm name was changed from R. Suydam to Suydam, Jackson & Peck.

One year later, in 1825, Peck was bought out and the firm became Suydam & Jackson.

In 1830 Suydam & Jackson moved from 140 Pearl Street to 78 Pearl Street, and the name was again changed, this time to Suydam, Jackson & Co. (Interestingly, another firm also occupied the space at 78 Pearl Street - Suydam & Kevan - a partnership of Richard Suydam with Alexander Kevan. This latter firm closed about 1844-45 when Suydam retired.)

Richard Suydam was another brother of the Rynier and John Suydam who founded R. & J. Suydam in 1791 at 10 Albany Pier (later 10 Coenties Slip).

A VF specimen of HT 1 with two deep digs above the back of the head realized $1650 in the PCAC June 3, 2000 sale, lot 1. The edge is diagonally reeded on HT 1.

HT #	Rarity	Year	Metal	Size		VG	VF	EF	Unc
4	R8	(1834)	Brass	27mm			17,600.	25,000.	

Jackson bust right, ANDREW JACKSON / . PRESIDENT OF THE US . around. Rv: ELECTED A.D. 1828 / We (etc., the same as reverse of HT 5). Only 2 specimens are known. The Gil Steinberg specimen in VF, holed (shown above) fetched $17,600 in Stack's Sept. 1989 sale, lot 215. The other known piece is in a southwestern U.S. collection, ex-Wayte Raymond.

HT #	Rarity	Year	Metal	Size	VG	VF	EF	Unc
5	R3	(1834)	Brass	27mm	40.00	250.	500.	900.
5A	R8	(1834)	White Metal	27mm	—	—	May not exist	

HT #	Rarity	Year	Metal	Size	VG	VF	EF	Unc
6	R2	(1834)	Brass	27mm	40.00	225.	400.	1000.

					VG	VF	EF	Unc
6A	R6	(1834)	Silvered Brass					
				27mm	45.00	325.	600.	1000.
6B	R7	(1834)	Copper	27mm	—	350.	—	—

The Lindesmith specimen of HT 6 realized $45 in the Dec. 1961 Kabealo auction, but only $52.90 in the B&M March 2000 sale!.

Reverse reads: ELECTED A.D. 1829. Andrew Jackson actually was elected in 1828.

HT 4, 5, 6

DeWitt (see Bibliography) attributes these tokens to the political campaigns of 1834.

Remark: These Patriotic tokens are generally listed as they were by Lyman Low with the exception that they have been grouped by general design and the listing within that listing follows Low's sequence. Tokens are illustrated actual size. As many varieties are hard to attribute enlarged illustrations with helpful notes appear at the end of the section.

Dates listed within parentheses do not appear on tokens but have been attributed as having been issued that year.

Large Shield

7	R5	1833	Brass	26mm	150.	500.	750.	1200.

Period after N of N. Orleans. Reeded edge.

7A	R8	1833	Brass	26mm	—	600.	—	—

(PCAC Dec. 9, 1995 sale, lot 079.) Plain edge.

An AU HT 7 brought $924 in the Hayden July 2000 sale.

Small Shield

HT #	Rarity	Year	Metal	Size	VG	VF	EF	Unc
8	R6	1833	Brass	26mm	300.	600.	800.	1500.

No period after N. Comes with upset and non-upset reverse. Well struck obverses command a premium. Reeded edge.

Running Boar

HT #	Rarity	Year	Metal	Size	VG	VF	EF	Unc
9	R1	1834	Copper	28.6mm	5.00	45.00	90.00	325.

An Unc MS-63 specimen fetched $529 in March, 2000! Another realized $476.10. A third fetched $345 in Jan. 2001.

HT #	Rarity	Year	Metal	Size	VG	VF	EF	Unc
10	R3	1834	Brass	28.5mm	25.00	150.	200.	300.
10A	R3	1834	Silvered Brass	28.5mm	20.00	150.	200.	600.

NOTE: Pig's snout points to C of CREDIT. Jackson narrow shoulders. HT 10 is on thick planchet, 10A on thin planchet.

HT #	Rarity	Year	Metal	Size	VG	VF	EF	Unc
11	R2	1834	Copper	28.5mm	16.50	60.00	180.	600.
11A	R7	1834	Svd/Br	28.5mm	—	400.	—	—

NOTE: Pig's snout points between H of PERISH and C of CREDIT. Jackson wide shoulders.

WARNING: White metal cast copies exist!

Obverse 9, Reverse 11

HT #	Rarity	Year	Metal	Size	VG	VF	EF	Unc
12	R5	1834	Brass	29mm	100.	350.	500.	1200.
12A	R6	1834	Silvered Brass	29mm	—	350.	700.	1500.

Obv. Similar to 9. Rev. Number 11

HT #	Rarity	Year	Metal	Size	VG	VF	EF	Unc
13	R7	1834	Copper	28.5mm	2000.	4000.	5000.	—

The "victory" at New Orleans, and the "glory" due to Jackson's military successes, was a favorite theme of his friends, and the boastful way in which they rehearsed his exploits excited the unceasing and satirical jests of his opponents. (See No. 4 and notes under Nos. 25 and 30.) This was struck as a counterfoil to No. 14, as is evident from a comparison of the reverse legend on No. 14 with the obverse legend of this.

HT #	Rarity	Year	Metal	Size	F	VF	EF	Unc
13R	R1	1824	Copper-coated lead alloy	29mm	—	—	2.00	5.00

Modern (post-1960) replica, made of the wrong metal and carrying an erroneous date. The edge is irregular, similar to that on electrotype copies.

WHIG VICTORY

Dies by Robert Lovett

HT #	Rarity	Year	Metal	Size	VG	VF	EF	Unc
14	R5	1834	Brass, engrailed edge	25.7mm	125.	400.	775.	1200.

The edge may be described as engrailed or diagonally left reeds.

HT #	Rarity	Year	Metal	Size	VG	VF	EF	Unc
14A	R6	1834	Brass	25mm	135.	400.	800.	1300.
14B	R8	1834	Silver	25mm	—	—	May not exist	
14C	R8	1834	Silver	27mm	—	—	—	7500.

(14C is struck over 1833 quarter dollar)

HT 14A, recently re-rated Rarity 6 from 4, realized only $412.50 in EF in the PCAC June 21, 1996 sale, lot 003. Plain edge.

Obv. Rays are short and heavy.

HT #	Rarity	Year	Metal	Size	VG	VF	EF	Unc
			Edges are reeded					
15	R6	1834	Copper	27mm	600.	1500.	3500.	5000.

HT #	Rarity	Year	Metal	Size	VG	VF	EF	Unc
			Buckled dies - reeded edge					
15B	R6	1834	Copper	27mm	500.	1600.	2500.	3500.
			Buckled dies - plain edge					
15C	R6	1834	Copper	27mm	500.	1600.	2500.	3500.
			Different dies					
15D	R8	1834	White Metal	27.4mm	—	3000.	4500.	5500.

HT #	Rarity	Year	Metal	Size	VG	VF	EF	Unc
15E	R8	1834	Brass	27mm	—	3500.	—	—

An Unc specimen of HT 15 realized $5,300 at auction March 27, 1981. HT 15D appeared in the New Netherlands Coin Co. sale in 1953.

An F-VF specimen of HT 15E fetched $3,300 in the Dec. 1991 Gold Medal sale. It is of a third obverse die type.

A VF specimen of HT 15 fetched $1,430 in the 1989 Steinberg sale, while another brought $1,050 in the 1995 PCAC58 sale. Another VF fetched $1,350 in PCAC 1998 sale.

An EF-AU specimen of HT 15D fetched $4565 in 1999 PCAC Centola sale, lot 6 (reeded edge).

DANIEL WEBSTER

HT #	Rarity	Year	Metal	Size	VG	VF	EF	Unc
16	R1	1841	Copper	28mm	5.00	15.00	35.00	200.
	Plain edge.							
16A	R9	1841	Copper	28mm	—	—	250.	—
	Reeded edge.							

| 17 | R1 | 1841 | Copper | 28mm | 5.00 | 15.00 | 35.00 | 200. |

| 18 | R1 | 1841 | Copper | 28mm | 5.00 | 15.00 | 30.00 | 200. |

Daniel Webster was a strong advocate of the United States Bank, and his speech on the subject in May, 1832, was an important one, while that of September, 1837, in the Senate, in opposition to the Sub-Treasury Bill is regarded as "one of the most effective of all his arguments on the subjects of currency and finance." His defense of the Constitution in January, 1830, in a famous speech, won for him the title of "Defender of the Constitution," to which this token alludes. As the leader of the opponents of Jackson's policy, Webster's name appears on several of their tokens, and it is interesting to note that his first great speech in favor of the United States Bank was met by the token issued by its adversaries and the first described in this work, which declared "The Bank must perish" but "the Union must be preserved," yet the Union had no more strenuous upholder than the great supporter of the Bank.

Lightning inside wreck

HT #	Rarity	Year	Metal	Size	VG	VF	EF	Unc
19	R5	1841	Copper	28mm	75.00	200.	550.	1000.

20B Rusted dies - rigging weak

HT #	Rarity	Year	Metal	Size	VG	VF	EF	Unc
20	R1	1841	Copper	28.5-29mm	5.00	17.50	30.00	275.
20A	R7	1841	Silver	29mm	—	2800.	4000.	6000.
20B	R2	1841	Copper	29mm	5.00	17.50	30.00	275.
20C	R9	1841	Copper	29mm	—	—	575.	—

Struck over South American token. (Kirtley Feb. 1991 list)

HT 20

Daniel Webster was born in Salisbury, N.H., 18 January, 1782. Graduating from Dartmouth in the class of 1801, he at once began the study of law in Salisbury, and in 1804 entered the office of the Hon. Christopher Gore, of Boston. He practiced a few years in New Hampshire, until elected to the House of Representatives in the National Congress by his native state. He withdrew from political life at the close of his second term and removed to Boston in 1816. Six years later he was again sent to Congress as a Representative from Massachusetts, and in 1828 was chosen Senator, and served until he became Secretary of State under Fillmore in 1850. He died at Marshfield, Mass., 24 October, 1852.

HT #	Rarity	Year	Metal	Size	VG	VF	EF	Unc
21	R2	1841	Copper	28.8mm	7.00	20.00	115.	250.

HT #	Rarity	Year	Metal	Size	VG	VF	EF	Unc
22	R1	1841	Copper	29.1mm	5.00	15.00	35.00	225.
22A	R4	1841	Gilt Copper	28.5mm		Not contemporary		

HT 22

About 90% of these have a slight break in the obverse die between the letters C and Y in CURRENCY, and on a few it extends to the ship, with another break through D in CREDIT, and sometimes continuing through CONSTITUTION. A third and still rarer break is visible at E in CURRENCY.

An Unc MS-63 specimen of 22 fetched $555.45 in B&M March, 2000 sale!

HT #	Rarity	Year	Metal	Size	VG	VF	EF	Unc
23	R4	1841	Copper	28.5mm	30.00	75.00	200.	450.

A choice AU realized $280.50 in the Hayden July 2000 sale.

Dies by John Gibbs

HT #	Rarity	Year	Metal	Size	VG	VF	EF	Unc
24	R3	(1838)	Copper	27.5mm	40.00	200.	350.	800.

An EF specimen of HT 24 realized only $135 in the 1995 PCAC58 sale.
A gilt specimen was reported in 1997; not verified as an original.

A CONTEMPORARY ACCOUNT OF THE HARD TIMES TOKENS

The *Niles' National Register* for Nov. 25, 1837, extracts several press cuttings from the *New York Journal of Commerce, The Washington Globe,* and a letter from the solicitor of the Treasury reflecting upon the copper ''cents'' then in circulation:

From *New York Journal of Commerce:*

Copper coin. There are great quantities of copper pieces in the market which circulate as cents, but which are not so. They are generally too light; but the worst part of their construction is the bad metal they are made of, and their consequent tendency to become foul. Worst of all, they are a vile debasement of the current coin, by which individuals very improperly make a large profit at the public expense, their spurious coins being generally sold by the bushel, at 50 to 62 1/2 cents the hundred.

They are all stamped with some device other than that of the national cent; for, to put on that would subject the operator to consequences not profitable. It is quite time for the public to refuse this trash altogether. A very discriminating spirit has been manifested in regard to *paper* change by the butchers and all those dealers who control such matters. The consequence is, that we have a comparatively sound currency, by which very little will be lost when the banks resume specie payments, and the paper change is expelled from the market.

The notes of the city of Newark are now the only notes which circulate freely in our market. All the notes of self-created loan companies, or by whatever name they may go, are, and ought to be rejected. We hope the same course will be pursued with the dirty ''no cents'' which are attempted to be put forth so plentifully.

From *Niles' National Register.*

The Washington ''Globe'' says: ''Most of the coins referred to are stamped with political caricatures, and other federal devices. An emission of them hails the inauguration of *Daniel Webster* as president in 1841, while others contain inscriptions insulting to the late and present president of the United States.

''There really seems to be no bounds to the limits of federal enterprise in the manufacture of spurious substitutes for money.''

(Author's comment: The comment above, made in 1837, seems to refer to the Webster Credit Current [and Currency] tokens, HT 16 to 23, since there are no political medalets hailing Webster's ''election'' as president. If it does, it would indicate these 1841-dated pieces were struck in 1837.)

From *Niles' National Register*, Nov. 25, 1837:

From the same paper **(The Washington Globe)** of the 23rd inst. we extract the following letter upon the subject, from the solicitor of the Treasury to N. Williams, Esq., district attorney of Maryland:

'Office of the Solicitor of the Treasury, Nov. 17, 1837,

'Sir: The secretary of the Treasury has referred to this office a communication received from Baltimore, transmitting the enclosed copper coin. It is stated to be a specimen of such as are extensively put in circulation there, and advertised in the newspapers by a commission house, which is retailing them to any one who applies for them. I have to request that you will cause inquiry to be made into the truth of these statements, and if such be the fact, institute the proper legal proceedings without delay.

'The second section of the Act of 8th May, 1792, provides that ''no copper coins or pieces whatsoever, except the said cents and half cents, being those coined at the mint of the United States, shall pass current as money, or shall be paid, or offered to be paid, or received in payment, for any debt, demand, claim, matter, or thing whatsoever; and all copper coins or pieces, except the said cents and half cents, shall be paid, or offered to be paid, or received in payment, contrary to the prohibition of the aforesaid, shall be forfeited; and every person by whom any of them shall have been so paid . . . shall also forfeit the sum of ten dollars . . .''

'Very respectfully yours, H.D. Gilpin, Solicitor of the Treasury, to N. Williams, Esq., U.S. Attorney, Baltimore.'

(Author's comment: We cannot know what the enclosed token was, but it seems certain it was one of the political HTT's.)

THE CONSTITUTION

Comes with upset and non-upset reverse

HT #	Rarity	Year	Metal	Size	VG	VF	EF	Unc
25	R1	1834	Copper	28.6mm	7.00	25.00	100.00	250.
25A	R3	1834	Silvered Copper	28mm			Not contemporary	
25B	R7	1834	Copper	30mm	—	70.00	—	—

As 25, on larger flan. (Donald Miller coll.)

The quotation, ''A plain system'' etc., is a sharp satire on the professed Jeffersonian Democracy of Jackson. In his speeches and public documents he was constantly upholding the doctrines of the third President, who was ''the very embodiment of democracy,'' and to whom all titles of honor, even that of Mr., were distasteful, who dressed in the plainest style, and whose inauguration was pre-eminently ''void of pomp;'' but the brilliant war record of Jackson was ever on the lips of his party followers. Somewhat egotistic in his way of expressing himself, due rather to his sense of the dignity and powers of his high office than to any great personal vanity, the satirists delighted to portray him in a dress suit, awkwardly brandishing his weapon, or in full uniform as a General, with epaulets and sword, and all the ''pomp'' of war, with ''My glory,'' or some similar phrase added, as on No. 9 above, and others.

WILLIAM SEWARD

HT #	Rarity	Year	Metal	Size	VG	VF	EF	Unc
26	R4	(1834)	Brass	27mm	45.00	200.	300.	1000.
26A	R6	(1834)	Silvered Brass	27mm	—	200.	350.	1500.

It is difficult at this distance of time to fix the date of this and the two following tokens, or to give an entirely satisfactory explanation of the legends on Nos. 13 to 16. While the extract below from a Democratic newspaper of May, 1835, shows that the Verplanck token was a Whig issue of 1834, yet Verplanck had been elected to Congress by the Democrats (1825-1833), his term having then but lately expired. But Seward and Stillwell were also the candidates of a party which called itself Whig, and were defeated by William L. Marcy in 1834, who was elected by the Democrats. This may indicate that the Seward token was struck either in 1834, when he was first a candidate, or in 1838, when he was successful. Admitting however that it was not struck until 1838, does not remove all difficulties; for since Seward and Verplanck were both rival candidates against Marcy, the legends express what were the hopes of the friends of each in 1834, yet each is called a ''Whig token.''

A possible explanation is found in the fact that the opponents of Jackson had at that time divided into two groups; one, called National Republicans, under the lead of Henry Clay, charged the President with overriding the Constitution, and other political crimes, while the other, under John Tyler, called ''States Rights'' men, opposed a high tariff, a National Bank, etc., and ''agreed with the National Republicans in nothing except hostility to the President.'' The National Republicans began to call themselves Whigs in 1834, and the followers of Tyler soon took the name of States Rights Whigs. The two divisions had nearly come together in 1836, but did not unite in season to agree on Presidential nominations, and Van Buren was elected. Let us therefore suppose that the factions opposing Jackson, the one led by Seward and the other by Verplanck, put out both tokens in 1834, under which date they are placed; the latter faction, as a newspaper cutting of the period shows, claimed to be the special ''friends of the Constitution and the laws,'' and called theirs the ''Constitutional ticket''; apparently both factions were included under the general name of Whigs by their political adversaries who supported Jackson.

HT #	Rarity	Year	Metal	Size	VG	VF	EF	Unc
27	R5	(1834)	Brass	28mm	100.	300.	475.	1200.

HT #	Rarity	Year	Metal	Size	VG	VF	EF	Unc
27A	R5	(1834)	Silver plated before striking		100.	300.	900.	1700.

HT #	Rarity	Year	Metal	Size	F	VF	EF	Unc
28	R3	(1834)	Brass	27.1mm	75.00	150.	250.	1500.
28a	R7	(1834)	Copper	28mm	—	—	May not exist	
29	R7	(1834)	Brass	28mm	1200.	3000.	3500.	6000.
29A	R7	—	Brass	27mm	1000.	2500.	3000.	5000.

NOTE: HT 29 has the reverse of number 30 below.
An EF specimen of 29 fetched $1870 in 1990 and $2750 in 1999 (Krause coll.). A VF realized $1140 in June 2000.
A Good specimen of HT 27 was valued at $50 in the May 2001 Hayden sale.

GULIAN VERPLANCK

HT #	Rarity	Year	Metal	Size	VG	VF	EF	Unc
30	R2	(1834)	Brass	27.3mm	45.00	125.	260.	450.
30A	R7	(1834)	Copper	28mm	—	—	—	Rare

NOTE: 30A was lot 259 in the Dunham sale.

30B	R4	(1834)	Silvered Brass	28mm	40.00	125.	300.	750.

An HT 30 in AU was lot 542 in the B&M Frontenac 1991 sale, and was lot 005 in PCAC June 1996 sale, where it realized $176.
NOTE: Though HT 30 identifies its portrait as that of Gulian C. Verplanck, comparison of the portrait with that on 28, (supposedly William H. Seward) reveals that they are more or less identical.

In an article in *The Times*, May 2, 1835, headed "And all their triumphs shrink into a coin," this piece is referred to, and the extracts below, which are copied from it, give the reasons for including this and the three preceding tokens in this list, as they prove that these pieces formed a part of the circulating medium: —

"A few brief years will pass away, and with them almost every trace of the existence of the Whig party. That party, however, in the pride of its power and confidence of its success, adopted the same plan for perpetuating its name that has been adopted by kings and princes. The story of their accession and their continuance in power is told by the coins and medals circulated during their reigns.***We have in our possession a coin of the grand Whig emission of 1834. On one side is an eagle, surrounded by the words "a faithful friend to our country," and on the other, an image surrounded by the words "Gulian C. Verplanck, our next Governor." It is made — most appropriately — of brass, symbolical of the modesty of the party with which it was issued. What a treasure will such a coin be to the antiquary a hundred years hence! — How will he pore over its image and superscription, and puzzle himself with most learned doubts as to its history and character! — At what epoch of the republic was it issued? What great event was it intended to commemorate, and who was the great man whose name, otherwise unrecorded — it has preserved for a hundred years? It speaks of Gulian C. Verplanck, "our next Governor." He was probably the governor-elect. The people had chosen him, but he had not yet entered upon the duties of his office. ***Why should a coin be struck off with his name and head on it? In all other countries it is the possessor and not the heir to the throne whose effigy is stamped on the coin of the realm. In looking over the almost interminable list of governors of the different States, the name of Gulian C. Verplanck can not be found. ***Most unfortunately, the coin bears no date, and for aught that appears to the contrary, it might have been issued anterior to the revolution. You cannot refer it to contemporary history, for the simple reason that you have no means of judging when it was issued. *** It is valuable because it is rare, and because from its most incomprehensible character, it will constantly call forth the discussions of antiquaries and virtuosi. It may be that in the wreck of matter of a hundred years, a few files of very old newspapers may survive. Possibly the very paper containing this article may chance to have a better fate than its brethren and furnish an addition to some collection of old and perhaps good for nothing trumpery. — Here then will be a key to unlock the mystery, and the quid nuncs of a hundred years hence will learn that in 1834, there flourished a mighty party called the great universal Whig party of the world, a party which lived and flourished on anticipation — celebrated victories which were to be won, but never were won, rejoiced over successes, which like the waters near the lips of Tantalus, were ever at hand but never reached, and struck medals in honor of governors who were never elected. ***We will mention by way of conclusion that the Verplanck Coinage of 1834 is becoming scarce. The pieces are at a premium, even now, the knowing ones among the Whigs having called in all they could possibly command."

1) William H. Seward was born in Florida, N.Y., 16 May, 1801. He was educated at Union College, and soon after attaining his twenty-first year was admitted to the Bar, where he achieved a high reputation as a criminal lawyer. Joining the Anti-Masonic party in the Morgan excitement, he was elected to the State Senate in 1830, and in 1832 made an able speech in favor of the United States Bank. Defeated as the Whig candidate for Gov-

ernor in 1834, he won the position in 1838 by a majority of 10,000, and was the first representative of his party to hold that office. The remainder of his life was spent in the political arena, with the exception of the period from 1842 to 1849. In the latter year he was chosen United States Senator, and served until he became Secretary of State under President Lincoln, in 1861. He died at Auburn, 10 October, 1872.

2) Gulian Crommelin Verplanck was born in New York in 1786. He was distinguished as a scholar and writer rather than as a politician, though his first work, published anonymously, was "The State Triumvirate, a Political Tale," which was a brilliant political satire, and appeared in 1819. He was soon appointed Professor of Christian Evidences in the General Theological seminary (Protestant Episcopal), New York, but was elected to Congress in 1825 and served until 1833. Political life was however distasteful to him, and he returned to literary pursuits. He is best known by his annotated edition of Shakespeare, published in 1846, which was highly praised. Verplanck was chiefly instrumental in passing two Acts while in the State Senate of New York, that greatly increased his popularity; one was that which exempted from attachment the goods of non-resident debtors, and the other for the more permanent establishment of the State Hospital, — both of which were productive of good results. He died in March 1870.

ILLUSTRIOUS PREDECESSOR

HT #	Rarity	Year	Metal	Size	VG	VF	EF	Unc
31	R3	1837	Copper	28.5mm	25.00	200.	350.	650.
31B	R7	1837	Thin oversize planchet		75.00	300.	450.	750.

An EF-AU specimen of HT 31 fetched $400 in the 1995 PCAC58 sale.

HT #	Rarity	Year	Metal	Size	VG	VF	EF	Unc
32	R1	1837	Copper	29mm	5.00	25.00	50.00	150.

HT #	Rarity	Year	Metal	Size	VG	VF	EF	Unc
33	R1	1837	Copper	28.5mm	5.00	15.00	50.00	125.
33A	R8	1837	Silver	28.5mm	—	—	—	7500.

Probably not a Bushnell product.

Photo enlarged

A33	R5	1837	Copper	29.5mm	—	—	60.00	—

As 33, but borders of denticles, not beads, and donkey's ear does not touch I in IN. (Boller and Dave Wilson colls.)

HT #	Rarity	Year	Metal	Size	VG	VF	EF	Unc
34	R1	1837	Copper	28.8mm	5.00	20.00	30.00	135.
34C	R8	1837	Copper	28.7mm	—	600.	875.	—

Obverse as 34. Rv: Blank. Weight 10.6 grams. Plain edge. This is a minting error blank reverse, not a planed-off blank. (PCAC May 1997 sale, lot 001; fetched $577.50; Gale July 1997 sale, page 10)

Whatever truth there may have been in the charges of weakness and subservience to Jackson and his friends which were brought against Van Buren by his political enemies, it is now generally admitted that his financial ability was great, and as Fiske says, "The principal achievement of his administration was the divorce of Bank and State." To his successful "experiment" is due the establishment of the Subtreasury system, which finally took shape in 1846. The Independent Treasury Bill was introduced in Congress, September 2, 1837, and rejected, but was passed with some modifications in 1840, and though repealed under Tyler, at length became the established Government policy, without regard to party. Briefly the experiment was to withdraw the Government funds from State Banks,— private institutions chartered under State Laws, — and place them in the hands of United States Government officers. The result of this was to separate the Government funds from all others, and to free its Treasury from any dependence upon the banks in its fiscal operations; the collection, safe-keeping, transfer and disbursement of the public money was to be performed solely by agents of the Government, — called "Fiscal Agents," — and all payments by or to the Government were made in specie. One can but wonder at the opposition these sound financial principles aroused.

The tortoise with a safe on its back on the tokens has been said to allude to the slow progress which the experiment made, and the running jackass to Van Buren's rapid growth in popularity — which is doubtful. The withdrawal of public funds from the banks, with other reasons, led to a contraction of the currency and great changes in apparent values, which under the loose methods that had previously obtained, may be said to have been the apparent causes of "Hard Times." The true causes lay further back, and are easily discernible by the student of history.

LIBERTY - NOT ONE CENT

HT #	Rarity	Year	Metal	Size	VG	VF	EF	Unc
35	R2	1837	Copper	27.2mm	30.00	125.	300.	700.

HT #	Rarity	Year	Metal	Size	VG	VF	EF	Unc
36	R3	1837	Copper	27.4mm	35.00	150.	250.	800.

HT #	Rarity	Year	Metal	Size	VG	VF	EF	Unc
37	R4	1837	Copper	28mm	50.00	400.	600.	1000.

Bushnell fantasy

HT #	Rarity	Year	Metal	Size	F	VF	EF	Unc
38	R7	1837	Copper	28mm	—	—	2000.	2300.
39	R7	1837	Copper	28mm	—	—	1900.	2200.

NOTE: HT 39 has the full lower serif of the ONE's 'E'.

HT #	Rarity	Year	Metal	Size				Unc
39A	R8	1837	Silver	28mm	—	—	—	6000.

Bushnell fantasy

HT #	Rarity	Year	Metal	Size	F	VF	EF	Unc
40	R7	1837	Copper	28mm	—	—	1800.	2100.
40A	R8	1837	Silver	28mm	—	—	—	6000.
40B	R7	1837	Struck over HT 42					
				28mm	—	—	2000.	2500.

NOTE: Bushnell series were made in very small numbers about 20 years later than the dates they bear. See note following HT 74.

Bushnell fantasy

HT #	Rarity	Year	Metal	Size	VG	VF	EF	Unc
41	R7	1837	Copper	28mm	—	—	2000.	2500.
41A	R8	1837	Silver	28mm	—	—	—	6000.

HT #	Rarity	Year	Metal	Size	VG	VF	EF	Unc
42	R1	1837	Copper	28mm	5.00	25.00	40.00	150.

Dies cut by John Gibbs

HT #	Rarity	Year	Metal	Size				
43	R8	1837	Copper	28mm		3000.	4000.	—

Only three pieces known.

Dies cut by James G. Moffet

44	R3	1837	Copper	28-1/2mm	20.00	100.	300.	900.

HT 45 in UNC.

HT #	Rarity	Year	Metal	Size	VG	VF	EF	Unc
45	R2	1837	Copper	28mm	10.00	50.00	90.00	275.

A silver-washed copper version reported 1997; not verified as original.

HT #	Rarity	Year	Metal	Size	VG	VF	EF	Unc
46	R2	1837	Bronze	28.1mm	5.00	12.00	30.00	165.
46A	R1	1837	Copper /Brass	28.1mm	5.00	12.00	30.00	165.

Enlarged   **Drawing of 3/5**

HT #	Rarity	Year	Metal	Size	VG	F	VF	EF
46R	R3	1837/57	Copper	28.1mm	10.00	20.00	50.00	150.

As 46, but diecutter recut a 3 over the 5 in a careless manner. The enlarged illustration and drawing of the 3-over-5 clearly evidence the variety. Discovered 1996 by Denton V. Curtis, Chandlers Ford, England.

Researcher Wesley S. Cox of Columbia, Mo., had acquired 24 specimens of HT 46R by 2001. Cox also has located two specimens of a partially filled '3' punch, and argues that 46R may have resulted from a die breakdown rather than a die recutting. Since HT 46 is common, further study of specimens seems inevitable; the collecting of Hard Times tokens is one of the brightest aspects of exonumia.

The comparative scarcities of HT 46 and HT 46R are radically altered above, due to a census of typical dealer inventory conducted recently by Wesley S. Cox Sr. He determined that HT 46R was almost three times as common as HT 46 (24 versus 9, or 62.5% vs. 37.7%).

Of all examples studied, the average measured 28.1mm diameter, smallest 28.0mm and largest 28.4mm. Average mass was 8.74 grams, with a wide weight range of 7.63 to 9.33 grams. Specific gravity ranged from 8.30 to 9.18, Cox stated.

All examples examined had plain edges and coin alignment, indicating excellent Scovill quality control on striking.

The metallic content of 30 pieces in Cox' possession is very enlightening:
Yellow brass – 3
Brass, copper-plated by electroless process – 17
Red brass or bronze (indistinguishable) – 9
Red copper – 1

The sampling may be too small to be scientific, but it would seem 76.7% of HT 46 and 46R may be copper-plated brass.

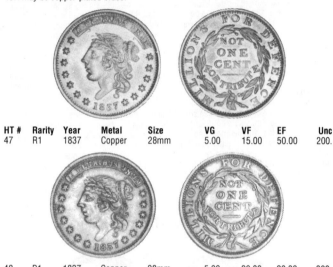

HT #	Rarity	Year	Metal	Size	VG	VF	EF	Unc
47	R1	1837	Copper	28mm	5.00	15.00	50.00	200.

48	R1	1837	Copper	28mm	5.00	20.00	90.00	300.
48A	R4	1837	Silvered Copper	28mm		Not contemporary		

Obverse as that of HT 47.

HT 47 and 48 occurs with both coin and medal alignment. This feature is common in Hard Times tokens and has no rarity significance.

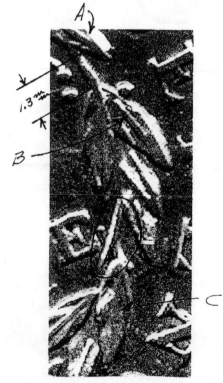

HT 47 and 49

HT #	Rarity	Year	Metal	Size	VG	VF	EF	Unc
49	R1	1837	Copper	28mm	5.00	35.00	65.00	300.

Reverse as that of HT 47.
A BU part orange HT 49 realized $460 in Jan. 2001.

HT #	Rarity	Year	Metal	Size	VG	VF	EF	Unc
52	R1	1837	Copper	28mm	5.00	25.00	40.00	300.

NOTE: All tokens HT 45 thru HT 52 were struck by Scovill in Waterbury, Conn.

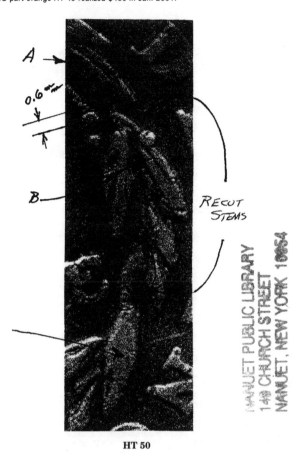

HT 50

Bushnell fantasy

HT #	Rarity	Year	Metal	Size	VG	VF	EF	Unc
53	R7	1837	Copper	28.5mm	—	—	1800.	2200.
53A	R8	1837	Silver	28.5mm	—	—	—	6300.

Bushnell fantasy

HT #	Rarity	Year	Metal	Size	VG	VF	EF	Unc
54	R7	1837	Copper	29mm	—	—	2000.	2500.
54A	R8	1837	Silver	29mm	—	—	—	6300.

Bushnell fantasy

HT #	Rarity	Year	Metal	Size	VG	VF	EF	Unc
55	R7	1837	Copper	29mm	—	—	2200.	2600.
55A	R8	1837	Silver	29mm	—	—	—	6300.

Weight of 55A 7.785 grams. Specific gravity 10.27.

When Scovill's repunched or cut in the berry stem at top of leaf B, they reduced the distance between leaf A and B by at least half. The berry atop leaf C in 47 and 49 was virtually omitted in 50. Also note clear dot after E of TRIBUTE has deteriorated on 50. (Enlargement photos and markings by Wesley S. Cox)

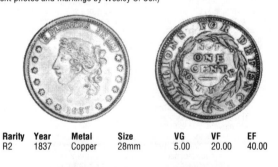

HT #	Rarity	Year	Metal	Size	VG	VF	EF	Unc
50	R2	1837	Copper	28mm	5.00	20.00	40.00	200.

HT #	Rarity	Year	Metal	Size	VG	VF	EF	Unc
56	R1	1837	Copper	28mm	6.00	15.00	37.50	250.

Note: See blowups at end of this chapter for reverse of HT 56!

Reverse of HT 48.

"Shinplasters" have been referred to in the Introduction. The name was applied to bills of irresponsible banks and private parties. The device of the phoenix rising from flames seems to mean that the paper money was only fit to be burned, and that with its destruction new life would spring from its ashes. The date, November, 1837, is that of a convention held in New York on the 27th of that month, by representatives of leading banks in nineteen states to fix a date for resumption. They met again the 16th of April, 1838 and decided to resume specie payments the 10th of May following, which was successfully accomplished after a suspension of exactly one year. (See No. 65.)

HT #	Rarity	Year	Metal	Size	VG	VF	EF	Unc
51	R2	1837	Copper	28mm	5.00	45.00	60.00	225.

HT #	Rarity	Year	Metal	Size	VG	VF	EF	Unc
57	R1	1837	Copper	28mm	5.00	12.00	40.00	150.

Reverse of HT 48.

HT #	Rarity	Year	Metal	Size	VG	VF	EF	Unc
58	R1	1841	Copper	28mm	5.00	15.00	30.00	300.

NOTE: HT 56, 57, 58, 61 and 62 are Scovill strikes.

| 58B | R6 | 1841 | Copper | 28mm | — | 150. | — | — |

As 58, double struck CURRENT and DEFENCE. (Gale July 1997 sale, page 11)

Bushnell fantasy

| 59 | R7 | 1841 | Copper | 28mm | — | — | 2000. | 2500. |
| 59A | R8 | 1841 | Silver | 28mm | — | — | — | 6000. |

Bushnell fantasy

| 60 | R7 | 1841 | Copper | 28mm | — | — | 2000. | 2750. |
| 60A | R8 | 1841 | Silver | 28mm | — | — | — | 6000. |

MINT DROP

HT #	Rarity	Year	Metal	Size	VG	VF	EF	Unc
61	R2	1837	Copper	28mm	5.00	20.00	50.00	460.

HT #	Rarity	Year	Metal	Size	VG	VF	EF	Unc
62	R1	1837	Copper	28mm	6.00	15.00	75.00	430.

| 63 | R1 | 1838 | Copper | 29mm | 8.00 | 30.00 | 60.00 | 400. |

HT #	Rarity	Year	Metal	Size	VG	VF	EF	Unc
63A	R9	1838	Copper	29mm	—	—	600.	—

HT 63 overstruck on HT 72.

An AU specimen of 63A fetched $810 in a Jan., 2001 eBay auction.

| 64 | R1 | 1841 | Copper | 28mm | 6.00 | 15.00 | 25.00 | 300. |

"Bentonian Currency" was hard money as opposed to paper. The friends of the United States Bank who favored the issue of Government paper for circulation, were constantly ridiculing their opponents by squibs in the newspapers of the day. The *Virginia Advocate*, for example, had the following in an article headed. "Who would not be a Jackson man?" — "Have you been seven times spurned by the people when you offered to serve your country, and are you in want of the wherewithal to make the pot boil? — try the hard money tack, and jingle a few Benton yellow jackets at everybody but your creditors, and it's odds if you don't rise to an embassy or a department. It is the short cut to fame, to wealth and power; and one has hardly time to put on a clean shirt . . . before he writes his name . . . on the milky way of 'glory.' . . . This Jacksonism is a crucible which like that of the astrologer, turns all baser metals to gold . . . Oh, what it is to be a Jackson man!" On the other side, Benton, in a letter written from St. Louis, in August, 1837, praised Jackson for accumulating eighty million of hard money in the country — enabling the Government to be independent, raising prices for farm products and prophesied good times, etc. He quoted Jefferson as having, in 1792, charged the Federalists with a scheme to banish gold and silver from circulation and deluge the States with paper money — which would have been accomplished in 1837 were it not that "Jackson's *policy balked this system* in the moment of its anticipated triumph," and he closed his letter by saying, "I think his successor (Van Buren) is '*made of the stuff* to sustain that policy, etc." Only a few months later, the policy of Jackson and Van Buren, or rather the heroic methods by which its supporters attempted to carry it out, regardless of the laws of business, — for the policy itself was sound — with other causes, brought the entire country to the verge of ruin. But the crash of 1837 and the Hard Times which followed were by no means solely due as the Whig leaders would have it believed — to the overthrow of their policy and the "mint drops" or hard money of Jackson and Van Buren: they were only the culmination of evils which had long been threatening disaster. The wild speculations which accompanied the rapid development of Western lands from 1820 onward, intensified by the building of railroads, as Fiske tells us; the miserable banking system of the period; the inflation of the currency by the issue of worthless bills and "shinplasters," were all potent causes. When speculation was checked, and "cheap money" abolished, prosperity returned. For this the Whigs claimed the glory, but it was due nevertheless to the "experiments" which they satirized so severely.

HT 63 - LOCO FOCO

The occurrence to which allusion appears on this token was briefly mentioned in the introductory remarks. At a meeting in Tammany Hall, on the evening of 29 October, 1835, there was a split in the party over the Congressional nominee. The friends of each had endeavored to pack the meeting; great confusion attended the efforts of the chiefs and their followers to obtain control, amid which the gas was turned off, it was alleged through the connivance of the janitor with one faction. Their opponents, however, if they did not themselves instigate the move, were equal to the occasion, and somewhat singularly, had come prepared with loco-foco matches and candles, and the room was speedily relighted. The *Morning Courier* and *New York Enquirer* dubbed the antimonopolists, who had used the matches, "Loco-focos," and the name was speedily affixed to the whole Democratic party.

MAY TENTH

HT #	Rarity	Year	Metal	Size	VG	VF	EF	Unc
65	R2	1837	Copper	28mm	5.00	23.00	70.00	250.

HT #	Rarity	Year	Metal	Size	VG	VF	EF	Unc
66	R1	1837	Copper	28mm	6.00	15.00	40.00	150.
66A	R2	1837	Copper	28mm	8.00	20.00	50.00	150.

NOTE: On 66A, both sides face the same way. On 66, each side is in inverse relation to the other.

HT #	Rarity	Year	Metal	Size	VG	VF	EF	Unc
67	R1	1837	Copper	28mm	6.00	25.00	40.00	285.
67F	R9	1837	Copper	—mm	4000			

Crude contemporary counterfeit!

A contemporary struck copy of 67, in only Good-VG, made from crude dies, fetched an astounding $4070 in PCAC Nov., 1999 Centola sale, lot 17. It had originally appeared in the 1989 Gil Steinberg sale by Stacks, lot 266, where it was hammered down at $2310. It is probably Rarity 9.

Such a piece might not be considered a counterfeit, but rather a separate variety.

HT #	Rarity	Year	Metal	Size	VG	VF	EF	Unc
68	R1	1841	Copper	28mm	6.00	15.00	25.00	250.

NOTE: HT 64, 65, 66, 66A, 67 and 68 are Scovill strikes.

I TAKE THE RESPONSIBILITY

HT #	Rarity	Year	Metal	Size	VG	VF	EF	Unc
69	R1	1837	Copper	28-1/2mm	5.00	20.00	45.00	175.

HT #	Rarity	Year	Metal	Size	VG	VF	EF	Unc
70	R1	(1833)	Copper	28-29mm	6.00	20.00	40.00	150.
70A	R3	(1833)	Copper Gilt	28-29mm	20.00	125.	300.	700.

HT #	Rarity	Year	Metal	Size	VG	VF	EF	Unc
71	R2	(1837)	Brass	29mm	10.00	50.00	125.	300.

HT 70

Recent research has shown that this token is probably the first cent-sized political type token which achieved wide circulation, and it opened the door for a flood of similar items. The die was cut by Edward Hulseman in Attleboro, Mass. in the fall of 1833, and the tokens were struck by the button-makers, Robinson's Jones & Co. of Attleboro, who were Hulseman's employers 1833-1836.

The tokens of this and later types (HT 69, 71 and 72) refer to Jackson, who is shown with sword and purse. The next year, Jackson is seen on another Hulseman-designed token (HT 25) with sword and purse in a different stance.

The feeling which led to the adoption of the sword and purse device continued for some time after the Whigs had taken the reins of government. The *Albany Argus* for October 1, 1842 said: "The liberties of the country were alarmingly threatened under Mr. Van Buren's administration by a union of the purse with the sword in the same hands."

The dates of issue of numbers 69 and 71 are somewhat uncertain, though they are after 1833. The issue date on 72 could be as late as 1842.

HT #	Rarity	Year	Metal	Size	VG	VF	EF	Unc
72	R2	(1837-42)	Copper	29mm	5.00	25.00	100.	250.

This is an inferior copy of Low 51 (no H under safe).

HALF CENT

Dies by E. Hulseman

HT #	Rarity	Year	Metal	Size	VG	VF	EF	Unc
73	R2	1837	Copper	23.5mm	20.00	75.00	125.	400.

Dry weight 5.18 to 5.24 grams. Specific gravity 8.71 to 8.80.

73F	R8	1837	Tin*		12.00	—	—	—

*Tin-based alloy with lead impurity, specific gravity 7.59.
Old cast counterfeit with coloration of tarnished solder. (Wesley Cox coll.)

AMERICAN SILVER

HT #	Rarity	Year	Metal	Size	F	VF	EF	Unc
74	R8	1837	German Silver	26mm	—	—	30,000	35,000

Obverse has an American eagle displayed, head left, AMERICAN SILVER above. Reverse reads in three lines: TOKEN/25 CENTS/1837.

This piece was first introduced to the public by the late Charles I. Bushnell in his work (referred to in the Introduction), published in 1858. It next appeared in his collection of coins, which was dispersed by auction in 1881. Low purchased the piece for a collector and no other was known to him. Low had no hesitancy in stating that it is unique and was struck from dies made by Bushnell's order. Low held a similarly unfavorable opinion of HT numbers 38, 39, 40, 41, 53, 54 and 55, but in these he thought a partner was admitted, and a very limited number of each was struck in copper and probably only single specimens in silver.

However, Wayte Raymond believed HT 74 was struck for Feuchtwanger, not Bushnell. It went into the F.C.C. Boyd collection.

We now feel certain this was a Feuchtwanger pattern.

A second specimen is now known, and possibly a third. Verified specimens are in the John Ford and Donald Partrick collections.

MARTIN VAN BUREN

HT #	Rarity	Year	Metal	Size	F	VF	EF	Unc
75	R2	(1840)	Copper	28mm	40.00	75.00	150.	400.
75A	R3	(1840)	Brass	28mm	40.00	125.	200.	500.
75B	R4	(1840)	Silvered Copper	29mm	50.00	125.	300.	700.

HT #	Rarity	Year	Metal	Size	F	VF	EF	Unc
76	R6	(1840)	Brass	23mm	1500.	2600.	3500.	—

HT #	Rarity	Year	Metal	Size	F	VF	EF	Unc
77	R5	1840	Copper	24mm	175.	500.	700.	1500.
77A	R6	1840	Brass	24mm	175.	500.	700.	1500.
77B	R8	1840	Gilt/Cop	24mm	275.	600.	800.	—

Numbers 77, 77A and 77B always occur holed. 77 has either a plain or diagonally reeded edge, while 77A and B have a plain edge. These pieces may not have seen currency use.

HT #	Rarity	Year	Metal	Size	F	VF	EF	Unc
78	R4	(1836)	Gilt Brass	26mm	100.	175.	700.	1500.
78A	R7	(1836)	White Metal	26mm	300.	500.	1000.	1500.

Bust right, M. VAN BUREN and 26 stars around. (The 26th state, Michigan, was admitted Jan. 26, 1837, but its admission was certain in 1836, when the election campaign took place.) Reverse: Temple of Liberty, DEMOCRACY AND OUR COUNTRY around. (DeWitt MVB 1836-4. Mc Sorley 12.)

As 77-77B above, these may not have seen currency use. They are so similar in size and fabric to the other Van Buren pieces, however, that they should not have been omitted by Low. Low must have known of them, as they are Bushnell number II.

Almost all HT 75 thru 78A exist holed only!

Probably 78 was issued gilt. A fully gilded Unc. specimen fetched $1650 in 1998!

An 80% gilt piece in EF made $715 in 1998!

HT #	Rarity	Year	Metal	Size			EF	Unc
800	R8	(1840)	Brass	24mm	—	—	525.	—

Bust left. Around: MARTIN VAN BUREN . BORN DEC: 5. 1782. Rv: U.S. flag on Liberty cap-topped staff waves right. Around: DEMOCRATS TO THE POLLS, AND VICTORY IS OURS. (DeWitt MVB 1840-10; McSorley 35)

The McSorley sale specimen in July, 1998 fetched $512.50 in EF holed. These extremely rare pieces were issued holed. Struck by Joseph F. Thomas of Newark. As with HT 75 thru 78A, they may not have seen currency use.

HT #	Rarity	Year	Metal	Size	VG	VF	EF	Unc
801	R8	(1837)	WM	33.3mm	—	—	1750.	2700.

Bust right. Around: THE PRINCIPLES & PRUDENCE OF OUR / FORE FATHERS. Rv: Farmer plowing left. Around: WHO CAN JUSTLY APPRECIATE LIBERTY & EQUALITY / THE / (arc of 11 stars) / DEMOCRACY / (arc of 15 stars). Plain edge. (DeWitt MVB 1836-2; Satterlee 53; McSorley 11; 1864 McCoy sale; 1922 Lynch sale)

The McSorley specimen, in holed Unc., realized $2530 in 1998. This piece is the rarest of all Van Buren medalets; Satterlee notes only a few were struck, probably in autumn, 1837 to counter the severe criticism of Van Buren's handling of the financial panic that had its roots in the summer of 1836 and reached crisis proportions in May, 1837.

HT #	Rarity	Year	Metal	Size				Unc
801A	R9	(1837)	Copper	33.3mm				Ex. Rare

As last, but in Copper. (Thomas Elder 1922 Lynch sale, lot 61)

HT #	Rarity	Year	Metal	Size	VG	VF	EF	Unc
803	R7	(1836)	WM	30mm	—	—	400.	450.

Bust right. Around: MARTIN VAN BUREN & DEMOCRACY / (arc of 6 stars) . Rv: OUR / NEXT / PRESIDENT. (DeWitt MVB 1836-3; Satterlee 57)

HENRY CLAY

HT #	Rarity	Year	Metal	Size	VG	VF	EF	Unc
79	R2	(1840)	Copper	27.4mm	15.00	45.00	125.	600.
79A	R3	(1840)	Brass	27.8mm	20.00	50.00	125.	600.
79B	R8	(1840)	Gilt/Brs	—	—	—	200.	—

Dies were cut by John B. Gardiner, whose initials I.B.G. are under the truncation of Clay's right-facing toga-clad bust. Obverse reads: HENRY CLAY, AND THE AMERICAN SYSTEM. Reverse has UNITED / WE / STAND in three lines within laurel wreath. DeWitt HC 1840-1; Bushnell 37.

Clay was the National Democrat or Whig nominee in 1824, 1832 and 1844, and he sought the nomination in 1836, 1840 and 1848. Clay's dismal record was approached only by William Jennings Bryan, Democrat nominee in 1896, 1900 and 1908, and aspirant for the Presidency in 1904.

HT #	Rarity	Year	Metal	Size	F	VF	EF	Unc
802	R6	1844	WM	31.4mm	—	—	—	150.

Toga-clad bust left. Around in two concentric circles: H. CLAY THE MAN OF THE PEOPLE . THE STAR OF THE WEST . / (26 6-pointed stars) 1844. Rv: Seated Liberty, radiant, nude child with torch at her side. On scroll below: UNITED WE STAND DIVIDED WE FALL. (DeWitt HC 1844-25; McSorley 50)

The McSorley specimen, in holed Unc. as issued, realized $148.50 in 1998. Struck by William M. Wagner. (Wagner re-used the reverse die for 1848 campaign medalets of Lewis Cass and Zachary Taylor).

HT #	Rarity	Year	Metal	Size	VG	F	VF	Unc
804	?	1844	Brass	24mm				Scarce

Toga-clad bust left. Around: HENRY CLAY / 1844 (under truncation) / * BORN APRIL 12. 1777 *. Rv: Within flowering wreath: THE NOBLE / & / PATRIOTIC / DEFENDER / OF / PROTECTION. Reeded edge. (DeWitt N/L; Satterlee N/L; similar to DeWitt HC 1844-35 but with much larger bust and differing inscription)

Note: The illustration shows the campaign token in a retaining bezel of about 1mm width, thus measures 26mm. (Photo courtesy Charles M. Kirtley)

Struck by Joseph F. Thomas, Newark, N.J. First reported in a 1980's Kirtley auction.

HT #	Rarity	Year	Metal	Size	VG	F	VF	Unc
805	R5	1845	Brass	24mm	—	30.00	40.00	—

Head left. Around: HENRY CLAY ELECTED PRESIDENT A. D. 1844. Rv: Boy rides horse left toward a mill. Around: THE MILL-BOY OF THE SLASHES / INAUGURATED / MARCH 4TH 1845. (DeWitt HC 1844-33; Bushnell 44; Satterlee 151)

Gilt brass specimens are known; relatively common.

Issued in 1844, obviously, since Clay was neither elected in November nor inaugurated the next March.

HT #	Rarity	Year	Metal	Size	VG	F	VF	Unc
806	?	1845	Copper	24mm				Scarce

Bust left. Around: HARRY OF THE WEST / .*. 1845 .*. Rv: Within oak and olive wreath: THE / PROTECTOR / OF HOME / INDUS-TRY. (DeWitt 1844-34; Bushnell 36; Satterlee 156)

Also known in gilt brass (Ramsey McCoy sale, lot 1069). This piece almost certainly never saw currency use.

HT #	Rarity	Year	Metal	Size	VG	F	VF	Unc
807	R3	1844	Brass	24mm	10.00	20.00	35.00	

Bust left. Around: HENRY CLAY THE ASHLAND FARMER 1844 / BORN APRIL 12, 1777. Rv: Balance scales with WHIGS outweighing DEMOCRATS. Around: WEIGHED IN BALANCE & FOUND WANTING / 1840. Issued holed for suspension. (DeWitt HC 1844-36; Hayden 1027 & 1028)

808	R3	(1844)	Brass	24mm	10.00	20.00	35.00	

Bust left. Around: HENRY CLAY THE FARMER OF ASHLAND / BORN APRIL 12, 1777. Rv: Within wreath: THE NOBLE & PATRI-OTIC SUPPORTER OF THE PEOPLES RIGHTS. Apparently issued unholed, though extant copies are usually holed. (DeWitt HC 1844-37; Hayden 1029)

WILLIAM HENRY HARRISON

An entire series of holed election medalets of the 1840 campaign, all with similar designs (military bust left on obverse, log cabin on reverse), listed by Doyle DeWitt as WHH 1840-23 through 1840-27, appeared in copper, brass and other metals. Some measure 29mm, the size of a U.S. large cent. Though possibly none did so, all may well have circulated alongside the other tokens of the period as a cent. Many show signs of circulation.

Some Harrison 24mm political medalets use a pair of scales and the legend WEIGHED IN THE BALANCE AND FOUND WANTING. These could have served duty as half cents. (DeWitt WHH 1840-46 to 48)

HT #	Rarity	Year	Metal	Size	VG	F	VF	EF
810	R6	(1840)	WM	30.8mm	—	—	185.	

Military bust right. Around: MAJOR GEN. WM. H. HARRISON. Rv: Liberty places a wreath on a stack of arms. Around: RESOLUTION OF CONGRESS APRIL 4, 1818 * / BATTLE OF THAMES / OCT. 5. 1813. Plain edge. (DeWitt WHH 1836-1; Satterlee 81; McSorley 13, fetched $193.60 in holed EF in 1998)

810A	R6	(1840)	GS	30.9mm			165.	—

As last, in German Silver. (McSorley 14 realized $165 in holed VF-plus)

810C	R8	(1840)	Copper	30.7mm	—	—	—	450.

As last, struck over U.S. Large cent. Dates examined: 1838, illegible. Only 2 pcs. known. (DeWitt WHH 1836-2; McSorley 15)

This type is known struck on a 30mm silver planchet and on a large 38mm copper planchet.

Though DeWitt and other writers ascribe this series to the 1836 campaign, it is more likely they were for Harrison's 1840 campaign. The medalet is a mediocre copy of the Moritz Furst Congressional gold medal, Julian MI-14, awarded to Harrison for his victory over the British and Indians at the Thames River in Ontario.

The McSorley specimen overstruck on an illegible-date Large cent fetched $440 in July, 1998.

812	R4	1841	Brass	25.6mm	—	45.00	60.00	—

Similar to last, but smaller bust, embroidery decoration on collar. (DeWitt WHH 1840-37)

Battle of the Thames

Major General Harrison, commanding regular U.S. troops and Kentucky mounted militia numbering 3,500 men, flanked the British positions by crossing the west end of Lake Erie into Canada. The British under Major General Henry Proctor (800 men) and the Indians under Tecumseh (1,000 braves) thereupon evacuated Detroit and Fort Malden, despite protests from Tecumseh, the great Shawnee chief.

The Americans pursued the retreating force and caught up with them at Chatham on the north bank of the Thames. The U.S. infantry attacked the center of the British line on October 5, 1813, while Colonel Richard Johnson's Kentucky cavalry charge caused the British right to collapse. The Indians held their ground until Tecumseh was killed, when they broke and fled.

American casualties numbered 15 killed and 30 wounded. The British suffered 12 killed, 22 wounded and 477 prisoners. Indians casualties, while heavy, are not known.

Johnson later became vice president of the U.S. (1837-41), and Harrison president (1841).

By a strange twist of fate, Gen. William Henry Harrison, Whig, and Col. Richard Mentor Johnson, Democrat, were on opposing sides in the bitter political campaign of 1840. Johnson, Martin Van Buren's vice president, was seeking re-election. Harrison won, was inaugurated president March 4, 1841 and died of pneumonia on April 4, 1841.

HT #	Rarity	Year	Metal	Size	VG	F	VF	Unc
811	R3	1841	Gilt/Cop	25.6mm	—	25.00	33.00	—

Youthful-appearing military bust left, three straps and four buttons on coat. Around: MAJ. GEN. W. H. HARRISON / *** 1841 *** / (arc of 20 stars). Rv: Eagle displayed, U.S. shield on its breast, olive branch and three arrows in its talons. On scroll above: GO IT TIP. On scroll below: COME IT TYLER. Border around all of 26 stars. Plain edge. (DeWitt WHH 1840-28; Satterlee 87; Bushnell 17; Wesley Cox coll.; PCAC Oct., 2000 sale, lots 1258-1259)

811A	R3	1841	Brass	25.6mm		25.00	35.00	—

As last.

Wesley Cox deduced that John B. Gardiner prepared the dies for this piece (see photographic enlargements in Die Evidence section). Weight 6.01 grams. Specific gravity of gilt copper piece is 8.74. Medal alignment.

DeWitt lists eight additional minor varieties of this token as WHH 1840-29 through 1840-36. These are unimportant variations, showing that Gardiner used many dies to create his campaign pieces, changing the placement of straps, buttons, etc.

HT #	Rarity	Year	Metal	Size	VG	F	VF	EF
817	R5	1841	Brass	24mm	—	85.00	125.	175.

Military bust left. Around: MAJ. GEN. W. H. HARRISON / * BORN FEB. 9. 1773 *. Rv: Sidewheeler steamer right, flying a flag waving left reading 1841. Around: STEAM BOAT VAN BUREN / LOCO-FOCO / LINE / FOR SALT RIVER DIRECT. Plain edge. (WHH 1840-43; Satterlee 96; Bushnell 18; PCAC March 20, 1999 sale, lot 291, fetched $79.20 in AU)

The satire on this token is biting. The term "loco foco" has been explained under HT 63.

"For Salt River Direct" recalls an early 19th century American colloquialism. A person who was in dire straits was said to be "up Salt River." A 20th century vulgarism summed it up about the same – "up shit creek without a paddle."

Thus the "steamboat Van Buren of the Loco-Foco Line headed for Salt River direct in 1841" translated to disaster for Van Buren's candidacy in the 1840 election and Harrison's inaugural in 1841.

Interestingly, a later token type of 1850 issued by S. T. Suit of Jefferson County, Kentucky – Miller Ky 36 – refers to "Kentucky currency, Salt River bourbon, for medicinal use only."

Struck at Belleville Mint. This token is much more scarce than its auction records indicate. (See *Numismatic News* for July 4, 2000, pgs. 24 and 28).

HT #	Rarity	Year	Metal	Size	VG	F	VF	EF
814	R4	1840	Brass	25mm	15.00	25.00	40.00	60.00

Thin-necked military bust left, three straps and no buttons on coat, no stars on epaulet. Point of truncation close to O of BORN. Around: MAJ: GENL. (smaller L) W. H. HARRISON / BORN FEB. 9. 1773. Rv: Log cabin has door with three planks, and cider barrel has three hoops at each end. Around: THE PEOPLES CHOICE / IN THE YEAR / 1840. Plain edge. (DeWitt WHH 1840-51; Satterlee 101 variety)

| 814A | R6 | 1840 | Svd WM | 24.5mm | — | — | 50.00 | 75.00 |

As last, in Silvered White Metal.

Struck by E. E. Pritchard.

HT #	Rarity	Year	Metal	Size	VG	F	VF	EF
818	R2	1840	Gilt/Brass	23.1mm	—	25.00	30.00	45.00

Small military bust left. Around: MAJ. GENL_ W. H. HARRISON / BORN FEB. 9. 1773. Rv: Log cabin with window and stippled door of four planks. Prominent door latch. Flag and smoke from chimney both blow right. Tree at left, cider barrel and tree at right. Around: THE CHOICE OF THE PEOPLE. In exergue: IN THE YEAR / 1840. Plain edge. (DeWitt WHH 1840-53 variety; Satterlee 103 variety; Wesley Cox coll.)

This piece differs on obverse from WHH 1840-55, which has a larger bust, with point of the larger bust almost touching R of BORN. The facial expression on 1840-55 is also very different.

Wesley Cox deduces this token was struck by Edward Hulseman in New York City (see photographic enlargements in Die Evidence section). Weight 4.45 grams. Specific gravity 8.59. Medal alignment.

HT #	Rarity	Year	Metal	Size	VG	F	VF	EF
819	R3	1840	Brass	23mm	18.00	30.00	40.00	—

Military bust left, GEN. WM. H. HARRISON / BORN FEB. 9. 1773. around. Rv: Balance scales, tipped in favor of WHIGS over DEMOCRATS. Around: WEIGHED IN THE BALANCE AND FOUND WANTING. Plain edge. Issued holed. (DeWitt WHH 1840-46; PCAC Oct. 28, 2000 sale, lot 1261, fetched $26.40 in Fine)

This relatively common variety has the point of the bust opposite the R in BORN. The size of a U.S. Half cent, it could have circulated as such.

HT #	Rarity	Year	Metal	Size	VG	F	VF	EF
815	R4	1840	Brass	24mm	20.00	30.00	45.00	70.00

Military bust left. Three stars on epaulet. Four straps and two buttons on stippled coat. Around: MAJ. GENL. (smaller L) W. H. HARRISON / BORN FEB. 9. 1773. Rv: Log cabin. Four planks and prominent latchkey in door. Flag at left flies right, smoke from chimney at right blows left. Cider barrel at right has four hoops at each end. Bushes at both ends of cabin. Around: THE PEOPLES CHOICE / IN THE YEAR / 1840. Plain edge. (DeWitt WHH 1840-54; Satterlee 102)

| 815A | R6 | 1840 | WM | 24mm | — | — | 65.00 | 100. |

As last, in White Metal.

Pieces are known in silvered brass. Dies for these pieces were used so long they were retouched, leading to many minor varieties. The varieties are of little valuation consequence.

Illustration enlarged 3.5 times!

HT #	Rarity	Year	Metal	Size	VG	F	VF	EF
820	?	(1840)	Copper	28.6mm	—	—	—	—

Military bust left. Around: MAJ. GEN. W. H. HARRISON / BORN FEB. 9. 1773. Rv: Log cabin, tree and cider barrel at left, flag flying right atop roof peak. Around: THE PEOPLES CHOICE / THE HERO / OF / TIPPECANOE. Plain edge. Weight 7.17 grams. Specific gravity 8.93. (DeWitt WHH 1840-27)

This cent-sized copper could have served duty as token coinage. The irregular hole at top was made after issuance, probably for wear.

This token is shown enlarged 3.5 times, with numerals added to show how our colleague Wesley Cox compared letter and numeral fonts with other known tokens, to reveal that the diesinking firm of Bale & Smith of New York City prepared this piece.

On the following page, Cox' photo enlargements of letter comparisons are shown. This will assist the catalog's user to understand the complexity and thoroughness of the die-evidence study to which Hard Times tokens in this volume have been subjected.

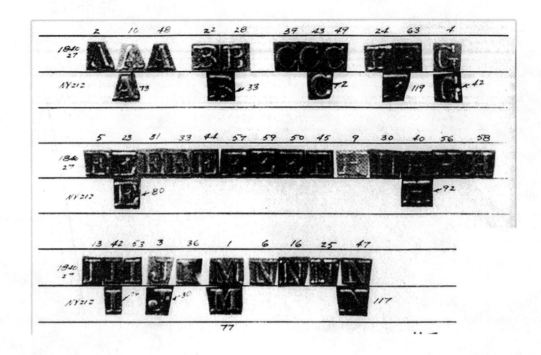

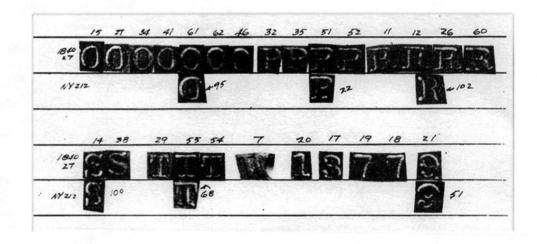

HT 820 (DeWitt WHH 1840-27) obverse and reverse letters compared with Rulau-E NY 212 (Doremus, Suydam & Nixon) letters. NY 212 is a known Wright & Bale striking of the 1831-33 period, now renumbered as HT 901A.

AM I NOT A WOMAN

HT #	Rarity	Date	Metal	Size	VG	F	VF	EF
81E	R8	1838	Copper	28.4mm	—	—	—	200.

As HT 81, but struck 5% off center at top. (B&M March, 2000 Lindesmith sale, lot 1120, in EF)

| 81G | R9 | 1838 | Copper | 28.4mm | — | — | 125. | — |

As HT 81, but ctsp small eagle perched on a 5-leaf branch, a star on its breast. Rv: Same ctsp as on obverse. (Lot 1122 in Bowers & Merena March 23-24, 2000 sale of the Lindesmith collection)

HT #	Rarity	Year	Metal	Size	VG	VF	EF	Unc
81	R1	1838	Copper	28.3mm	35.00	85.00	125.	500.
81A	R3	1838	Copper	27mm	35.00	85.00	150.	550.
81B	R8	1838	Svd/Cop	28mm	—	—	200.	—

An AU HT 81 made $297 in PCAC June, 2000 sale, lot 11. A part red Unc. 81 made $517.50 in Stack's Jan., 2001 sale.

BEEHIVE

HT #	Rarity	Year	Metal	Size	VG	F	VF	EF
81H	R9	1838	Copper	28.4mm		—	—	75.00

As HT 81, but crudely ctsp with two large serif letters H, and a small punch above the date. Most likely stray personal initials.

HT 81G is unpublished. It is doubtful the counterstamp is relevant to the slavery issue; it resembles a gunsmith marking.

Lot 1121 in the Lindesmith sale offered four examples of HT 81, respectively in EF (1) and VF (3) grades. These fetched, respectively, $135, $75, $67 and $67.

AM I NOT A MAN

HT #	Rarity	Year	Metal	Size	VG	F	VF	EF
82	R8	1838	Copper	28mm		—	—	29,500.35,000.

Three pieces of HT 82 are known; ex-Ricard, ex-Miller and ex-Fuld.

The question of slavery and its abolition had at this time found a permanent place in politics, and to a large number of people in the North such sentiments were particularly pleasing. Hence, the shrewd selection of the device of the kneeling slave, to popularize the introduction of a profitable token and to advance the cause of freedom.

The slavery question became a national issue in 1838. On August 1, 1838, local legislatures in Jamaica, Barbados, Grenada, St. Vincent, St. Kitts, Nevis, Montserrat and British Virgin Islands abolished Negro apprenticeship, and this boosted the morale of U.S. anti-slavery societies.

Kneeling male slave tokens, undated, with clasped hands on reverse, are earlier English pieces; relatively common. Value in VF = $100 and in Unc = $210.

Thanks to the research of Eric P. Newman, collectors may now know a good deal more about the background of HT 81 and 82. His conclusions are summarized here:

In late 1837 the American Anti-Slavery Society, located at 143 Nassau Street, New York, commissioned the firm of Gibbs Gardner & Co. of Belleville, N.J. to strike copper tokens (HT 81, the Kneeling Female piece). The tokens probably cost the AASS about 50 cents per hundred, as they contained copper then worth 39.5 cents per hundred.

Beginning May 4, 1833, the AASS published a weekly newspaper, *The Emancipator*, published by Charles W. Denison and edited by Joshua Leavitt. In its issue of Nov. 23, 1837, *The Emancipator* ran an advertisement offering the Female Slave tokens at $1 per hundred. Made of good copper and with a device on reverse similar to legal U.S. cents, they sold well.

The ad also said that it was proposed to issue Kneeling Male Slave tokens as well, and this accounts for the few pattern pieces of HT 82, which were never produced for circulation.

U.S. Mint Director Patterson moved quickly to suppress the circulation of HT 81, and it is apparent that by late December, 1837, he had succeeded in doing so. No further ads for the Female Slave tokens appeared in the AASS weekly or in other Journals, but since the number of pieces of HT 81 still surviving is quite large, they may well have been distributed by middlemen who paid about 62 cents per hundred for them in early 1838.

Gibbs Gardner & Co. were selected by the AASS in part because John Gibbs' Belleville Mint had also struck the 1833 Liberia cent tokens for another American anti-slavery group in Maryland.

The AASS actually distributed a British anti-slavery medal in the U.S. in 1835, selling for 25 cents each, the 1834 Emancipation Jubilee Medal.

HT #	Rarity	Year	Metal	Size	F	VF	EF	Unc
83	R4	1838	Brass	28.4mm	50.00	90.00	200.	400.
83A	R4	1838	Copper	28.4mm	50.00	90.00	200.	400.

The date on this token clearly places it in the Hard Times era, yet it has never been published as such. In 1954 Donald M. Miller considered adding it to the HTT listing, as did R.B. White in 1973.

White brought up the possibility of this token having an English origin, and some experts seemed to agree. Both pieces have Plain edges.

The Bangs Merwin sale catalog of the Groh collection (Feb. 28-29, 1860) listed HT 83A (copper) as lot 496, showing that in 1859 the Beehive piece was considered by Groh an American token. This was the judgement of the period, and may well mitigate today's opinions.

We received a copy of the Groh catalog for the first time only in early 1997 through the kindness of Q. David Bowers.

Close observation of the die work on HT 83 and 83A led our colleague Wesley S. Cox to determine that these *indeed* are American Hard Times tokens, the product of the Scovill Manufacturing Co. We quote directly from Cox' written analysis:

"The case of the letters on HT 83 and HT 83A (the same dies) is the same size as the letters used by the Scovills for "E PLURIBUS UNUM" on their Liberty head dies and the letters on the obverse of the Merchants Exchange die (HT 291)." Cox then offers photographic evidence of enlarged letter examinations of HT 83 and 291. He continues:

"There is one more clue suggesting HT 83A is a Scovill strike. One example I possess was struck on a brass planchet and then chemically plated with copper (electroless plating). Approximately 75 per cent of the Scovill tokens listed by Rulau as copper were struck on brass (planchets) and then copper plated. The study of the Hard Times tokens metals is ongoing and very far from complete."

HT #	Rarity	Year	Metal	Size	F	VF	EF	Unc
A83	R7	(1800-20)	Brass	28.3mm		—	85.00	

The beehive design is quite different from HT 83. The legend around reads: BY INDUSTRY WE LIVE / BY PERSEVERANCE, EXCEL. Reeded edge.

The illustrated piece is in the collection of Denton V. Curtis, Chandlers Ford, Hampshire, England.

The numeral "1000" has no discernible connection with the Hard Times era of which we are aware.

We now possess conclusive evidence that HT A83 is not a Hard Times token, but a British token of the 1800-1820 period. It is a scarce specimen of a very little-known class of British pieces called "school counters."

Dr. Andrew Bell (1753-1832), an Anglican clergyman, began an experimental education system in 1798 which included "counters" (tokens) as rewards for merit by students. An entire decimal system was introduced on these copper pieces and the highest value, 1000, was called a "chiliad."

Only a few schools ever used Bell's system and its counters, and thus they are virtually unknown even in England. My late friend and colleague, Roy N. P. Hawkins, wrote up the few (20) pieces of this type known to him in an obscure journal, the *Doris Stockwell Memorial Papers No. 2*, published in 1975 by BANS (British Association of Numismatic Societies). The 9-page article was titled "School Counters for Marks of Merit."

A83 was Hawkins number 0101 (copper, 28mm), issued by the "Society of Industry." Hawkins reported a second 28mm variety with the same beehive but the words REWARD / OF / MERIT replacing 1000 on reverse. (Research courtesy Dr. Ronald Ward, Rockville, Md.)

LAND LIMITATION

HT #	Rarity	Year	Metal	Size	VG	F	VF	EF
830	R8	(1844)	Silver	27mm		—	200.	—

LAND (downward arc) / LIMITATION (upward arc) ctsp on Spanish-American 2-reales. Examined: 1797-Mo-FM and 1812-NG-M. (Brunk 23795; R. Merchant coll.)

HT #	Rarity	Year	Metal	Size	VG	F	VF	EF
831	R9	(1844)	Copper	29mm	—	—	175.	—

Similar ctsp on U.S. 1844 Large cent.

For a full explanation of the Land Limitation scheme of the year 1844, see the Introduction to this Hard Times reference, tying this counterstamp and the VOTE THE LAND FREE markings together.

These Land Limitation prepared punches may also have an early Mormon connection. An old pamphlet by Frederick W. Evans of Mount Lebanon, N.Y. is entitled *A Shaker's View on the Land Limitation Scheme and Land Monopoly, and Mormon Persecution.*

VOTE THE LAND FREE

HT #	Rarity	Year	Metal	Size	VG	F	VF	EF
833	R5	(1844)	Copper	29mm	—	70.00	—	100.

VOTE THE LAND / FREE ctsp on U.S. Large cent. Dates examined: 1796, 1798, 1808, 1812, 1816, 1817, 1818, 1819, 1824, 1825, 1827, 1828, 1829, 1831, 1833, 1834, 1835, 1836, 1837, 1838, 1839, 1840, 1841, 1842, 1843, 1844, 1845, 1846, 1847, 1848. There are least 63 genuine pieces reported. (DeWitt MVB 1848-3; Duffield 1387; Brunk 41255; Sterling Rachootin coll.; Rulau Y1)

The 1844 Land Limitation scheme's supporters had specifically called for counterstamping coins as a method of advertising "free land," Dave Bowers learned.

Only 1 each of dates 1845-48 has been reported, and none of these actually examined by my colleagues or myself. The bulk of the specimens are dated 1840-44.

HT #	Rarity	Year	Metal	Size	VG	F	VF	EF
834	R7	(1844)	Silver	27mm	125.	—	225.	—

Similar ctsp on Spanish-American 2 reales. Reported: 1781, 1811-Mo, 1813, 1819 and PTS mint with date worn off. Only 5 pcs. known. (DeWitt MVB 1848-4 and 1848-5; Rulau Y2; PCAC June 16, 2001 sale, lot 152)

| 835 | R9 | (1844) | Silver | 25mm | — | — | 225. | — |

Similar ctsp on U.S. 1843 Seated Liberty quarter. (Ex-Levine, Van Ormer; Rulau Y2A)

| 836 | R9 | (1844) | Copper | 32mm | — | — | 150. | — |

Similar ctsp on England 1826 penny, KM 693. (Hartzog July 1996 sale)

| 837 | R9 | (?) | Copper | 29mm | — | — | 95.00 | — |

Similar ctsp on U.S. 1816 Large cent. Rv: L. W. GODDARD ctsp incuse twice on other side of coin. (Bowers coll.)

Foreign silver coins flooded the country beginning in 1834 as regular U.S. silver coins were snapped up by speculators and hoarders as bullion, and thus the legalization of foreign coins by the Act of 1793 permitted a torrent of Spanish-American, British and other coins.

These pieces were not simply political medalets; they were also a circulating medium and thus included in this catalog.

CAUTION: Recent fakes exist ctsp from single-letter punches! Originals are struck from one punch.

COUNTERSTAMPS

HT #	Rarity	Year	VG	F	VF	EF
84	R8	(1837)	—	—	200.	—

OLD HICKORY SPECIE WANTED ctsp on a U.S. Large cent. (Hallenbeck 15.503; Brunk 30180)

| 85 | R8 | 1837 | — | — | 125. | — |

LIBERTY / 1837 ctsp on U.S. 1819 Large cent. (Steinberg 1982 sale; Brunk 24480)

| 86 | R8 | (1834) | — | — | 125. | — |

REX AND JACKASS / THE HERO OF NEW ORLEANS ctsp on a U.S. Large cent. (DeWitt CD 1838-20; Brunk 33970)

HT #	Rarity	Year	Metal	Size	VG	F	VF	EF
A86	R9	(?)	Copper	29mm	—	—	50.00	—

AM / (Anchor) / (Anchor) / (Rooster left) / (5-pointed Star) ctsp on U.S. 1833 Large cent. (Kirtley Feb. 4, 1997 sale, lot L009)

HT #	Rarity	Year	Metal	Size	VG	F	VF	EF
B86	R9	(1840)	Copper	29mm	—	—	100.	—

Log cabin with flag flying atop its roof, in relief, ctsp on U.S. 1827 Large cent. (PCAC McSorley Nov. 1997 sale, lot 500; Brunk N/L; DeWitt N/L)

| C86 | R9 | (1840) | Copper | 29mm | — | — | 10.00 | — |

TIPP ** TYLER ctsp with indiv. letter punches on U.S. 1837 Large cent. (PCAC McSorley Nov. 1997 sale, lot 501)

HT #	Rarity	Year	Metal	Size	VG	F	VF	EF
D86	R9	1827	Silver	26mm	—	—	275.	—

GEN. / ANDREW / JACKSON. / 1827 from individual letter-punches ctsp on Spanish-American 1802-Mo-FT 2-reales, KM 91. (PCAC July 10-11, 1998 sale, lot 3, ex-McSorley; realized $275)

Cataloger H.J. Levine speculated that this piece might have been a visitation commemorative. General Jackson ran for president in 1824, 1828 and 1832.

Though clearly pre-Hard Times period, we felt this counterstamp belonged with the HT 84 to 88 grouping.

HT #	Rarity	Year	Metal	Size	VG	F	VF	EF
E86	R9	(?)	Copper	29mm	—	30.00	—	—

JACKSON ctsp three times, the incusings crossing each other, on U.S. 1828 Large cent. (PCAC July 10-11, 1998 sale, lot 4, ex-Charles McSorley; fetched $27.50)

HT #	Rarity	Year	Metal	Size	VG	F	VF	EF
87	R9	1837	—	—	—	—	200.	—

From Andrew Jackson Pres- / ident of the U.S. to *engraved* on U.S. 1836 Capped bust half dollar. Andrew Jackson / Ellis / of New Haven Conn / Feb. 22d / 1837 *engraved* on opposite side.

A male child, Andrew Jackson Ellis, was born April 29, 1836 at New Haven township, New Haven, Conn., to William H. and Susan Ellis. It is possible this is the person to whom President Andrew Jackson presented his engraved coin, but we have been unable to trace the importance of William H. Ellis to receive such honor.

An Andrew Jackson Ellis (1803-62) lived in Gallatin, Tenn., only 15 miles from The Hermitage, President Jackson's home. Present Ellis family genealogists, however, can determine no connection to Connecticut from their ancestor who was the second of five generations of Ellises to live in Gallatin 1789-1916. Charles Ellis on July 11, 2001 wrote: "I suspect my A.J. Ellis may have known President Jackson"

HT #	Rarity	Year	VG	F	VF	EF
88	R9	1837	—	—	100.	—

1837. / The true / currency *engraved* on obverse of U.S. 1805 Bust quarter. Rv: Initials I L are *engraved*. (Charles Kirtley Jan. 19, 1993 sale, lot P001)

Undoubtedly a contemporary reference to the financial panic of 1837.

ANIMAL HORN BOX

HT #	Rarity	Year	Metal	Size	F	VF	EF	Unc
90	—	(1830s)	Bone	75x45mm	—	—	200.	—

This oval box is made of animal horn bound together with brass pins. Brass hinge permits opening of box at top. Top is etched: JACKSON'S / (Reversible effigy of Andrew Jackson and jackass heads) / BEST. Bottom is etched: INVERT ME / FOR BETTER OR WORSE / ASS OR HUMAN / TAKE YOUR CHOICE. (L.B. Fauver coll. until Nov. 1987)

Enlargement numbers refer to HT numbers as given in text.

HT 31.

Basic design.

Basic design. A running mule.

33.

Corner of safe opposite right part of X in EXECUTIVE; the perpendicular strap on end passes through the exact center of handle; rosettes are smaller and less leaf-like; the ground and grass are different; date small, 7 above G in agent.

32.

The jackass and ground beneath, on this and the two varieties following, are longer than on the preceding; right ear points to right part of first L in ILLUSTRIOUS; left ear between and beyond the letters I, which begin the two lines over the animal. The eye of the donkey is large.

34.

As figure 31 with word FINANCIERING instead of EXPERIMENT. Proportions of safe are slightly different from preceding; the straps on end pass through handle a little left of its center.

33.

The right ear points to the second L in ILLUSTRIOUS; the left touches top of I in IN. Left foot points at P in PREDECESSOR; left hind foot nearly touches R in same word. Periods, smallest of this type.

34

The right ear in same position as on 33; to the left similar to 32; I in IN touches ear below its point. O in FOLLOWbelow I in ILLUSTRIOUS; both hind feet rest squarely on ground.

A33.

As 33, but borders are denticles, not beads. Donkey's ear does not touch I in IN.

49.

No obvious letter distortion, though worn. As reverse of HT 47. Right stems as original. (See blowup after HT 50 in text.)

35.

Same reverse on HT 36.

37.

NOT ONE CENT is higher in wreath, which has nine berries outside, four inside.

Recut
Stem

Recut
Stem

50.

Retouched die. Stems recut at points indicated. Die failing at ILL of MILLIONS in points shown by arrows. Dot after E of TRIBUTE almost disappeared. (See blowup after HT 50 in text.)

41.

A star has been added on each side of FOR and a dash below CENT.

42.
The wreath has six berries outside, seven inside.

38.
E PLURIBUS UNUM. Above head, chaplet of laurel leaves, plain hair cord. Thirteen stars, small 1837 lowest curl terminates right below neck, opposite the first star.

HT 35.
Thirteen stars, a break on the obverse die runs from the leaves on the head through the eye to the third star & then to the second.

40.
Same but Beaded hair cord; lowest curl short and over 37 which is large.

36.
Smaller head, fifteen stars, two of them small, separated by date.

41.
Motto framed. Forming a scroll.

37.
Coronet inscribed UNITED within a circle of twelve stars.

44.
Inferior design and execution. Heavy masculine features; large lettered motto; lowest curl terminates right, above space between 7 and *.

46.

Nose sharp; point of bust above 1 in date; lowest lock horizontal (only instance) with curl terminating right; above 7; end of scroll beneath second U in UNUM.

45.

Chin & point of bust short; curl on and below neck, both terminate left, the latter above 37.

42.

Letter of the motto smaller; plain hair cord lower curl large, terminates right above 7 in date; six stars left (others have 7).

47. & 48.

Curl on and below neck, both terminate at left; end of scroll under N in UNUM, which is double-cut at bottom.

HT 44.

The wreath has four berries outside (two opposite second E in DEFENCE), and four inside. First letters in ONE and CENT are weak occasioned by high relief of check on obv.

46.

The wreath has four berries outside (one opposite first E in DEFENCE and another, very small, on the leaf which points to C), and six inside; a small dot after TRIBUTE.
The stem of the leaf pointing to N in NOT, on sharp impressions, has the appearance of a berry, and probably was intended for such; this with the distinct one below it, would match the pair that are opposite, on the inner side of wreath, but so seldom does it appear with distinctness that we forbear to count it as a berry.

48. & 56.

The wreath has five berries inside, three outside (one opposite second E in DEFENCE).

51.   (not shown)

The wreath has six berries inside, two outside.

59.
The wreath has three berries outside and four inside; the berries are larger and letters smaller.

40.
Die altered to ONE and the berries increased to seven outside and eight inside.

60.
A small six-pointed star has been added on each side of FOR and one small berry to inside of wreath.

53.
Wreath has three berries outside, six inside.

295.
On HT 295 the second word on the scroll is spelled PLURIBUS, while on HT 297 it is spelled PIUBIBUS in error. Note that the S and N of the scroll motto are cut backwards.

45.
The wreath has three berries outside, six inside (in three pairs); without dash below CENT.

38.
ONF instead of ONE, and without dash below CENT. Wreath has six berries outside, six inside.

HT 49.
Lower curl further from 7; end of scroll under second U in UNUM.

53.
Basic design for 53, 54 and 55.

19.
Six pointed star; letters larger; water more turbulent; lightning above; one flash ends under A in VAN; the top of the promontory is opposite the same letter; the ship is without bowsprit and has a straight deck.

55.
Lightning added above the ship and a fire topmast and main-topmast falling forward.

20.
CURRENT instead of CURRENCY; the top of the stern on a line with the left part of the second R in the same word; a small stump of bowsprit.

69.
Letters & date larger, stars smaller and six-pointed bowsprit points to star before V.

16.
Basic design * Webster *

18.
Six pointed star; letters larger; water more turbulent; lightning above; one flash ends under A in VAN; the top of the promontory is opposite the same letter; the ship is without bowsprit and has a straight deck.

20.
Better executed, a crosstree below the lower sail on the mainmast; the flag on the foremast extends only to the middle of R in WEBSTER; the stars are very small.

23.

Leaf before and after WEBSTER, instead of a star.

22.

Two stays from the bowsprit to the foremast; foretop mast-staysail set, as are eight other sails; the top of the flagstaff on the stern is opposite R in CREDIT.

21.

* CREDIT 1841 CURRENCY *, straight deck, inscribed CONSTITUTION. Four stays from the bowsprit to the foremast; the top of the flag is opposite E in CREDIT; the stars are small.

ALABAMA

E. & I. BRAGAW
Mobile, Ala.

See these tokens under Newark, New Jersey, HT 207 thru 207B.

HUNT PYNCHON & JACKSON
Mobile, Ala.

HT #	Rarity	Year	Metal	Size	VG	F	EF	Unc
98	R8	(1835)	Brass	27mm	2000.	5000.	8000.	—

HUNT, PYNCHON & JACKSON / HARDWARE AND CUTLERY. Anvil, Etc. (Miller Ala 1)

The partners were Jonathan Hunt, who appears in the 1830 and 1840 census reports; George A. Pynchon, who appears in the 1830 census, and someone named Jackson. The Jackson could be either of these men from the 1830 census: John H., Samuel or S. F. Jackson. Directory confirmation is lacking.

The card may be among the rarest of all Hard Times merchant pieces. It appeared in none of the major sales of the 1980's or 1990's, and was missing from the Dr. B. P. Wright collection.

CIRCULATION AS MONEY

In the 1837-1842 period, almost 26% of the Large cent-sized pieces in circulation in the United States were Hard Times tokens, the balance being perhaps 3% foreign coppers of about 29mm size, and just 71% U.S. Mint cents.

STICKNEY & WILSON
Montgomery, Ala.

HT #	Rarity	Year	Metal	Size	VG	VF	EF	Unc
99	R8	(1835)	Brass	27.3mm	800.	3000.	6000.	—

STICKNEY & WILSON / (ornament) / Alabama / (ornament) / * MONTGOMERY *. Rv: DRY GOODS GROCERIES / CLOTHING / (leaf device) / — HATS & SHOES — / * HARDWARE CROCKERY *. (Miller Ala 27; PCAC June 1991 sale, lot 23)

Henry G. Stickney and Joseph W. Wilson ordered brass tokens in 1835 from Scovill Mfg. Co., Waterbury, Conn., for their general mercantile business in Montgomery. The firm was out of business by Nov. 11, 1839.

Research by Cindy Grellman and H. Joseph Levine permits us to assign this token issue with certainty to the Hard Times era. It had previously been listed in our *U.S. Merchant Tokens 1845-1860*.

We have increased this token's rarity from R7 to R8. Only two pieces have appeared at auction in the 20th century. A VF specimen was lot 316 in the 1925 W. W. C. Wilson collection sale. The second, in VF-EF, is the Brand-Zeddies-Krause specimen, which realized $5720 in the PCAC Nov. 13, 1999 Centola sale, lot 71.

The Brand-Zeddies piece had fetched only $440 in a B&M sale, but was resold by buyer H. Joseph Levine to Chester L. Krause for $3850 in June, 1991.

CONNECTICUT

S. NORTH
Berlin, Conn.

HT #	Rarity	Year	Metal	Size	VG	F	VF	EF
565	R9	(1830-50)	Copper	29mm	100.	—	150.	

S. NORTH — BERLIN, CON. / OURAM ctsp on U.S. 1820 large cent. (Koppenhaver Nov. 1983 sale, lot 19; Brunk 29860; Rulau Conn 110)

Simeon North was one of America's most successful early 19th century gunsmiths. Born in Berlin, Conn. on July 13, 1765, he started life as a farmer. In 1795 he purchased a water mill on adjoining land and started manufacturing scythes. In 1799 he started the manufacture of pistols. In April 1813, following a large order for 20,000 pistols, North built a large arms factory at Middletown, Conn. which operated in conjunction with his older Berlin shop about six miles distant. In 1828 North halted the manufacture of pistols and concentrated on making rifles.

From 1828 to 1850 Simeon North made Model 1817 and later Hall-patent breech-loading flintlock rifles and percussion carbines. The "Hall-North carbine," Model 1833, was a .58 caliber smoothbore to carry 24 balls to the pound, 45 inches in length, weighing 8 pounds 4 ounces and complete with a rod bayonet. They were the first percussion arms obtained by the Army ordnance department and they cost $20 each under the contract of June 1833.

Almost all of North's arms were stamped with logos such as: S. NORTH or US / S. NORTH / MIDLtn / CONN or some variation with a date such as 1826 or 1833 included. So far as we can determine, he did not mark weapons with the logo S. NORTH — BERLIN, CON. / OURAM, so we must assume that this marking was from one of his ancillary lines manufactured at the Berlin works, perhaps scythes or some other implements.

The North counterstamp is more properly included in my Hard Times Tokens reference; research is continuing.

N. PRATT JR.
Essex, Conn.

It is likely that one of the Nathan Pratt Jr. hallmarks appearing on coins was stamped in the Hard Times era. See Rulau-E Conn 8 to B8B in the EAT section of *Standard Catalog of U.S. Tokens 1700-1900*.

CHAMBERLAIN WOODRUFF & SCRANTON (and) HOTCHKISS HALL & PLATT
Fair Haven, Conn.

HT #	Date	Metal	Size	VG	F	VF	Unc
580	(1837)	Brass	30mm	10.00	30.00	100.	300.

CHAMBERLAIN WOODRUFF & SCRANTON / GREAT / CASH / DRY / GOODS / ESTABLISHMENT / . FAIR HAVEN. Rv: HOTCHKISS HALL & PLATTS / SPLENDID / OF / GROCERIES / ASSORTMENT / * LONG BRICK STORE *. Plain edge. (Wright 465; Miller Conn 5)

HT #	Date	Metal	Size	VG	F	VF	Unc
580A	(1837)	Brass	30mm	10.00	30.00	95.00	300.

As 5. Reeded edge. (Kovacs coll.)

HT #	Date	Metal	Size	VG	F	VF	Unc
580B	(1837)	Silvered Brass	30mm	10.00	30.00	100.	350.

As 5. Plain edge. (Wright 161)

HT #	Date	Metal	Size	VG	F	VF	Unc
581	(1837-41)	Copper	30mm	—	—	100.	400.

As 5. Plain edge. (Slabaugh coll.; Miller Conn 5D)

According to Wesley Cox' die evidence study, 580-581 were struck 1837-1841 by Scovill Mfg. Co., Waterbury, Conn. See the rosette blowup for HT 581 above.

T. D. B.
Hartford, Conn. (?)

This ctsp was erroneously attributed to T. D. Boardman in the 6th edition, HT B99. See under HT mavericks, HT 448.

BOLLES & CHILDS
Hartford, Conn.

HT #	Rarity	Year	Metal	Size	VG	F	VF	EF
100	R9	(1840)	Silver	26.5mm	—	—	—	500.

BOLLES & CHILDS ctsp on Spanish-American 1796-PTS-PP 2-reales, well worn. The stamp is from a die, incused. (Rulau coll.; Brunk 4197)

HT #	Rarity	Year	Metal	Size	VG	F	VF	EF
A100	R9	(1840)	Copper	23mm	—	—	—	425.

Similar ctsp on U.S. 1809 Half cent. (PCAC Nov. 13, 1999 sale, lot 72; realized $412.50 in EF)

Bolles & Childs were silversmiths, jewelers and dry goods merchants operating in Hartford only in 1840. Their work is published by Louise Conway Belden and Ralph & Terry Kovel (see Bibliography). Several references give their hallmark incorrectly as BULLES & CHILDS.

The firm was connected with Bolles & Hastings, operating circa 1841-48 in Hartford. The various partners were Edward W. Bolles, Lucius B. Childs and Gerry Hastings.

Lucius B. Childs and John C. Dickinson formed Childs & Dickinson 1841 in Hartford. Childs died 1844 and the firm disappears from directories. In 1842 they advertised as "wholesale dealers in staple and fancy dry goods, silver and German silver spoons, spectacles, jewelry, cutlery, combs, needles etc." They probably did not manufacture items they sold. (Rainwater 1998 report)

COLLINS & CO.
Hartford, Conn.

HT #	Rarity	Year	Metal	Size	VG	F	VF	EF
108D	R9	(1830's)	Copper	29mm	—	—	100.	

COLLINS & CO. / HARTFORD / CAST STEEL / WARRANTED ctsp. on U.S. 1820 Large cent with unrelated ctsp added on reverse: H. NORTON. (B&M Taylor sale of April 4, 1997, lot 1272; Brunk 8875)

Samuel Collins built a profitable axe factory in Hartford in 1826; possibly the first in America. He had a large plant in Collinsville, Conn. (Re: Barlow, Brunk)

J. C. FRANCIS
Middletown, Conn.

HT #	Rarity	Year	Metal	Size	VG	F	VF	EF
520	R9	(?)	Copper	29mm	—	—	85.00	

J. C. FRANCIS in relief within toothed rect. depression ctsp on worn U.S. Large cent. (R. Merchant coll.)

Julius C. Francis (1785-1858) was a silversmith in Middletown who entered into partnership with Edmund Hughes titled Hughes & Francis, 1807-09.

This piece could be Early American or Hard Times era; it is reported here for the first time. It is not known how long Francis worked alone after 1809.

DAVENPORT
New Haven, Conn.

HT #	Rarity	Year	Metal	Size	VG	VF	EF	Unc
101	R3	(1835)	Copper	28mm	10.00	45.00	85.00	300.

FOBES & BARLOW

HT #	Rarity	Year	Metal	Size	VG	VF	EF	Unc
102	R2	(1835)	Copper	28mm	7.00	25.00	60.00	250.

There is a John M. Barlow in the 1840 census.

WILMOT

New Haven, Conn.

HT #	Rarity	Year	Metal	Size	VG	F	VF	EF
103	R8	(1837-46)	Copper	29mm	—	100.	—	175.

WILMOT in relief within toothed rectangular depression ctsp on U.S. 1795 or 1837 Large cent. (Rulau coll.; Brunk 43680)

Both Samuel Wilmot (1777-1846) and his son, Samuel Wilmot Jr. (1808-1846), used this hallmark in their silversmith business. This firm had been known as Wilmot & Stillman about 1800. Samuel Wilmot also worked in Georgetown, S.C. and Charleston, S.C.

A relative (?), T. T. Wilmot, was also a silversmith in New Haven about 1810.

D. B. HEMPSTED

New London, Conn.

HT #	Rarity	Year	Metal	Size	VG	F	VF	EF
521	R9	(1825-35)	Copper	29mm	—	—	100.	

D. B. HEMPSTED ctsp incuse on U.S. 1803 Large cent. (Ganter 962; R. Merchant coll.)

Daniel Booth Hempsted (1784-1852), son of Revolutionary War veteran Captain Samuel Booth Hempsted, began working as a silversmith about 1806 in the Spencer & Hempsted firm (with Asa Spencer). About 1821 this firm became Daniel B. Hempsted & Co. (with Asa Spencer and Nathaniel Saltonstall) in Eatonton, Georgia until ca 1825. The hallmark on silver spoons on this ctsp was in use 1825-35 in New London, Conn.

The newspaper *New London Gazette* on April 21, 1835 advertised the firm's services and products, one reason we assign this piece to the Hard Times era. In 1852 Hempsted's son, Daniel B. Hempsted Jr. took over the business until 1882. In 1882 a grandnephew of the same name continued the business.

Hempsted in his earlier career had used a quite different hallmark: * H * in relief within rectangular depression, according to Belden. The book *Images of Connecticut Life* by Ronna L. Reynolds (1978) gives the story of Daniel Booth Hempsted's life and times.

T. K.

Norwich, Conn.

HT #	Rarity	Year	Metal	Size	VG	F	VF	EF
A103	R7	(1830's)	Copper	29mm	—	—	75.00	

T K in relief within rect. depression ctsp on U.S. Large cent. Examined: 1817, 1818, 1820, unknown date. (PCAC July 1993 sale, lot 1073)

Mark Greengold attributed this to silversmith Thomas Kinney (1796-1836) of Norwich, who in his later career moved to Cortland, N.Y. The mark matches one of those listed by Kovel (see Bibliography).

BENEDICT & BURNHAM

Waterbury, Conn.

HT #	Rarity	Year	Metal	Size	VG	VF	EF	Unc
104	R3	1837	Copper	27.5mm	12.00	70.00	100.	300.

The store card of Benedict & Burnham of Waterbury, Conn. The firm was a creator of Hard Times tokens for other merchants. In later years, especially circa 1845-1857, the company pro-

duced a number of store cards for various merchants. In 1887 the firm supplied the U.S. government with 20,000 pounds of planchets for the striking of copper-nickel 5-cent pieces.

Aaron Benedict and Joseph Burton started manufacturing bone and ivory buttons in Waterbury in 1812. Under the name A. Benedict a reorganized firm in 1823 began making gilt buttons. Benedict & Coe succeeded in 1829, and sheet brass manufacture was added. In 1834 it became Benedict & Burnham (Aaron Benedict, Gordon W. Burnham, Bennet Bronson, Alfred Platt and others), and copper, zinc and nickel alloys were added.

On Jan. 14, 1843, the firm became Benedict & Burnham Mfg. Co. In 1895 Benedict & Burnham absorbed Holmes, Booth & Haydens Co. (organized 1853), another early token issuer of Waterbury.

J. M. L. & W. H. SCOVILL

Waterbury, Conn.

HT #	Rarity	Year	Metal	Size	VG	VF	EF	Unc
105	R3	1837	Copper	28.5mm	20.00	125.	200.	340.

HT #	Rarity	Year	Metal	Size	VG	VF	EF	Unc
106	R2	1837	Copper	28.5mm	—	15.00	27.50	50.00

R on reverse. 1952 reissue from replica dies.

HT #	Rarity	Year	Metal	Size	VG	VF	EF	Unc
107	R7	(1830's)	Brass	27.5mm	70.00	200.	250.	550.

Obv: J.M.L. & W.H. SCOVILL / GILT & PLATED / BUTTON / MANUFACTURER / WATERBURY . CON. in five lines. Rv: * GILT BUTTONS OF EVERY DESCRIPTION / SHEET BRASS / PLATED METAL / & / GOLD PLATE. Only 6 to 8 pcs. known. Plain edge.

HT #	Rarity	Year	Metal	Size	VG	VF	EF	Unc
107a	R8	(1830's)	Brass	27mm	—	250.	400.	

As 107, but crudely Reeded edge. (Boller coll.; Miller coll.)

The reverse is similar to but from a different die than the reverse of HT 105, though the planchet is a bit smaller.

Token authority Dr. George Fuld possesses copies and photocopies of Scovill 1830-1845 correspondence which sheds much light on the firm's involvement with Hard Times tokens.

A holed EF HT 107a made $341 in a May 2001 Hayden sale.

SCOVILL'S DOUBLE GILT

Waterbury, Conn.

HT#	Rarity	Year	Metal	Size	VG	F	VF	EF
108	R9	(1830's)	Copper	29mm	—	—	75.00	—

SCOVILL'S DOUBLE GILT ctsp in circular fashion on U.S. 1826 Large cent. (Brunk 35945)

Scovill Mfg. Co., founded 1802, made brass buttons throughout its earlier years. This stamp is one of its many button "backmarks," This backmark was last used about 1840 (Tice, pg. 29).

H. KINGSBURY
Willamantic and Norwich, Conn.

HT #	Rarity	Year	Metal	Size	VG	F	VF	EF
518	R9	(1844)	Copper	29mm	—	—	60.00	—

H. KINGSBURY in relief within rect. depression ctsp on U.S. 1830 Large cent. (R. Merchant coll.)

Louise C. Belden illustrates this mark as that of one H. Kingsbury, silversmith, who engraved script AMF and 1844 on fiddle-end silver salt shovel in the Winterthur Museum. This same salt shovel later was engraved JWH / 1889 on the handle's back.

Green (1989) lists a vendor of watches named H. A. Kingsbury in Norwich and a Henry A. Kingsbury, jeweler, in Willamantic, most likely the same person, but, like Belden, gives no activity dates. Robert Merchant acquired a coin silver teaspoon with this same maker's mark.

Quite possibly this piece postdates the Hard Times period.

C. C. & S.
(Curtis Candee & Stiles)
Woodbury, Conn.

HT #	Rarity	Year	Metal	Size	VG	F	VF	EF
109	R9	(1831-35)	Copper	29mm	—	—	65.00	—

C. C. & S. in relief within rectangular depression ctsp on U.S. 1829 Large cent. (Brunk 6380)

This silversmith hallmark of Curtis Candee & Stiles appears in Belden's work. The partners were Daniel Curtis, Lewis Burton Candee and Benjamin Stiles. The partnership lasted only 1831-1835; it succeeded Curtis & Candee 1828-1831.

C. C. & S. also used other hallmarks. Lewis Burton Candee lived 1806-1861.

O.H. MUNSON
Yalesville, Ct.?

HT #	Rarity	Year	Metal	Size	VG	F	VF	EF
550	R9	(1839-40?)	Silver	32.5mm	—	—	400.	—

O.H. MUNSON in relief within curved-arc, toothed rect. depression ctsp on U.S. 1828 Bust half dollar. (Brunk 29900)

HT #	Rarity	Year	Metal	Size	VG	F	VF	EF
551	R9	(1839-40?)	Silver	27mm	—	—	400.	—

Similar ctsp on U.S. 1805 Bust quarter.

HT #	Rarity	Year	Metal	Size	VG	F	VF	EF
552	R9	(1839-40?)	Copper	28.5mm	—	—	100.	—

Similar ctsp on 1835 Hard Times token, HT 216 of Lansingburgh, N.Y.

HT #	Rarity	Year	Metal	Size	VG	F	VF	EF
553	R8	(1849)	Copper	29mm	—	—	100.	—

Similar ctsp on U.S. 1824 or 1834 or 1849 Large cent. (Thoele coll; Bowers coll. ex- Del Bland)

Possibly a Yalesville pewterer's touch of about 1840. Kerfoot's "American Pewter" illustrates a similar touch of John Munson, active in pewter and Britannia ware 1846-1852, and possibly later.

This ctsp is also reported on U.S. 1833 and 1834 Bust half dimes.

DELAWARE

E. JEFFERIS
Wilmington, Del.

HT #	Rarity	Year	Metal	Size	VG	F	VF	EF
522	R9	(1832-39)	Copper	29mm	—	—	350.	—

E. JEFFERIS in relief within rect. depression ctsp on U.S. 1827 Large cent. (Robert Merchant coll.)

Emmor Jefferis (1804-92) was born in Chester County, Pa. He opened his own silver-smith business 1827 in Wilmington, Del., and the same year married Ann Robinson. On Feb. 3, 1832 Jefferis took over the business of Joseph Draper (1800-64) when Draper, another issuer of counterstamps, moved west to become Cincinnati's first silverware manufacturer.

The Draper business in Wilmington had been founded before 1826 by Henry J. Pepper and sold to Draper in 1826. In 1832 Jefferis was located at 77 Market Street.

Jefferis formed a partnership with James Guthrie in 1840 (Guthrie & Jefferis). Guthrie had been a silversmith since he purchased the gold and silver business of G. J. Wolf at 41 Market Street in 1822.

UNCIRCULATED

As used in this reference, the "Unc" equates approximately to Uncirculated Mint State 63 in the U.S. coin series. Unc prices are based upon the desire of Hard Times token collectors to obtain part red, no problem specimens.

GEORGIA

I. GILBERT
Augusta, Ga.

HT #	Rarity	Year	Metal	Size	VG	F	VF	EF
110	R7	(1829-33)	Copper	28.5mm	1000.	1500.	2500.	4000.

I. GILBERT'S SADDLERY WAREHOUSE / NO. 301 / BROAD STREET / AUGUSTA / GEO. / W&B NY. Rv: SADDLERY OF EVERY DESCRIPTION / WHOLESALE / AND / RETAIL. (Low 315; Rulau-E Ga 1)

HT #	Rarity	Year	Metal	Size	VG	F	VF	EF
110A	R7	(1829-33)	Brass	28.5mm	800.	1500.	2500.	—

As 110 (Low 316; Rulau-E Ga 2)
A porous VG specimen of 110A realized only $440 in an Oct. 1996 sale.

J. & D. MORRISON
Augusta, Ga.

HT #	Rarity	Year	Metal	Size	G	VG	F	VF
111	R8	(1829-33)	Copper W&B NY	28mm	1300.	2000.	5000.	10,000.

Like the Gilbert token above, the Morrison piece properly belongs in the Early American token category.

Only four specimens are known, the ANS specimen (multilated) and three in private hands. In the Gold Medal sale of Dec. 1991, lot 031 was a specimen in only Fair-Abt Good condition, yet it realized $1,100.

A poor specimen (Zeddies) was offered at $850 by Kirtley in Feb., 1991. A nice specimen is in the Alan V. Weinberg coll.

J. A. & S. S. VIRGIN
Macon, Ga.

HT #	Rarity	Year	Metal	Size	VG	F	VF	EF
113	R9	(1835-37)	Copper	29mm	—	—	200.	

J. NALLE / N. YORK / M. BENEDICT / J.A. & S. S. VIRGIN / MACON, GEO ctsp on U.S. 1835 Large cent. (Brunk 29240 / 3310 / 41210; formerly Rulau USTT Ga-Ma 13)

Jonathan Ambrose and Samuel Stanley Virgin worked as silversmiths in Macon 1834-1837, according to Kovel.

J. Nalle has not been identified.

Martin Benedict was a New York City silversmith and jeweler 1823-1845. See his listing in the EAT section of the *Standard Catalog of U.S. Tokens 1700-1900* (Rulau-E NY 65).

LOUISIANA

A number of the Louisiana store cards of the Hard Times period have been shown by Wesley Cox' die-evidence studies to have been produced by James Bale of New York or by the Bale & Smith partnership from 1835 on.

HT 121 and 121A were struck by Bale after the Wright & Bale partnership dissolved in 1833, as was HT 123 (Puech, Bein & Co.). HT 117 (Folger), HT 120 (Henderson, Walton), HT 128 (Walton & Co.) and HT 129 and 129A were produced by the Bale & Smith partnership, though only HT 117 bears the B&S NY signature.

Both Georgia's HT 110-110A (Gilbert) and 111 (Morrison) resulted from the work of Wright & Bale, and each bears the W&B NY signature.

It is probable that more of the Louisiana Hard Times cards emanated from Bale and his associates, but this has not yet been proven.

GASQUET, PARISH & CO.

HT #	Rarity	Year	Metal	Size	VG	VF	EF	Unc
118	R6	(1835-41)	Brass	28mm	300.	1200.	2500.	3500.

W.A. Gasquet & Co. operated as a dry goods store 1830-35, becoming Gasquet, Parish & Co., foreign and domestic dry goods at 47 Chartres Street in 1835.

It was located at 18 Chartres Street in 1841 and in 1842 became Gasquet & Conrey. Thus this token is clearly within the Hard Times period. (See "New Orleans Store Cards in the Ante-Bellum Days" by Sidney K. Eastwood, in *TAMS Journal* for Oct. 1966.)

DAQUIN BROS.
New Orleans, La.
ALL ARE 10-SIDED

HT #	Rarity	Year	Metal	Size	VG	F	VF	AU
115	R5	(1835-42)	Brass	23mm	150.	250.	700.	1200.
			With or without period after PAIN					
115A	R7	(1835-42)	Lead	23mm	600.	900.	1700.	2500.
			No period after PAIN					

HT #	Rarity	Year	Metal	Size	VG	F	VF	AU
116	R6	(1835-42)	Brass	23mm	150.	250.	530.	1000.

GOOD FOR on one line; period after PAIN.
HT 115 and 116 are from differing dies. The stars are smaller on 116.

Louis D'Aquin operated his bakery from 1824 at 120 Chartres Street and other locations. In 1835 it became D'Aquin Brothers at 36 New Levee Street until 1853. The partners in 1842 were F.B. D'Aquin and Adolph D'Aquin.

The firm became F. Daquin & Co. in 1853, the partners being F. Daquin, G. Montegut and L.L. Brown. Brown was sole owner 1856-61. A successor firm was in business after the Civil War.

HENDERSON & GAINES

HT #	Rarity	Year	Metal	Size	F	VF	EF	Unc
119	R7	(1838-42)	Brass	33mm	2000.	4000.	4500.	5000.
119A	R8	(1838-42)	WM	33mm	—	—	4500.	6500.

A VF-minus specimen of 119 was lot J048 in the Kirtley Feb. 10, 1998 sale. A VG holed specimen fetched $1719.25 in the B&M March 2000 Lindesmith sale!

HENDERSON, WALTON & CO.

HT #	Rarity	Year	Metal	Size	VG	VF	EF	Unc
120	R7	(1835)	Brass	33mm	500.	2000.	2500.	4000.

NATHAN C. FOLGER

HT #	Rarity	Year	Metal	Size	VG	F	VF	EF
117	R7	1837	Brass	34mm	3000.	5000.	9000.	12,000.
			B & S = Bale & Smith.					

J. HALL WALKER & WALTON

HT #	Rarity	Year	Metal	Size	VG	F	VF	EF
121	R8	1834	Brass	33mm	2000.	4000.	7500.	8500.
121A	R8	1834	WM	33mm	2000.	5000.	7500.	8500.

KOHN DARON & CO.

BRASS, 27MM, PLAIN EDGE

HT #	Rarity	Year		VG	F	EF	Unc
431	R7	(1835)		100.	250.	500.	800.

Large 4-petaled ornament at center, wavy rule above and below - all within beaded central circle. Around: KOHN DARON & CO above. Laurel and oak wreath below. Rv: Within open-top oak wreath: GOOD / FOR / ONE / LOAD. (Miller Tenn 28)

BRASS, 27MM, REEDED EDGE

HT #	Rarity	Year		VG	F	EF	Unc
431A	R8	(1835)		—	550.	850.	1100.

As last. (Zeddies coll.; Miller Tenn 28A; PCAC June 1991 sale, lot 24)

Scovill Mfg. Co., Waterbury, Conn., correspondence dated March 30, 1835, refers to "brass medals (like J. A. Merle & Co. of New Orleans) one side Kohn Daron & Co. — other, Good For One Load." (Research by H. Joseph Levine)

Since 1920 and its attribution to Memphis by Edgar H. Adams, these tokens have been considered Tennessee issues. Due to research by Ray W. Brown published in the *TAMS Journal* for October, 1996, they are repositioned as New Orleans tokens.

Brown found that in 1834 the firm of J. Kohn & Bordier were commission merchants at 28 Bienville St. and the next listing in 1838, contained an entry for Kohn, Daron & Co., merchants, at 28 Bienville St. Thus the tokens, issued in 1835, must have coincided with the beginnings of the Kohn-Daron partnership. Brown also found confirmations in the 1830 and 1840 census records for New Orleans.

Thus Tennessee loses its only struck Hard Times entry. We have decided not to renumber the issue, however, as too many collectors use the HT numbers.

JOHN A. MERLE & CO.

HT #	Rarity	Year	Metal	Size	VG	F	VF	Unc
122	R5	(1835-41)	Brass	27mm	200.	300.	550.	2000.

Reeded edge.

Four VF-EF pieces were auctioned 1989-92, realizing respectively $550, $374, $550 and $350. An AU specimen was estimated at $800.

PUECH, BEIN & CO.

HT #	Rarity	Year	Metal	Size	F	VF	EF	Unc
123	R8	1834	Copper	25.5mm	—	17,000.	—	—

James Puech and John D. Bein were in business as partners in New Orleans beginning 1834. Only 2 pieces known (Partrick, ANS).

The pedigree of HT 123 is Tilton (1880), Gould (1950), Fuld, John Ford, Ray Byrne, Levine sale, Dave Bowers. Another is in ANS collection.

Puech's hardware store opened 1823.

LOW NUMBERS

For veteran collectors still using the century-old "Low" numbering system, there is a conversion chart of the "HT" numbers in the Introduction to this reference.

PB CTSP ON SPANISH SILVER SEGMENTS

(Planters Bank)

Enlargement of the Stamp

HT #	Rarity	Year	VG	F	VF	EF
124	R6	(1811-15) on quarter of clipped-down 8-reales	350.	1000.	1400.	2800.

HT #	Rarity	Year	VG	F	VF	EF
125	R6	(1811-15) on quarter of 8R (15 pieces known)	800.	900.	1200.	—
126	R8	(1811-15) on quarter of counterfeit 8R	—	900.	1200.	3800.
126A	R7	(?)	—	1500.	—	—

As 126, but additional ctsp BAD applied. Only 4 known. (Brunk 1740)

Planters Bank withdrew these cut segments from circulation 1815-1817, according to Robert Leonard's latest research.

A new die, HT A126, was discovered in 2001. P. B. in rectangle. Rv: NOUVELLE . ORLEANS . in concentric circles. Rare!

Steinberg Sale 289, EF, fetched $1155 in Oct. 1989 for HT 126.

NOTE: Imitations of these cut segments exist!

Number 124 weighs 4.9 grams.

Number 125 equals 2 bits, or 25 cents, and weighs 6.7 grams. The counterstamp appears on a quarter cut segment of an 8-reales (dollar) silver coin.

The obverse counterstamp is a script PB in a chain circle of 16 links. Reverse stamp shows an eagle displayed at center, with NOUVELLE ORLEANS around.

There are 5 obverse and 3 reverse dies known.

NOTE: Robert Leonard and Gregory Brunk dispute any connection between Puech Bein and numbers 124, 125 and 126.

Planters Bank was in business 1811-1826.

HT 126 is reported struck over counterfeit Mexico 1812 Monclova (KM-202), 1811 Zacatecas and 1811-14 Morelos SUD 8-reales. Only four specimens overstamped BAD are known, these being worth $1500 each. The Monclova piece realized $3872 in the 1987 Norweb sale, lot 1412!

0-0-0-0-0

The following observations by Karl Moulton appeared in the Aug.-Sept. 2000 issue of *Rare Coin Review*, courtesy of Q. D. Bowers, publisher:

"Based on U.S. Mint Director Robert L. Patterson's letters, he knew there were 69,232 quarters struck in 1815. Many of them were shipped to Bailey Blanchard, the head cashier at Planter's Bank in New Orleans, on or before the 16th of December 1815. Although the original correspondence from Blanchard is missing, the story can now be easily pieced together.

"Immediately after the 'Battle of New Orleans' in January 1815, the British soon departed and the French arrived in rather substantial numbers. Naturally, they brought their own money which was not French but consisted primarily of Spanish 'bits' (12-1/2 cents) and 'two-bit' (25 cents) pieces. Several years earlier, beginning in 1811 or so, Planter's Bank had remedied this foreign exchange problem in their own way. They physically cut down Mexican 8-reale 'SUD' pieces into four equal pie-shaped sections and counterstamped the initials PB (for Planter's Bank) with an eagle on one side, while the other side displayed 'Nouvelle Orleans,' which is New Orleans in French. Both counterstamps have finely detailed circular scrollwork around the outside edges.

"As we shall see, Bailey Blanchard is the one person responsible for reviving the United States quarter denomination, because of his insistence on quarter dollars being coined from his bank's bullion deposit. Since Congress had not officially discontinued them, the U.S. Mint was forced to comply with his request."

0 - 0 - 0 - 0 - 0

Planters Bank issued bank notes in $5, $10, $20, $50 and $100 denominations from about 1811 to sometime in the early 1820's. These notes were hand-signed by cashier Bailey Blanchard and president William Harrison. All are rare; Haxby (1988) was aware of no surviving $20 or $50 notes.

Planters Bank issued bank notes in the 1811-1826 period; it closed in 1826. Known issued notes include $5 1821, nature scene; $10 1819, female reclining against cotton bale; $100 1817, reclining female with ships at left. In 1988 these notes were valued at $150 in VG, $250 in VF, and were not known in crisp Unc.

Surviving U.S. Mint correspondence from 1815 reveals that Planters Bank had shipped many of their cut quarter segments to Philadelphia that year, along with other bullion, for coinage into U.S. quarter dollars. (See *Rare Coin Review* for Aug. 2000, pgs. 24-25)

Planters Bank, a well run institution, went out of business in 1826. In 1827 the cotton planters opened a new banking entity to replace it, called Consolidated Association of Planters of Louisiana. This bank fell victim to the 1837 financial panic, was bailed out by the state of Louisiana, and eventually had its charter revoked when Louisiana's state bonds were themselves defaulted in Dec., 1842.

VALETON & CO.

BRASS, 23MM, 10-SIDED

HT #	Rarity	Year	F	VF	EF	Unc
127	R9	(1842-43)	—	9000.	—	—

WALTON & CO.

HT #	Rarity	Year	Metal	Size	VG	F	EF	Unc
128	R8	(1841-44)	Brass	33mm	500.	1600.	3000.	5000.

WALTON WALKER & CO.
New Orleans, La.

HT #	Rarity	Year	Metal	Size	VG	VF	EF	Unc
129	R7	1836	Brass	34mm	2000.	7500.	8500.	10,000.
129A	R8	1836	WM	34mm	—	—	8500.	10,000.

MAINE

R. FITTS
Bangor, Maine

HT #	Rarity	Year	Metal	Size	VG	F	VF	EF
581	R9	(1830's)	Copper	29mm	—	—	75.00	—

R. FITTS in coin-wide logotype ctsp incuse on U.S. Large cent. Examined: 1795, 1802. (Brunk 14350; Bowers coll.)

George Fitts was a Bangor clockmaker in the 1830's. The relationship of R. Fitts must be established, but the first initial could in fact be a misformed or misstruck G, Bowers reports.

Tentative attribution.

C. B. S.
(Cyrus B. Swift)
Kennebec County, Maine

HT #	Rarity	Year	Metal	Size	VG	F	VF	EF
523	R8	(ca 1843)	Copper	29mm	—	65.00	—	—

Very large, crude C. B. S. ctsp incuse on U.S. Large cent. Examined: 1828, 1829. 2 pcs. known. (Thoele coll.)

Cyrus B. Swift was born in Kennebec County, Maine, Feb. 7, 1817, the son of Alfred and Betsey Swift. On May 14, 1843 he married Martha J. Nelson in a civil ceremony in Kennebec County.

His descendants include C. A. Swift, a locksmith and carriage maker in East Montville, Maine in 1871, and another C. A. Swift, blacksmith in Bangor, Maine in 1871.

Tentative attribution.

CIRCULATION AS MONEY

In the 1837-1842 period, almost 26% of the Large cent-sized pieces in circulation in the United States were Hard Times tokens, the balance being perhaps 3% foreign coppers of about 29mm size, and just 71% U.S. Mint cents.

L. BAILEY
Portland, Maine

HT #	Rarity	Year	Metal	Size	VG	F	VF	EF
130	R8	(1839)	Copper	29mm	—	—	125.	—
130A	R9	(1839)	Silver	39mm	—	—	800.	—

130: L. BAILEY ctsp on U.S. 1839 or worn Large cent. (Brunk 1850)

130A: Similar ctsp on U.S. 1795 Bust silver dollar. (Bob Stark, University of Delaware, report)

Lebbeus Bailey has been identified by both Dwight B. Demeritt and Frank Sellers as a Portland gunsmith. On Feb. 20, 1839, in collaboration with John B. Ripley of Claremont, N.H. and William B. Smith of Cornish, N.H., he obtained U.S. patent no. 1084 for a magazine rifle.

As lot 3114 in the 1993 B&M Kovacs sale, HT 130A fetched $825.

Two silversmiths named Lebbeus Bailey worked in Portland, one living 1763-1827, and his son, 1791-1849. Both made clocks.

H.C. JENNYS

HT #	Rarity	Year	Metal	Size	VG	F	VF	EF
131	R9	1835	Copper	29mm	—	27.50	—	—

H.C. JENNYS, 1835 / PORTLAND / FORGET ME NOT ctsp on U.S. Large cent. (Koppenhaver Feb. 26, 1998 sale, lot 246)

The 'L' in PORTLAND is inverted. This piece could well be a love token item, even though not engraved.

A. LOWELL
Portland, Maine

HT #	Rarity	Year	Metal	Size	VG	F	VF	EF
578	R9	(1834-40)	Silver	27mm	—	—	75.00	—

A. LOWELL in relief within rect. depression ctsp on Mexico 1834-Zs-OM 2-reales, KM-377.13. (Robert Merchant coll.)

Owner Merchant purchased this piece on the Internet from a Bangor, Maine antique dealer. Attribution of this piece is rather difficult, as it seems it may be an unrecorded hallmark of silversmith, watch and clock maker Abner Lowell who worked in Portland from 1830 to 1875. Ensko, Belden and Fredyma silversmith references have him at Portland; Belden says in the Lowell & Senter partnership 1830-70. Kovel depicts this mark as about 1830 but does not identify its user.

Henry Thoele attributes this to a completely different person, jeweler Abner Lowell, who appears in the 1850 census as 37 years of age, single, born in Massachusetts and practicing his trade in Dracut, Middlesex Co., Mass.

Tentatively, we place it in Portland, Maine in the Hard Times period. Should that prove accurate, this Abner Lowell likely was born Jan. 10, 1812 in Portland, the son of John Lowell and Sally Adams Lowell. More research is required.

(BALTIMORE TOKEN)
Baltimore, Md.

Some of these anonymous ship-and-shield tokens were probably emitted in the Hard Times era. They are all listed together in the EAT section of the *Standard Catalog of U.S. Tokens 1700-1900* (Rulau-E 7, 8 and 9).

JOHN L. CHAPMAN
Baltimore, Md.

HT #	Rarity	Year	Metal	Size	VG	F	VF	Unc
132	R5	(1834-40)	GS	17mm	150.	200.	400.	—

133	R6	(1834-40)	GS	17mm	200.	270.	500.	—
			Soda, BALT					
134	R7	(1834-40)	GS	17mm	—	1000.	2500.	—

Same as 133, ctsp '2' (for two sodas). (PCAC June 2001 sale, lot 25)

John Lee Chapman was born at Fell's Point, Baltimore, in 1812. He began business as a druggist in 1834 at the southeast corner of Baltimore and South Streets, moving in 1841 to the opposite side of South Street. About 1846, with his brother Jonathan Chapman, he took over the glass manufacturing firm formerly conducted by his uncle George Chapman. This lasted until the outbreak of the Civil War.

Chapman was elected mayor of Baltimore in 1862, 1864 and 1866. In 1869 he was appointed naval officer of the Port of Baltimore by President Grant, and later became superintendent of the U.S. bonded warehouse there. He died Nov. 18, 1880.

HT 132 shows on obverse an eagle, and reads ONE SODA in center on reverse. The HT 133 token is similar, but there are 13 stars around the eagle, and BALT is incused below.

There are also two other tokens of Chapman (Miller Maryland 30 and 31) which probably are later than the Hard Times period.

JAMES COLE

Dies by James Bale

HT #	Rarity	Year	Metal	Size	VG	VF	EF	Unc
135	R5	(1835)	Copper	23mm	100.	375.	500.	700.
135A	R5	(1835)	Brass	23mm	100.	300.	400.	600.
136	R8	(1835)	Ctsp. F.W.		—	—	200.	—
137	R8	(1835)	Ctsp. ICE		—	—	200.	—

NOTE: The ship reverse of the Cole Cards, muled with a shield in circle of 13 stars, is known as the Baltimore Token, Brass, 23mm. It may precede the Hard Times era, or possibly may be a proper addition to the general types of HT Tokens. See numbers 7 to 8D in Miller's 'A Catalogue of U.S. Store Cards or Merchants Tokens.'

From 1833 to 1845 Cole was an official of Baltimore harbor. He was born in 1802. He was harbor master 1833-39 and was state wharfinger 1845.

He operated a grocery on South Wolfe Street, Fell's Point, in 1835-36 while harbor master, and the tokens may be connected with this period. He was a hotelkeeper in Fell's Point 1847-49, and again a grocer on Wolfe Street 1849-51.

Selling his grocery in 1851, he tried life as a ship's captain and pilot 1851-60, then farmed in Anne Arundel County 1860-66. He opened a Baltimore restaurant at 721 So. Broadway 1866-69, then farmed and took life easy until his death in 1882.

In a late-1990 auction, VF specimens of 135 fetched $242 and $198, respectively.

H. HERRING

HT #	Rarity	Year	Metal	Size	VG	F	VF	Unc
139	R8	1834	WM	35mm	—	15,000.	—	Rare

Fair Mount

Henry Herring opened his famed Fair Mount Hotel and Gardens in May, 1834 on the summit of Hampstead Hill. This eastern section of the city became known as Fair Mount, later the Jackson Square area. Herring was the proprietor 1834 to 1845.

HOUCK'S PANACEA
Baltimore, Md.

HT #	Rarity	Year	Metal	Size	VG	F	VF	EF
140	R7	(1836)	Silver	27mm	350.	—	500.	—

HOUCK'S / PANACEA / BALTIMORE in relief within oblong depression ctsp on U.S. Draped or Capped Bust quarter. (Dates examined: 1805, 1807, 1818, 1819). 6 pieces known. (Brunk 20140)

| 141 | R4 | (1836) | Silver | 32.5mm | 350. | — | 500. | — |

Similar ctsp on U.S. Draped or Capped Bust half dollar. (Dates examined: 1795, 1805, 1806, 1807, 1808, 1809, 1810, 1811, 1812, 1813, 1814, 1817, 1818, 1819, 1821, 1822, 1823, 1824, 1826, 1827, 1827/6, 1828, 1829, 1829/7, 1830, 1831, 1832, 1833, 1834, 1834-Small date — small stars, 1838 LD-SL, 1835, 1836, 1845). At least 90 specimens reported. (Van Ormer sale 2693, 2694)

In a recent B&M sale, an 1835 piece fetched $1452.

HT #	Rarity	Year	Metal	Size	VG	F	VF	EF
142	R7	(1836)	Silver	39mm	1200.	—	2000.	—

Similar ctsp on early U.S. silver dollar. (Dates examined: 1795,

1700, 1800, 1834). 4 specimens reported. (Van Ormer sale 2695, 2696; Kenney 228)

143 R7 (1836) Silver 27mm 600. — 900. —
Similar ctsp on Spanish-American 2-reales, (Dates examined: 1741, 1775-PTS-JR, 1777-PTS-PR, 1784, 1793, 1793-LMA, 1794, 1804, date worn off). 11 specimens reported. (Ulex 304; Van Ormer 2691)

143A R9 (1836) Silver 21mm — — 1750. —
Similar ctsp on Spanish-American 1797-Mo 1-real. (Krause coll., ex-Vlack; PCAC Nov. 1999 sale, lot 70, realized $1760)

144 R7 (1836) Silver 38mm 500. — 1200. —
Similar ctsp on France 5-francs. (Dates examined: 1795-1803 type, Craig 138; 1824-A; 1834). Only 4 pieces reported.
145 R9 (1836) Silver — — 800. —
Similar ctsp on Prussia silver thaler, date not known. (Brunk 20140FF). Apparently unique; not examined.
145F R9 (1836) Silver 39mm 800. —
Similar ctsp on Brazil 1821 960-reis.

Interestingly, one collection, that of Stewart P. Witham, contained 14 Houck counterstamps on Bust half dollars. In 1955 George Fuld possessed 20 such pieces of differing dates, but no records were kept. These pieces (HT 141) are seldom seen and consistently bring high prices.

Dr. Jacob Houck was born in Frederick, Md., where he became a leading merchant. He came to Baltimore in 1828 and had a dry goods business at 121 West Baltimore St.

In 1834 Houck placed on the market his "Botanic Panacea," which sold for $1.50 a bottle. The counterstamps probably emanate from about 1836.

Houck's laboratory in 1840 was at 10 So. Charles St., then moved to 16 Hanover St., then 15 So. Liberty St., and in 1850 he was at 357 West Baltimore St. In 1851 Henry T. Houck had become proprietor, at 8 So. Eutaw St.

Houck's Panacea was "prepared solely from vegetable matter" by Jacob Houck, 16 Hanover St., and according to his full page advertisement in Matchett's *Baltimore Director*, 1842, "it may be taken with perfect safety by all ages and in all diseases." Undoubtedly this counterstamp exists on other silver coins of the Hard Times era.

In later years Jacob Houck may have permitted others to prepare his popular panacea for sale under some licensing arrangement. Recently we encountered this advertisement in the 1855 city directory of Nashville, Tenn.:

"Houck's Panacea. Dr. A. G. Goodlet, mfr. & proprietor of: Houck's Improved Panacea and Goodlet's Vegetable Lineament. 29 1/2 No. Cherry St., Nashville, Tenn.

"These remedies have popular favor in the South and North. And should be in use in every family."

Some medicine bottles of the 1850's read: "Houck's / Vegetable Panacea / Nashville Tenn." and "Houck's / Vegetable Panacea / Goodletsville, Tenn."

Bottle in Gregory Brunk collection.

Prepared Solely from Vegetable Matter, by

JACOB HOUCK,

BALTIMORE,

Which may be taken with perfect safety by all ages and in all diseases; its cures are for the following diseases:—Dyspepsia, Loss of Appetite, Indigestion, Inflammation of the Stomach, Heart Burn, Diarrhœa, Dysentery or Flux, Piles, Fistula, Obstructed Menstruation, Ague and Fever, Bilious or Remittent Fever, Typhus Fever, Scarlet Fever, Small Pox, Erysipolous or St. Anthony's Fire, Asthma, Pleurisy, Measlés, Yellow Fever, Costiveness, Wind on the Stomach or Bowels, Cholera Morbus, Consumption, Influenza, Colds, Coughs, Inflammation of the Chest, Palsy, Gout, Rheumatism, Inflammatory Sore Throat or Quinsey, Whooping Cough, Thrush or Sore Mouth, Putrid Sore Throat, Croup, Inflammation of the Heart, Dropsy, Rickets, Diseases of the Liver, Jaundice, Difficulty of making Urine, Gleet, Hysterics, Nervous and Scrofulous Affections of the Members and Ligaments, Mercurial and Venereal Diseases, Ulcers, Sores, Affections of the Skin, and all diseases arising from Impure Blood,.&c.

Price per Bottle, $1.50.

The above medicine can be obtained at

No. 16, corner of German and Hanover streets,

With proper directions for using.

☞ A liberal discount made to persons who buy to sell.

S. JACKSON

Enlarged

HT #	Rarity	Year	Metal	Size	VG	F	VF	EF
A145	R9	(1835)	Copper	23mm	200.	—	450.	—

S. JACKSON (curved) / BALTIMORE ctsp on U.S. 1834 Half cent. (Schenkman report; Van Ormer report; Russ Sears report; Brunk 21395)

S. Jackson was listed in the 1833 directory as a cutler and maker of surgical instruments located at the corner of Liberty and German (now Redwood) Streets. In the 1835 directory Shadrach was described as a sawyer located on Douglas Street. In the 1846-47 directory Samuel Jackson is listed as a cutler and maker of surgical instruments. The next item may or may not be connected to either.

HT #	Rarity	Year	Metal	Size	VG	F	VF	EF
B145	R9	(1835)	Copper	23mm	200.	—	450.	—

S. JACKSON ctsp on U.S. 1835 Half cent. (Brunk 21390)

DR. LEACH

HT #	Rarity	Year	Metal	Size	VG	F	VF	EF
146	R9	(1845-51)	Silver	32.5mm	—	4000.	—	—

DR. LEACH / BALTO. ctsp on U.S. 1824 Bust half dollar. (Brunk 24065)

Dr. Leach practiced dentistry 1845-51.

RANDALL & CO.

GERMAN SILVER, 15MM

HT #	Rarity	Year		VG	F	VF	Unc
147	R6	(1840-42)	Plain edge	20.00	75.00	200.	350.
147A	R5	(1840-42)	Reeded edge	20.00	75.00	200.	400.

The obverse reads in five lines: MONUMENT / (flower) / RANDALL & CO / BALT / SQUARE. On reverse, Battle Monument is at center, with MINERAL WATER above and CITY HOTEL below.

HT #	Rarity	Year	Metal	Size	VG	F	VF	EF
148	R9	(1840-42)	Lead	22mm	—	—	7000.	—

Dudley A. Randall & Co. is listed in the directories of 1840-1842 in Barnum's City Hotel. Monument Square, Baltimore. Unique. Die trial. Ex-Williams, Fuld, Schenkman.

6 BALTM.

Baltimore, Md.

HT #	Rarity	Year	Metal	Size	VG	F	VF	EF
149	R7	(?)	Copper	23mm	150.	—	200.	—

6 (five dotted lines) / BALTM. ctsp on U.S. Half cent. Examined: 1797, 1809, 1825, 1828, 1834. (Brunk 2260).

The five dotted lines have been described as a fire grate or as an oyster shucker's crate. It was apparently issued by a Baltimore merchant, possibly in the HT period.

MASSACHUSETTS

H M & E I RICHARDS
Attleboro, Mass.

HT #	Rarity	Year	Metal	Size	VG	VF	EF	Unc
150	R2	1834	Copper	28.5mm	5.00	35.00	100.	200.

HT #	Rarity	Year	Metal	Size	VG	VF	EF	Unc
151	R2	(1834)	Copper	28.5mm	6.00	20.00	125.	250.

Cousins Herve Manning and Edmund Ira Richards formed their company in 1830. H. M. was then only 18, and E. I. just 15. Their career as Hard Times token manufacturers from 1834, utilizing the services of Edward Hulseman, the engraver at Robinson's Jones & Co. in the same city, is now in doubt. We believe they merely distributed Robinson products.

H. M. left in 1837 for Philadelphia, E. I. continuing alone.

ROBINSON'S JONES & CO.
Attleboro, Mass.

HT #	Rarity	Year	Metal	Size	VG	VF	EF	Unc
152	R2	1833	Copper	28.5mm	4.50	20.00	40.00	150.

HT #	Rarity	Year	Size	VG	VF	EF	Unc
153	R1	1833 Slanting 1 in 1833	28.5mm	4.00	12.00	40.00	200.
153A	R7	1833 Svd/Cop	28.5mm	—	300.	—	—

Robinson's Jones & Co. received the American Institute medal for their metallic buttons in the fall of 1833, and promptly issued these tokens to advertise their triumph. The dies were cut by Edward Hulseman at about the same time that he cut the dies for HT 70, the first of the "I Take The Responsibility" political tokens.

Robinson's Jones & Co. traces its formation to Col. Obed Robinson, a blacksmith who made gunlocks during the Revolutionary War. He began making kitchen clocks after 1783, and in 1807 formed a partnership with David Brown to manufacture jewelry.

In 1812 Obed and his son Otis Robinson produced U.S. Army buttons without buttonmaker backmarks, and this 1812 initiative launched the first Robinson button enterprises. Otis Robinson, Virgil Blackinton and a skilled British immigrant buttonmaker, Edward Price, later formed their own button firm, which lasted to 1820.

Two others of Obed's sons, Richard and Willard, plus their brother-in-law Virgil Blackinton, began making glass buttons in Attleboro in 1813. Richard Robinson, the principal, turned to metal buttons for the Army artillery in 1820 with his brother Willard, admitting William Henry Jones and Horace M. Draper as partners by 1826.

Robinson's Jones & Co. was organized in 1828 in Attleboro, Mass. and reorganized as R. & W. Robinson in 1836. Robinson's Jones employed Edward Hulseman as an in-house engraver 1833-1836, after which Hulseman removed to New York City.

This premier button-making firm is now credited with manufacturing the earliest large-circulation Hard Times tokens, such as HT 70, 25, 152, 153 and 428 (the latter the 1833 Ephraim Hathaway token.)

R. & W. ROBINSON

HT #	Rarity	Year	Metal	Size	VG	VF	EF	Unc
154	R3	1836	Copper	28.5mm	8.00	35.00	70.00	270.

A points between Y and O. Date close to buttons.

HT #	Rarity	Year	Metal	Size	VG	VF	EF	Unc
155	R1	1836	Copper	28.5mm	5.00	12.00	80.00	160.

A points to Y. Date distant from buttons.

HT #	Rarity	Year	Metal	Size	VG	VF	EF	Unc
155A	R6	—	Silvered Copper	28.5mm	50.00	100.	200.	400.

HT #	Rarity	Year	Metal	Size	VG	VF	EF	Unc
156	R4	1836	Copper	28.5mm	40.00	200.	250.	400.

New-York

The NEW YORK on all obverse dies pertains to the location of the American Institute, issuer of the medal reproduced there.

Willard Robinson was one of the partners. He married a girl of the H. M. & E. I. Richards family. The R. & W. Robinson firm was reorganized from the earlier Robinson's Jones & Co. firm in 1836. In 1848 they were succeeded in turn by D. Evans & Co. (Daniel Evans was the striker of the Rhode Island series of Civil War token mulings depicting hunting scenes).

Documentary evidence shows that some of the 1836 Robinson cards were actually struck in 1839.

S.B. SCHENCK

HT #	Rarity	Year	Metal	Size	VG	VF	EF	Unc
157	R1	1834	Copper	28.5mm	4.50	20.00	40.00	140.

W.P. Haskins

HT #	Rarity	Year	Metal	Size	VG	VF	EF	Unc
157C	R9	1834	Copper	29mm	—	400.	—	—

Both sides struck over an HM & El Richards token, HT 150 (PCAC58 sale, lot 024).

HT #	Rarity	Year	Metal	Size	VG	VF	EF	Unc
158	R1	1834	Copper	28.5mm	4.50	20.00	50.00	175.
		This Machine						
158A	R7	(1834)	Svd/Cop	28.5mm	—	—	90.00	—

HT #	Rarity	Year	Metal	Size	VG	VF	EF	Unc
159	R2	(1834)	Copper	28.5mm	6.00	20.00	125.	250.
		Richards						
160	R2	(1834)	Copper	28.5mm	8.50	30.00	120.	300.
		Peck & Burnham						

Woodworth's Patent Planing Machine, manufactured in Attleboro, Mass. by S. B. Schenck, was made famous by its appearance on a number of Hard Times tokens of 1834 and later.

In 1870, the successor firm, John B. Schenck & Son, received the 60.1mm silver American Insitute of New York medal "for the best Woodworth planing & moulding machine." The George Hampden Lovett-engraved medal appeared as lot 1527 in the B&M June 22-23, 2000 sale in Chicago.

J. L. COOPER
Location not known

HT #	Rarity	Year	Metal	Size	VG	F	VF	EF
A160	R9	(?)	Copper	28.6mm	—	—	—	100.

Ctsp J. L. COOPER near bottom center of HT 158. (B&M March 2000 Lindesmith sale, lot 1130)
Unpublished token, discovered 2000.

GRAVES & HATCH
Location not known

Illustration enlarged.

HT #	Rarity	Year	Metal	Size	VG	F	VF	EF
161	R7	(1850's)	Copper	28.5mm	—	100.	—	—

Ctsp. GRAVES & HATCH / CAST-STEEL. Name curved. (Brunk 16950; Krause coll., ex-Vlack)
| 161A | R9 | (1850's) | Copper | 29mm | — | 100. | — | — |

Similar ctsp on U.S. 1851 Large cent, but name straight.
| 161B | R9 | (1850's) | Copper | 29mm | — | 75.00 | — | — |

GRAVES & HATCH ctsp on U.S. 1802 Large cent. (Brunk 16947)
161-161B were thought to be Hard Times pieces, but in fact are from the USMT period. Toolmakers.

I. TRASK
Beverly, Mass.

HT #	Rarity	Year	Metal	Size	VG	F	VF	EF
524	R9	(1831-35)	Copper	29mm	—	150.	—	-

I. TRASK in relief within rectangular depression ctsp on U.S. 1819 Large cent. (Thoele coll.)
Israel Trask was a coppersmith, pewterer and buttonmaker in Beverly, Mass., active from 1816 through 1835. This piece might properly belong in the Early American tokens section.

Israel Trask married Elizabeth Porter in Beverly on Feb. 12, 1815, according to the Mormon Genealogical Library.

D. B. BOWLER
Boston, Mass.

HT #	Rarity	Year	Metal	Size	VG	F	VF	EF
525	R8	(1830's)	Copper	23mm	—	—	135.	—

D. B. BOWLER in relief within rectangular cartouche ctsp on U.S. Half cent. Examined: 1808, 1809. Only 2 pcs. known. (Koppenhaver Feb. 2, 1980 sale, lot 857; Robert Merchant coll.)
| 525A | R9 | (1830's) | Copper | 29mm | — | — | 150. | — |

Similar ctsp on U.S. 1804 Large cent.
The exact matching mark is depicted in Belden for jeweler and silversmith D. B. Bowler of Boston, who advertised in the 1830 Boston directory. Earlier, about 1809-15, Kovel reports this craftsman was located in Providence, R. I.

Belden reports the Ineson-Bissell collection contains this marking on a broad fiddle-end spoon engraved script D W, originally owned in Cambridge, Mass.

EXCHANGE COFFEE HOUSE
Boston, Mass.

See this ctsp 1838 Large cent in USMT section under Mass 702.

FARNSWORTH, PHIPPS & CO.

HT#	Rarity	Year	Metal	Size	F	VF	EF	Unc
162	R3	(1829-33)	Copper	28.5mm	40.00	125.	—	300.

FARNSWORTH PHIPPS & CO. / NO 85 / KILBY STREET / BOSTON. Rv: DEALERS / IN / BRITISH FRENCH / INDIA AND / AMERICAN / DRY GOODS. Tiny W. & B. - N.Y. flanks DRY GOODS. (Wright 356; Low 314; Storer 366; Rulau-E Mass 38)
This token spans the Early American and Hard Time eras. Struck by Wright & Bale of New York, who were in partnership May 1829 to October 1833.

J. JONES

HT #	Rarity	Year	Metal	Size	VG	F	VF	EF
A162	R9	(1837)	Copper	23mm	80.00	—	125.	—

J. JONES in relief within rect. depression ctsp on U.S. 1804 Half cent. Surrounding the J. JONES stamp are 14 counterstamps consisting of a relief S within small depression. (Charles Kirtley Oct. 1985 sale, lot 307; Brunk 22020; ex-Maurice Gould, Sol Taylor)

HT #	Rarity	Year	Metal	Size	VG	F	VF	Unc
B162	R8	(1837)	Copper	29mm	80.00	—	125.	—

Similar ctsp on U.S. Large cent, minus the S stamps. Dates examined: 1795, 1830, unknown. 3 pieces known.

HT #	Rarity	Year	Metal	Size	VG	F	VF	Unc
C162	R9	(1837)	Silver	18mm	100.	—	150.	—

Similar ctsp on U.S. 1837 dime. Unique?

HT #	Rarity	Year	Metal	Size	VG	F	VF	Unc
D162	R9	(1837)	Copper	29mm	75.00	—	125.	—

Similar ctsp on Canada token. (Brunk 22020S)

The S-within-depression punch was a common one in the silversmith trade to indicate "sterling."

Attributed to John B. Jones, born 1782, died 1854. He began business as a silversmith in 1809. He was a member of all these firms:

Jones & Aspinwall (Zalmon Aspinwall) 1809
Jones & Pierce (John Pierce) 1810
Jones & Ward (Richard Ward) 1813-16
John Jones 1816-22
Baldwin & Jones (Jabez L. Baldwin) 1816-20
John B. Jones & Co. (S. S. Ball) 1838
Jones Low & Ball (John J. Low, S. S. Ball) 1839-46
Jones Ball & Poor (S. S. Ball, Nathaniel C. Poor) 1846-53
Jones Ball & Co. (S. S. Ball) 1853-55

John B. Jones died in 1854. His son's last partnership was succeeded by Shreve Brown & Co. 1857-69 and then Shreve Crump & Low, 1869 to the present.

J. B. JONES

HT #	Rarity	Year	Metal	Size	VG	F	VF	EF
G162	R8	(1839)	Copper	29mm	100.	—	125.	—

J. B. JONES in incused logotype (1819) or in relief hallmark (1818), ctsp on U.S. Large cent. Examined: 1818, 1819. 2 pieces known. (Brunk 22035; Bowers coll.)

The son of John B. Jones (see above), John B Jones Jr. was in business for himself 1821-34 and in various partnerships 1835-56.

WM. H. MILTON

HT #	Rarity	Year	Metal	Size	VG	F	VF	Unc
163	R1	(1830-34)	Copper	28.5mm	4.50	12.00	30.00	200.
163A	R1	(1830-34)	Copper	28.5mm	5.00	12.00	30.00	200.

As 163, but periods after HALL, CLOTHING and WAREHOUSE.

WM. H. MILTON & CO.

HT #	Rarity	Year	Metal	Size	VG	VF	EF	Unc
164	R1	(1835-44)	Copper	29.1mm	5.00	12.00	60.00	150.
			WAREHOUSE					
164A	R8	(1835-44)	S/Brass	28.5mm	—	—	200.	450.

HT #	Rarity	Year	Metal	Size	VG	VF	EF	Unc
165	R2	(1835-44)	Copper	28.5mm	5.50	15.00	60.00	175.
			WAREHOUSE					

HT #	Rarity	Year	Metal	Size	VG	VF	EF	Unc
166	R4	(1835-44)	Brass	28.5mm	8.50	15.00	60.00	—
			WAREHOUSE*					
166A	R8	(1835-44)	S/Brass	28.5mm	—	—	200.	450.

Milton's store was in the left front of Fanueil Hall on the first floor, a very popular spot even with tourists in 1997. It was pictured in 1837 in England's "Bartlett's Views of America."

PECK & BURNHAM

HT #	Rarity	Year	Metal	Size	VG	VF	EF	Unc
167	R2	(1834)	Copper	28.5mm	8.00	20.00	75.00	225.

HT #	Rarity	Year	Metal	Size	VG	VF	EF	Unc
168	R2	(1834)	Copper	28.5mm	6.00	15.00	120.	300.
			Schenk Rev.					

Peck & Burnham were located at 54 Hanover St., the address on the tokens, from 1832 through 1835. In 1836 the firm apparently dissolved, and Abel G. Peck was located at 15 Central with a dry goods firm. (Abel G. Peck & Co. were at 6 Kilby St. in 1837-1845, then at 35 and 57 Kilby St. in 1846-1847).

W. D. PHYFE

HT #	Rarity	Year	Metal	Size	VG	F	VF	EF
A168	R9	(1830's)	Silver	39mm	—	—	400.	—

W D PHYFE (incused) / PURE SILVER COIN (italics, in relief in rect. depression) / Boston (in relief in rect. depression) - ctsp in three separate stamps on Kingdom of Italy 1813-B silver 5-lire. (Hartzog sale of Dec. 1, 1980, lot 1811; B&M Taylor sale of March 26-28, 1987, lot 1295; Brunk 32010).

William Phyfe was a silversmith who carried on his trade in Boston in the 1830's, and then in New York City 1840-50. From 1844-1850 he was part of the silversmith firm of Eoff & Phyfe with Garret Eoff.

The stamp W D PHYFE was created from single letter punches. Boston is on reverse.

CIRCULATION AS MONEY

In the 1837-1842 period, almost 26% of the Large cent-sized pieces in circulation in the United States were Hard Times tokens, the balance being perhaps 3% foreign coppers of about 29mm size, and just 71% U.S. Mint cents.

ROXBURY COACHES

HT #	Rarity	Year	Metal	Size	F	VF	EF	Unc
169	R3	1837	GS	18.7mm	100.	200.	300.	700.

JOHN ELIOT SQUARE, ROXBURY, MASSACHUSETTS. An old print showing two omnibuses of the Roxbury Coaches

HT #	Rarity	Year	Metal	Size	VG	VF	EF	Unc
169A	R8	1837	Copper	18.7mm	—	—	—	Electro

The Roxbury Coaches were those which ran through what later became Washington Street, Boston, over "the Neck," to the top of the hill in Roxbury where once stood the old church in which Apostle Eliot preached in New England's early days. The Norfolk House, a famous hostelry on the opposite side of the street, was their stopping place in John Eliot Square until the line was discontinued.

The coaches were long omnibuses carrying 16 to 20 persons inside, drawn by four horses. At first they made hourly trips from Roxbury to downtown Boston and were called "Roxbury Hourlies." The fare was 25 cents each way. Handsomely painted, their sides bore names — *Regulator, Conqueror* and *Aurora,* the latter with a goddess in a cloud-borne chariot on its yellow sides.

Horace King managed the business 1832-1851, later finding opposition from coaches of one Mr. Hobbs which made more frequent trips. The Roxbury Coaches succumbed to "progress" about 1856.

WILLIAM RUTTER

HT #	Rarity	Year	Metal	Size	F	VF	EF	Unc
170	R7	(1831-35)	Copper	29mm	400.	650.	950.	1500.

William Rutter's Red Store on Fulton St. at Cross St., mentioned on the cards, was attributed to the 1831-1835 period by Howland Wood in 1913 on sound deductive reasoning. Rutter, a man of many parts, was in business in Boston from 1813 to 1863 in a number of partnerships and alone. Only about 22 pieces were struck. Plain edge.

1813 William Rutter, LYNN ST. (Grocer)
1816 William Rutter / Asa Hayes, 4 TOWN DOCK (Traders)
1818 William Rutter & Co. (David Manley), 17 BRAY'S WHARF
1821 William Rutter & Co. (William Manley) TOWN DOCK
1823 William Rutter, 1 TOWN DOCK (Trader)
1825 William Rutter, BIXBY & VALENTINE'S WHARF (Trader) and 1825 Rutter, Gaylord & Co. (Charles Gaylord, Mathew M. Teprell), 6 ANN ST. (Booksellers & Stationers)
1826 William Rutter, BIXBY & VALENTINE'S WHARF (Trader) but out of Gaylord & Hatch, Booksellers & Stationers and into Freeman, Rutter & Co. (John Freeman), 46 NO. MARKET ST. (Stationers) 1827 William Rutter, 152 ANN St. (Variety Store)
1829 William Rutter & Co. (Reuben Mossman & Artemas Tirrill), CROSS ST. (Paper Rags, Junk)
1830-35 William Rutter (alone), CROSS ST. (Variety Store)
1835-39 William Rutter, SNOW'S WHARF (Junk)
1839-63 William Rutter, 221 BROAD ST.
(Fulton Street, formerly under water, was platted in 1828 on new land fill. It received the name Fulton in 1831.)

H. L. WEBSTER & CO.

HT #	Rarity	Year	Metal	Size	VG	F	VF	EF
A170	R9	(1835-42)	Copper	29mm	—	—	100.	—

H L Webster & Co in relief in slanting letters within rect. depression ctsp on U.S. 1835 Large cent. (Kirtley Nov. 1991 sale, lot Q002)

In the example above, the 'L' of the stamp is blundered and appears like an 'S' tilted left.

Henry L. Webster was a silversmith operating in Boston circa 1826-42 and also in Providence, R.I. circa 1831-64. Born 1808, he died in 1864.

In Providence he was a partner of famed Jabez L. Gorham (Gorham & Webster 1831-37; Gorham, Webster & Price 1837-41; Jabez Gorham & Son 1841-50; Webster & Knowles 1852-64).

The H. L. Webster & Co. mark seems to have been used only in Boston. The mark matches punches shown in Louise C. Belden's *Marks of American Silversmiths* and the Kovels' silversmith reference.

ALFRED D. WILLARD
Boston, Mass.

HT #	Rarity	Year	Metal	Size	F	VF	EF	Unc
171	R1	(1835)	Copper	28.5mm	4.50	11.00	50.00	125.
171A	R9	(1835)	WM	28.5mm				Possible fake!

BUNKER HILL FAIR
Charlestown, Mass.

HT #	Rarity	Year	Metal	Size	F	VF	EF	Unc
A171	R7	1840	Copper	43mm	—	90.00	200.	—

Battle scene and death of Gen. Joseph Warren. BUNKER HILL / 17 JUNE 1775. Under truncation: MITCHELL BOSTON. Rv: Monument, clouds around. SUCCESS TO THE FAIR / SEPt. 8 1840. (Storer 981)

HT #	Rarity	Year	Metal	Size	F	VF	EF	Unc
B171	R5	1840	WM	43mm	—	55.00	90.00	—

As A171.

This piece is also known in Lead. There are other medals commemorating this 1840 fair, some of which depict William Henry Harrison, then a candidate for president on the Whig Party ticket.

LOW NUMBERS

For veteran collectors still using the century-old "Low" numbering system, there is a conversion chart of the "HT" numbers in the Introduction to this reference.

MAVERICK COACH
East Boston, Mass.

HT #	Rarity	Year	Metal	Size	VG	VF	EF	Unc
172	R3	1837	GS	18.7mm	100.	275.	500.	850.
172A	R8	1837	Copper	18.7mm	—	—		Electro

The reverse die was preserved and used to make Rhode Island Civil War token mulings.

W. W. PETTEE
Foxboro, Mass.

HT #	Rarity	Year	Metal	Size	VG	F	VF	EF
600	R8	(1840's)	Copper	29mm	60.00	—	80.00	—

W. W. PETTEE ctsp on U.S. Large cent. Examined: 1818, 1822, 1828. (Brunk 31835)

HT #	Rarity	Year	Metal	Size	VG	F	VF	EF
601	R9	(1840's)	Copper	29mm	—	—	100.	—

(Eagle) / W. W. PETTEE ctsp on U.S. 1800 Large cent. (R. Merchant coll.)

HT #	Rarity	Year	Metal	Size	VG	F	VF	EF
603	R8	1841	Copper	29mm	75.00	—	100.	—

W. W. PETTEE CAST STEEL 1841 ctsp on U.S. Large cent. Examined: 1822, 1828, 1839. (Brunk 31840)

William W. Pettee, machinist, appears in the 1861 Boston directory. The same man (?) appeared at Foxboro, Mass. in the 1850 census. The latest ctsp found for this person is on an 1839 cent.

WM. WILSON
Greenfield, Mass.

HT #	Rarity	Year	Metal	Size	VG	F	VF	EF
557	R9	1844	Silver	18mm	—	100.	—	—

Wm WILSON.S / PATENT / 1844 (inverted) ctsp incuse on U.S. 1839 Seated Liberty dime. (Brunk 43825)

The only reported specimen is holed at both 3 and 9 o'clock, Brunk formerly (1987) numbered this piece 43830.

William Wilson received a patent for a flat iron. The 1844 *Annual Report of the Commissioner of Patents* listed has name as "Wm Wilson," just as in this counterstamp.

F. LAMSON (and) MERRIMACK HOUSE
Lowell, Mass.

HT #	Rarity	Year	Metal	Size	VG	F	VF	EF
173	R9	(1840's?)	Copper	28.5mm	—	200.	—	—

F. LAMSON in relief within rect. depression ctsp eight times on obverse of S. B. Schenck 1834 Hard Times token of Attleboro, Mass. (HT 158). Rv: On reverse of token are seven stamps, all in relief within rectangular depressions, top to bottom: MERRIMACK / HOUSE / LOWELL / LOWELL / F. LAMSON. At left: NASHUA. At right: BOSTON. (B&M Patterson March, 1985 sale, lot 1716; Brunk 23760)

The Merrimack House in Lowell has been traced. The presence of the names Nashua and Boston may indicate some connection (stagecoach service?). Search of Nashua directories offers no help.

There was a Merrimac House in Boston at least 1853-1863. In 1853 it was at the corner of Dutton and Emery Henry was proprietor. In 1863 it was at corner Merrimac and Friend, with James L. Hanson proprietor.

Francis Lamson and J.M. Tarr were jewelers at 98 Merrimac in 1853.

We are tentatively assigning a Hard Times-era provenance to this piece. Lamson and Merrimac (K) House probably were in business earlier than 1853. (Research courtesy Paul G. Pettazoni, Chelmsford, Mass.)

R. LYMAN

HT #	Rarity	Date	Metal	Size	VG	F	VF	EF
173C	R9	(?)	Copper	29mm	—	75.00	—	—

R. LYMAN in rectangular cartouche ctsp on reverse of U.S. 1825 Large cent. (Brunk 25360; Rulau MV 196)

R. Lyman was a silversmith in Lowell in 1840.

S.L. WILKINS
Lowell, Mass.

HT #	Rarity	Year	Metal	Size	F	VF	EF	Unc
174	R1	1834	Copper	28.5mm	7.00	50.00	80.00	225.
		Lafayette H						

Samuel L. Wilkins advertised in 1832 that he had for sale a large assortment of French and American paper hangings in addition to his normal clothing and shoe stock. In 1836 he moved to number 21 Merrimack St., where he stayed six or seven years. He then retired from business and moved to Medford, Mass.

The standing figure of Lafayette, cut by Edward Hulseman, is based on Ary Scheffer's celebrated painting which attained great popularity in the United States at that time. Lafayette died in 1834.

J. EASTON
Nantucket, Mass.

HT #	Rarity	Year	Metal	Size	VG	F	VF	EF
526	R8	(1828-38)	Copper	29mm	—	—	85.00	—

J. EASTON in relief within rectangular depression ctsp on U.S. Large cent. Examined: 1803, 1808. Only 2 pcs. reported. (Brunk 12873; R. Merchant coll.)

James Easton II (1807-1903) was born in Providence, R.I., and apprenticed to silversmith William Hadwen in Nantucket ca 1824-28. He purchased Hadwen's business in 1828.

In 1830 he formed Easton & Sanford (with Frederick S. Sanford) in Nantucket 1830-38. Their silverware shop was at 62 Main Street in 1833.

FRANCIS L. BRIGHAM
New Bedford, Mass.

HT #	Rarity	Year	Metal	Size	F	VF	EF	Unc
175	R6	1833	Copper	28.5mm	200.	400.	675.	1250.
		Beaded borders outside circle						
175A	R9	1833	Copper	28.5mm	—	—	3000.	—
		Struck over HT Token 70						

HT #	Rarity	Year	Metal	Size	F	VF	EF	Unc
176	R3	1833	Copper	28.5mm	40.00	175.	350.	500.
		Beads only						

HT #	Rarity	Year	Metal	Size	F	VF	EF	Unc
176A	R5	1833	Silvered Copper				Not Contemporary	

"Cheapside" was the name given in the Hard Times period to that portion of Pleasant Street, New Bedford, which formed the east side of what was then called Market Square, fronting a large granite building used for a market, public meetings and the like. "Cheapside," parallel with Purchase Street, a block away, was bordered by the long, one-story building, shown on the token, and was a favorite resort for shoppers. Francis L. Brigham was in 1836 (according to the New Bedford directory) a dentist, having an office at 24 Purchase Street, and he was engaged in that profession when he died, 18 September, 1845, aged nearly 43. Just when he abandoned the selling of dry goods and took up dentistry, does not appear. He was remembered for some slight eccentricities.

DOW

New Bedford, Mass.

HT #	Rarity	Year	Metal	Size	VG	F	VF	EF
A176	R8	(1836 ?)	Copper	28.5mm	—	—	100.	—

DOW ctsp on Francis L. Brigham 1833 Hard Times token. (Storer 1473; Brunk 12003)

Dow was the successor to Brigham, possibly about 1836.

J. D. MANN (and) L. AMES JR.

North Bridgewater, Mass.

HT #	Rarity	Year	Metal	Size	VG	F	VF	EF
D176	R9	(1840's)	Copper	29mm	—	—	200.	—

J. D. MANN / L. AMES JR. / N. BRIDGEWATER (in a single punch) ctsp on U.S. 1838 Large cent. (Kirtley Sept. 1992 sale, lot 5134)

This stamp likely has a connection to the Ames family of gunsmiths of North Bridgewater, Mass., founded by John Ames in 1776, and carried on after 1803 by his sons David (1761-1847) and Oliver (active until 1820's).

However, we can find no record of an L. Ames Jr. or a J. D. Mann.

N - BRIDGWATER

(Perkins)

North Bridgewater, Mass.

HT #	Rarity	Year	Metal	Size	VG	F	VF	EF
177	R9	1841	Silver	40mm	—	—	—	450.

N-BRIDGWATER / 1841 ctsp on Spanish-American 1814 8-reales of Ferdinand VII. (Van Ormer sale 2556).

178	R9	1841	Silver	38mm	—	—	—	450.

Similar ctsp on Spain 1814-Crowned C-CJ 8-reales of Cadiz Mint, Craig 136.2. (Stanley Steinberg Nov. 1985 sale; Brunk 5175)

178A	R9	(1840's)	Copper	29mm	—	—	225.	—

BRIDGEWATER ctsp on U.S. 1798 Large cent. (Brunk 5170)

178B	R9	(1840's)	Copper	29mm	—	—	225.	—

BRIDGEWATER in arc ctsp on U.S. 1817 Large cent. (Robert Merchant coll.)

The stamps on these pieces are typical of the Perkins family of gunsmiths of North Bridgewater, Mass., who frequently misspelled the locale as BRIDGWATER on their punches to mark guns. The date '1841' may be an actual issue date, or may refer to the Model 1841 rifles produced for the Army Ordnance Dept.

Rufus Perkins of North Bridgewater received a contract in 1808 for 2,500 muskets to be delivered by 1813. Some of these are marked BRIDGEWATER.

James Perkins and Adam Kinsley of nearby Bridgewater had received a contract for 2,000 French Charleville-pattern muskets in 1798 and some of these were stamped BRIDGWATER / 1809.

The Model 1841 rifle (sometimes called the "Mississippi rifle" or the "Yager rifle"), a muzzle-loading .54 caliber percussion weapon, was first prepared at the Harpers Ferry (Va.) Armory in 1841, and the weapon's lockplate received stamps from a number of gunmakers who also counterstamped coins. Some of the contractors' marks were:

HARPERS FERRY / 1845 / AW/P VP (eagle head).
REMINGTON'S / HERKIMER / N.Y. / US / 1849.
ROBBINS / KENDALL & / LAWRENCE / US / WINDSOR, VT. / 1847.
ROBBINS / & / LAWRENCE / US / WINDSOR, VT. / 1850.
TRYON / US / PHILADA / PA / 1848.
E. WHITNEY / US / N. HAVEN / 1851.

George W. Tryon, Eliphalet Remington and Eli Whitney's names will conjure up many associations (Whitney was a gun inventor as well as inventor of the cotton gin, for example).

Additional information is needed on just who was operating the North Bridgewater arms works in/after 1841.

Stanley Steinberg attributed this mark to the gun manufactory of David and John Ames of North Bridgewater (now Brockton, Mass.). John Ames had been appointed the first superintendent of Springfield Arsenal in Mass. by President George Washington.

The Rulau gunsmith listing in *U.S. Merchant Tokens 1845-1860* (2nd ed.) shows N. P. Ames at Springfield Arsenal 1839-45 but the Ames Mfg. Co. at Chicopee Falls 1835-85.

It is possible the Van Ormer and Steinberg pieces are one and the same — both are Ferdinand VII. The author has not examined them.

L. POMEROY

Pittsfield, Mass.

Lemuel Pomeroy gunsmith ctsps dated 1835 and 1842 are clearly Hard Times tokens, but cannot be dissociated from their 1825 and 1826 precursors of similar type. All may be found in the Early American tokens section, Rulau-E Mass 70 thru 73, of the *Standard Catalog of U.S. Tokens*.

E. CURRIER

Salem, Mass.

HT #	Rarity	Year	Metal	Size	VG	F	VF	EF
527	R9	(1825-44)	Copper	29mm	—	—	200.	—

E. CURRIER in relief ctsp on U.S. 1802 Large cent. E. C. in relief ctsp on reverse of the coin. (R. Merchant coll.)

Edmund M. Currier (1793-1853) began working as a goldsmith and silversmith in Hopkinton, N.H. 1815-25, gradually adding clock and watch making from 1817 on. In 1825 he removed to Salem, Mass., advertising in newspapers there.

He worked alone in Salem 1825-37, then in partnership of Currier & Foster (with George B. Foster, 1810-81) in the 1837-40 period, and again alone 1840-53. From 1846 on he was a clockmaker only, abandoning the silversmith work.

COCHRAN'S MANY CHAMBERD RIFLE

Springfield, Mass.

HT #	Rarity	Date	Metal	Size	VG	F	VF	EF
A178	R9	(1836-41)	Copper	29mm	—	—	200.	—

COCHRAN'S / MANY / CHAMBERD (sic!) / NON RECOIL / & / PATENT / RIFLE / SPRINGFIELD / MASS. ctsp on U.S. 1820 Large cent. (Doty pg. 99; Bowers coll.; Brunk 8500)

John Webster Cochran (1814-1874) was one of America's most prolific inventors of guns, cannon, explosive shells and revolvers. He lived in New York. His weapons were made under contract by others; e.g. turret guns by Cyrus B. Allen in Springfield, Mass. 1830-1840, and cartridge carbines by Eli Whitney Jr. in New Haven, Conn. 1841-1888.

Cochran's first patent (Oct. 22, 1834) was for a revolving cannon; his next (April 28, 1837) for a turret gun. Twenty-four more patents followed, the last (Nov. 7, 1876) for a revolver.

He had several patents for a "breechloading firearm" in the 1859-1874 period which could have been rifles such as that mentioned on the token, but we believe this is a Hard Times-era issue. The "many chambered nonrecoil rifle" was the C. B. Allen-produced turret gun, as the stamp appeared on the gun's topstrap.

J. CUMMINGS

HT #	Rarity	Year	Metal	Size	VG	F	VF	EF
183	R8	(1840's)	Copper	28mm	—	—	75.00	—

J. CUMMINGS / SPRINGFIELD, MASS. ctsp on Canadian token. (Brunk 10270)

John Cummings was a gunsmith at 18 Kingsley Street in Hartford, Conn. 1841-43, according to authorities Gardner, Sellers and Kauffman. Just when he was at Springfield, Mass. is not known.

SPRINGFIELD (ARMORY)

Springfield, Mass.

HT #	Rarity	Year	Metal	Size	VG	F	VF	EF
590	R9	1832	Copper	29mm	—	—	150.	—

SPRING / FIELD / US / 1832 ctsp incuse on U.S. Large cent. (Van Ormer April 1985 sale; Rulau-E Mass 84; Brunk 37745)

591	R9	1833	Copper	29mm	—	—	150.	—

SPRING / FIELD / 1833 / US / (Eagle) ctsp incuse on U.S. Large cent, worn ca 1816.

592	R9	1836	Copper	29mm	—	—	150.	—

SPRING / FIELD / 1836 ctsp incuse on U.S. 1817 Large cent. (Bowers report)

The Springfield Armory, the first national arsenal, opened 1795, and its recorded markings span dates from 1799 through at least 1870.

The specific marking SPRINGFIELD 1836 in various versions was applied to U.S. flintlock pistols, Model 1836, made thereafter under contract to various films. For example R. Johnson of Middletown, Conn. had a June 1836 contract to deliver 300 pistols at $9 each and a March 1840 contract for 15,000 pistols at $7.50 each.

Each date-marking signified a firearms contract. Only those falling in the Hard Times period are cataloged here. For a detailed catalog of earlier Springfield Armory issues, see Rulau-E Mass 80 thru 85 in the EAT section of *Standard Catalog of U.S. Tokens 1700-1900*.

SPRINGFIELD BRIDGE
Springfield, Mass.

HT #	Rarity	Year	Metal	Size	VG	F	VF	EF
C178	R7	(?)	Cardboard	Rect 60x34mm ?	150.	200.	250.	—

* Occurs in red, yellow or green cardboard, all equally scarce. Within rectangular leaf border: SPRINGFIELD BRIDGE / -o- / Pass for a One Horse Vehicle, with / not more than three persons. / July 18 (vertical) / G. Dwight (ink signature) / Agent. Rv: Blank. (Smythe 1592)

These passes could postdate the Hard Times era, which ended 1844.

GIBBS TIFFANY & CO.
Sturbridge, Mass.

HT #	Rarity	Year	Metal	Size	VG	F	VF	EF
179	R7	(1835-38)	Copper	29mm	—	250.	—	—

GIBBS TIFFANY & CO. ctsp on U.S. 1826 Large cent. (Rich Hartzog coll.)

A179	R8	(1835-38)	Copper	29mm	—	—	250.	—

GIBBS TIFFANY & CO. / STURBRIDGE MASS. ctsp on U.S. 1800 or 1817 Large cents.

HT #	Rarity	Year	Metal	Size	VG	F	VF	EF
180	R8	1836	Copper	29mm	—	—	900.	—

(Eagle) / E. HUTCHINGS & CO. / AGENTS BALTO / GIBBS TIFFANY & CO. / STURBRIDGE MASS. / CAST-STEEL / 1836 ctsp on U.S. Large cent. (Brunk 20880; Russ Sears coll.)

NOTE: Hutchings was in business only 1835-1838. Gibbs Tiffany was in business 1820-1850.

Gibbs Tiffany made popular under hammer pistols. Hutchings was an agent for them.

JOHN J. ADAMS
Taunton, Mass.

HT #	Rarity	Year	Metal	Size	VG	F	VF	Unc
181	R1	(1835)	Copper	28.5mm	6.00	15.00	40.00	140.
181A	R6	(1835)	Brass	28.5mm	35.00	75.00	150.	600.

Donald Miller coll. contains brockage of HT 181, possibly unique. Assigned number 181X.

HT #	Rarity	Year	Metal	Size	VG	F	VF	Unc
181B	R9	(1835)	Silver	32.5mm	—	—	2000.	—

Obverse die overstruck on one side of a U.S. 1811 half dollar.

CROCKER BROS. & CO.
Taunton, Mass.

Photo enlarged

HT #	Rarity	Year	Metal	Size	VG	F	VF	EF
182	R3	(1830's)	Copper	28.5mm	25.00	60.00	85.00	175.
182A	R7	(1830's)	WM	28.5mm	—	1000.	1400.	1700.

HT 182A in VF from the Wayte Raymond coll. fetched $1430 in a Bowers & Merena 1990 sale.

Documentary evidence shows that some of the Crocker Brothers tokens were still being struck in Attleboro in 1839.

H. W. C.
Massachusetts

HT #	Rarity	Year	Metal	Size	VG	F	VF	EF
184	R9	(?)	Silver	32.5mm	—	—	35.00	—

H. W. C. / MASS ctsp on U.S. 1824 Bust half dollar. (Sol Taylor coll.; Brunk 17620)

A similar ctsp on U.S. 1829 Large cent was reported as Brunk 17605. Attribution to HT period is tentative.

MISSOURI

H. M. BROWN
St. Louis, Mo.

HT #	Rarity	Year	Metal	Size	VG	F	VF	EF
186	R9	(1838-41)	Silver	32.5mm	—	—	800.	—

H. M. BROWN / ST LOUIS MO ctsp on U.S. 1803 Draped Bust/ Heraldic Eagle half dollar. (Brunk 5486)

Henry M. Brown, born in 1814, was a gunsmith in St. Louis from 1838 to 1850, according to DeWitt Pourie's unpublished studies of St. Louis firearms makers, quoted by Frank M. Sellers (see Bibliography).

The 1838-1841 dates assigned this great rarity are based on Kauffman's 1952 work.

HUCKEL, BURROWS & JENNINGS
St. Louis, Mo.

HT #	Rarity	Year	Metal	Size	VG	F	VF	EF
187	R8	1836	Brass	29mm	4000.	7000.	9000.	11,000.
187A	R8	1836	S/Brass	29mm	—	7000.	9000.	11,000.
187B	R8	1836	WM	29mm	2000.	5500.	9000.	11,000.

HT #	Rarity	Year	Metal	Size	VG	F	VF	EF
188	R8	1836	Brass	29mm	3500.	6500.	8500.	10,000.

HUCKEL erased on die.

188A	R8	—	WM	29mm	2000.	5500.	8500.	10,000.

HT 187-188A are not known in uncirculated condition.

Bale & Smith of New York engraved and struck the cards of Huckel, Burrows & Jennings, HT 187 and 188, as evidenced by die links to the B&S cards struck for New Orleans in this same period.

Close examination of the choice specimens in the American Numismatic Society collection reveals that the name HUCKEL was erased on the die before HT 188 and 188A were struck, but the erasure left clear evidence of what had been there.

It must be assumed that partner Huckel left the firm in or soon after 1836.

J. MASSOT

SILVER, 38MM

HT #	Rarity	Year	VG	F	VF	EF
189	R9	1840		600.	—	—

J. MASSOT / 1840 ctsp on obverse of France 1792-D ecu (6-livres) of Louis XVI, Craig 93.4. ST. LOUIS ctsp on reverse of the coin. (Frank Kovacs coll.; Brunk 26440)

189A	R9	1840			350.	—

Similar ctsp on France 1799 (An 8) 5-francs, Craig 138. This piece made $240 at a 1990's auction.

Joseph Massot was a wholesale grocer on South Fourth Street 1840-1847. The St. Louis directories of 1840, 1842, 1845 and 1847 give differing descriptions of his address, which seems to have been unchanged — 155 So. Fourth (east side), between Cedar and Mulberry.

J. S. PEASE & CO.
St. Louis, Mo.

See the tokens of this hardware importer under New York City, HT 282 and A282, with their partner-agent, L. G. Irving.

UNCIRCULATED

As used in this reference, the "Unc" equates approximately to Uncirculated Mint State 63 in the U.S. coin series. Unc prices are based upon the desire of Hard Times token collectors to obtain part red, no problem specimens.

NEW HAMPSHIRE

S. E. BROWN
Concord, N.H.

HT #	Rarity	Year	Metal	Size	VG	F	VF	EF
528	R9	(1844-48)	Silver	27mm	—	—	200.	—

S. E. BROWN in relief within ribbon-shaped depression ctsp on Spanish-American 1797-PTS-PP 2-reales, KM-71. (Robert Merchant coll.)

This is one of the hallmarks used by Seth E. Brown, silversmith, watchmaker and jeweler who did business in Concord, N.H. 1844-1848 and then in Boston 1849-1864. While in Boston, Seth E. Brown did work for the large Jones Ball & Co. manufacturing jewelry firm, of which he was a partner 1855-64. He is believed to have died in or after 1868.

Brown's more usually encountered hallmark is: Seth E. Brown in relief italics within long oval depression.

HASELTON & PALMER
Dover, N.H.

HT #	Rarity	Metal	Size	Year	VG	VF	EF	Unc
192	R2	1837	Copper	28.5mm	7.00	15.00	50.00	250.

A.C. Smith.

A.C. SMITH
Dover, N.H.

HT #	Rarity	Year	Metal	Size	VG	VF	EF	Unc
193	R2	1837	Copper	29.1mm	7.00	15.00	50.00	250.

Haselton & Palmer

H. TOWLE
Haverhill, N. H.

HT #	Rarity	Year	Metal	Size	VG	F	VF	EF
900	R7	(1835)	Copper	29mm	150.	-	225.	-

H. TOWLE in relief within rectangular depression ctsp on U.S. Large cent. Dates examined: 1802, 1807. Only 4 or 5 pcs. known. (Brunk 40335; Rulau-E NH 2; Bowers coll.; Rulau coll.)

Henry Towle (1788-1867) was born the son of Simon Towle and Eleanor Hall Towle. In 1805 he arrived in Haverhill, N. H. and soon set up as a silversmith on Main Street. He remained in Haverhill until his death, March 28, 1867.

(Research on this craftsman has been difficult, but is partially explained by the opus of Henry N. Flynt and Martha Gandy Fales for The Heritage Foundation.)

It is possible there is a conection between H. Towle and Anthony F. Towle, founder of the Towle Mfg. Co. of Newburyport, Mass., though the official Towle Mfg. Co. history published in 1908 does not mention any silversmith predecessors to their founder.

A.F. Towle and William P. Jones founded Towle & Jones in 1857. This became A.F. Towle & Son (Edward B. Towle) in 1873, and Towle Mfg. Co. in 1882.

G. N. GALE
Lisbon, N. H.

HT #	Rarity	Date	Metal	Size	VG	F	VF	EF
566	R9	(1838)	Silver	27mm	30.00	—	45.00	—

G. N. GALE in relief within toothed rect. depression ctsp on Spanish-American 1784-Mo-FM 2-reales. WEAVER incuse is ctsp on reverse. (Van Ormer sale 2653; Brunk 15560;Rulau-E Mav 19S)

| 566A | R8 | (?) | Copper | 29mm | 30.00 | — | 45.00 | — |

Similar ctsp on 1807, 1826 or 1837 U.S. Large cent.

| 573 | R9 | (1838) | Copper | 29mm | — | — | 35.00 | — |

G. N. GALE incused, from shaped prepared punch, ctsp on U.S. 1835 Large cent. (Erwin Lein coll., Bethpage, N.Y.; Rulau-E Mav 19V)

| A573 | R9 | (1838) | Copper | 29mm | — | — | 45.00 | — |

G. N. GALE in relief within toothed rect. depression ctsp on U.S. 1807/6 Large cent. (Bowers coll.)

Supposedly Gale was a New Hampshire goldsmith, Van Ormer reported. No verification has been found in gold/silver references.

G. N. Gale appears in the 1830 federal census under Lisbon, Grafton County, New Hampshire.

NATHL. MARCH
Portsmouth, N.H.

HT #	Rarity	Year	Metal	Size	VG	VF	EF	Unc
194	R1	1837	Copper	29.1mm	5.00	17.50	50.00	170.

William Simes

Nathaniel March was born in Portsmouth on June 14, 1807. He became a junior partner in the firm of Childs & March, the successor to Childs & Sparhawk. Childs left the firm soon thereafter, and business was then conducted as Nathaniel March & Co. until about 1839. After that time the business was conducted simply in his personal name, Nathaniel March. He died July 9, 1846, after which the trade was continued by Samuel A. Badger.

William Simes was born in Portsmouth on April 9, 1806. He entered business in 1828. At different times Thomas E. Call and Henry F. Gerrish were partners. His business was sold in 1860 to Moulton & Blaisdell, who continued the trade for many decades thereafter. In 1861 and 1862 William Simes was elected mayor of Portsmouth. A third nomination was subsequently declined. The token issued jointly by March and Simes is believed to have been struck by Robinsons Jones & Co. of Attleboro, Mass.

WILLIAM SIMES & CO.

HT #	Rarity	Year	Metal	Size	VG	VF	EF	Unc
194	R1	1837	Copper	29.1mm	5.00	17.50	50.00	170.

Nathl March

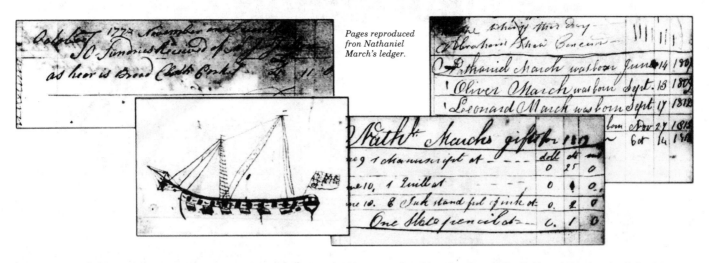

Pages reproduced from Nathaniel March's ledger.

An old ledger containing entries by Nathaniel March from 1809 on was found in a Hampton Falls, N. H. antique shop by Q. David Bowers and published in Rare Coin Review for Sept.-Oct. 2000. Entries as early as 1772 for one John Jackson appeared.

E.F. SISE & CO.
Portsmouth, N.H.

HT #	Rarity	Year	Metal	Size	VG	VF	EF	Unc
195	R1	1837	Copper	28.5mm	4.00	17.50	37.50	200.

Edward F. Sise, founder of the firm of general commission and forwarding merchants which issued this card, was born in Dover, N.H. on Sept. 19, 1799, and died May 25, 1868. The firm advertised itself as importers of crockery and glassware and dealers in coal.

The "Co." was E.F. Sise and John Walker, but after Sise's withdrawal about 1854, Walker continued the business in partnership with William H. Sise and Joseph Sise. Walker retired in 1883. Joseph Sise died in 1894. This firm occupied the same premises from 1822 until at least 1895, according to Lyman H. Low.

NEW JERSEY

HOWELL WORKS GARDEN

Allaire, N.J.

HT #	Rarity	Year	Metal	Size	VG	VF	EF	Unc
200	R4	1834	Copper	22mm	45.00	200.	400.	750.

Grapes, Signum. Well struck EF reverse is worth more, $450.

| 201 | R3 | (1835) | Copper | 27mm | 150. | 350. | 450. | 600. |

Rose, Token

A Fine-plus HT 201 with word Token complete, Hayden 639 in May 2001, was valued at $200 up. The word is usually weakly struck.

| 201A | R9 | (1835) | Copper | 29mm | — | 3000. | — | Rare |

Similar, ctsp on 1820 U.S. cent

The Howell Works had its origin in an establishment called the Monmouth Furnace, founded in Howell, Monmouth Co., N.J. (now Allaire), in 1814. About 1822 James P. Allaire took possession, changing the name to Howell Works, under which title they were carried on for about twenty-five years. Mr. Allaire died in 1858. A few years before his death it became the Allaire Works, famous for its marine engines, etc., the fine workmanship of which gave them a wide reputation. In this concern the well known John Roach began his career.

Just what relation the Garden had to the Works does not appear, but it was connected with them in some way, we have on good authority. From the device the tokens bear it was very likely a social resort of the workmen, under control of the company.

These tokens, as well as Howell Works "shin plasters" for various denominations, were used as currency. The paper bills were engraved by Rawdon, Wright, Hatch and Co., of New York, and were for 6 1/4, 12 1/2 cents, $1, $2, $3, $5 and $10, and possibly other denominations, payable to bearer and signed by the president of the "Howell Works Co."

J. GIBBS, MANUFACTURER

Belleville, N.J.

HT #	Rarity	Year	Metal	Size	VG	F	VF	EF
202	R6	(1841)	Copper	28mm	350.	600.	1000.	1600.

John Gibbs was senior partner of Gibbs Gardner & Co. and a master of the Belleville Mint. He is profiled elsewhere (see Index).

I. GIBBS USM STAGE

HT #	Rarity	Year	Metal	Size	VG	F	VF	EF
203	R8	(1835)	Brass	23mm	2000.	2500.	5000.	7500.

One Ride

The I. Gibbs USM Stage piece could have been issued as early as 1831. An advertisement in an 1831 newspaper publicized John Gibbs' Belleville to Newark (3 miles) and Belleville to New York (8 miles) stages. John Gibbs moved to New York in 1846.

Previous editions of this catalog listed the I. Gibbs piece under New York City, but we now believe that Atwood was in error in assigning it there, as the headquarters of the stage line apparently was in Belleville, New Jersey.

T. DUSEAMAN

HT #	Rarity	Year	Metal	Size	VG	VF	EF	Unc
204	R1	(1837)	Copper	28mm	10.00	40.00	75.00	400.
204A	R6	—	Gilt/C.	28mm	80.00	—	300.	—

Breton 670

Lindesmith has discovered that the Duseaman design was originally a button die by Hugh Wishart of New York City. The 1828-29 Longworth directory lists Jane Wishart, widow of Alexander, at 97 Charlton. Hugh Wishart was a goldsmith ca 1784-1822.

T.D. SEAMAN

Belleville, N.J.

HT #	Rarity	Year	Metal	Size	VG	VF	EF	Unc
204B	R5	(1837)	Copper	27.6mm	170.	500.	875.	3000.

T.D. Seaman operated a hotel in Belleville around 1837 and also apparently engaged in trade as a butcher. He was probably the same as one Tobias D. Seaman who was proprietor of the Mechanics' Hotel, 188 Broad Street, Newark, N.J., from about 1845 to 1850 and, following that, in 1851 the South Ward Hotel at 398 Broadway in Newark.

It is probable that HT 204 bearing the name DUSEAMAN was in reality issued for Seaman. The workmanship is very crude and for this reason the piece was probably rejected by Seaman when he first saw it. A diecutter at the Belleville Mint simply added an extraneous U in place of the period between the D and SEAMAN, creating the *DUSEAMAN* name. After the U was added the piece was suitable for general purposes and could be sold to anyone in quantity. As such pieces sold for less than a cent but circulated at the value of one cent each, a profit was to be made. As such it circulated in Canada.

A choice toned AU specimen of this rare card (HT 204B) fetched $2200 in the 1989 Gil Steinberg sale. A near EF specimen realized only $275 in the PCAC May 1997 sale, lot 008.

An EF specimen made $859.63 in the B&M March 2000 Lindesmith sale, lot 1133.

HT #	Rarity	Year	Metal	Size	F	VF	EF	Proof
C204	R8	(1909)	Brass	45mm	—	—	—	175.

In 1909 Thomas L. Elder prepared an imitation Agriculture & Commerce Bas Canada bouquet sou die and had it struck in various metals, both on normal sized planchets and large 45mm flans. Illustrated is the James Henderson specimen in brass proof on a 45mm uniface planchet with plain edge.

BERGEN IRON WORKS

Lakewood, N.J.

STARS

BRASS, 21.4MM, PLAIN EDGE

HT #	Rarity	Year	Metal	Size	VG	VF	EF	Unc
205	R2	1840	*Store*		30.00	100.	250.	500.
205X	R9	1840			—	—	—	—

Brockage of eagle obverse intaglio on reverse. (Stanley Miller coll.)

COPPER, 21.4MM

HT #	Rarity	Year	Metal	Size	VG	VF	EF	Unc
205A	R4	1840	*Store*		30.00	125.	200.	600.
205B	R6	1840 *Store*	Silvered Copper			Not contemporary		

CIRCLES

COPPER, 22MM

HT #	Rarity	Year	Metal	Size	VG	VF	EF	Unc
206	R4	1840 O Store O			30.00	100.	265.	600.

HT #	Rarity	Date	Metal	Size	VG	F	VF	EF
A206	R9	1840	Copper	22mm	40.00	—	—	—

As 206, but large X in relief within circular depression, ctsp on each side. Resembles a pewterer's quality mark. (Kirtley April 15, 1997 sale, lot Q058; realized $27.50)

The Bergen Iron Works was located in what is now Ocean County, New Jersey, at a place once known as Bricksburg and now called Lakewood. They were at a point where the railroad crosses Metetecunk River, about four miles from the north end of Barnegat Bay. In the 1830's the forges and furnaces of central New Jersey were engaged in treating "bog ores" — but when the abundant mines of Pennsylvania were developed the mines in New Jersey ceased operations.

The tokens were apparently issued by the company store to supply currency for their workmen and store patrons.

Bergen Iron Works apparently was associated with wildcat notes through two banks and a general store — the Ocean Bank of Bergen Iron Works and Union Bank of Tom's River. These wildcat institutions were controlled in 1851 by the Snyder family of Bergen Iron Works.

E. & I. BRAGAW

Newark, N.J. & Mobile, Ala.

HT #	Rarity	Year	Metal	Size	VG	F	VF	EF
207	R7	(1830's)	Copper	28mm	350.	600.	1500.	3000.

Illustration enlarged!

HT #	Rarity	Year	Metal	Size	VG	F	VF	Unc
207A	R7	(1830's)	Brass	26.6mm	350.	800.	2000.	3000.

E. & I. BRAGAW. HAT MANUFACTURERS. / NEWARK N: J. / AND / MOBILE / ALABAMA / (tiny) W & B NYC. Rv: HATS & CAPS OF EVERY DESCRIPTION / WHOLESALE / AND / RETAIL. (Wesley S. Cox coll. in holed F+ condition; bid in Oct. 1998 for $231)

The reverse of HT 207-207B is very similar to the reverse of HT 235, also a Wright & Bale product, but letter spacing etc. are different. Researcher Cox found that 207A had specific gravity 8.87, the color of old cartridge brass, perhaps an alloy of copper, zinc and a small amount of lead. Diameter 26.6mm. Dry weight 6.32 grams.

HT #	Rarity	Year	Metal	Size	VG	F	VF	Unc
207B	R7	(1830's)	WM	28mm	350.	800.	2000.	3000.

Elias and John Bragaw were listed as "wholesale hatters" at 348 Broad "and at Mobile, Ala." until 1836. The partnership broke up in 1836, Elias continuing the business in Newark and John going into business for himself in Mobile.

The tokens, cut by Wright & Bale, would have been issued in the 1829-33 period.

Elias Brevoort Bragaw was born June 15, 1800 at Newton, Sussex County, New Jersey, the son of Richard Bragaw and Elizabeth Painter, his wife. He married Alethea Williams on Dec. 24, 1824 at Newark, Essex County, N.J.

NEW JERSEY TURNPIKE

Non-Local

HT #	Rarity	Year	Metal	Size	VG	F	VF	EF
199	R7	(?)	Cardboard	*Rect 64x22mm	—	30.00	—	—

* White cardboard; black printing.
NEW JERSEY TURNPIKE 2 / Two Horse Team. / Sec'y. Rv: Blank. (Kirtley report)

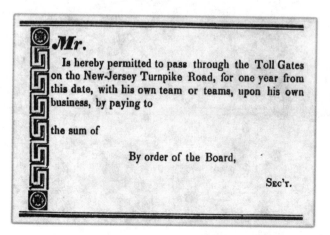

A surviving paper ticket of the same issuer, not filled in by ink, gives slightly more perspective to the cardboard two-horse team ticket. (Courtesy Charles E. Kirtley)

NEW YORK

WHITCOMB. ADAMS
Adams, N.Y.

HT #	Rarity	Year	Metal	Size	VG	F	VF	EF
574	R8	1838	Silver	27mm	50.00		75.00	

WHITCOMB. ADAMS (script) in relief within shaped rect. depression ctsp on Spanish-American 1819 and worn-date 2-reales. (Van Ormer sale 2502; Brunk 42935; Rulau-E Mav 59)

The worn-date piece is also ctsp 1838. Adams, Mass. had been suggested for these pieces. Henry Whitcomb appears in Adams, Jefferson County, N.Y. in the census records for 1830 and 1840.

A possible descendant, H. Whitcomb, appears in the 1882 gazetteer under watches and jewelry.

BOGARDUS
Albany, N.Y.

HT#	Rarity	Year	Metal	Size	VG	F	VF	EF
A210	R8	(1830's)	Copper	29mm	65.00	—	100.	—

BOGARDUS ctsp on U.S. Large cent. Examined: 1803, 1831. (Brunk 4140)

Peter H. Bogardus worked as a silversmith in the 1830's in Albany, according to Kovel. The dates 1833 and 1834 are firm, directories indicate.

S. D. BROWER

HT#	Rarity	Year	Metal	Size	VG	F	VF	EF
E210	R9	1827	Copper	29mm	—	—	400.	—

S. D. BROWER / ALBANY / 1827 ctsp on U.S. 1797 Large cent. (Brunk 5315; Bowers coll.)

S. Douglas Brower was a silversmith 1837-50 in Albany. He also labored at his trade in Troy, N.Y. 1832-36 and had an outlet in New York City ca. 1834.

ERIE CANAL TRANSPORTATION
Albany, N.Y.
and Rochester, N.Y.

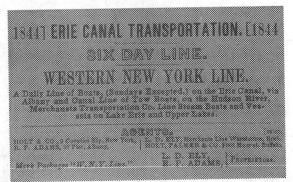

HT #	Rarity	Year	Metal	Size	VG	F	VF	Unc
E210	?	1844	xx	71x53mm	—	—	35.00	

1844]ERIE CANAL TRANSPORTATION[1844 / - / SIX DAY LINE (in open letters) / WESTERN NEW YORK LINE / (nine lines of smaller type). Rv: Blank. (Kirtley Sept. 22, 1997 sale, lot H076) xx Black printing on whitish cardboard.

Owners L.D. Ely and R.P. Adams had agents in New York City and Buffalo, according to this ticket.

C. JOHNSON
Albany, N.Y.

HT #	Rarity	Year	Metal	Size	VG	F	VF	EF
209	R8	(1840-41)	Copper	29mm	60.00	—	90.00	

C. JOHNSON in relief within rect. depression ctsp on U.S. Large cent. Examined: 1802, 1840. (Brunk 21810)

The hallmark may be that of Chauncey Johnson, silversmith, in Albany 1824-1841, according to Kovel (see Biblio.). Johnson was in business alone 1824-1831; in the partnership C. & A. W. Johnson 1831-38; alone again 1838-41.

N. SAFFORD
Albany, N.Y.

HT #	Rarity	Year	Metal	Size	VG	VF	EF	Unc
210	R4	(1830's)	Copper	26.6mm	20.00	85.00	160.	350.

TEMPERANCE / N. SAFFORD / 280 / NORTH MARKET ST. / ALBANY / HOUSE. Rv: ACCOMMODATIONS FOR / MERCHANTS / AND / TRADERS / IN / GENERAL / . PRIVATE FAMILIES. (Wright 930)

HT #	Rarity	Year	Metal	Size	VG	VF	EF	Unc
210A	R7	(1830's)	WM	26.6mm	—	350.	625.	1000.

As 348. Plain edge.

The Temperance movement commenced in this country as early as 1808-1813 in New York and Massachusetts. The movement, originally calling only for abstinence from distilled spirits (whiskey, brandy and rum), spread rapidly under the influence of the churches. By its apogee in 1833 there were 6,000 local Temperance societies in the country.

A few Temperance advocates who were innkeepers offered "temperance house" facilities to abstaining travelers. N. Safford of Albany was such an innkeeper.

In 1840 the Washington Temperance Society, demanding total abstinence from all alcoholic beverages, was formed. In 1846 the Maine Law was passed, prohibiting the sale of intoxicants in the state of Maine. The Order of Good Templars, an international body, was formed at Utica, N.Y. in 1851. The Woman's Christian Temperance Union (WCTU), founded in Cleveland in 1874, used political methods as well as moral persuasion and health education to accomplish its aims. Prohibition was adopted in the U.S. Constitution in 1919, but it was repealed in 1933.

Safford is not in the 1830 census. Tokens were struck by James Bale, either alone or with Wright or Smith. The lettering is distinctive to Bale.

J. COCHRAN
Batavia, N.Y.

HT #	Rarity	Year	Metal	Size	VG	F	VF	Unc
211	R7	1844	Copper	28mm	5000.	6500.	10,000.	—

James H. Cochran was a bell founder and a very ingenious mechanic, who is said to have 'made the first cent coined in the U.S.,' though what this latter phrase refers to we have not discovered. Only four specimens of his 1844 token are known, all supposedly struck over other coins.

Benjamin Franklin is said to have visited his earlier shop, in Philadelphia.

In the 1840's his workshop and residence were on Bank St., Batavia. He died at age 83 in Batavia, Genesee County, N.Y.

Only two of the four known specimens have ever been sold at public auction. The best-known piece appeared in Frossard's Dec. 1896 sale (lot 486), and then in Ben Green's July 1912 sale (lot 10006), where it was purchased by George Hetrich. It passed later to Donald M. Miller, Q. David Bowers, Rossa & Tanenbaum and to a private New York collector.

A Fine specimen appeared in Henry Chapman's Nov. 1910 sale (lot 651), where Virgil Brand purchased it. Much later it was lot 011 in the Dec. 1986 sale by H. Joseph Levine. Then it was sold for $4675 in the Oct. 1989 Steinberg sale by Stack's Inc.

LOW NUMBERS

For veteran collectors still using the century-old "Low" numbering system, there is a conversion chart of the "HT" numbers in the Introduction to this reference.

E. STILLMAN
Brookfield, N.Y. and Burlington , Vt.

HT #	Rarity	Year	Metal	Size	VG	F	VF	EF
540	R7	(1835-)	Copper	29mm	200.	—	400.	—

E. STILLMAN ctsp on U.S. Large cent. Examined: 1803, 1820, 1823, 1835. 4 pieces known. (Rulau Ct-St 4; Brunk 38420)

541	R9	(1835-)	Silver	21mm		—	400.	

Similar ctsp on Spanish-American 1789 1-real. (Rulau Ct-St 5; Rulau Mav 327)

A541	R9	1810	Copper	29mm	—	—	400.	—

STILLMAN (curved) / U.S. / 1810 ctsp incuse on U.S. Large cent, worn, ca 1800. (Bowers coll., ex-F.C.C. Boyd, J.J. Ford)

Ethan Stillman, born in Westerly, N.Y. in 1768, worked as a youth in New York Iron Works and later was a shoemaker. In 1790-97 he resided in Burlington, Vt. In 1798 he moved to Farmington, Ct., where he and his brother Amos got a government contract to produce 500 muskets; this was completed 1803.

In 1808 he received a contract for 2200 more muskets and in 1818 moved his gun-smith operations to Brookfield, N.Y. He was in business there at least until 1835. The stamp matches his 1808 musket lockplate markings.

Previously these pieces were attributed to an early 19th century silversmith of Stonington, Ct. (Research courtesy Bill Groom)

Almost certainly Ethan Stillman issued A541 from his Burlington, Vt. location, before his move to Brookfield, N.Y.

BROOKLYN UNION FERRY CO.
Brooklyn, N.Y.

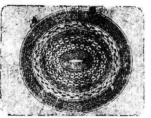

HT #	Rarity	Year	Metal	Size	VG	F	VF	EF
E211	?	(1840's?)	Cardboard	*Rect 28x24mm	—	20.00	—	35.00

* Rectangular cardboard, color not reported.
Steam ferry left, FOOT / PASSENGER around, all within wide oval border labeled: BROOKLYN UNION / FERRY Co. Ornamentation in all four corners. Rv: Banknote-type guilloche in oval format.
It is possible this ticket postdates the Hard Times period by a few years.

FULTON FERRY
Brooklyn, N.Y.

HT #	Rarity	Date	Metal	Size	VG	F	VF	EF
B211	R8	1837	Cardboard	Rect 78x28mm	—	—	225.	—

Sketch of the ferry from Brooklyn to Manhattan circa 1830. The ungainly round steam-powered ship 'Brooklyn' is seen entering the Manhattan docking area, with New York harbor in background. Stabilizers something like outriggers enable the unwieldy craft to avoid tipping, although this ferry must have been "docked" during strong storms. (Sketch courtesy U.S. Encyclopedia of History)

Within ornate printed border: FULTON FERRY COMMUTATION / For- - Cart, / TILL FIRST OF MAY, 1837. (pinecone-like ornament). Signed in ink between words For--Cart: J. Michaels. Rv: Blank. (B&M 1985 Patterson sale, lot 1477)

James Michaels. Issued shortly before the famous May 10, 1837 suspension of specie payments in New York. The Patterson collection sale specimen, ex-David Proskey and F.C.C. Boyd, realized $176 on March 26, 1985.

McLANAN

HT #	Rarity	Date	Metal	Size	VG	F	VF	EF
584	R9	(1830's)	Copper	29mm	—	—	75.00	

McLANAN ctsp incuse multiple times on U.S. 1827 Large cent. Also ctsp with oval silversmith's punches several times. (Maurice M. Gould sale, lot 4663)

James B. McLanan was a silversmith in Buffalo in the 1830's. In 1836-37 he was in the Myer & McLanan silversmith partnership there with Henry B. Myer.

Myer was a seasoned silversmith, operating in Newburgh, N.Y. 1818-35 and Buffalo 1836-48.

PATTERSON BROS.

HT #	Rarity	Year	Metal	Size	F	VF	EF	Unc
212	R2	(1838-39)	Copper	28.5mm	15.00	35.00	65.00	250.
212A	R2	(1838-39)	Engrailed Edge		15.00	35.00	65.00	250.

John Patterson, principal, and James Patterson made up Patterson Brothers, hardware, at 170 Main Street in the 1839 directory. The business was known as John Patterson, hardware, and crockery, at 170 Main Street in the 1844 directory, and James Patterson is listed as a clerk there, John Patterson resided at 350 Washington in 1844, and James Patterson boarded at the same address, the directory reveals.

Neither Patterson appeared in the 1830 census.

Very Good specimens of 212 and 212A sell for $8.

W.A. THOMSON
Buffalo, N.Y.

HT #	Rarity	Year	Metal	Size	VG	F	EF	Unc
213	R4	(1838-39)	Copper	38mm	15.00	35.00	100.	400.

Anvil and hammer in center, NO. 9 on side of anvil. W.A. THOMSON above, WEBSTER BUILDINGS / BUFFALO below. Reeded edge. (Miller NY 25)

HT #	Rarity	Year	Metal	Size	VG	F	EF	Unc
214	R5	(1843-44)	Copper	33mm	20.00	70.00	150.	400.

Anvil in center, W.A. THOMSON ** above, BUFFALO N.Y. below. Rv: Teakettle in center, IMPORTERS above, OF HARDWARE below. Reeded edge. (Wright 1142; Miller NY 26)

New Amsterdam village (later Buffalo) was a going concern in 1803, but was burned to the ground by the British in 1813. In 1832 Buffalo became a city; it then had 10,000 population. Its 1836 population totaled 16,000.

Thomson was a clerk 1835-38, in the latter year for Patterson Brothers hardware.

William A. Thomson is listed in the 1839 directory, in hardware at 9 Webster Block, which helps to date the larger token to the 1838-39 period.

In the 1844 directory Thomson, hardware and cutlery, is at 7 and 9 Webster Block and also at 164 Main Street. The smaller token probably emanates from Thomson's expanded operations period, as it is without address. Thomson also appears in the 1840 census, but cannot be located in the 1820 or 1830 census reports. By 1847-49 the firm was known as Thomson Brothers after the admission of Hugh Thomson.

Thomas L. Elder in "A Plea for American Token Collecting" (1915) said that the two Thomson cards were issued "between 1840 and 1845." We still do not know the source of his claim, but our foray in April, 1984 into Buffalo records at the Mormon Genealogical Library in Salt Lake City proves that Elder was very close to accurate. The assumption of the Fulds much later that these pieces emanated from the 1820's - which we repeated in the first two editions of *Early American Tokens* — is now proven inaccurate and we can confidently assign both tokens to the Hard Times period.

L. ROBINSON
Chittenango, N.Y.

HT #	Rarity	Year	Metal	Size	VG	F	VF	Unc
215	R5	(1848-58)	Copper	28mm	80.00	150.	200.	400.

L. ROBINSON / -OF- / *COMPOUND* / MAGNETS / MANUFACTURER. RV: *RIFLE. TRIMMINGS* / -AND- / GUNNERY / CHITTENANGO. N.Y. Reeded edge. (Wright 906)

HT #	Rarity	Year	Metal	Size	VG	F	VF	Unc
215A	R9	(1848-58)	Copper	28mm	—	—	1500.	

Plain edge.

HT #	Rarity	Year	Metal	Size	VG	F	VF	Unc
215B	R8	(1848-58)	WM	27.5mm	—	—	1000.	1750.

As 215. Plain edge.

HT #	Rarity		Metal	Size			F	
216C	R8		Copper	26mm			600.	—

As 215, but smaller planchet. (Krause coll.)

The tokens of L. Robinson have been determined to be of later issuance than has been thought for many years. They are store cards of Luther Robinson, who made percussion halfstock rifles in Chittenango from 1848 through 1858.

The store cards belong in *U.S. Merchant Tokens 1845-1860*. They are rare, and will probably retain much of their price, though some of that price level was attained by association with the Hard Times period.

A variety of 215B with extra thick planchet appeared in the Dec. 1991 Gold Medal sale in EF+ and fetched $800.

HALL & ELTON
Geneva, N.Y.

HT #	Rarity	Date	Metal	Size	VG	F	VF	EF
564	R9	(1841)	Copper	29mm	—	200.	—	—

HALL & ELTON (incuse) ctsp on U.S. 1806 Large cent. (Brunk report; Bowers coll.)

Abraham B. Hall and A.D. Elton advertised their plated ware in 1841. The punch matches one in Belden, page 210.

W. BESSAC
Hudson, N.Y.

HT #	Rarity	Year	Metal	Size	VG	F	VF	EF
A450	R9	(1830's)	Copper	29mm	200.	—	300.	—

W. BESSAC ctsp on U.S. 1833 Large cent. (Brunk 3515)

HT #	Rarity	Year	Metal	Size	VG	F	VF	EF
B450	R9	(1830's)	Copper	28mm	200.	—	300.	—

Similar ctsp on Hard Times token, HT 353.

| C450 | R9 | (1830's) | Copper | 29mm | | | 300. | — |

BESSAC / McDONALD ctsp incuse (unrelated styles of stamp) on U.S. 1803 Large cent. (Bowers coll.)

An H. W. Bessac is listed as a silversmith in Hudson 1823-1825. Belden gives another mark for H. W. Bessac.

J. I. TOBEY

Hudson, N.Y.

HT #	Rarity	Year	Metal	Size	VG	VF	EF	Unc
A215	R9	(1830's)	Copper	29mm	—	800.	—	

J. I. TOBEY / HUDSON within two rectangles, ctsp on U.S. 1794 Large cent. (Tanenbaum coll.; Brunk 40223)

J. I. Tobey had a store from about 1827 onward on Warren Street (Main Street) and Cherry Lane, according to Columbia County Records for the 1830's. In 1827-28 Tobey was a Hudson alderman. Tobey made wooden planes.

J. BURRITT & SON

Ithaca, N.Y.

HT #	Rarity	Year	Metal	Size	VG	F	VF	EF
530	R9	(1838)	Silver	32.5mm		600.		900.

J. BURRITT / & SON / ITHACA ctsp on U.S. 1809 Bust half dollar. (Brunk 6120; Rulau NY 2165)

| 531 | R9 | (1838) | Copper | 28.5mm | — | 300. | | 450. |

Similar ctsp on 1837 Hard Times token. (Bosco Apr. 1989 sale, lot 017; Rulau NY 2166)

| 532 | R9 | (1838) | Silver | 32.5mm | — | 600. | — | 900. |

J. BURRITT / & SON ctsp on U.S. 1834 half dollar. (Brunk 6110; Rulau NY 2167)

Joseph Burritt was a silversmith who came to Ithaca from Connecticut in 1816. His son, Joseph C. Burritt, joined the firm in 1838. The business became Burritt, Clark & Co. about 1864 and was then at 34 Oswego Street.

These pieces were formerly listed under the USMT section as 1840's products.

WALSH'S GENERAL STORE

Lansingburgh, N.Y.

HT #	Rarity	Year	Metal	Size	VG	F	VF	Unc
216	R1	1835	Copper	28.5mm	5.00	10.00	20.00	300.
	Plough							

				217		**218**		
HT #	Rarity	Year	Metal	Size	VG	VF	EF	Unc
217	R1	1835	Copper	28.5mm	5.00	20.00	40.00	350.
	Lafayette H							
218	R1	1835	Copper	28.5mm	5.00	20.00	40.00	300.

LANSINBURG (Sic!), straight.

These tokens were issued by Walsh's general store in Lansingburgh, Rensselaer County, New York. The motto SPEED THE PLOUGH, IT FEEDS ALL refers to the interest in horticulture and farming shown by the owner, Alexander Walsh, who conducted the store more than 30 years. His so-called "Plough Penny" circulated freely all over northern New York from 1835 on.

Locally Walsh's enterprise was known as Walsh's Museum due to the interesting and unusual variety of stock it contained. Walsh was very prominent; in 1825 he accompanied Governor DeWitt Clinton on the first boat in ceremonies opening the Erie Canal and received a silver medal from that event. He was an admirer of the Marquis de Lafayette, who visited the U.S. in 1825 and is depicted on two of Walsh's tokens. In 1839 Henry Clay was a guest in his Lansingburgh home. He retired from business in 1846. He died Aug. 4, 1849. Walsh does not appear in 1820 census, but he is in 1830 census.

Imitation dies for the plough side of HT 216 were made for Thomas L. Elder. In 1909 Elder caused to be struck several uniface tokens in various metals from these dies, both in normal size and on dollar sized flans. The imitations read PLOW instead of PLOUGH.

The 45mm proof brass item illustrated above is from the James Henderson collection. It is one of several known.

A. HENSHAW

Newark, N.Y.

HT #	Rarity	Year	Metal	Size	VG	F	VF	EF
A218	R9	1837	Copper	29mm	—	—	1500.	—

A. HENSHAW in relief within long rectangular depression ctsp on U.S. 1822 Large cent. Large 1837 in single numeral-punches incused below. (Charles Kirtley Nov. 1991 sale, lot Q041; Brunk 19257; Kirtley June 18, 1996 sale, lot AD8)

HT #	Rarity	Year	Metal	Size	VG	F	VF	EF
B218	R9	(1837 ?)	Silver	27mm	—	—	2200.	—

Same Henshaw ctsp on Spanish-American 1789-Mo-FM 2-reales coin. Incused above is: O. BENNETT and incused below is: LYONS. (Brunk 3380)

Orra Bennett (1800-65) was a maker of percussion halfstock guns at Lyons, N.Y. from 1848 until his death 17 years later.

One Joseph Henshaw is known to have been a gunsmith and engraver in New York City 1830-36 and then in Newark, N.Y. 1836-on. (Some gunsmith references give Newark, N.J., but we believe Newark, N.Y. is correct.)

Newark and Lyons are nearby communities in Wayne County, New York, both on the New York State Barge Canal which runs from North Tonawanda to the Mohawk River east of Little Falls.

One of the two known A. HENSHAW counterstamps surfaced in 1991 and had never previously been published; the silver piece was purchased by Brunk 1975, ex-J. W. Carberry, Ralph Goldstone, Maurice Gould. Whether the A. Henshaw of the stamps was the Newark gunsmith is not known, but the body of circumstance is too strong to ignore. Tentative attribution.

A218 fetched $1500 in the 1996 Kirtley sale, against estimate of $750-$1250!

W. ADAMS

New York, N.Y.

HT #	Rarity	Year	Metal	Size	VG	F	VF	EF
F218	R9	(1831-42)	Copper	28.5mm	30.00	—	50.00	—

W. ADAMS / NEW YORK ctsp on Hard Times token. (Brunk 370)

William Adams, silversmith, worked in New York 1831-1842. His shop was at 10 Elm Street in 1835. Adams was president of the Board of Aldermen in 1842. He moved his shop to Troy, N.Y. 1844-1850.

ALLCOCK & ALLEN CO.

HT #	Rarity	Year	Metal	Size	VG	F	VF	EF
J218	R9	(?)	Copper	28.5mm	—	—	150.	—

ALLCOCK & ALLEN CO / 519 BROADWAY / NEW YORK ctsp on U.S. Hard Times token. (Brunk 600)

Silversmith on Broadway, Kovel says. The firm was known as Allcock & Allen 1810-1820.

HENRY ANDERSON

New York, N.Y.

HT #	Rarity	Year	Metal	Size	VG	VF	EF	Unc
219	R2	1837	Copper	28.1mm	5.00	17.50	30.00	200.

A 50% red Unc. HT 219 made $300 in May, 2001.

An ad from the New York Transcript for Sept. 14, 1835.

N. ANDRUS & COMPANY

HT #	Rarity	Year	Metal	Size	VG	F	VF	EF
A219	R9	(1837)	Silver	32.5mm	—	—	250.	—

N. ANDRUS & COMPANY ctsp on U.S. 1834 Bust half dollar, which had earlier (ca 1835) been ctsp by Barnes & Potter, HT 233. (Brunk 1000)

This firm of silversmiths was active 1834-1837.

ASTOR HOUSE

New York, N.Y.

HT #	Rarity	Year	Metal	Size	VG	F	VF	Unc
905	R8	(1840's)	GS	28mm			Ex. Rare	

5 (large, shaded) / Cts. / ASTOR HOUSE. Rv: Same as obverse, from different die with C of Cts. touching the large numeral 5. Reeded edge. Only 1 specimen thus far examined. (Rulau NY 43; Charles Litman coll.)

The famous old 5-story Astor House fronted on Broadway, occupying all the street front from Vesey St. to Barclay St. Its rooms overlooked the large plaza formed by Ann St. and Park Row ending across Broadway. By crossing just one street, hotel guests could visit St. Paul's Church, Barnum's Museum, Park Theatre, American House or the city hall fountain.

Early in the 18th century the space occupied by Astor House had been Drovers' Inn, resort of the Colonial sporting gentry. About 1800 leading stores occupied the site, but these gave way quickly to residences of the wealthiest merchants – John Jacob Astor, John G. Coster and Philip Lydig. In 1830 John Jacob Astor, the "fur king," determined to build the finest hotel in the country on that Broadway block. Astor bought out all his neighbors, though he reportedly had to pay Coster $20,000 more than his home was appraised for by Coster's own friends.

The Astor House was completed in 1836, the marvel of its age. In 1836 its rooms cost the unheard-of price of $1 per day. Among its guests were Andrew Jackson, Gen. Sam Houston, Daniel Webster, Washington Irving, Charles Dickens, Jenny Lind and, for a few days beginning Feb. 19, 1861, Abraham Lincoln.

A huge banquet was held here for Prince de Joinville on Nov. 26, 1840. On St. Valentine's Day, 1844, there was held the first of the "Bachelors' Balls," long remembered for their brilliance. As can be seen, the "Hard Times" had little enough effect on the upper classes of New York.

The token above, unpublished until May, 2001, may postdate the Hard Times period by a few years, but we believe it was issued and used before 1849. It seems to be made of a metal not unlike Feuchtwanger's composition.

ATWOOD'S RAILROAD HOTEL

HT #	Rarity	Year	Metal	Size	VG	F	VF	EF
220	R6	(1835-8)	Copper 3 Cents, Bale & Smith	26.5mm	200.	250.	500.	1250.
221	R7	(1835-8)	Copper 3 Cents, Bale & Smith	25mm	200.	400.	850.	1400.

HT #	Rarity	Year	Metal	Size	VG	F	VF	Unc
222	R9	(1835-8)	Fire Gilt 3 Cents, Bale & Smith	20mm	—	—	—	3000.
222A	R9	(1835-8)	Copper	20mm	—	—	2000.	—

Numeral 57 ctsp retrograde on obverse. (PCAC Dec. 9, 1995 sale, lot 093)

HT #	Rarity	Year	Metal	Size	VG	F	VF	Unc
223	R8	(1835-8)	Brass 3 Cents, Bale & Smith	26.5mm	—	—	1500.	2000.
223A	R9	(1835-8)	Brass Uniface (obv.)	26.5mm	—	—	—	750.

HT #	Rarity	Year	Metal	Size	VG	VF	EF	Unc
224	R8	(1835-8)	WM	26.5mm	—	1000.	2000.	3000.
224A	R8	(1835-8)	Silver	26.5mm	—			May not exist

J. W. B. (James W. Beebe)

HT #	Rarity	Year	Metal	Size	VG	F	VF	EF
225	R7	(1834-35)	Copper	29mm		70.00		

J. W. B. in relief within rectangle ctsp four times on obverse of U.S. 1820, 1834, 1838 or 1842 Large cent. (Sol Taylor coll.)

225A	R9	(1835-41)	Copper	29mm		150.		

J. W. BEEBE in relief within rect. depression ctsp on U.S. 1810 Large cent. (Bowers coll.)

Beebe appears in directories as a silversmith 1835-1849.

Earlier HT 225 had been assigned to Joseph W. Boyd, a N.Y.C. blacksmith, listed 1812-1824.

BAILLY, WARD & CO.

HT #	Rarity	Year	Metal	Size	VG	F	VF	Unc
226	R8	(1832-43)	WM	27mm	1400.	1800.	2500.	—
226A	R8	(1832-43)	Silver	27mm			2000.	—

An about Fine 226 fetched only $632.50 in an Oct. 1996 auction.

In the B&M 1990 Zeddies sale a Fine specimen of 226 realized $1650. PCAC June 2000 sale, lot 28, measured only 24.2mm; it fetched $1166 in Fine.

BALE & SMITH

HT #	Rarity	Year	Metal	Size	VG	F	VF	Unc
227	R7	(1835-8)	Copper	25mm	300.	700.	1450.	2250.
			Bale & Smith, NY					
227A	R8	(1835-8)	WM	25mm	—	—	2000.	3000.
			Bale & Smith, NY					
228	R7	(1835-8)	Copper	25mm	—	—	1800.	3500.
			B & S, NY					
228A	R8	(1835-8)	WM	25mm	—	—	2500.	3500.
			B & S, NY.					

This firm of die sinkers and medallists was at 68 Nassau Street 1835 to 1838.

HT #	Rarity	Year	Metal	Size	VG	F	VF	Unc
229	R9	(1833-5)	WM	19x23mm	—	—	1100.	—

Minerva Head, BALE N.Y. signature. (Die trial)

JOHN BARKER

HT #	Rarity	Year	Metal	Size	VG	F	VF	EF
230	R7	(1829-33)	Brass	19mm	750.	1500.	2000.	3000.

A Washington head is right within olive wreath. AMERICAN REPOSITORY OF THE FINE ARTS around. Reverse: JOHN BARKER / 16 MAIDEN LANE / DEALER IN / MUSIC PRINTS / & / FANCY / STATIONARY. Only 5 to 9 pieces are known. (Baker 511; Miller 57; Low 338; Levick 243)

Cut by Wright & Bale, which dates it to the 1829-1833 period.

BARNES & POTTER

HT #	Rarity	Year	Metal	Size	VG	F	VF	Unc
231	R8	(1835)	Copper	29mm	150.	—	300.	—

The countermark on a U.S. cent reads: BARNES & POTTER / N. YORK / 1835. (Duffield 1392 in "A Trial List of Countermarked Modern Coins of the World"; Brunk 2430). Dates examined: 1827.

232	R7	(1835)	Copper	29mm			300.	

BARNES & POTTER ctsp on U.S. Large cent.

233	R9	(1835)	Silver	32.5mm			450.	

BARNES & POTTER ctsp on U.S. 1834 half dollar. (Brunk 2420)

The firm of Barnes & Potter appears in the 1835 directory only. They were watch case makers, at 6 Lincoln Green. The senior partner was Charles L. Barnes. The other partner may have been Samuel S. Potter, a brass founder located at 63 Willett in 1835.

J. H. & A. BENEDICT

New York, N.Y.

HT#	Rarity	Year	Metal	Size	VG	F	VF	EF
A233	R9	(1820-39)	Copper	29mm	—	—	65.00	—

J. H. & A. BENEDICT ctsp on U.S. 1819 Large cent.

B233	R9	(1820-39)	Silver	27mm	—	—	100.	—

Similar ctsp on Spanish-American 1796-Lima-IJ 2-reales.

According to Kovel (see Bibliography), this silversmith firm operated in New York City in the 1820's and 1830's. About 1830 a J. H. Benedict operated a silversmithy in Skaneateles, N.Y.

This piece was newly reported in 1996. It is quite possible it belongs in the Early American tokens section.

G. BOYCE

HT #	Rarity	Year	Metal	Size	G	VG	F	EF
234	R8	(1832-41)	Copper	29mm	—	—	—	250.

G. BOYCE / N. YORK in relief ctsp on U.S. 1831 or 1833 Large cent. (The countermark is in two separate stamps, N. YORK being curved) (Brunk 4680; Bowers coll.)

Gerardus Boyce (1795-1880) was a silversmith in New York City beginning about 1814. The mark is his hallmark. (See "The Book of Old Silver" by Seymour B. Wyler.)

J. & L. BREWSTER

New York, N.Y & New Orleans, La.

HT #	Rarity	Year	Metal	Size	VG	VF	EF	Unc
235	R6	(1832-3)	Gilt/Cop	26.5mm	200.	400.	900.	1400.

W & B NY. (B&M Vlack sale, Nov. 16, 1996, lot 2291)

HT #	Rarity	Year	Metal	Size	VG	VF	EF	Unc
235A	R7	(1832-3)	Brass W & B NY	26.5mm	200.	500.	900.	1400.
236	R7	(1833)	Gilt/Cop Bale, NY	26.5mm	300.	600.	900.	1400.
236A	R7	(1833)	Brass Bale, NY	26.5mm	300.	600.	900.	1400.

Listed at 166 Water Street in New York in 1835-36. They were at 176 Water Street 1840-41. The Wright & Bale and Bale alone signatures help date these cards. Wright and Bale split before October 1833.

HT 235 and 235A are struck from different dies. Letter spacing is different.

BROMBACHE

New York, N.Y.

HT #	Rarity	Year	Metal	Size	VG	F	VF	EF
529	R9	(?)	Copper	29mm	—	85.00	—	—

BROMBACHE / NEW YORK in relief ctsp on worn U.S. 1798 Large cent. (Litman coll., ex-Don Miller)

DAVID C. BUCHAN

The token issues of chairmaker Buchan (HT 237-238A, Low 224-226) are from 1831 and may be found in our *Early American Tokens* reference.

LOW NUMBERS

For veteran collectors still using the century-old "Low" numbering system, there is a conversion chart of the "HT" numbers in the Introduction to this reference.

CENTRE MARKET

New York, N.Y.

HT #	Rarity	Year	Metal	Size	VG	F	VF	Unc
239	R1	1837	Copper	28mm	5.00	15.00	25.00	90.

Scroll Under 2nd U in Unum

HT #	Rarity	Year	Metal	Size	VG	F	VF	Unc
240	R1	1837	Copper	28mm	5.00	15.00	30.00	140.

Scroll Under N in Unum

HT #	Rarity	Year	Metal					
240A	R8	1837	Lead counterfeit?	Rare	—	—	—	

Broadway at the Bowling Green in Manhattan in 1835. The fenced green is at right. The four mansions at left, No. 1 Broadway on the corner and its next three companions were built by, respectively: Captain Archibald Kennedy, Judge John Watts, Philip Livingston and city clerk Frederick Van Cortlandt. The Kennedy House and Watts House (No. 3 Broadway) became famed museum-like attractions later, but here they represented the residences of some of New York's elite.

CLINTON LUNCH

HT #	Rarity	Year	Metal	Size	VG	VF	EF	Unc.
A240	R6	(1835-45)	Brass	19.5mm	100.	450.	800.	1100.

Cuirassed bust left in crested Greek helmet. Rv: Eagle displayed, U.S. shield on its breast, head turned right. Seven stars in arc above, o CLINTON. LUNCH o below. (Rulau-E NY 161)

HT #	Rarity	Year	Metal	Size	VG	VF	EF	Unc.
B240	R5	(1830-45)	GS	19.5mm	100.	330.	450.	850.

As last, (Wright 197; Rulau-E NY 162)

The center of the reverse is usually weakly struck.

These tokens, long attributed to the Early American period are repositioned to the Hard Times era. Though attributed to New York by Tilton, Wright, Adams, Raymond and others, the site could never be verified through city directory evidence.

In a little-noticed paragraph in the October 1911 *The Numismatist* (pp 368-369), collector J. Coolidge Hills of Hartford, Conn. advanced the attribution to his city.

Clinton House, or Clinton Hotel, had a lower part used as a lunchroom in the 1830's and 1840's, Hills reported. The Clinton hotel continued in business until near the end of the 19th century.

We discount a Hartford connection, however, since our collaborator Steve Tanenbaum recently discovered a review in the New York City newspaper circa 1835 which described the type of food served and the prices charged for food at the Clinton Lunch. Directory evidence is still lacking, but we now believe the rare Clinton Lunch tokens — as always reported — are from New York and also can be safely attributed to the Hard Times era.

German silver tokens appear with some regularity in auction sales. In the May 1981 PCAC sale, a VF realized $425. A BU specimen was auctioned for $775 in 1988. In the 1989 Gil Steinberg sale, a BU piece, probably the finest known specimen, made $852.50. In the same Steinberg sale another piece in VF fetched $165.

Brass pieces appear less often. An AU specimen in the PCAC May 1982 sale realized $320. In the 1990 Chris Schenkel sale, an unholed EF piece fetched only $154. A VF specimen fetched $363 in the 1996 Kirtley Oct. sale. A choice AU piece fetched $1045. in the PCAC Nov. 1999 sale.

COLLINS READY MADE LINEN & FANCY STORE

HT #	Rarity	Year	Metal	Size	VG	F	VF	EF
241	R8	(1834-41)	Brass	25.5mm	750.	1500.	2500.	4000.

William Collins was at 67 Maiden Lane 1838-39. He was at 69 Maiden Lane 1845-46. This card was cut by Robert Lovett, Sr., who used the same obverse on his own HT card. (Sotheby's 433). Weight 4.74 grams.

J. H. CONNOR

HT #	Rarity	Date	Metal	Size	VG	F	VF	EF
A241	R9	(1833-38)	Silver	32.5mm	—	—	500.	—

J. H. CONNOR ctsp on U.S. 1829 Bust half dollar. (Brunk 9250).

John H. Connor was a New York silversmith 1833-38, and a partner of Garret Eoff 1833-35. Connor & Eoff were located at 6 Little Green Street.

His name is misspelled Conner in some references.

J. CRAWFORD

HT #	Rarity	Year	Metal	Size	VG	F	VF	EF
242	R8	(1837-41)	Copper	29mm	150.	—	200.	—

J. CRAWFORD in relief within rectangular depression ctsp on U.S. Large cent. Dates examined: 1807, 1827, 1833. (Hallenbeck 3.757; Brunk 9990)

John Crawford was a silversmith in New York City 1815-41. He opened a Philadelphia operation 1837-43 and may have closed his New York firm in/after 1843. Directory listings show his New York addresses:

92 John Street	1815-20
227 Grand	1832-33
99 Chrystie	1834-41

We have not yet determined his Philadelphia location(s).

Unless specimens with later-dated host coins surface, it seems reasonable to conclude that New York was the home of HT 242. (References: Ensko and Kovel silversmith chronologies; New York City directories; Kenneth Hallenbeck; Gregory Brunk)

H. CROSSMAN

HT #	Rarity	Year	Metal	Size	F	VF	EF	Unc
243	R2	1837	Copper	28.5mm	10.00	40.00	200.	425.

HT #	Rarity	Year	Metal	Size	F	VF	EF	Unc
244	R2	1837	Copper	29mm	9.00	30.00	70.00	250.

Henry Crossman was a manufacturer of umbrellas at 92-1/2 Chatham St. 1830-1841, after which he was located at various other addresses. The firm became H. Crossman & Co. in 1857 while at 63 Liberty St. In 1860 it was at 94 Warren St.

W.D. CRUMBIE

HT #	Rarity	Year	Metal	Size	VG	F	VF	EF
245	R7	(1844-6)	GS	19mm	200.	250.	500.	1000.
245A	R7	(1844-6)	Blank Rev. —	—	—	250.	500.	1000.

At the corner of Bowery and Houston 1844-46. This was a soda water check.

D. & CO.
(DeForest & Co.)
New York, N.Y.

HT #	Rarity	Year	Metal	Size	VG	F	VF	EF
533	R8	(ca 1840)	Copper	29mm	85.00	—	—	—

D. & Co. in relief within small rectangular depression cts on U.S. 1840 Large cent. The "o" of Co. is at upper position with the period below it. (Ganter 881; Robert Merchant coll.)

Hallmark of DeForest & Co., New York City silversmiths circa 1827-1840 or a bit later. The mark exactly matches that given in Ensko, Kovel and Green.

DeForest & Co. apparently were successors to DeForest & Fowler (1827-1828), with Gilbert Fowler.

T. DARBY

HT #	Rarity	Year	Metal	Size	VG	F	VF	EF
246	R8	(1830's)	Copper	29mm	—	150.	—	200.

T. DARBY / -.- / NEW YORK ctsp on U.S. Large cent. Examined: 1816, 1831. (Brunk 10700)

Thomas Darby was a coppersmith in the 1830's. In the 1829 city directory he was listed as a brassfounder at 158 Bowery. In the 1834 listing he is a coppersmith at the rear of 160 Bowery.

DARROW
New York, N.Y.

HT #	Rarity	Year	Metal	Size	FG	F	VF	EF
A246	R9	(?)	Copper	23mm	—	—	50.00	

DARROW in relief within rect. depression ctsp on U.S. 1807 Half cent. (Brunk 10745)

This may well be one of the recorded marks of Edmund Darrow, a silversmith who worked in New York 1843-61 (and thus is more likely to be positioned in our *U.S. Merchant Tokens 1845-1860*.

It could also be the mark of silversmith David Darrow of New York, active circa 1825, or of John F. Darrow of Catskill, N.Y., active circa 1818.

This piece is assigned tentatively to the HT period until more can be learned about it.

DAY NEWELL & DAY

HT #	Rarity	Year	Metal	Size	F	VF	EF	Unc
247	R6	(1834-5)	Copper	26.5mm	150.	400.	750.	900.
247A	R8	(1834-5)	Brass	26.5mm	150.	500.	900.	1200.

| 248 | R6 | (1834-5) | GS | 26.5mm | 300. | 600. | 1300. | — |

These locksmiths were at 589 Broadway 1834-35.

J.H. DAYTON

HT #	Rarity	Year	Metal	Size	VG	VF	EF	Unc
249	R2	1837	Copper	28mm	7.00	35.00	90.00	200.

P.B. & S. DEVEAU

HT #	Rarity	Year	Metal	Size	F	VF	EF	Unc
250	R2	1837	Copper	28mm	10.00	40.00	65.00	370.

HT #	Rarity	Year		F	VF	EF	Unc
251	R8	1837 Obv. 250, Rev. 61		3500.	4000.	5350.	—
252	R8	1837 Obv. 250, Rev. 52		3700.	—	5500.	—

P.B. & S. Deveau were located at 156 Chatham Square, New York City, from 1831 to 1850, after which they moved to 74 Forsyth Street, where they stayed until 1858.

Number 251 uses a MINT DROP reverse, and 252 a NOT ONE CENT reverse.

There are only 3 known specimens of HT 251. One in very Good realized $3520 in the PCAC Nov. 1999 sale, lot 66, ex-Krause coll. A VG/F example fetched $3000 in 1981, and a VF/EF specimen brought $5280 in the PCAC 1986 Leidman sale.

DOREMUS, SUYDAM & NIXON

HT #	Rarity	Date	Metal	Size	F	VF	EF	Unc
901	R5	(1831-33)	Copper	26-1/2mm	35.00	110.	350.	—

Inscription both sides. 209 PEARL ST., with period after NIXON. N-YORK. (Low 306; Rulau-E NY 211)

| 901A | R5 | (1831-33) | Brass | 26-1/2mm | 35.00 | 110. | 250. | — |

Same as 211. (Low 307)

| 902 | R5 | (1831-33) | Copper | 26-1/2mm | 35.00 | 110. | 210. | — |

Similar to 211, but no period after NIXON. N. York (Low 308; Rulau-E NY 213)

| 902A | R6 | (1831-33) | Brass | 26-1/2mm | 35.00 | 110. | 350. | — |

Same as 213. (Low 309; Rulau-E NY 214)

| 902B | R6 | (1831-33) | Brass | 26-1/2mm | 35.00 | 110. | 500. | — |

Same as 214. Reeded edge. (Low 309A)

This dry goods firm issued a number of tokens spanning the Early American and Hard Times periods. The cards listed above may have been struck for D.S. & N. by Wright & Bale. Trested's business was sold by his widow, Ann, to Wright & Bale on May 25, 1829, and W&B NY (later BALE NY and B&S NY) began to appear on tokens for D.S.&N. Some 1832-33 pieces were included as Low 310-311 under Rulau's *Hard Times Tokens*, still at the 209 Pearl Street address.

HT #	Rarity	Date	Metal	Size	F	VF	EF	Unc
253	R5	(1832-33)	Copper	26.5mm	150.	300.	750.	—

As 214, W.&B. N.Y. on obverse. Rv: LINENS SHEETINGS & DAMASKS in center. (Low 310; Rulau-E NY 215)

| 254A | R6 | (1832-33) | Silv/Bs | 26.5mm | — | — | 300. | |

As 215.

| 254B | R8 | (1832-33) | Gilt/Bs | 26.5mm | — | 150. | 300. | 1000. |

| 254 | R5 | (1832-33) | Brass | 26.5mm | 50.00 | 80.00 | 300. | — |

As 215. (Low 311; Rulau-E NY 216)

| 255 | R4 | (1834-35) | Brass | 26.6mm | 50.00 | 80.00 | 300. | — |

50 & 52 Wm. St. Bale NY

| 256 | R4 | (1834-35) | | | 50.00 | 100. | 200. | — |

Hyphen Between N-Y

| 257 | R4 | (1836) | Copper | 26.6mm | 50.00 | 175. | 300. | — |

37 & 39 Nassau St.

| A258 | R6 | | Brass | 28mm | | | 200. | — |

| 258 | R4 | (1836-38) | Brass | 26.5mm | 50.00 | 100. | 300. | — |

B & S NY

| 258A | R4 | (1836-38) | Copper | 26.5mm | 50.00 | 100. | 300. | — |

Reeded edge

| 258B | R8 | | Gilt/B | 28mm | — | | 300. | — |

Plain edge

| 258C | R8 | (1836-38) | Gilt/B | 28mm | — | — | 200. | 325. |

Reeded edge. (Hayden 644)

William C. Dusenberry was a watchmaker and silversmith in New York 1819-1834. This hallmark matches that illustrated in Belden.
This could be an Early American period token.

C. C. DYER

HT#	Rarity	Year	Metal	Size	VG	F	VF	EF
E259	R5	(1840)	Copper	29mm	50.00	—	75.00	—

C. C. DYER ctsp on U.S. Large cent. Examined: 1794, 1798, 1803, 1811, 1816, 1817, 1818, 1819, 1820, 1822, 1824, 1826, 1827, 1828, 1829, 1830, 1831, 1833, 1835, 1836, 1837, 1838, 1840, 1847, worn dates. There are 53 pieces reported. (Brunk 12650; Ganter sale 904-905; Gary Pipher coll.; Henderson coll.; Bowers coll.)

HT#	Rarity	Year	Metal	Size	VG	F	VF	EF
E259A	R8	(1840)	Silver	16.5mm	60.00	—	90.00	—

Similar ctsp on U.S. Draped Bust 1825 and Capped Bust 1833 half dime. The latter measures only 15.5mm.

HT#	Rarity	Year	Metal	Size	VG	F	VF	EF
E259C	R8	(1840)	Silver	21mm	60.00	—	90.00	—

Similar ctsp on Spanish-American 1-real. Examined: 1798, worn date.

| E259D | R8 | (1840) | Silver | 27mm | 50.00 | — | 75.00 | — |

Similar ctsp on Spanish-American 2 reales, dates not known. 3 pieces reported.

| E259F | R9 | (1840) | Copper | 29mm | 30.00 | — | 45.00 | — |

C. C. DYER / MYERS ctsp on U.S. 1803 Large cent. (Brunk 12650/29080)
Charles C. Dyer is listed in the 1843-1856 directories as a saw filer and tool maker at 510 Greenwich Street. Both large and small size varieties of the stamp are known on coins, the large being more common.
Dyer appears in the 1840 census in the 8th ward.
Gregory Brunk reasons that since 52 pieces have surfaced with only one host coin dated later than 1840, that these ought to be considered HT era tokens.
(See our notes under H. Rees of Philadelphia for a similar situation)

EVERDELL

HT#	Rarity	Year	Metal	Size	VG	F	VF	EF
K259	R8	(1835-36)	Copper	29mm	—	150.	—	250.

EVERDELL in relief within curving scroll-shaped depression ctsp on U.S. Large cent. Examined: 1818, 1831, 1847. (Brunk 13610; Rulau-E NY 217; Frank Kovacs coll.; Bowers coll.)
William Everdell was a diesinker at 135 William St. in the 1836 directory.
William Everdell was christened at Trinity Church parish in New York City on March 18, 1798, the son of William James and Mary Everdell, according to Mormon Genealogical Library records.

DR. L. FEUCHTWANGER

HT#	Rarity	Year	Metal	Size	VG	F	VF	EF
260	R7	(1831-36)	GS	27mm	800.	2500.	2900.	3500.

Dr. L. FEUCHTWANGER / AMERICAN / SILVER / COMPOSITION / 377 / BROAD-WAY, / NEW-YORK. in seven lines of text. Rv: HOUSE & HOUSEHOLD, FURNITURE. / INSTRUMENTS / (Rosette) / BEER PUMPS / PILLARS, GRATES / SPOONS, FORKS / (Rosette) / & DINNER SETS. in eight ines. (Levick 1884 sale, lot 418, fetched $8; Wright 314; Miller 240)
An EF specimen HT 260, weight 104.1 grains, fetched only $715 in a 1991 Bowers & Merena sale. In the same sale, an AU HT 261 realized only $660. However, a VF-EF specimen of HT 260 realized $2860 in the PCAC June 2000 sale, lot 31.

HT #	Rarity	Year	Metal	Size	F	VF	EF	Unc
259	R4	(1840-44)	Gilt/B	27.3mm	45.00	75.00	150.	300.

Nassau St.

| 259A | R3 | (1840-44) | Brass | 26.5mm | 40.00 | 100. | 150. | 300. |

NOTE: HT 256 comes in two different die varieties with different letter spacing.

THE DOREMUS-SUYDAM DRY GOODS FIRMS

Thomas C. Doremus and Rynier Suydam were in business as Doremus & Suydam, dry goods store, at 171 Broadway, at least from 1821 to 1826. This became Doremus, Suydam & Co. at 171 Broadway, 1826-1828.
The firm became Doremus, Suydam & Nixon, dry goods, still at 171 Broadway, 1829-1830. The new partner was John M. Nixon. This firm was at 209 Pearl St. 1832-1833; 50 and 52 William St. 1834 until December 31, 1835. According to a note in the 1835-36 directory, the firm moved on New Year's Day, 1836, to 37 and 39 Nassau St. Its address in 1840-1841 was 39 Nassau St., corner Liberty.
The firm name became Doremus & Nixon 1844-1849, still at 39 Nassau St., corner Liberty. In the 1850's the address changed to 21 Park Place. Dated tokens at the latter address are known bearing either 1853 or 1861.

o o o

Another firm which apparently did not issue any tokens was composed of Lambert and Cornelius R. Suydam, who may have been related. L. & C. Suydam, merchants, were at 212 Pearl St. 1821-1822; 71 Maiden Lane 1826-1828; 111 Pearl St. 1829-1830.

o o o

A third firm was composed of Richard Suydam and Daniel Jackson. This firm, Suydam, Jackson & Co., Indian contractors, issued HT 1 and varieties, a pro-Andrew Jackson political token of 1832. Richard Suydam started business alone in 1811.
Suydam & Jackson, merchants, were at 140 Pearl St., 1825-1830. They became known as Suydam, Jackson & Co. and were located at 78 Pearl St., 1830-1845.

o o o

Henry (Hy) Suydam and William Boyd were in business as Suydam & Boyd, dry goods, at 183 or 187 Broadway (there is a discrepancy in the 1830 directory) 1829-1830; then at 187 Pearl St., corner Cedar, 1831-1834; then at 157 Pearl St., 1834-1837. Store cards were issued from the latter two locations, spanning the Early American and Hard Times token periods.

o o o

In addition to Suydam & Boyd, above, there was another firm, Boyd & Suydam!

o o o

Ferdinand Suydam (another brother of Rynier, John and Richard) formed the firm of F. Suydam in 1808 at 37 Front St. In 1809 William Boyd became a partner. Later in 1809 they moved to 21 South St. and became Boyd & Suydam. This lasted until 1834.
In 1834 the business became Suydam, Sage & Co., and this failed about 1851. No tokens were issued.

o o o

Henry (Hy.) Suydam & Co. went into business 1800 at 45 Front St. He admitted a partner, John Wilson, in 1804, and it became Suydam & Wilson. S&W dissolved in 1834, Wilson retiring. This firm in 1834 became Suydam, Sage & Co., which failed about 1851. No tokens were issued.

o o o

The founders of all these Suydam (Dutch) businesses were Rynier and John Suydam, who created R. & J. Suydam in 1791 at 10 Albany Pier. Albany Pier was renamed Coenties Slip before 1794.
In 1794 the firm split. John Suydam, his brother Henry Suydam and Henry J. Wyckoff formed Suydam & Wyckoff.
Rynier Suydam resurfaced in Doremus & Suydam about 1821.
Meanwhile Suydam & Wyckoff were at 11 & 13 Coenties Slip 1794-1821, and 31 South Street 1821. This firm remained there until 1835.

The Doremus-Suydam firms were large issuers of store cards from the 1820's to 1861 or later. Their dates of issuance are approximately:

Miller NY 211-214A	209 Pearl St.	1831-1835
HT 253-254	209 Pearl St.	1832-1833 (W&B NY)
HT 255-256	50 & 52 William St.	1834-1835 (BALE NY)
HT 257	37 & 39 Nassau St.	1836
HT 258-258A	37 & 39 Nassau St.	1836-1838
HT 259-259A (NY 219-219A)	39 Nassau St.	1840-1844
NY 222-223 (Doremus & Nixon)	39 Nassau St.	1844-1849
NY 224-224B	21 Park Place	1850-1853
NY 225-229 (mulings)		1853-1861

W. C. DUSENBERRY

HT#	Rarity	Year	Metal	Size	VG	F	VF	EF
A259	R9	(1830-34)	Copper	29mm	—	—	60.00	—

W. C. DUSENBERRY / NEW YORK ctsp on U.S. 1826 Large cent. (Brunk 12550)

UNCIRCULATED

As used in this reference, the "Unc" equates approximately to Uncirculated Mint State 63 in the U.S. coin series. Unc prices are based upon the desire of Hard Times token collectors to obtain part red, no problem specimens.

HT #	Rarity	Year	Metal	Size	VG	F	VF	EF
261	R7	(1837-38)	GS	27mm	800.	2500.	2900.	3500.

FEUCHTWANGER / AMERICAN / SILVER / COMPOSITION / 2 / CORTLANDT St / NEW-YORK. in seven lines of text. Rv: Same as reverse of HT 260. (Miller 241; Hayden 645 in AU)

An AU clipped specimen of HT 261 fetched $1650 in the PCAC June 2000 sale. Less than 10 pieces of each, HT 260 and 261, exist.

NOTE: A muling in lead of the two obverses (address side) has been reported to exist. The authenticity of the report, and the specimen, have not been verified.

Die evidence study of the lettering and symbols (rosettes, beaded bordering, etc.) has led our colleague Wesley Cox to conclude that both HT 260 and 261 were engraved and struck by James Bale and his associates. The letters, numerals and symbols match those used on HT 117, 162, 258, 269, 279 and 332, for example.

Cox used 10-times enlargement photos of these pieces in his unpublished studies.

This conclusion draws attention to the maker(s) of HT 262, 263 and 264, and especially to the profuse varieties of HT 268. About these Cox writes: "All of the other Feuchtwanger tokens require more study. There is a device link between HT 262 (3-cent, arms) and HT 309 (R. E. Russell), but until I can study ANS scan images, I will not know if these two tokens can be linked to Bale & Smith."

"The Feuchtwanger 1-cent tokens (HT 268) may be an unascribable Pandora's box, and as noted in the *Standard Catalog*, some of them may have been issued long after 1837. The letter styles of varieties 2A, 3E, 6G and 6I, for example, do match each other or those of Bale & Smith."

Cox is planning to publish an eventual complete die-link and rarity monograph on the 15 reported obverses and reverses of the 1-cent Feuchtwanger tokens, HT 268, with illustrations of tokens at 7-times and of identifying features at 10-times.

The other Feuchtwanger 3-cent tokens (HT 265 through 267) were struck in / about 1855 to 1864, as noted below.

NOTE: For a complete background on Feuchtwanger and German silver, see Appendix II.

HT #	Rarity	Year	Metal	Size	VG	VF	EF	Unc
265	R7	1837	GS	24.2mm	—	—	3800.	4500.
		3 Three Cents						
265A	R9	1837	GS	25mm			PROOF	6600.
266	R8	1837	Copper	25mm	—	—	—	3500.
		Die Trial.						

NOTE: 266 is struck uniface (eagle side) over a British Conder token. 265 was struck in proof circa 1855-1860. A triple struck Proof HT 265, offered as Low 119A, realized $6600 in 1989.

HT #	Rarity	Year	Metal	Size	F	VF	EF	Unc
267	R6	1864	GS	25mm	—	—	2000.	3000.
267A	R9	1864	GS	25mm	—	—	2200.	

As 267, double struck. (Hayden Oct. 2000 sale, fetched $2200 in AU)

NOTE: 265, 265A, 266 and 267 are Civil War era pieces with HT die links. They cannot be disassociated from the Feuchtwanger 3-cent pieces they imitate.

FEUCHTWANGER'S COMPOSITION

REEDED EDGE

HT #	Rarity	Year	Metal	Size	VG	VF	EF	Unc
262	R3	1837	GS	25mm	200.	600.	900.	1400.
262A	R7	1837	Lead	25mm	—	900.	1500.	2000.

HT #	Rarity	Year	Metal	Size	F	VF	EF	Unc
262B	R8	(1837)	WM	25mm			Ex. Rare	

As HT 262, in White Metal. (Miller 246A)

262E	R8	(?)	GS	25mm			Ex. Rare	

Obverse as reverse of HT 262. Rv: Blank, but ctsp PASSAIC I P. (Miller 246C)

We have never examined specimens, nor seen an auction catalog or fixed price listing of 262B or 262E other than in Donald Miller's 1962 catalog. Passaic is, of course, a city in New Jersey, but no explanation springs to mind.

On the off chance that Passaic might be a person, we checked the Mormon Genealogical Library's internet access, but found the earliest U.S. person with this surname was Joseph Passaic (1887-1937) of Caldwell, N.J.

Miller misdescribed Adams 246 (HT 262, Arms of New York) in his catalog, though he had the Low number (117) correct.

Dr. Lewis Feuchtwanger

Feuchtwanger Cent Varieties HT 268

REEDED EDGE
Many Varieties

HT #	Rarity	Year	Metal	Size	VG	VF	EF	Unc
268	R1	1837	GS	18.5mm	20.00	50.00	135.	300.

NOTE: Specimens fully struck on obverse are worth up to double the Unc price!

Obv. 1. Coarse denticles. Large date close to ground above, the 3 exceptionally large, the 7 very high. Snake's tongue almost vertical. Seven tail feathers, four of them touching the ground.

Obv. 2. Similar treatment of the eagle to preceding. In date 18 low, small, closely spaced; 37 much larger, higher, also closely spaced. Eight tail feathers, five touching ground.

263	R5	1837	GS	25mm	800.	1800.	2500.	5000.
264	R8	1837	Copper	25mm	—	—	4000.	

HT 268

FEUCHTWANGER CENTS

REVERSE "A"
ONE very wide spaced
ONE CENT recut, doubled

REVERSE "E"
N's crumbled

REVERSE "G"
N in ONE crumbled at base

REVERSE "I"
E in ONE high at base
T has curving base

IMAGES 10X SIZE

Obv. 3. Date closely spaced, from smaller punches as on all to follow, and in a straight line on top. The 7 frequently shows crumbling between horizontal and upright; rim breaks down at lower right. Seven tail feathers, first two and fourth (latter recut) touching ground.

Obv. 4. In date 3 low, rather distant from 7 and often joined to it at top by a line. Loop in snake's tail left of date; in all other dies loop is above 18. Snake's tongue very long, very deeply forked. Eagle's head droops. Eight tail feathers, three touching ground.

Obv. 5. Date widely and evenly spaced; slightly curved bar in ground directly above 83. Seven tail feathers, only the second barely touching ground; fourth recut at tip.

Obv. 6. Closely spaced date, bottoms in a straight line; 83 a little apart. Dash to left from upper serif of 1. Base of eagle's neck smooth. Seven tail feathers, four of them touching ground.

Rev. A. One very widely spaced. Small O's in COMPOSITION. A and P recut.

Rev. B. Stems end in marked claws. S in COMPOSITION very defective at top. Upright of F recut. N in COMPOSITION recut.

Rev. C. Star too close to final S in FEUCHTWANGER'S. Two upper berries within right branch arise from innermost leaves almost at tips.

Rev. D. O in ONE too low. Right bow plainly overlaps left one. Right ribbon almost touches both S and I.

Rev. E. IT about touch. E in ONE, T in CENT (left top) and P in COMPOSITION clearly recut N's in ONE CENT crumble.

Rev. F. ER joined at bases. Left stem, divided like a penpoint, touches M.

Rev. G. Thirteen berries, the extra one just right of bow. Berry near base of T in CENT attached to a leaf. Star too close to final N in COMPOSITION. Stems end in claws though not too distinctly. M P O spaced apart. Develops a crack through HTWANG, and another from wreath through final N to edge. N in ONE crumbles at base.

Rev. H. Thirteen berries, extra one just left of bow. E in ONE top high at top and base. Crude recutting NE CEN; crumbling develops on these letters.

Rev. I. Thirteen berries, extra one just left of bow, and looking more like an extra stem. E in CENT heavily recut. E in ONE high at base but in line with N at top.

Die combinations and rarity:	
1A	R4
2A	R5
3B	R3
3C	R8
3D	R7
3E	R3
3G	R6
4E	R3
4F	R8
5G	R2
5H	R1
6G	R1
6I	R1

HT #	Rarity	Year	VG	F	VF	Unc
268	R2	1837 One Cent	25.00	45.00	100.	350.
	R3		28.00	50.00	120.	375.
	R4		35.00	100.	135.	400.
	R5		75.00	120.	170.	500.
	R6		100.	125.	220.	600.
	R7		—	300.	350.	700.
	R8		—	500.	900.	1800.

NOTE: Dr. Lewis Feuchtwanger in 1837 petitioned Congress to adopt his "Feuchtwanger's Composition" (German silver, a white, tarnishable copper-zinc nickel alloy) for the U.S. copper cent, reducing it to 18.5mm. The petition, supported by Senator Thomas H. Benton, was rejected by Mint Director Patterson in 1838.

The German-born Feuchtwanger (1807) was at 377 Broadway 1831-1837; 2 Cortlandt Street 1837-1838; 7 Gold Street 1839; 320 Broadway 1840; 1-1/2 Wall Street 1842-1843; and 2 Wall Street 1843. He published a book on gems 1872, and died in 1876. At the 377

Broadway address he struck his first store card (Low 247), but in 1837, at the 2 Cortlandt St. address, he emitted the second card (HT 261) and all the One and Three Cent private patterns.

Robert Lindesmith opined that die combinations 5G, 5H, 6G and 6I may have been struck during the Civil War, since the 1858 Bushnell and 1859 Cogan lists do not mention them. Walter Breen saw more than 65 specimens of 6I, commonest of all HT 268 varieties.

One of the largest collections of Feuchtwanger 1 and 3-cent tokens to appear in recent years were the 7 3-cent and 141 1-cent pieces of the Rogers M. Fred Jr. holdings, auctioned by Bowers & Merena Galleries Nov. 13-14, 1995. Prices realized altered several valuations.

A perfect Unc MS-63 specimen of die 6-G fetched $595 in March, 2000!

HT #	Rarity	Year	Metal	Size	VG	F	VF	Unc
268A	R9	1837	Silver *	18.5mm	—	—	7500.	—

As HT 268, from die pairs not used in any other combination. Discovered only in May, 2001. Probably a pattern. Q. David Bowers purchased this piece from Rossa & Tanenbaum, the discoverers, for $5,000. Plain edge (all HT 268 varieties are reeded edge).

* Certified after analysis by Civil War Token Society.

Feuchtwanger Cent Brockage
Enlarged 50%
Value = $200

FEUCHTWANGER-MILTON CONNECTION ?

Coin dealer Jonathan K. Kern, Lexington, KY., discovered a steel die about 1984 which he showed to the author. The oval die measures 43 by 35mm and carries a signature at upper right: I. Milton F. (John Milton fecit — made it). Kern sold this die for an oval medal to Q. David Bowers in 2001 for a reported high 4-figure sum.

Milton was a London, England diesinker of the 1790's. The eagle-on-serpent device is precisely the same, even to fine details, as that used by Dr. Feuchtwanger on this cent and 3-cent tokens some 40 years afterward. A charitable view might be that both Milton and Feuchtwanger copied the device from some illustration in an as-yet-undiscovered book, but the more likely explanation is that Dr. Feuchtwanger simply copied Milton's device for his token issues.

For further comments on Feuchtwanger, see the appendix in this reference on makers of tokens. The good doctor was not above using the ideas and inventions of others.

W. FIELD

HT #	Rarity	Year	Metal	Size	VG	VF	EF	Unc
269	R7	(1835)	Copper	28mm	1000.	2500.	4500.	5500.
270	R7	(1835)	Copper	30mm	1000.	2500.	4500.	5500.

FIFTH WARD MUSEUM HOTEL

HT #	Rarity	Year	Metal	Size	VG	F	EF	Unc
271	R9	(1847-51)	Brass	26mm		400.		

FIFTH WARD / (rays) / MUSEUM / (rays) / HOTEL. Rv: 2 / 6 (two shillings sixpence). Plain edge. (Sotheby's 440)

One specimen is in the American Numismatic Society collection. Since the hotel was located near the Hudson River piers, many of the patrons would have been British seamen or visitors.

Fifth Ward Museum Hotel was opened in 1826 at West Broadway and Franklin by Thomas Riley. A hotel and popular dining salon, it contained an Americana collection stressing Colonial history.

The hotel's intersection was a busy one in the 1830-1850 period.

An excellent history of the hotel, by Werner G. Mayer, was published in the *TAMS Journal* for June 1978 under the title "Riley's Fifth Ward Museum Hotel." An excerpt of this article appears below.

Exhibits were housed in the hotel's largest room, one flight up from the main entrance. The room was jammed with glass cases containing Riley's collection of relics, and the walls were covered with paintings of great statesmen and soldiers along with displays of their weapons and uniforms. However, the authenticity of some of the items was questionable. Featured was the Hawaiian club that was supposed to have disposed of Captain Cook, Chief Tecumseh's rifle, Andrew Jackson's pipe, and other curiosities.

Most of the exhibits were genuine, including a remnant of William Pitt's statue. Erected in 1766 by grateful American colonists who appreciated Pitt's efforts on their behalf in the English Parliament, it was later dismantled by the British (in retaliation for the 1776 destruction of King George's statue by the colonial Sons of Liberty). British soldiers cut the head and one arm off the Pitt statue, then dumped it into the Collect Pond. Some years later, Riley recovered the statue — minus the head and arm — and placed it in front of his hotel.

After Riley's death (in 1858) and the subsequent razing of the hotel, the statue was acquired by the New York Historical Society, where it remains on exhibit.

The hotel intersection was a busy one in the 1830-50 period. For many years, it was used as the site for periodic musters and contests by the New York City volunteer firemen, and in 1834 — on George Washington's birthday — a Liberty Pole was erected outside the hotel. A replica of a Liberty Pole erected by the Sons of Liberty just before the Revolutionary War, the spire was 174 feet tall and was used by the volunteer firemen in pumping contests to see which company could pump the highest stream of water. The record — 137 feet — was set in 1855 by the famous fire engine, the Mankiller.

Hand-pumping was exhausting work, and the firemen could maintain peak efficiency for only about five to ten minutes. The Liberty Pole was torn down in the year of Riley's death.

In the picture of the hotel are two sets of railroad tracks on West Broadway. City records show that the tracks were installed about 1850 and were used by the Sixth Avenue (Yount & Ward) and the Eighth Avenue (Finch, Sanderson & Co.) railroads, represented by Adams store card numbers 1005 and 250, respectively. The two railroads used a common track at the hotel, but separated uptown on Canal Street.

G. S. GELSTON

New York, N.Y. (and)

M. MILLER

Charleston, S.C.

HT #	Rarity	Year	Metal	Size	VG	F	VF	EF
534	R9	(1835-39)	Copper	29mm			Rare	

G. S. GELSTON in relief within rect. depression / M. MILLER in relief within rect. depression, ctsp on U.S. 1835 Large cent. (R. Merchant coll.)

HT #	Rarity	Year	Metal	Size	VG	F	VF	EF
A534	R9	(1850's)	Copper	29mm	—	—	60.00	—

G. S. GELSTON in relief within rect. depression ctsp on U.S. 1853 Large cent. (Brunk 15937)

George S. Gelston was a New York City silversmith, in business alone 1830-37, as Gelston & Co. 1837-39, in Gelston Ladd & Co. (with William F. Ladd) 1839-44, and in Gelston & Treadwell 1844-49. His address after 1833 was 189 Broadway.

Matthew Miller was a Charleston, S.C. silversmith 1835-40. The Miller attribution is tentative.

W. GIBBS, AGRICULTURIST

HT #	Rarity	Year	Metal	Size	VG	F	VF	EF
272	R6	(1837-40)	Copper	27.6mm	250.	300.	500.	800.

AGRICULTUREIST (sic!)

GREEN & WETMORE

The token issues of Green & Wetmore, hardware dealers of Washington & Vesey Streets, were released in the 1825-32 period and may be found cataloged in *Early American Tokens* section as Rulau-E numbers 288 through 290.

HALLOCK & BATES

HT #	Rarity	Year	Metal	Size	VG	F	VF	Unc
275	R4	(1834-7)	Brass	29.8mm	15.00	30.00	90.00	300.

Reeded edge. Specific gravity 8.71.

| 276 | R8 | (1834-7) | Blank Rev. | 29.8mm | — | 100. | 200. | 500. |
| A276 | R6 | (1834-7) | Copper | 28mm | — | — | 70.00 | — |

May not exist.

HALLOCK, DOLSON & BATES

HT #	Rarity	Year	Metal	Size	VG		VF	EF	Unc
277	R4	(1838-40)	Brass	29.8mm	12.00		30.00	125.	250.

Hallock & Bates were at 234 Pearl St. 1835-37. The other partnership does not appear in the New York directories. Reeded edge.

Researcher Wesley S. Cox Sr., who has done extensive study on die variations of struck tokens of the Hard Times period, has proven that Scovill Mfg. Co. of Waterbury, Conn. prepared HT 275, 276, and 277. WILLIAM is misspelled WILLAM on reverse of HT 277 (on left above).

DR. J. G. HEWETT

COPPER, 29MM

HT #	Rarity	Year	VG	F	VF	Unc
278	R4	(1837-8) Thick Planchet, 12 grams, 2.8mm	50.00	100.	150.	550.

HT #	Rarity	Year	VG	F	VF	Unc
279	R3	(1837-8) Thin Flan, 7 grams, 1.64mm	40.00	75.00	100.	500.

Dr. Jonas G. Hewett was at 68 Prince St. 1837-38. By 1850-51 he was at 100 Spring St.

B. HOOKS

Enlarged

HT #	Rarity	Year	Metal	Size	VG	F	VF	EF
280	R8	(1833-5)	Copper Bale	18mm	750.	2000.	3800.	7500.
280A	R8	(1833-5)	Silver	18mm	—	—	4000.	4500.
280B	R7	(1833-5)	S/Cop	18mm	750.	2000.	3500.	4000.

HT #	Rarity	Year	Metal	Size	VG	F	VF	EF
281	R7	(1833-5)	Copper	18mm	—	1000.	1750.	3000.

Ctsp. Small Dog. Blank reverse. 4-5 known.

| 281A | R9 | (1833-5) | "Tin" | 18mm | | May not exist. | | |

Blank reverse. (N.S.P. 1859 catalog, no. 161)

Photo Enlarged

| 281B | R9 | (1833-35) | Copper | 17.2mm | — | — | 3500. | — |

As 281, but without dog counterstamp. The name BALE has been mostly erased from the die. (PCAC June 3, 2000 sale, lot 38)

Located at 276 Broome Street, presumably. Dated on the evidence of Bale's signature. This card (280) was listed as Bushnell 76.

The obverse of the token shows a bust of Benjamin Franklin in fur cap facing left. BALE below bust, five stars at bottom. The reverse reads in five lines: B. HOOKS / 276 / BROOME / STREET / CORNER OF ALLEN ST.

The countermarked variety, HT 281, has a small dog figure counterstamped in front of the head; the reverse of this piece is blank. 281 in EF fetched $2585 in PCAC Nov. 1999 sale, lot 67.

GEORGE C. HOWE

HT #	Rarity	Year	Metal	Size	VG	F	VF	EF
A281	R8	(1838-42)	Copper	29mm	—	100.	—	175.

GEORGE C. HOWE in relief within rect. depression ctsp twice on U.S. 1808 or 1818 Large cent. (Brunk 20360; Doty page 102)

HT #	Rarity	Year	Metal	Size	VG	F	VF	EF
B281	R9	(1838-42)	Copper	29mm	—	100.	—	175.

GEO. C. HOWE in relief within rect. depression ctsp on U.S. 1837 Large cent. (Brunk 20355)

George C. Howe apparently began as a silversmith about 1810, according to Kovel. In directories Stebbins & Howe (Edwin Stebbins) appear 1827-40 as jewelers and watchmakers. G. C. Howe & Co. is listed 1837-38; Howe & Guion 1839-40 (also as silver platers); then G. C. Howe & Co. again 1841-42. In 1849 he advertised as a watchmaker at 143 Chester St.

Both stamps match the descriptions given in Belden.

IRVING, L. G. & PEASE, J.S.

New York, N.Y. & St. Louis, Mo.

HT #	Rarity	Year	Metal	Size	VG	F	VF	EF
282	R6	(1844-46)	Brass	27.3mm	500.	1000.	1900.	2600.
282A	R8	(1844-46)	Brass	27.3mm	500.	1100.	2000.	2750.

Arm with raised hammer above anvil, both facing left. Around: HE WHO LIVES BY THE SWEAT OF HIS BROW SELDOM LIVES IN RUIN. / J. S. PEASE & Co-St- LOUIS / L. G. IRVING, / N – YORK. Rv: J. S. PEASE & Co. / St. LOUIS / Mo. / IMPORTERS / OF / HARDWARE / & / CUTLERY. Plain edge. Struck without collar. Weight: 6.791 grams. Medal alignment.

| A282 | R8 | (1844) | Brass | 27.3mm | | | 2500. | |

As 282, but outer circular legend ends LIVES IN VAIN rather than LIVES IN RUIN. The sentiment in this error variety may have been rejected by Pease.

Though we have listed this piece under New York City, we believe it more properly belongs under St. Louis, Missouri. The legend would seem to indicate that hardware importer Pease was headquartered in St. Louis and partnered with Irving, where shipments arrived. See the enlargement of an ANS digital image of this token in the appendix containing Cox' die-evidence studies.

Irving was on 19th St. near Third Ave. in New York 1844-46. The store cards apparently were cut by Bale & Smith.

There are two die varieties: Legend on Irving side reads HE WHO LIVES BY THE SWEAT OF HIS BROW SELDOM LIVES IN RUIN, or LIVES IN VAIN.

GEORGE A. JARVIS

New York, N.Y.

HT #	Rarity	Year	Metal	Size	VG	VF	EF	Unc
283	R2	1837	Copper	28.5mm	10.00	40.00	65.00	250.

Stars on Rev.

| 284 | R1 | 1837 | Copper | 28.5mm | 8.00 | 25.00 | 40.00 | 250. |

Leaves on Rev.

One George A. Jarvis married Catharine A. Jarvis on Sept. 2, 1833 in the famous old Trinity Church parish in New York City. This may or may not be the token issuer.

WM. G. JONES

HT #	Rarity	Year	Metal	Size	VG	VF	EF	Unc.
285	R8	(1836-7)	Copper	26.5mm	165.	250.	600.	900.

HT #	Rarity	Year	Metal	Size	VG	VF	EF	Unc.
285A	R6	(1836-7)	Brass	26.5mm	100.	400.	700.	850.

Jones' Union Coal office was at the corner of Chambers and Washington Streets 1835-1839. The workmanship of this piece is similar to HT 257 (by Bale & Smith). The brass pieces were gilded. Reeded edge.
1823-24 58 WALL ST.
1835-39 COR. CHAMBERS & WASHINGTON STS.
1844-45 58 WALL ST.
1845-46 MERCHANTS EXCHANGE (6 WALL ST.)

H. LAW

HT #	Rarity	Year	Metal	Size	VG	VF	EF	Unc
286	R2	(1834-5)	Copper	29mm	15.00	50.00	125.	325.

Law, a baker, was at 187 Canal St. in 1834-35 only.

LEVERETT & THOMAS

HT #	Rarity	Year	Metal	Size	F	VF	EF	Unc
287	R5	(1833-5)	Copper	28.5mm	125.	200.	300.	600.
287A	R8	(1833-5)	Brass	28.5mm	150.	300.	600.	1250.

They were at 235 Pearl St. only in 1833-35.
In 1836 Leverett & Thomas were designated one of the agent firms for distribution of Scovill buttons and other products in New York, chosen by Scovill's then principal depot agent, Joseph Chamberlin.
In a surviving letter in the Scovill archives from J. M. L. "Lamson" Scovill to Chamberlin dated Feb. 13, 1836, Scovill notes some of the dealers of Scovill-Buckingham butt hinges who carried these on consignment. Included were Leverett & Thomas (which Scovill misspelled as 'Leverit'); Smith Starr & Co.; Atwater & Pomeroy; Pettibone & Long.

LOVETT, SEAL ENGRAVERS

HT #	Rarity	Year	Metal	Size	VG	F	VF	EF
288	R7	(1833-39)	Brass	25mm	700.	1200.	3000.	4500.

Weight 4.89 grams. Reeded edge. (Sotheby's 435)
Robert Lovett Sr., a fine engraver was at:
1824-25 249 Broadway
1833-34 67 Maiden Lane
1850-55 5 Dey Street
His card is the same type as the Collins piece, HT 241. An AU specimen fetched $3900 in the B&M Zeddies sale, Nov. 1990, lot 4241.

S. MAYCOCK & CO.

HT #	Rarity	Year	Metal	Size	VG	VF	EF	Unc
289	R2	1837	Copper	28.5mm	10.00	40.00	90.00	225.

HT #	Rarity	Year	Metal	Size	VG	VF	EF	Unc
290	R1	1837	Copper	27.7mm	7.00	30.00	65.00	150.

MERCHANTS EXCHANGE

HT #	Rarity	Year	Metal	Size	VG	F	VF	Unc
291	R1	(1837)	Copper	28mm	6.00	15.00	20.00	200.

6 Berries in, 4 out

292	R7	(1837)	Copper	28mm	800.	1250.	2200.	4000.

5 Berries in, 3 out

The EF Oechsner specimen fetched $4675 in 1988! The EF Middendorf piece realized $2900 in 1990. The EF Gil Steinberg specimen brought a mere $1540 in 1989.

HT #	Rarity	Year	Metal	Size	VG	F	VF	Unc
293	R1	(1837)	Copper	28mm	6.00	15.00	30.00	250.
	No Dash under Cent							

294	R1	(1837)	Copper	28.8mm	5.00	8.50	30.00	175.

Both the Merchants Exchange and the Tontine Building are mentioned on HT 291-294. Behind these names is one of the most unusual business arrangements America has ever seen. A "tontine" was a legal device whereby survivors split an inheritance at some point specified, and those unfortunate enough to die earlier get nothing.

The Tontine Coffee House building, at the corner of Wall and Water Streets in New York, was commenced in 1792 and completed in 1794. It and a large amount of surrounding land were owned by an association of 203 city merchants and other prosperous persons, who had subscribed at $200 per share. Thus the initial capital was $40,600.

The Tontine scheme was to be divided equally when the original 203 holders had been reduced by death to just seven! Share purchasers often named their children, not themselves, as the share owners. Meanwhile, shareholders shared the income of the entity, which owned a good portion of what was then the 2nd Ward (bounded by Pine St., Nassau St., East River, and Gold and George Sts.). The first five trustees for the 203 shareholders, who were to meet every year in the Tontine Coffee House, were John Broome, Gulian Verplanck the Elder, John Delafield, William Laight and John Watts.

The Tontine was also a hotel, and rented street shop space to certain merchants, such as John R. D. Huggins, the famed hairdresser who kept his shop there 1794-1800. The Tontine's charter was signed Nov. 4, 1794.

The largest room in the Tontine housed the Merchants Exchange 1794-1825, but it soon outgrew its quarters, with bargaining being conducted in the bar, etc. A supposedly fireproof Merchants Exchange building was erected 1827 on Wall Street, but it was destroyed in the Great Fire of 1835.

From 1797-1812 the Tontine Coffee House served from 11 AM to 1 PM punch, lemonade, crackers, cheese, and codfish at their splendid bar. The merchants called this "lunch." The Gulian C. Verplanck of HT 30 (born 1786) and William Bayard (born 1791) were original shareholders as children. The Tontine Coffee House was renamed the Tontine Building in 1843.

The Tontine scheme was a sort of "Russian roulette." When the 203 were reduced to 7, the survivors were to divvy up the loot. A complete list of the original 203 appears in Volume 4 of "The Old Merchants of New York City," pages 223-225 (see Bibliography). By 1862, 70 years after the plot was hatched, it was found that a family named De Peyster had bought up some two-thirds of the outstanding shares.

JAMES G. MOFFET

HT #	Rarity	Year	Metal	Size	VG	VF	EF	Unc
295	R2	(1837)	Copper	29mm	7.00	30.00	60.00	225.
			PLURIBUS. No six-petal rosettes					
295A	R8	(1837)	Overstruck on	—	—		375.	—
			Moffet token					

The famous Tontine Coffee House on Wall Street, at the corner of Water Street, housed the Stock Exchange from 1792 to 1825. It is the white building, second from the left, in this Smithsonian Institution painting.

HT #	Rarity	Year	Metal	Size	VG	VF	EF	Unc
296	R2	(1837)			—	—	—	—

PLUBIBUS. No rosettes.

NOTE: Confirmation of this variety will require discovery of a perfect specimen!

| 297 | R2 | (1837) | Copper | 28.7mm | 5.00 | 20.00 | 50.00 | 150. |

Six-petal rosettes. PIUBIBUS

Moffet was at 121 Prince St. 1832-37 and it was from this address that he struck his own tokens, as well as those of Samuel Maycock and Henry Crossman.

HT 297 comes in 28.7mm (normal) and 30mm sizes.

In 1802 James G. Moffet in New York rolled brass between rolls turned by power from cattle harnessed to a sweep, according to William Lathrop, *The Brass Industry*, (Mount Carmel, Conn., 1926). Moffet thus was a pioneer in American sheet brass.

A man named Abel Porter was the first to do rolling, Lathrop adds.

J. & W. MOIR

HT #	Rarity	Date	Metal	Size	VG	F	VF	EF
F297	R8	(1839-44)	Copper	29mm	60.00	—	90.00	—

J & W MOIR in relief within rect. depression ctsp on 1800 and worn Large cents. 2 pieces known. (Brunk 28165)

John and William Moir were silversmiths and watchmakers in New York 1839-1844, according to Belden. John Moir continued alone in business 1844-1870

J. MOORE

New York, N.Y. (?)

HT #	Rarity	Date	Metal	Size	VG	F	VF	EF
A297	R9	(1830's)	Copper	23mm	60.00	—	90.00	—

J. MOORE in relief within rect. depression ctsp on U.S. 1825 or 1826 Half cent. (Brunk 28330)

| B297 | R9 | (1830's) | Copper | 29mm | 60.00 | — | 90.00 | — |

Similar ctsp on U.S. 1810 Large cent. (PCAC July 1993 sale, lot 995)

Gregory Brunk previously attributed this mark to a N.Y.C. silversmith based on the mark's appearance. Jared L. Moore (active 1825-44) or John C. Moore (active 1832-44) might qualify, but the marks do not seem to match any published hallmarks. Also reported on a U.S. 1810 half dollar.

Tentative, and dubious, attribution.

N-YORK & HARLAEM RAILROAD COMPANY

GERMAN SILVER, 18MM, OCTAGONAL

HT #	Rarity	Year	VG	VF	EF	Unc
298	R6	(1835-8) B & S NY	100.	250.	500.	750.
299	R6	(1835-8) Ctsp. Rosette	200.	400.	700.	900.
300	R7	(1853-8) Ctsp. Dog	250.	500.	600.	900.

Enlarged

COPPER, 18MM, OCTAGONAL

HT #	Rarity	Year	VG	VF	EF	Unc
301	R8	(1835-8) Ctsp. Leaf	—	1000.	3000.	4000.

PEWTER, 19MM, OCTAGONAL

HT #	Rarity	Year	VG	VF	EF	Unc
A300	R8	(1835-8) Ctsp. Leaf	550.	700.	2200.	—

(Atwood pattern 998D; PCAC Nov. 1999 sale, lot 77)

Enlarged to show fine detail

This first railway in Manhattan was chartered in April 1831. Service along Fourth Avenue and Bowery began November 1832. From 1832-1839 the fare was 6 cents to 12-1/2 cents.

All tokens struck by Bale & Smith.

We have learned that pewter copies of HT 298 are just that, copies, but are listed because they are collected.

A 1916 article on this railroad was reprinted in *The Fare Box*, journal of the American Vecturist Association, which gives some additional details. The 1831 charter permitted the company "to construct a single or double track railway" on various streets in New York City. On May 12, 1836, the company was authorized to unite with any railroad or canal company organized under New York state law, at any point which the directors of the two companies agreed upon.

Subsequent legislation empowered the firm to extend its railroad from the Harlem River through Westchester County to intersect with the proposed Albany & New York Railroad. The company was also authorized to build a drawbridge across the Hudson River. (See David E. Schenkman's "Early New York Token Appeals to Several Groups" in *Numismatic News* for Feb. 13, 2001.)

NEW YORK CONSOLIDATED STAGE CO.

CARDBOARD, 29x48MM, RECTANGULAR

HT #	Rarity	Year	VG	VF	EF	Unc
A301	R8	(1830's)	50.00	100.	—	—

Large ornate 2 in cartouche. Around: New York / Consolidated / STAGE CO. Rv: Large script signature within cartouche: T. P. Jeremiah, above small printed: Treasurer. Tiny imprint near bottom: D. W. LEE 83 NASSAU ST. (Dave Wilson collection; John Coffee attribution; Eric Newman report; B&M 1985 Patterson sale, lot 1486)

CARDBOARD, 30x49MM, RECTANGULAR

HT #	Rarity	Year			VG	VF	EF	Unc
B301	R8	(1830's)			50.00	100	—	—

Similar to A301, but 4. Signature on reverse is J. Daurphler (?).

These cardboard tickets, presumably either for transportation or for small change, were discovered in a hoard of mid-19th century paper notes of New York and New Jersey. It is possible this is an 1850 product.

EDWIN PARMELE

HT #	Rarity	Year	Metal	Size	VG	VF	EF	Unc
302	R7	(1834-39)	Brass	18.5mm	1000.	4400.	5000.	6000.

The liquor store was at 340 Pearl St. 1834-39. Only 4 pieces are known, all in private hands.

A damaged VF specimen of HT 302 was lot 015 in PCAC June 1996 sale, where it fetched $4400. The last Parmele token, HT 302, had appeared at auction 20 years earlier (the Otto Sghia specimen in VF with planchet cracks) and fetched $1200 in 1976.

An Unc. specimen sold in Orlando, Fla. about 1994 for $5000.

PEALE'S MUSEUM

HT #	Rarity	Year	Metal	Size	VG	VF	EF	Unc
303	R5	1825	Copper	34.5mm	50.00	125.	400.	700.
303A	R8	1825	WM	34.5mm	1500.	—	—	Ex.Rare

Rubens Peale established his museum in 1825 in the Parthenon, at 252 Broadway opposite City Hall. The Long Room contained snakes, lizards and an Egyptian mummy. Another gallery contained paintings. Lectures and special appearances were made. In 1831 the museum was renovated and enlarged. HT 303 was used 1825-1841.

Tickets for a whole family for one year were $10; single admissions were 25 cents. The copper ADMIT THE BEARER checks may have been used for annual subscribers. The museum was sold to P.T. Barnum in 1843.

Rubens' father, Charles Willson Peale, opened the Philadelphia Museum in 1784, incorporating it in 1821. This museum issued two different types of ADMIT checks, both probably pre-dating the HT period. Rubens' brother, Franklin Peale, became chief coiner of the U.S. Mint in 1839.

PHALON'S HAIR CUTTING

HT #	Rarity	Year	Metal	Size	VG	VF	EF	Unc
304	R2	1837	Copper	28.5mm	15.00	45.00	90.00	200.

Edward Phalon probably began his business as a hair dresser at 161 Chatham Street in 1834. From then until 1860 he changed location at least 11 times, one address being the 35 Bowery address on the token. In 1842 he was opposite St. Paul's at 214 Broadway, where he sold the "Amazon Toupee" for which (along with his "Wigs and Scalps") the American Institute awarded him a silver medal in 1841, and their first premium in 1842.

In 1848 he was at 61 Broadway, where his extensive advertisements touted "Chemical Hair Invigorator." At the height of his prosperity he occupied an elegant shop in the St. Nicholas Hotel, where his prices for services and cosmetics matched the brilliance of the numerous mirrors, gilded frames, marble basins, and silver-plated fixtures which adorned the salon. Here he remained until the hotel closed.

His "Night Blooming Cereus" was the best known, and last, of his successes before he retired. Low interviewed him in 1886 but Phalon could provide little information about his store card.

An 1849 advertisement for Edward Phalon's "Chemical Hair Invigorator" indicates that Phalon opened his 197 Broadway "bathing and hair cutting rooms" in May, 1843.

PIKE & SONS

HT #	Rarity	Year	Metal	Size	VG	F	VF	EF
587	R9	(1836)	Copper	29mm	—	—	100.	—

Within oval logotype, but with all lettering **in relief and retrograde**, is ctsp PIKE & SONS / OPTICIANS / 166 BROADWAY NY. (Brunk 32120; Bowers coll.)

Possibly for use as a seal, issued on formation of the firm in 1836?

This firm made ivory draftsmen's rules and surveyors' compasses. (Barlow 1991, 172 and 207)

ABRAHAM RIKER

HT #	Rarity	Year	Metal	Size	VG	VF	EF	Unc
305	R1	(1837)	Copper	28mm	5.00	30.00	70.00	175.

5 Berries in, 3 out

HT #	Rarity	Year	Metal	Size	VG	VF	EF	Unc
306	R3	(1837)	Copper	28mm	10.00	100.	200.	300.

6 Berries in, 2 out

Abraham Riker & Co. loaned $10,000 to the U.S.A. in 1813 to aid the war against England.

ROBERT B. RUGGLES

Beaded border

HT #	Rarity	Year	Metal	Size	VG	VF	EF	Unc
307	R1	(1832-35)	Copper	28.5mm	8.00	25.00	80.00	175.
			Plain edge.					
307A	R3	(1832-35)	Reeded edge	27.9mm	12.50	30.00	110.	275.

307A weighs 9.07 grams.

HT #	Rarity	Year	Metal	Size	VG	VF	EF	Unc
307B	R9	(1832-35)	Thin flan, Reeded		—	—	—	—
			(1996 Vlack sale, lot 2310)					
307D	R8	(1832-35)	Brass	28.5mm	—	—	250.	—
			Formerly HT 307B.					

HT 307-307D were struck by Wright & Bale. The distinctive rosettes on reverse serve as W&B mintmarks.

Plain raised border

HT #	Rarity	Year	Metal	Size	VG	VF	EF	Unc
308	R2	(1835-38)	Copper	28.5mm	8.00	15.00	60.00	250.
			Plain edge. Bale NY					
308A	R3	(1835-38)	Reeded edge		8.00	15.00	90.00	250.
308B	R7		Diagonal reeding		—	100.	250.	—

No border

HT #	Rarity	Year	Metal	Size	VG	VF	EF	Unc
308E	R8	(1835-38)	Copper	26mm	—	250.	—	—

Small, thin planchet. Diagonal reeding. Tiny denticles at reverse border. This appears to be a muling of HT 308B reverse with HT 307 obverse, struck on an undersized flan. (B&M Vlack sale, Nov. 1996, lot 2311)

R.E. RUSSELL

HT #	Rarity	Year	Metal	Size	VG	F	VF	Unc
309	R5	1837	GS	19.5mm	250.	400.	600.	1300.

(PCAC Oct. 2000 sale, lot 42, in holed VF, fetched $330)

SANS SOUCI

HT #	Rarity	Year	Metal	Size	VG	VF	EF	Unc
310	R8	(1838-40)	Lead	18mm	300.	750.	1000.	—

Eagle with drooping wings, head turned right. Rv: SANS SOUCI across center, branch above and below. (Miller NY 769)

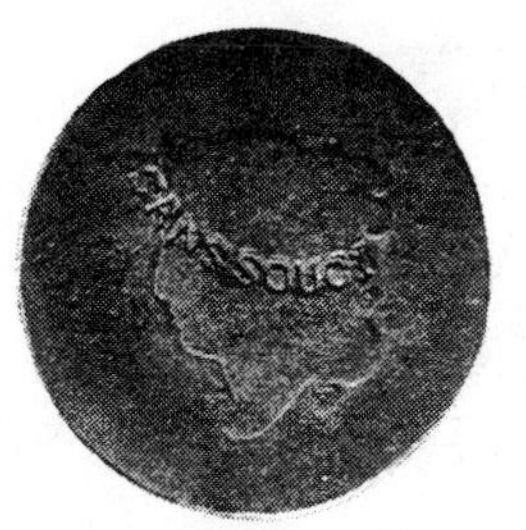

HT #	Rarity	Year	Metal	Size	VG	F	VF	EF
310B	R9	(1838-40)	Copper	29mm	—	—	400.	—

SANS SOUCI (curved) ctsp on U.S. Large cent of 1820's-30's, date worn. (Hayden Nov. 1998 sale, lot 698)

The 1839-40 *Longworth's American Almanac, New York Register and City Directory* lists Sans Souci under the proprietorship of Asa Hinckley at 61 Broadway. It is not listed in any other years in the New York city directories and thus may be confidently assigned to the Hard Times period. (Research by David Schenkman)

HT #	Rarity	Year	Metal	Size	VG	VF	EF	Unc
310E	R9	(?)	Lead	18mm	—	1000.	—	—

Obverse as 310. Rv: Large script monogram, possibly LB or PB.

SMITH'S CLOCK ESTABLISHMENT

HT #	Rarity	Year	Metal	Size	VG	VF	EF	Unc
311	R2	1837	Copper	28.5mm	20.00	75.00	150.	250.
			Hour Hand Right of X					
312	R8	(1837)			—	—	—	Rare
			Clock side only					
312B	R7	—	S/Copper	28.5mm	—	—	150.	450.

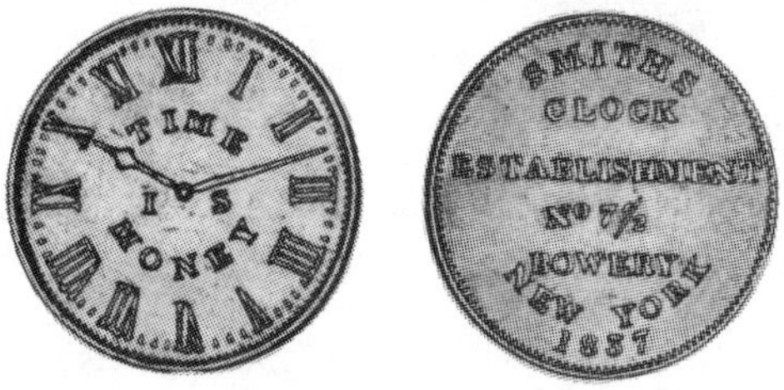

HT #	Rarity	Year	Metal	Size	VG	VF	EF	Unc
313	R3	1837	Copper	28.5mm	20.00	75.00	175.	450.
			Establishment straight					

314	R1	1837	Copper	28.5mm	15.00	60.00	100.	325.
			Establishment Curved					

CIRCULATION AS MONEY

In the 1837-1842 period, almost 26% of the Large cent-sized pieces in circulation in the United States were Hard Times tokens, the balance being perhaps 3% foreign coppers of about 29mm size, and just 71% U.S. Mint cents.

HT #	Rarity	Year	Metal	Size	VG	VF	EF	Unc
315	R1	1837	Copper	28.5mm	15.00	60.00	100.	175.
			Small ornaments flank 7-1/2					
316	R1	1837 Dotted Circle				Probably does not exist		

HT #	Rarity	Year	Metal	Size	VG	VF	EF	Unc
317	R1	1837	Copper	28.5mm	20.00	65.00	75.00	275.
			Large Ornaments					
317A	R7	—	Gilt/C	28.5mm	—	—	250.	450.

Andrew B. Smith advertised in the *New York Examiner* in June 1837 that he was located at the corner of the Bowery and Division Street, New York, "up stairs, third story, entrance 7-1/2 Bowery." In Nov. 1838 the style of the firm was changed to A.B. Smith & Co.; in 1841 the partnership was conducted as Smith & Brothers, and they announced they had established a branch of the business at 9 North Fifth Street, Philadelphia.

Die trial pieces exist.

SQUIRE & MERRITT

Obv. 1 - Small letters. S of STT over space between O and R of YORK. R of ROPE directly under S of SHIP, and S of MAKERS directly under S of CHANDLERS.

Obv. 2 - Small letters. S of STT directly over R of YORK. R of ROPE directly under S of SHIP, and S of MAKERS directly under S of CHANDLERS. Period under 2nd T of STT.

Obv. 3 - Large letters. O of ROPE under S of SHIP, and R of MAKERS under S of CHANDLERS. Period under 2nd T of STT.

Rev. A - Small letters. N of NAILS over I of IMPORTERS.

Rev. B - Large letters. N of NAILS over M of IMPORTERS.

OBV. 1   **REV. A**

COPPER, 27MM REEDED EDGE

Var. 1-A - Thin planchet, beaded border, milled edge, 5 grams, 27mm

HT #	Rarity	Year	F	VF	EF	Unc
318	R5	(1836)	50.00	150.	300.	600.
		COPPER, 27MM, PLAIN EDGE				
318A	R4	(1836)	50.00	100.	200.	550.
		"175" INCUSED				
		Very thick planchet - plain edge - 12 grams				
319	R7	(1836) Copper	Rare	—	350.	500.
		Thin planchet, milled edge - 5 grams				

HT #	Rarity	Year		F	VF	EF	Unc
319A	R7	(1836) Copper		—	200.	—	—
		Small 175 incused. Thick planchet.					
320	R8	(1836) Silver		Rare	—	1000.	1500.
320A	R3	(1836) Copper		50.00	100.	150.	400.
		"1836" INCUSED					

HT #	Rarity	Year	F	VF	EF	Unc
321	R6	(1836) Copper	100.	200.	350.	550.
		Var. 2-A - Thin planchet, beaded border, plain edge, 5 grams, 27mm				
322	R4	(1836) Copper	75.00	150.	225.	400.
		Thick planchet - 8 grams				
323	R5	(1836) Copper	85.00	175.	225.	400.
		Var. 3-B — Thin planchet, dentilated border, PLAIN EDGE, 5 grams, 27MM				

REEDED EDGE

HT #	Rarity	Year	F	VF	EF	Unc
324	R6	(1836) Copper	100.	225.	275.	400.
324A	R4	(1836) Copper	75.00	200.	275.	400.
		Plain edge				

REEDED EDGE - "175" INCUSED

HT #	Rarity	Year	F	VF	EF	Unc
325	R4	(1836) Copper	75.00	100.	200.	400.

HT #	Rarity	Year	Metal	Size	G	VG	VF	EF
326	R9	(ca 1834-37)	Silver	40mm		—	2500.	

L.L. SQUIRE / N-YORK ctsp. on obverse of U.S. 1795 silver dollar. Rv: L.L. SQUIRE / J. MERRITT / N-YORK ctsp on reverse of the 1795 silver dollar. Low 395 may be unique. (Van Ormer sale 2850, ex-H. Chapman, Stephen Nagy, A.A. Grinnell, Ed Rice, James J. Curto, David Schenkman, Roy Van Ormer; Brunk 37830)

This firm of ship chandlers was at 175 South St., corner Roosevelt, from 1831-37. Lewis L. Squire and Jacob T. Merritt issued HT store cards circa 1836, and Squire alone issued tokens from 1840 until 1855.

HT 324A measures 26.8mm and weighs 7.08 grams.

J. MERRITT

HT #	Rarity	Year	Metal	Size	VG	F	VF	EF
327	R9	(1834-37)	Silver	32.5mm	—	—	350.	

N-YORK / J. MERRITT ctsp on U.S. 1819 half dollar. The punches match Low 395. (Van Ormer 1748, ex-Schenkman 1984; Brunk 27430)

328	R8	—	Copper	29mm			300.	—

J. MERRITT / N. YORK ctsp on U.S. 1814 or 1829 Large cent. (Tanenbaum collection)

UNCIRCULATED

As used in this reference, the "Unc" equates approximately to Uncirculated Mint State 63 in the U.S. coin series. Unc prices are based upon the desire of Hard Times token collectors to obtain part red, no problem specimens.

L.L. SQUIRE

HT #	Rarity	Year	Metal	Size	VG	F	VF	EF
329	R7	(1840)	Copper	29mm	—	100.	—	175.

L. L. SQUIRE ctsp on reverse of U.S. Large cent. (Dates examined: 1798, 1803, 1823, 1828, 1831, 1839, 1845, 1847). 12 pcs. known. (Bowers coll.)

HT #	Rarity	Year	Metal	Size	VG	F	VF	EF
330	R8	(1840)	Copper	23mm	—	115.	—	160.

Similar ctsp on obverse of U.S. Half cent. Dates examined: 1806, 1828. (John Cheramy coll.; Brunk 37820)

| 331 | R9 | (1840) | Silver | 32.5mm | — | 550. | — | — |

Similar ctsp on obverse of U.S. 1806 Draped Bust half dollar. (Gamer-White PCAC specimen)

SILVER, 34MM

HT #	Rarity	Year	Metal	Size	VG	F	VF	EF
331A	R9	(1840)			—	—	380.	—

Similar ctsp on Spain 1821-Sr-LT 10 reales, Craig 138. (B&M Sept. 1985 sale, lot 3318)

The punch matches exactly the 'L. L. SQUIRE' punch used on HT 326, the counterstamped 1795 Silver dollar. The fact that Squire appears alone on this stamp may indicate that J. Merritt pulled out of the partnership before these pieces were issued, in or soon after 1840.

It is probable that other Squire, Merritt or Squire & Merritt counterstamps remain to be identified.

| A331 | R9 | (1840) | Silver | 27mm | — | — | — | 200. |

L. L. SQUIRE / N-YORK ctsp on Spanish-American 1775-Mo-FM 2-reales, KM-88.2. (Gary Mauer coll.)

STERLING CO.

New York, N.Y.?

HT #	Rarity	Year	Metal	Size	VG	F	VF	EF
561	R9	(?)	Copper	28.5mm	125.	—	200.	—

STERLING. Co (in prepared punch) ctsp on U.S. 1837 Hard Times token. (Brunk 38200)

| 561A | R9 | (?) | Copper | 29mm | 125. | — | 200. | — |

Similar ctsp on U.S. 1817 Large cent reverse. On obv. is stamped in indiv. letter-punches: ISRAEL L. GREEN / N. YORK / JULY 9TH / 1827. The latter is also listed as Rulau-E NY 285 and Brunk 17080.

This firm has not yet been traced. A firm of the same name began in Derby, Conn. in 1866, probably not connected.

SUYDAM & BOYD

COPPER, 26MM

HT #	Rarity	Year	VG	F	VF	EF
332	R5	(1831-4) 187 Pearl St.	40.00	80.00	150.	300.

BRASS, 26.1MM

| 332A | R8 | (1831-4) 187 Pearl St. | — | 125. | 200. | 300. |
| 333 | R5 | (1834-7) 157 Pearl St. | 40.00 | 80.00 | 125. | 200. |

Enlargements

HT 332, copper, measures 26.0mm in diameter. Dry weight 4.52 grams. Specific gravity 8.95.
HT 332A, brass, measures 26.1mm in diameter. Dry weight 4.28 grams. Specific gravity 8.58. Its color is basically "door-knob brass."
HT 333, brass, measures 26.0mm in diameter. Dry weight 6.141 grams.

BRASS, 26.5MM

| 333A | R6 | (1834-7) 157 Pearl St. | — | — | 175. | 250. |

Exists in Gilt Brass, EF $300.
This firm of dry goods merchants, consisting of Hy. Suydam and William Boyd, was at 187 Pearl St. 1831-34 and then at 157 Pearl St. 1834-37. (See Doremus, Suydam and Nixon entry.)
HT 332 is Wright 1080.
HT 332A is in Wesley S. Cox Sr. coll.
HT 333A appeared in B&M 1989 Saccone sale, lot 3173, and in B&M 1996 Vlack sale, lot 2318, the same coin, in bright AU (pictured).

EZRA B. SWEET

HT #	Rarity	Year	Metal	Size	F	VF	EF	Unc
334	R4	1837	Copper	27.5mm	50.00	160.	200.	350.

HT #	Rarity	Year	Metal	Size	F	VF	EF	Unc
335	R3	1837	Copper	28.5mm	45.00	140.	175.	325.

Thick Planchet

Ezra B. Sweet was in active business in New York from 1825 to 1852, changing his address 12 times. He was at 200 Canal Street from 1836 to 1839 when the tokens were issued. In addition to the business advertised on his cards, he was a bell-founder and plumber.

TISDALE & RICHMOND

HT #	Rarity	Date	Metal	Size	VG	F	VF	Unc.
A335	R9	(1833-34)	Copper	28mm	—	7500.	—	—

TISDALE & RICHMOND / KEEP / CONSTANTLY / ON HAND / SHOVELS, NAILS / HOLLOW WARE / PIG, & BAR IRON / &c. &c. &c. / No. 250 WATER ST., NEW YORK. Rv: TACK & BRAD PLATES / SHEATHING. / & BOLT. COPPER / TACKS, BRADS, / & SPARABILLS, / SUGAR KETTLES. / ROLLING MILL, / ROLLS &c. / &c. &c. / NAIL RODS, HOOP IRON & c. Plain edge. (Dr. Robert Schuman coll.)

Sparabill = Thin headless nails used to attach soles to shoes. They resembled a sparrow's bill.

Tisdale & Richmond are listed at 250 Water St. only 1833-34. They were at 210 Water St. 1834-35 and 218 Water St. 1835-36. They do not appear in the 1832 or earlier, or 1836 or later, directories.

This token, so far unique, was discovered by Charles Kirtley and researched by H. Joseph Levine in 1988. Dr. Robert Schuman first published it in *Rare Coin Review* no. 75 (1992) by Bowers & Merena Galleries.

VAN NOSTRAND & DWIGHT

HT #	Rarity	Year	Metal	Size	VG	F	VF	EF
336	R2	(1835-7)	Copper	26.5mm	10.00	15.00	25.00	165.

These book publishers were at 146 Nassau St. 1835-37. Reeded edge. Struck by Bale & Smith, New York.

C.H. WEBB, CONGRESS HALL

HT #	Rarity	Year	Metal	Size	F	VF	EF	Unc
337	R3	(1832-34)	Copper	26.5mm	25.00	40.00	150.	250.
337A	R3	(1832-34)	Brass	26.5mm	25.00	40.00	150.	200.
338	R3	(1832-34)	Copper	26.5mm	25.00	40.00	75.00	200.

Period after GENERAL

Charles H. Webb was proprietor of Congress Hall Hotel, at 142 Broadway, according to the 1833 directory. In the 1835 directory, Webb's address had changed to 438 Greenwich. The tokens were struck by James Bale.

RD. WILLIAMS, UNION HALL

HT #	Rarity	Year	Metal	Size	VG	VF	EF	Unc
339	R8	(1833-5)	Copper	19.5mm	1000.	3500.	4500.	5500.

The exact design of Richard Williams' Union Hall token reads: Obv: UNION HALL / B (hand with heart on palm) Y / RD. WILLIAMS / CORNER / OF / HENRY & OLIVER STS. Rev: GOOD FOR / REFRESHMENTS / AT THE BAR / BALE. (Sotheby's 439)

WRIGHT & BALE
New York, N.Y.

HT #	Rarity	Date	Metal	Size	F	VF	EF	Unc
340	R8	(1829-30)	Copper	30mm	4000.	9000.	—	12,000.

Fur capped bust of Franklin left, BENJAMIN FRANKLIN around. Below: WRIGHT & BALE. Rv: WRIGHT & BALE / ENGRAVERS / AND DIE CUTTERS / 68 WILLIAM ST. NEW YORK / ..... OF EVERY DESCRIPTION / CARDS OF ADDRESS / BOOKBINDERS TOOLS. (Rulau-E NY 1001)

HT #	Rarity	Date	Metal	Size	F	VF	EF	Unc
340A	R8	(1829-30)	Brass	30mm	4000.	9000.	—	12,000.

As 340. (Rulau-E NY 1000)

In July 1995, 340A with VF obv. and smooth rev. still fetched $1320!

HT #	Rarity	Date	Metal	Size	F	VF	EF	Unc
341	R4	(1832-33)	Copper	19mm	150.	300.	600.	750.

Head of George Washington right within large oak wreath. Rv: WRIGHT & BALE / ENGRAVERS / & DIE / CUTTERS / 68 NASSAU STREET / PLATES & ROLLS / FOR EMBOSSING / DIES & SEALS OF / EVERY / DESCRIPTION / NEW-YORK. Thick planchet. (Wright 1275; Rulau-E NY 1002)

HT #	Rarity	Date	Metal	Size	F	VF	EF	Unc
342	R5	(1832-33)	Copper	19mm	200.	300.	500.	800.

Same as 341, but thin flan. (Rulau-E NY 1003; Baker 594)

HT #	Rarity	Date	Metal	Size	F	VF	EF	Unc
342A	R8	(1832-33)	Silv/C	19mm	—	800.	—	—

As last. Only 2 known. (Rulau-E NY 1003A)

See Introduction to Hard Times section for an account of the Wright & Bale partnership, which lasted May 1829 to late 1833.

WOOD & FORCE
New York, N.Y.

HT #	Rarity	Year	Metal	Size	VG	F	VF	EF
343	R8	(1839-41)	Copper	29mm	90.00	—	135.	—

WOOD & FORCE / W & F in relief within rect. depressions ctsp on U.S. Large cents. Examined: 1822, 1829.

Jabez W. Force and a man named Wood were silversmith partners 1839-1841. Later Force was in business alone.

HENDERSON & LOSSING
Poughkeepsie, N.Y.

HT #	Rarity	Year	Metal	Size	F	VF	EF	Unc
344	R7	(1833)	Copper	19mm	300.	500.	700.	1200.

Washington head right within wreath. Rv: HENDERSON & LOSSING / CLOCK & WATCH / MAKERS / DEALERS IN / WATCHES / JEWELLERY / SILVER / & PLATED WARE / CUTLERY &C. / W&B POKEEPSIE NY. Plain edge. Thick flan, weight 3.05 to 3.12 grams. (Rulau-E NY 1017; Low 317; Baker 539; Sotheby's 430)

| 344A | R7 | (1833) | Copper | 19mm | 300. | 500. | 700. | 1200. |

As 344, but struck on Thin flan, weight 2.81 grams. (Sotheby's 430, ex-Zabriskie)

Only about 10 pieces are known of HT 344 and 344A. Which variation is more scarce is not known. The flan differences were first reported in Sotheby's June 1999 Zabriskie sale by catalogers David E. Tripp, Jonathan H. Mann and Donald L. Ackerman.

These cards were cut by Wright & Bale, whose initials W&B NY appear on the text side; a Washington head adorns the obverse.

Adam Henderson, a Poughkeepsie watchmaker, in 1826 took as an apprentice the orphan Benson John Lossing, then 13. When Lossing was 20, in 1833, he was made a partner in the newly-named Henderson & Lossing watch and clockmaking and jewelry firm.

Wright & Bale used their own store card obverse die (HT 340) to create the partnership's card.

Lossing gave up the watchmaking business at age 22, in 1835, becoming a journalist/editor and eventually one of America's most popular historians. He moved to New York City 1838. His masterwork, *Pictorial Field-Book of the Revolution*, filled with his own engravings of the 1775-83 war in two volumes, was published 1852 and reprinted 1855.

J. Weekes
Poughkeepsie, N.Y

HT #	Rarity	Year	Metal	Size	VG	F	VF	EF
579	R9	(1833-35)	Copper	29mm	—	—	100.	—

J. WEEKES ctsp incuse on U.S. 1816 Large cent. (Q. D. Bowers coll.)

James Weekes began advertising fancy goods on Main Street, Poughkeepsie on June 16, 1833. In an ad of April 23, 1834, he said he made his own Britannia ware, coffee and tea pots, soup ladles, molasses gates, beer mugs, tumblers, faucets, tableware, etc. His remaining goods, he advertised, "will be sold at auction March 4, 1835," after which he moved to Brooklyn, N.Y.

J. Weekes & Co. are listed in pewter references in New York City 1822 through 1858, in the later years as "tinware and tinman." There may have been two different pewterers named James Weekes contemporaneously.

AISTED
Rochester, N.Y.

HT #	Rarity	Year	Metal	Size	VG	F	VF	EF
B344	R8	(1830's)	Copper	29mm	75.00	—	125.	—

AISTED ctsp on U.S. Large cent. Examined: 1800, 1811 / 10, 1821. Only 3 pcs. reported. (Brunk 450; Thoele coll., ex-Stubler)

The last bearer of the surname Aisted in U.S. census records before 1882 was John Aisted, 4th ward, Rochester, in the 1830 census. Trade not known.

ETTENHEIMERS
Rochester, N.Y.

HT #	Rarity	Year	Metal	Size	F	VF	EF	Unc
567	R8	(1830's)	Brass	26mm	—	1500.	—	—

ETTENHEIMERS / WATCH & / JEWELRY / STORE. / 53 / BUFFALO ST. / o ROCHESTER, N.Y. o. Heavy beaded border on obverse. Rv: Blank but number 26 incused. Plain edge. (William Carr report, Medina, N.Y.; Rulau NY 1017A; Cox research)

So far as we know, the illustration and description above are the first time this rarity among American tokens has ever been fully cataloged. The Carr piece, holed at 3 o'clock, was sold by private treaty in the late 1980's. None of the early token catalogers ever saw the piece.

HT 567 is repositioned in the Hard Times era. It was formerly listed under the Merchant era (1845-60).

HIRAM JUDSON
Syracuse, N.Y.

COPPER, 28.5MM

HT #	Rarity	Year	VG	F	VF	Unc
345	R4	(1835-8) B & S NY	6.00	12.00	40.00	300.
346	R4	(1835-8) Thick Planchet	6.00	12.00	40.00	300.

NOTE: HT 345 has a Reeded edge. HT 346 has a Plain edge. HT 346 is known bearing a counterstamped numeral 1 (Rarity 9, value $950) or with counterstamped numeral 2 (value $300-$400). At this time it is not known what reason Judson had for placing these numerals on his tokens.

HT 346 weighs 9.08 grams.

HT #	Rarity	Year	Metal	Size	VG	F	EF	Unc
A346	R9	(?)	Copper	29mm	250.	400.	—	—

H. JUDSON /Gear) ctsp on U.S. 1826 Large cent. (Tanenbaum coll.; Brunk 22235)

| C346 | R9 | (?) | Silver | 26.5mm | 250. | 400. | — | — |

H. JUDSON / SYRACUSE /(Gear) ctsp on Spanish-American 1775-LME 2-real coin. (Tanenbaum coll.; Brunk 22240)

| D346 | R9 | (?) | Silver | 26mm | 250. | 400. | — | — |

H. JUDSON /Gear) ctsp on Spanish-American 1776-Mo 2-real coin. (Tanenbaum coll.)

By 1851 Hiram Judson is listed as a justice and commissioner. He does not appear after 1853.

W. H. HEPWORTH
Tonawanda, N.Y.

HT K346 and similar items are post-Civil War and may be found under the USTT Section.

O. & P. BOUTWELL
Troy, N.Y.

HT #	Rarity	Year	Metal	Size	VG	F	VF	EF
347	R7	1835	Copper	28mm	3000.	4200.	6000.	9000.

HT #	Rarity	Year	Metal	Size	VG	F	VF	EF
347A	R9	1835	Copper	31mm	—	—	—	9000.
			Struck on U.S. Large cent					
347B	R9	1835	Silver	27mm	—	—	—	10,000.

Struck on Spanish-American 1774-PTS 2-reales

A Fine-plus HT 347 realized only $3316.50 in the Hayden May 26, 2001 sale, lot 601.

BUCKLIN'S INTEREST TABLES

HT #	Rarity	Year	Metal	Size	G	VG	F	VF
348	R5	1834	Copper	28.5mm	125.	150.	400.	675.

BALE N.Y. signature appears on reverse.

HT #	Rarity	Year	Metal	Size	G	VG	F	VF
349	R5	1835	Copper	28.2mm	125.	400.	750.	1200.

2 Stars Under Head

In 1995-1996 sales, VG specimens of 349 made $121 and $81.10 respectively.

350	R7	1835	Copper	27.5mm	1500.	2500.	3000.	5000.

No Stars Under Head. In only About Good this piece fetched $650 in 1995. In VG, another made $1952 in Oct. 1996.

In 1999 a VF or better specimen of HT 350, the 1835 No Stars under head variety, was discovered by Charles Litman. There are two punchmarks left of the head, and the reverse is struck off-center, but this may be the finest known specimen of this crude rarity.

COPPER, 27.5MM, HEAD LEFT

351	R8	1835 No Stars on Obverse	—	—	—	8000.
352	R8	1835 Shapely Head, 28.5MM, 14 Stars	—	19,000.	—	—

HT 352 had been thought not to exist. John Ford, Donald Miller and George Fuld have not seen one in past 40 years. Two known 352's are hand altered.

The Virgil Brand VG specimen was sold privately in 1990 by Michael Brand Zeddies for $19,000, he revealed to the author in May, 1995.

COPPER, 28.5MM, NO HEAD

HT #	Rarity	Year		VG	VF	EF	Unc
353	R1	1835 T* under date		9.00	40.00	60.00	100.
354	R3	1835 Only 27MM		—	—	60.00	100.

HT #	Rarity	Year	Metal	Size	VG	VF	EF	Unc
355	R4	1835	Copper	28.5mm	100.	375.	1250.	1400.

TRUE ALB under date

An EF specimen realized $1,200 on March 27, 1981. Another realized $1210 on Nov. 13, 1999. A pitted Fine fetched $110 in 1999.

BUCKLIN'S BOOK KEEPING

West Troy, N.Y.

HT #	Rarity	Year	Metal	Size	VG	VF	EF	Unc
356	R2	(1835)	Copper	28.5mm	20.00	150.	300.	500.

COPPER, 29.5MM

357	R3	(1835) Large thin flan, 8-9 grams		20.00	60.00	150.	—

COPPER, 27MM

357A	R4	(1835) Smaller thin flan, 4-5 grams		35.00	60.00	150.	—

HT #	Rarity	Year	Metal	Size	VG	VF	EF	Unc
357B	R3	(1835)	Thick flan	8.77 grams 27.7mm	20.00	60.00	150.	—

HT #	Rarity	Year			VG	VF	EF	Unc
358	R4	(1835) Different head, smaller			30.00	60.00	150.	—

Isaac B. Bucklin was a schoolteacher in Troy in 1835-37, having his residence in what was then called West Troy, now a part of the city, giving special attention to instruction in bookkeeping, and printing and selling "Interest Tables." In 1839 and later he engaged in business as a stove-dealer, at 221 River Street, still residing in West Troy. The date of his death has not been ascertained.

A specimen of HT 356 of one of its varieties has been reported counterstamped J.M. BLANCHARD. (Duffield 1613; Brunk 4003)

CARPENTER & MOSHER
Troy, N.Y.

COPPER, 28MM

HT #	Rarity	Year		G	VG	F	EF
359	R6	(1835) River St. (no number)		3000.	3500.	4000.	6500.

An EF specimen fetched $6600 in 1989.

HT #	Rarity	Year		G	VG	F	EF
360	R7	(1836-37) 310 River St.		2000.	3500.	4000.	6500.

All are weakly struck.

W.P. HASKINS

COPPER, 28.5MM

HT #	Rarity	Year	VG	VF	EF	Unc
361	R4	1834 Lafayette H	30.00	100.	200.	400.

HT #	Rarity	Year	VG	VF	EF	Unc
362	R1	1834 Schenck	4.50	20.00	40.00	140.

William P. Haskins appears in 1830 census.

J. & C. PECK

HT #	Rarity	Year	Metal	Size	VG	F	VF	Unc
363	R1	(1835)	Copper	28.5mm	5.00	12.00	55.00	250.

An EF specimen made $126.50 in a 1997 auction.

HT #	Rarity	Year			VG	F	VF	Unc
364	R6	(1835) Eagle			400.	550.	1200.	—

HT #	Rarity	Year	Metal	Size	VG	F	VF	Unc
365	R7	(1835) Britannia seated			600.	800.	1200.	—

Types 364 and 365 are mulings of the Peck tin machine obverse with Canadian "blacksmith copper" types; 364 was numbered by Howland Wood ("The Canadian Blacksmith Coppers" in *The Numismatist* for April 1910) as 28, while 365 was not listed by Wood but was reported by Warren Baker, Montreal, Canada, to the author.

John Peck appears in 1830 census.

S. F. PHELPS

HT #	Rarity	Year	Metal	Size	VG	F	VF	EF
A365	R9	(1834-38)	Brass	29mm	—	350.	—	—

S. F. PHELPS ctsp on brass counterfeit of U.S. 1827 Large cent. (Brunk 31900)

Samuel F. Phelps was a silversmith in Troy 1834-38, according to the Kovels (see Bibliography).

LOW NUMBERS

For veteran collectors still using the century-old "Low" numbering system, there is a conversion chart of the "HT" numbers in the Introduction to this reference.

N. STARBUCK & SON
Troy, N.Y.

HT #	Rarity	Year	Metal	Size	VG	F	VF	EF
366	R6	(1835)	Copper	28mm	150.	250.	350.	600.

No Stars Under Head
A BU piece made $3300 in the 1989 Gil Steinberg sale.

| 367 | R8 | (1835) 2 Stars Under Head | | | | | May not exist | |

| 368 | R2 | (1835) | Copper | 29.2mm | 7.00 | 15.00 | 100. | 225. |

From study of HT 368 specimens, it is certain there were at least three strikings - normal, dies rotated 90 degrees, and dies rotated 180 degrees. All plain edge.

| 369 | | R7 | | (1835) George II in cuirass | 800. | 1000. | 1200. | — |

| 370 | | R7 | | (1835) Eagle | 600. | 700. | 900. | — |

HT #	Rarity	Year	Metal	Size	VG	F	VF	EF
371	R5	(1835)	Peck's tin machine		300.	400.	500.	750.

Types 369, 370 and 371 are mulings of the Starbuck reverse (screw design) with Canadian "blacksmith copper" types. They were numbered by Howland Wood ("The Canadian Blacksmith Coppers" in *The Numismatist* for April 1910) respectively as 25, 27 and 29.

A clipped VG specimen of 371 made $300 in the 1993 Greater New York sale.

Nathaniel and Charles Starbuck established a plough factory in Troy in 1818. The factory was on the west side of River Street south of the old Fulton Market. In April 1821 N. & C. Starbuck admitted Ephraim Gurley to the business, which became Starbuck & Gurley and bought out the Troy Air Furnace from Gurley and his partners.

Charles Starbuck died in 1823. By 1830 the firm became known as N. Starbuck & Sons, Troy Air Furnace. It was still in business in 1845.

TROY AND OHIO LINE
Troy, N.Y.

HT #	Date	Metal	Size	VG	F	VF	EF
B371	1837	Cardboard	Rect 81x47mm	—	150.	—	—

Within very wide printed border: 1837. / Troy & Ohio Line (Ohio handwritten in ink to replace crossed-out word Erie) / (double line) / Boat Sarah Louisa, / J. S. ROBINSON, MASTER. Rv: Blank. (B&M 1985 Patterson sale, lot 1492, ex-Proskey, F.C.C. Boyd)

| C371 | 1838 | Cardboard | Rect 62x32mm | — | — | 150. | — |

Within printed Greek fret border: 1838. / TROY & OHIO LINE / (two-horse drawn canal boat to left) / Boat Sarah Louisa, (large, boldface font) / J. S. ROBINSON, MASTER. (B&M 1985 Patterson sale, lot 1492)

Both B371 and C371, offered together on March 26, 1985, fetched $242 in aged, smudged condition but overall F-VF as seen in illustrations. These items are associated with the Erie Canal.

OSBORN
Utica, N.Y.

HT #	Rarity	Year	Metal	Size	VG	F	VF	EF
586	R7	(1830-44)	Copper	29mm	—	—	45.00	—

OSBORN in relief within toothed rect. depression ctsp on U.S. Large cent. Examined: 1803, 1816 (ca), 1844, unknown date. (Brunk 30307; B&M Nov. 1986 sale, lot 5085; Bowers coll.)

John Osborn, a silversmith of Utica, used a matching hallmark 1804-07, according to the Kovel reference. This Osborn was in partnerships: Butler & Osborn (1805-07); Rugg & Osborn (1804); and Osborn & Hammond.

Whether he worked until 1844 or had a successor who could have used the hallmark is unknown. Possible silversmith successors are Robert Osborn, Rochester, N.Y., ca 1847, and W.R. Osborn, Watertown, N.Y. ca 1850.

Tentative attribution.

N. ROTH
Utica, N.Y.

HT #	Rarity	Year	Metal	Size	VG	F	VF	EF
908	R9	(1837-45)	Copper	29mm	—	—	125.	—

N. ROTH ctsp on U.S. 1837 Large cent. (Brunk 35077)

| 908A | R9 | (1837-45) | Copper | 28.5mm | — | — | 125. | — |

Similar ctsp on Hard Times token, type not known. (Brunk report)

Nelson Roth was active as a silversmith and jeweler in Utica 1837-53. His address appearing in the 1853 city directory was 175 Genesee Street, "under the Museum." He was a wholesaler and retailer of watches, clocks, plated ware, etc. Born 1817 at Minden Township, Montgomery Co., N.Y.

NELSON ROTH,

No. 175 Genesee Street, (Under Museum,) Utica,

Wholesale and Retail Dealer in

GOLD AND SILVER WATCHES,

Fine Jewelry, Diamond Work, &c,

Also on hand a large assortment of

SILVER PLATED AND BRITANNIA WARE,

Girandoles, Table Cutlery, Clocks, &c.

——oo——

☞ SILVER SPOONS AND FORKS manufactured by the best of workmen, and the quality of the silver warranted equal to coin.

☞ WATCHES AND CLOCKS carefully repaired, and warranted to keep good time for a year.

S. & C.
(Storrs & Cooley)
Utica, N.Y.

HT #	Rarity	Year	Metal	Size	VG	F	VF	EF
E371	R8	(1841)	Silver	25mm	—	—	150.	—

S & C in relief within rounded-ends rectangular depression, ctsp on U.S. Seated Liberty quarter. Examined: 1840, 1841-O. (Brunk 35425; Donald Miller coll.)

Charles Storrs and Oliver Blanchard Cooley were silversmiths in Utica 1831-1839; Storrs died in 1839. Cooley (1808-44) entered into partnership with Horace P. Bradley, who had been an S & C partner, and Perry G. Tanner. The new firm, Tanner & Cooley, lasted only 1840-1842, but probably owned all the S & C punches for hallmarks.

Cooley died in 1844 and Tanner opened his own silversmith business in Cooperstown, N.Y. in 1844.

The S & C hallmark apparently was used by the T & C firm until about 1841. The attribution is tentative as the S & C mark on the coins does not match exactly the known markings listed in Kovel, Ensko etc.

SIBLEY & WATSON
West Mendon, N.Y.

HT #	Rarity	Year	Metal	Size	VG	F	VF	EF
372	R8	(1832-40)	Copper	28mm	12,000.	—	—	—

Struck over U.S. Cent

The overstrike reads in 12 lines: SIBLEY & WATSON . MACHINISTs . W . MENDON . / MONROE CO. N.Y. / MANU / FACTURE, / WOOL CARD / ING MACHINES / CONDENSERS / POWER, LOOMS / BROAD & NARRO / W. JACKS / JINNEYS / & C. (An unusual feature of this overstrike is that all '&' signs are lying on their side.)

Both Hiram Sibley (1807-88) and Don Alonzo Watson (1807-92) were born in Massachusetts, departing there for New York in the 1820's, where they are traceable to various locations until both ended up in West Mendon in 1832 as business partners. The partnership was dissolved in 1840.

Sibley, the mechanic, became sheriff, and later his name was given to the engineering building at Cornell Univ. because of a bequest, apparently resulting from his involvement with the Western Union Telegraph Co. and the Michigan Southern & Northern Indiana railroads.

Watson became involved in private banking in Rochester after the two dissolved their partnership, but the men did have subsequent joint business ventures.

The only known specimen of this token was discovered at an Ohio token show in 1980 by Dick Grinolds of Minnesota.

NORTH CAROLINA

J. MARTINE

Fayetteville, N.C.

HT #	Rarity	Year	Metal	Size	VG	F	VF	EF
373	R9	(1830-36)	Silver	19mm	300.	—	450.	—

J. MARTINE / FAYt N.C. in relief within a rectangle ctsp on U.S. 1820 Bust type dime. (Dom Mulrooney coll.; Brunk 26170; Rulau NC 100)

374	R8	(?)	Silver	32.5mm	400.	—	600.	—

Similar ctsp on U.S. Bust half dollar. Examined: 1828, 1829. 3 pcs. known. (Rulau NC 101)

374A	R9	(?)	Silver	27mm	300.	—	450.	—

Similar ctsp on Spanish-American 1802 2-reales.

CIRCULATION AS MONEY

In the 1837-1842 period, almost 26% of the Large cent-sized pieces in circulation in the United States were Hard Times tokens, the balance being perhaps 3% foreign coppers of about 29mm size, and just 71% U.S. Mint cents.

James Martine was a coppersmith who began business in Cumberland County in 1826. Fayetteville is the county seat.

Martine later became a pewterer in Fayetteville circa 1826-1836. He also sold medicines with S.J. Hinsdale, according the *The Story of Fayetteville* by James Oates.

James Martine was a director of Fayetteville Bank in 1849. Assuming the stamps are from his coppersmith and pewterer trade, they would belong in the Hard Times period.

Martine was a pewterer and coppersmith in Fayetteville from 1826 until at least 1836. One of his apprentices was William Bass, a black slave, who was freed in 1828. In 1829 Martine advertised in the *North Carolina Journal* that he sold "braziers, copper and tinware" (Ledli Laughlin, *Pewter in America*).

C. BECHTLER

Rutherfordton, N.C.

HT #	Rarity	Year	Metal	Size	VG	F	VF	EF
570	R9	(1834-40)	Gold	22.5mm	—	—	8000.	—

C. BECHTLER. N. C. ctsp on U.S. 1834 Bust $5 gold piece. Unique. (Brunk report)

Christopher Bechtler, a German immigrant metalsmith, manufactured pistols 1831-1852. He is best known as the founder of the Bechtler private mint for gold coins operating ca 1834-52 (with his son August from 1848 on).

It is believed the punch used on HT 570 may have been one of Bechtler's gunsmith markings.

UNCIRCULATED

As used in this reference, the "Unc" equates approximately to Uncirculated Mint State 63 in the U.S. coin series. Unc prices are based upon the desire of Hard Times token collectors to obtain part red, no problem specimens.

P. EVENS
Cincinnati, Ohio

HT #	Rarity	Year	Metal	Size	VG	F	VF	Unc
375	R6	(1830's)	GS	24mm	150.	300.	1000.	1700.

HT #	Rarity	Year	Metal	Size	VG	F	VF	EF
375A	R6	(1830's)	Brass	24mm	150.	400.	600.	1500.

375B	R8	(1830's)	Gilt/B	24mm	—	—	1150.	1500.

On 375B, the ornament above SELECTION is not a rosette, but a crosslike device. (Krause coll.)

HT #	Rarity	Year	VG	F	VF	Unc
376	R7	(1833-5) Bale NY	200.	300.	700.	1500.

GILT COPPER, 23.8MM

376A	R7	(1833-5) Bale NY	200.	300.	1100.	1500.

COPPER, 24MM

376B	R7	(1833-5) Bale NY	200.	300.	700.	1500.

GILT COPPER, 24MM

HT #	Rarity	Year	VG	F	VF	Unc
376C	R8	(1833-5) Bale NY			1100.	

As 376, but ctsp 25 CTS in relief within rect. depression, neatly placed between 149 and MAIN ST. Depression is 11mm long. (Gaylor Lipscomb coll.; PCAC June 2001 sale, lot 27)

Platt Evens is recorded as having been at these addresses:
1815-19 138 Main St.
1829-40 149 Main St.
1842-43 Main between 3rd & 4th (Evens and Farnham)
See *The Numismatist*, May 1917, page 198, for the Waldo C. Moore research on this issuer.

SCOVIL & KINSEY
Cincinnati, Ohio

HT #	Rarity	Year	Metal	Size	VG	F	VF	EF
A376	R9	(1836-37)	Silver	27mm	—	300.	—	—

SCOVIL & KINSEY in relief within rectangular depression ctsp on Spanish-American 1782-Mo-FF 2-reales, Mexico KM-88.2. (Russell A. Hibbs coll.; Brunk 1996 personal letter)

Pulaski Scovil and Edward Kinsey are listed as silversmith partners in directories only 1836-1837, though some sources erroneously report their business in 1830.

Edward Kinsey (1810-65) and his brother David Kinsey (1819-74) immigrated from Wales about 1833, and started their silverware manufactory about 1836, though Edward had begun his smithing in 1834. E. & D. Kinsey was dissolved 1862.

For later issues of the Kinseys, see the USMT Ohio numbers 19 and 19A.

The Scovil & Kinsey mark above exactly matches those in Ensko (1937) and Belden (1980). Pulaski Scovil may have been in business as early as 1830.

A. LOOMIS
Cleveland, Ohio

COPPER, 28.5MM

HT #	Rarity	Year	VG	F	VF	EF
377	R7	1843 Arrows R & L	2500.	3300.	4000.	4600.
377A	R8	1843 Struck on Cent	—	—	7000.	—
378	R8	1843 Arrows Right. 28MM	10,000.	—	—	—

CIRCULATION AS MONEY

In the 1837-1842 period, almost 26% of the Large cent-sized pieces in circulation in the United States were Hard Times tokens, the balance being perhaps 3% foreign coppers of about 29mm size, and just 71% U.S. Mint cents.

HT #	Rarity	Year	VG	F	VF	EF
379	R8	1843 No Rings in Beak	5000.	5800.	7500.	10,000.
379A	R8	1843 Silvered Copper	—	—	8000.	10,000.
379B	R8	1843 Double Struck, 20% shift	5000.	5800.	6500.	8000.

| 379C | R9 | 1843 Triple Struck on Cent | 3500. | — | — | — |

This overstrike has one auction record of $12,100! Now in ANA Museum.

COPPER, 30MM

| 380 | R6 | (1840's) 11 Stars Above | 100. | 150. | 400. | 650. |

HT #	Rarity	Year	VG	F	VF	EF
381	R5	(1840's) 6 Stars Above	100.	250.	480.	575.

381 is 30.7mm, plain edge.

| 381A | R8 | (1840's) Double Struck | — | — | 600. | 800. |
| 381B | R8 | (1840's) Fully Reeded Edge | — | — | 400. | 800. |

A reddish AU specimen of 381B fetched $675 in the PCAC58 sale in 1995.

HT #	Rarity	Year	VG	F	VF	EF
381C	R9	(1840's) Struck on 1827-37 Cent	—	—	2300.	—

Anson L. Loomis was born at Sangerfield, N.Y., April 6, 1812. He died in Nov. 1863. Loomis and his wife Charlotte apparently moved to Cleveland in 1836 from St. Louis. He started business about 1837 as a grocer, expanding into the wholesale grocery and liquor business in the early 1840's.

G. & A. Loomis, grocers, were at 14 Dock St. 1837-38. Anson Loomis, grocer and ship chandler, was at 24 Dock St. in 1841. A.L. Loomis & Co., wholesale grocery and liquors, was at 34 Merwin St. in 1843-47. Loomis does not appear in directories from 1848 on.

The three rings in the eagle's beak constituted Loomis' emblem and it appears on his surviving advertisements. Loomis was an active Mason in Cleveland City Lodge 15. He was made a Master Mason Jan. 16, 1842.

The dated tokens (HT 377-379) all bear the 1843 date. The undated pieces (HT 380, 381) also bear the 34 Merwin Street address, so they could not have been emitted later than 1847; they probably appeared in the 1842-44 period.

Two unique Loomis pieces, HT 379C and 381C, were reported for the first time in 1981. HT 379C realized $12,100 in the Hartzog sale, purchased by Kurt R. Krueger. HT 381C fetched $2,300 in the Chesterfield sale, purchased for Chester L. Krause by the author.

The Loomis cards are among the most difficult to obtain of any Hard Times tokens. Of HT 377, only 10 to 12 specimens are known, while of HT 378 there are just 2 specimens known. Only 4 pieces of HT 379 are known, and 5 pieces of all HT 379 varieties (379A, B and C).

Specialists Charles Kirtley and Alan Weinberg state that all Loomis cards have partially reeded edges.

BANK OF J.G. YOUNG

Piqua, Ohio

COPPER, 29MM, PLAIN EDGE

HT #	Rarity	Year	VG	F	VF	EF
382	R9	1837 Engr. on HT Token	—	—	40.00	—

BANK / OF / J G YOUNG / PIQUA crudely hand engraved on Low 17, an 1837-dated "Illustrious Predecessor" HT token. (Ned Drees collection, Covington, Ohio)

Joseph G. Young was Piqua (Miami County) town treasurer in the 1830's and 1840's, and apparently acted as a private banker as well. He and Moses B. Corwin formed a law partnership in Nov. 1832. In 1847 Young became the founder of the newly organized Piqua Branch, State Bank of Ohio.

The item above can hardly be considered a store card, yet its existence verifies the circulation of HTT's in western Ohio at this period. Piqua is about 31 miles north of Dayton.

Listing handmade pieces is, admittedly, dangerous because unscrupulous persons could "make their own." The specimen above has been in the Drees family since the 1890's.

J. DEMUTH

Bushkill, Pa.

HT #	Rarity	Year	Metal	Size	VG	F	VF	EF
383	R8	(1830's)	Copper	29mm	35.00	—	50.00	—

J. DEMUTH ctsp on U.S. Large cent. Examined: 1807, 1832. (Brunk 11380)

383A	R9	(1830's)	Silver	27mm	45.00	—	60.00	—

Similar ctsp on Spanish-American 2-reales.

383B	R9	1832	Copper	29mm	35.00	—	50.00	—

P. H / 1832 / J. DEMUTH / J D ctsp on U.S. 1800 Large cent.

383E	R8	(1830's)	Copper	29mm	35.00	—	50.00	—

J. DEMUTH / WARRANTED ctsp on U.S. Large cent. WARRANTED is in Italics capitals. Examined: 1801, 1823. (Brunk 11385)

383F	R9	(?)	Copper	29mm	35.00	—	50.00	—

DEMUTH / WARRANTED (latter in capital Italics) ctsp incuse on U.S. 1801 large cent. (Bowers coll.)

383G	R9	(1830's)	Silver	32.5mm	—	—	200.	—

Similar ctsp to 383E (WARRANTED in Italics) on U.S. 1825 Bust half dollar. (Robert Merchant coll.)

The Demuth family of gunsmiths operated in Pike and Lancaster Counties, Pa., from 1771 until at least 1832. The issuer above is most likely Jonathan Demuth, a percussion lock gun maker located in Bushkill, a small place in Pike County in 1828.

Other J. Demuths of Lancaster included John Demuth, 1771-1796, and Joseph Demuth, 1800-1813. Christopher Demuth of Lancaster operated 1790-1804, and William Demuth of Bushkill in 1820. This family made flintlock and percussion weapons.

Q. David Bowers attributes the Demuth counterstamps to one John Demuth, a tobacconist on East King Street, Lancaster, Pa., primarily because a gun on display in Old Sturbridge Village in Massachusetts is engraved "John Demuth" on its barrel, and another gun is known with "J. Demuth, Lancaster" on the plate. Gun historian Henry Kauffman could find no record of the tobacconist having been listed as a gunsmith, adding "it is possible he sold guns in his tobacco shop."

We will rely on the attribution of the ctsps to Bushkill, pointing out that Lancaster gunsmith John Demuth (born 1771) is the likely maker of both guns Bowers described, and he had removed to Maryland in 1796. The only other reported J. Demuth gunsmith, Joseph, was active in Lancaster 1800-1813, well before the established date 1832 associated with several of these stamps.

0 - 0 - 0 - 0 - 0 - 0

The Demuth family is of German origin. Some of its members emigrated to Herkimer County, N.Y. as early as 1710.

Alexander Demuth (born ca 1660 at Runkel an Lahn, Germany; married Anna Catherine ca 1690. The couple were in Palatine records 1710-12.

A woman named Demuth, married to Hans Wilhelm Altmann, died at Weitersweiler, Alsace, Aug. 17, 1666.

Dietrich Demuth (born Germany 1696) was in Herkimer County, N.Y. ca 1743. Captain George Demuth (1740-89), married Anna Weaver 1766; he died at Fort Schuyler, N.Y. 1789.

Albert Demuth in 1997 wrote "The Civil War Letters of Albert Demuth and Roster of the 8th Missouri Volunteer Cavalry" (176 pages).

Elizabeth Demuth, German immigrant in Pennsylvania, 1800.

J. DEMUTH (et al)

Bushkill, Pa.

HT #	Rarity	Year	Metal	Size	VG	F	VF	EF
384	R9	(?)	Silver	28mm	—	—	75.00	—

Six separate incuse punches, all in straight lines, ctsp on very worn bust-type Spanish-American 2-reales, which has been widened by the stampings. Ctsps, in descending order: M. HARRISON / J. DEMUTH / R. C. SEARLE. / WARRANTED (in capital Italics letters) / J. V. JENKINS / H. FENN. (Van Ormer 2684)

The J. Demuth and Warranted stamps probably belong together, as listed by Brunk 11385. Probably Jonathan Demuth, gunsmith of Bushkill, Pa. ca 1828-32, who also issued ctsps on his own.

R. C. Searle / Warranted (Brunk 35975). Trade not known.

M. Harrison is not otherwise reported.

J. V. Jenkins (Brunk 21605).

H. Fenn (Brunk 13970). Trade not known.

Bushkill is a small place on the Bush Kill (river), near the Delaware River border between Pa. and New Jersey.

S. FEATHER

Norristown, Pa.

Illustrations double normal size!

HT #	Rarity	Year	Metal	Size	VG	F	VF	UNC
408	R8	(1840-60)	Brass	21-22mm	750.	1000.	1500.	4000.

S FEATHER / G / 12 1/2 Cts. Rv: Blank (intaglio of obverse). Crude work. Thin, bracteate-like planchet. Plain edge. (Miller 163; Wright 308; Fuld "Token Pages" pp. 83-84; Litman coll., ex-Don Miller; *Numismatic News* for May 18, 1999, pg. 1; Karen Allen coll.)

The "2" in "12" was clearly recut on the die over a "1." The "dots" appearing below the G are mere blobs resulting from die irregularities. Sizes on extant specimens vary slightly.

A408	R9	(1840-60)	Copper	18.3mm	—	—	7500.	—

S FEATHER / G / (large blob) / 6 1/4 Cts. Rv: Blank. Thin planchet, similar to HT 408. Plain edge. (Litman coll.; ex-Don Miller)

While the 12 1/2-cent token has been known for many years, and misattributed by all writers to Philadelphia, the 6 1/4-cent denomination was publicized only in May, 1999. George Fuld reports the 12 1/2-cent token was called a "levy" in Pa., Md., Del., etc. – this term standing for "elevenpence" when the Spanish dollar was rated at 7 shillings 6 pence. About this time the dollar was rated only at 4 shillings 9 pence in England. In New England and New York 12 1/2-cents was a "shilling" and elsewhere a "bit."

Solomon Feather was born 1815, the grandson of Isaac Feather Sr., a Revolutionary War veteran of the battles of Long Island and Brandywine. The Feathers lived in Montgomery County, Pa. and were farmers and innkeepers. Solomon Feather first appears in the 1840 census in Pottstown, Pa., but soon afterward moved to Norristown where he opened a hotel. He is listed as a hotelkeeper in Norristown in both the 1850 and 1860 census records.

A present-day descendant, Albert E. Feather Sr. of New London, N.H., provided a copy of his family's history, entitled "The Feather Family in America – the Path to the Present." The Feathers in America descended from Peter Feather Sr., who was born 1725 in the Palatinate (Pfalz), Germany and died at Reading, Pa. in 1801.

Solomon Feather's hotel was called Railroad House, located 1860 at the corner of De-Kalb and Washington in Norristown.

S. ALFORD

Philadelphia, Pa.

HT #	Rarity	Year	Metal	Size	VG	F	VF	Unc
K384	R9	(1840)	Copper	29mm	—	—	100.	—

S. ALFORD ctsp on U.S. 1833 Large cent. (Brunk 575)

Samuel Alford was a silversmith active in 1840, according to Kovel. He was a descendant of silversmiths Samuel Alford (1759-1762) and Thomas Alford (1762-1764), both of Philadelphia.

LOW NUMBERS

For veteran collectors still using the century-old "Low" numbering system, there is a conversion chart of the "HT" numbers in the Introduction to this reference.

ISAAC BARTON & CO.
Philadelphia, Pa.

HT #	Rarity	Year	Metal	Size	VG	F	VF	Unc
385	R4	(1837)	Gilt/Brass	27mm	20.00	45.00	100.	350.

ISAAC BARTON & CO / NO 27 / SOUTH 2ND / STREET / (ornament) / * PHILADELPHIA *. Rv: IMPORTERS & DEALERS / WHOLESALE / (ornament) / DRY GOODS / (ornament) / & RETAIL / .IN FOREIGN & DOMESTIC. Plain edge. (Wright 60)

HT #	Rarity	Year	Metal	Size	VG	F	VF	Unc
385A	R8	(1837)	Gilt/Br	27mm	—	—	600.	800.

As last, but Reeded edge. (Koppenhaver Oct. 25, 1996 sale, lot 16, prooflike Unc.)

The reverse is similar to that on the cards of Hooper Martin & Smith (Pa 204) and Samuel & Joseph Harvey (Pa 202-203), with a change for the store's activity. Probably all three cards emanate from a single token-maker.

Isaac Barton & Co. was at 30 So. 2nd St. in 1833, then at 27 So. 2nd St., the address on the token, in 1837. In 1841-44 it was at 29 So. 2nd St.

A specimen of 385 exists with numeral 3 punched in above address.

S. C. BEMIS
Philadelphia, Pa.

HT #	Rarity	Year	Metal	Size	VG	F	VF	EF
385G	R9	(1838)	Copper	29mm	—	—	200.	

S.C. BEMIS ctsp on U.S. 1837 Large cent. (Brunk 3245)

Bemis appears in the 1838 city directory as a hardware dealer, maker of small tools and knives.

BENDER'S EATING SALOON
BRASS

HT #	Rarity	Year		VG	VF	EF	Unc
386	R7	(1837-44)	6-1/4 Cents	200.	500.	700.	900.
387	R7	(1837-44)	12 Cents	200.	500.	700.	900.
388	R7	(1837-44)	13 Cents	200.	500.	700.	900.

HT #	Rarity	Year		VG	VF	EF	Unc
389	R7	(1837-44)	19 Cents	200.	500.	700.	900.
390	R7	(1837-44)	22 Cents	200.	500.	700.	900.

HT #	Rarity	Year		VG	VF	EF	Unc
391	R8	(1837-44)	25 Cents	200.	500.	1000.	1300.
392	R7	(1837-44)	34 Cents	200.	500.	700.	900.
393	R7	(1837-44)	35 Cents	200.	500.	700.	900.
393A	R9	(1837-44)	37-3/4 Cents	200.	500.	1100.	—
394	R7	(1837-44)	38 Cents	200.	500.	700.	900.
395	R7	(1837-44)	44 Cents	200.	500.	700.	900.
396	R8	(1837-44)	62-1/2 Cents	200.	500.	1000.	1300.

HT #	Rarity	Year	Metal	Size	VG	F	VF	EF
397	R9	(1837)	Copper	29mm	600.	—	900.	1250.

BENDERS / S. E. COR. 3D & / PHILA / CHESNUT / EATING SALOON ctsp on U.S. 1802 Large cent. (Kurt Krueger Sept. 7, 1983 sale, lot 1697; Brunk 3250)

HT #	Rarity	Year	Metal	Size	VG	F	VF	EF
398	R9	(1844)	Copper	29mm	—	750.	—	1250.

BENDER'S STAR HOTEL. / CHAS. W. BENDER / PHILADA ctsp on U.S. 1838 Large cent. (Brunk 3260)

HT #	Rarity	Year	Metal	Size	VG	F	VF	EF
A398	R9	(1844)	Silver	27mm	—	—	1800.	

Similar ctsp on Spanish-American Mo-FM 2-reales of 1773-77 type, date worn, KM 88.2 (PCAC July 1998 sale, lot 391; realized $1760)

HT 386 through 396 are all incused on brass discs. The obverse reads: BENDER'S / S. E. COR. 3D & / PHILA / CHESNUT (sic!) / EATING SALOON. The reverse reads: GOOD FOR 38 CENTS (etc.). The 38-cent rarity appeared as lot 4603 in the B&M April 12, 1986 sale.

C. W. B(ENDER)

HT #	Rarity	Year	Metal	Size	VG	F	VF	Unc
399	R6	1842	GS	16mm	1500.	2000.	3600.	5800.
399A	R7	1842	Silver	14mm	2000.	2250.	4000.	6000.

Probably other denominations exist in this series. Numbers 386 to 396 likely were used in the 1837-1844 period.

Charles W. Bender does not appear in the 1833 directories. In 1836-37 he appears, with his business not stated, at 2 Chestnut Street (His residence in 1837 was at 3 Noble.)

Bender issued his tokens, HT 399 and 399A, in 1842. These contain a large star as central motif, and this can be explained when it is realized that, in 1842-48, C. W. Bender is found listed as proprietor of the Star Hotel at 71 Dock Street.

Bender is also believed to have been in business in the 1850's.

Discovery of HT 397 tends to confirm Bender as a Hard Times merchant. Other cataloguers had guessed he might be later — into the 1850's.

BOLIVAR

HT #	Rarity	Year	Metal	Size	VG	F	VF	EF
400	R8	(1828-48)	Silver	27mm	—	—	2000.	

BOLIVAR / 8TH AND CHEST STRT ctsp on Spanish-American 1784 or 1789-Mo-FM 2-reales. 2 known. (Brunk 4180)

HT #	Rarity	Year	Metal	Size	VG	F	VF	EF
400A	R9	(1828-48)	Silver	27mm	—	—	2000.	

Similar ctsp on U.S. 1807 Bust quarter. (PCAC Nov. 1996 sale, lot 020; fetched $2250)

HT #	Rarity	Year	Metal	Size	VG	F	VF	EF
401	R9	(1828-48)	Silver	27mm	—	400.	—	

BOLIVAR BOLIVAR / 8TH AND CHEST STRT ctsp on Spanish-American 178?-Mo-FF 2-reales. (Robert M. Ramsay coll.)

HT #	Rarity	Year	Metal	Size	VG	F	VF	EF
401R	R7	(?)	Brass	27mm	900.	—	2000.	3000.

BOLIVAR / 20 / 8TH AND CHEST STRT on 27mm brass disc. Uniface.

HT #	Rarity	Year	Metal	Size	VG	F	VF	EF
401S	R7	(?)	Brass	27mm	900.	—	2000.	—

Similar, but 50. (Smithsonian coll.)

The Bolivar House was operated by William Carels at 203 Chestnut Street from 1827 to at least 1848.

HT 401R fetched $3190 in a 1993 auction.

401T	R9	(?)	Brass	23.5mm	—	—	3000.	—

Similar to 401R, but 25. Rv: 25. Unique. (Krause coll., ex-Vlack)

401U	R9	(?)	Brass	23mm	—	—	3000.	—

Similar to 401T, but 13/. Rv: Blank. (Miller coll.)

401V	R9	(?)	Brass	23mm	—	—	3000.	—

Obverse similar to 401 T, but 6. Rv: BOLIVAR / 6 incused. (PCAC58 1995 sale, lot 069)

W. BROWN

HT #	Rarity	Year	Metal	Size	VG	F	VF	EF
A401	R8	(1837)	Copper	29mm	60.00	—	90.00	—

W. BROWN ctsp on U.S. Large cent. Examined: 1803, 1837, 1848. (Brunk 5560)

A401A	R9	(1837)	Copper	36mm	—	—	100.	—

Similar ctsp on England 1797 Cartwheel penny.

William Brown was a Philadelphia silversmith and watchmaker 1823-1837. His hallmark is recorded by Belden and Kovel (see Bibliography). From 1845-49 he may have been in Albany, N.Y.

BUEHLER'S & SMITH

BRASS, 29MM, REEDED EDGE

HT #	Rarity	Year	VG	F	VF	Unc
402	R6	(1837)	55.00	75.00	150.	550.

MARTIN BUEHLER. WILLIAM BUEHLER. EDWARD SMITH + / BUEHLER'S & SMITH / 192 / MARKET / STREET / PHILADA. Rv: IMPORTERS & DEALERS / HARDWARE / CUTLERY / & / HEAVY / GOODS / IN FOREIGN & DOMESTIC. (Miller Pa 60)

COPPER, 29MM, REEDED EDGE

402A	R7	(1837)	75.00	100.	150.	600.

As 404. (Miller Pa 61; Wright 1349)

GILT BRASS, 30MM, REEDED EDGE

402B	R7	(1837)	75.00	100.	150.	600.

As 404. (Miller Pa 62)

M. & W. Buehler were located at 192 High (Market) Street as early as 1833-1836, according to the article "Philadelphia Story of the American Retail Merchants, 1830," appearing in the August, 1975 issue of the journal *Just Buttons*. At this time the Buehler firm sold metal buttons, a common practice for hardware stores of the period.

The 1837 directory places Buehlers and Smith, as the hardware firm was known, at 192 High (Market) St. that year. Martin Buehler & Brother had an outlet in 1848 at 195 High St., according to the 1848 directory.

CATCH CLUB

COPPER, 27MM

HT #	Rarity	Year		VG	F	VF	EF
403	R7	(1830's) 12-1/2 Cents		200.	300.	450.	700.
403A	R8	As last, but silvered copper and 30.5mm (Boller coll.)					

Enlarged

				VG	F	VF	EF
		BRASS, 26MM					
405	R6	(1830's) 12-1/2 Cents		100.	300.	600.	900.
		SILVERED BRASS, 26MM					
405A	R7	(1830's) 12-1/2 Cents		—	—	—	900.
		BRASS, 26MM					
406	R6	(1830's) Ctsp BOOTH on Rev		100.	300.	500.	700.
		GILT COPPER, 26MM					
406A	R6	(1830's) Ctsp BOOTH on Rev		100.	300.	600.	1000.
		SILVERED BRASS, 26MM					
406B	R6	(1830's) Ctsp BOOTH on Rev		200.	300.	600.	1000.
		SILVERED BRASS, 26MM					
407	R7	(1830's) Issuer side blank		—	—	200.	350.

NOTE: No name on 407.

J. (Cannon)
Philadelphia, Pa. ?

SILVER

HT #	Rarity	Year	VG	F	VF	EF
A452	R9	(?)	100.	—	150.	—

J (Cannon right) ctsp on U.S. 1832 half dime. (Brunk 21230)

B452	R9	(?)	100.	—	150.	—

Similar ctsp on U.S. 1835 dime.

C452	R8	(?)	100.	—	150.	—

Similar ctsp on U.S. quarter. Dates examined. 1815, 1818, 1819.

HT #	Rarity	Year		VG	F	VF	EF
D452	R9	(?)		115.	—	165.	—

Similar ctsp on U.S. 1824 half dollar.

The issuer's name may have been J. Cannon; he used a view of a cannon to depict it. Probably issued before 1838, by which time most of the host coins were out of circulation since they contained too much silver for the standard of 1836.

James Cannon, tinsmith, 240 Callowhill in the 1849 city directory.

J. CURRY
Philadelphia, Pa.

HT #	Rarity	Year	Metal	Size	VG	F	VF	EF
538	R9	(1837-40)	Copper	29mm	—	—	200.	—

J. CURRY ctsp on U.S. 1837 Large cent. (Merchant coll.)

John Curry was in a silversmith partnership with Stephen L. Preston 1825-31. An invoice dated Nov. 18, 1831 shows he was in business alone on that date; the bill was to Mr. Skerrett for $34.85 for six silver forks. (At $5.81 per fork, these must have been very special indeed in 1831!)

In an advertisement placed in *Poulson's American Daily Advertiser* for Aug. 2, 1834, Curry's address was given as 76 Chestnut St. He remained in business alone until 1863, when a new Curry & Preston was founded with Preston Curry, and this may have ended 1864.

Kovel intimates Curry may have had a shop in Newburgh, N.Y. ca 1849. This is based on a 1939 report by George Barton Cutten, unverified.

Curry's only known registered hallmark is J. CURRY in relief within rectangular depression, sometimes followed by an eagle displayed, in relief, within rounded depression.

DERINGER
Philadelphia, Pa.

HT #	Rarity	Year	Metal	Size	VG	F	VF	EF
491	R9	(1841)	Copper	29mm	—	—	600.	—

DERINGER / PHILA ctsp on U.S. 1817 Large cent. (Doty pg. 99; Brunk 11465; Bowers coll.)

| 491A | R9 | (1841) | Silver | 32.5mm | — | — | 800. | — |

Similar ctsp on U.S. 1832 Bust half dollar.

| 491B | R9 | (1841) | Copper | 23mm | — | — | 650. | — |

Similar ctsp on U.S. 1808 Half cent. (John Battaglia coll.)

Henry Deringer Jr. (1786-1868) followed his father's footsteps as a gunmaker and inventor. He started the Deringer Armory in 1808 after moving from Richmond, Va. This firm was active until about 1870.

The tiny, easily-hidden handgun known as a deringer was his invention; one was used to assassinate Abraham Lincoln. "Deringer" entered the dictionary to describe a tiny handgun; there were many imitators.

DICKSON, WHITE & CO.

HT #	Rarity	Year	Metal	Size	VG	F	VF	UNC
485		(1837-38)	Copper	30mm	30.00	75.00	175.	350.

A watch. DICKSON, WHITE & CO. / 129 MARKET STREET / PHILADELPHIA. Rv: IMPORTERS / OF / WATCHES / JEWELRY / PLATED WARE / FANCY GOODS & C / JOHN DICKSON / WM H. WHITE, JNO. M. HARPER. (Wright 1396; Miller Pa 122)

| 486 | | (1837-38) | German Silver | 30mm | — | — | — | 500. |

As Pa 122.

| 487 | | (1837-38) | WM | 30mm | — | — | — | 500. |

As 123. Plain edge. (ANS coll.)

| 488 | R6 | (1837-38) | Brass | 30mm | — | — | 300. | 500. | 700. |

As 123. Plain edge. (ANS coll.) Miller Pa 123B

Dickson, White & Co., are listed in the directories only in 1837-1838.

HENRY DISSTON
Philadelphia, Pa.

HT #	Rarity	Year	Metal	Size	G	VG	F	EF
568	R9	(1844)	Silver	27mm	—	175.	—	250.

HENRY DISSTON / (eagle) / PHILADa. ctsp on Spanish-American 1781 2-Reales. (Brunk 11745; Miller Pa 124)

| 571 | R8 | (1840-44) | Brass | 23mm | — | — | 40.00 | — |

H. DISSTON./ * (Eagle) displayed, head turned left */ PHILa. Rv: Blank, but something (sawbolt, shank ?) has been ground off. (Joseph Whipple & Donald Miller colls.; Miller Pa 125)

Henry Disston, saw maker, rear of 99 Mullberry, in the 1844 city directory. He had been at 21 Broad St. in 1840-42. Disston used dies to stamp brass discs mounted on his tools to identify their maker.

Possibly the brass discs referred to above are HT 571.

The firm was still in business in 1976 as a supplier of saws and tools.

S. FEATHER

See this entry under Norristown, Pa.

GILBERT
Philadelphia, Pa. ?

HT #	Rarity	Year	Metal	Size	VG	F	VF	EF
575	R8	(1838-44)	Copper	29mm	—	—	35.00	—

GILBERT in relief within extremely small rect. depression ctsp on U.S. Large cent. Examined: 1830, 1838. (Brunk 16120; R. Merchant coll.)

| 576 | R9 | (1844) | Silver | 25mm | — | — | 50.00 | — |

Similar ctsp on U.S. 1844 Seated Liberty quarter.

Charles Gilbert was a silversmith in business in Philadelphia from 1835 on. This may be his hallmark, though it may be too small for this purpose.

GOODYEAR & SONS

HT #	Rarity	Year	Metal	Size	VG	F	VF	Unc
409	R8	(1828-29)	Brass	29.2mm	3000.		6000.	10,000.

DOMESTIC HARDWARE COMMISSION MERCHANTS * / MANUFACTURERS OF PATENT PITCHFORKS * / A / GOODYEAR / & / SONS / *** / PHILADA. Rv: * GILT & ANERICAN (sic!) BUTTONS OF ALL KINDS / IVORY COMBS PLATED WARE &C * / SCOVILLS / GILT / BUTTONS. Ornate border and flourishes on each side. Weight 8.362 grams. (Miller Pa 179; illustrated specimen in ANS collection)

Amasa J. Goodyear made gilt brass and pewter buttons on Fulling Mill Brook in Naugatuck, Conn. 1811-1827. From 1831 on he made forks, buttons, faucets, etc. in Naugatuck.

In 1808 Goodyear had opened a Philadelphia button outlet managed by his son Charles Goodyear. In the 1830 depression, Charles Goodyear was sentenced to debtors' prison after overextending credit to customers who failed to pay.

Charles Goodyear invented the vulcanization process for hardening rubber, and his brother Nelson Goodyear obtained U.S. patents on the process in 1849 and 1851. Nelson manufactured vulcanite buttons – and later tokens. (See HT 409)

These were the antecedents of today's Goodyear Rubber Co., one of the world's leading manufacturers of rubber products.

Goodyear Rubber Co. issued a number of tokens in New York in the 1876 period.

Cox' die-evidence studies conclude that the Amasa Goodyear token could only have been struck by Richard Trested, no earlier than 1826 when the A. Goodyear & Son firm was founded, and no later than Trested's death on January 13, 1829 – unless of course Trested's apprentice James Bale finished the striking process from his master's dies.

Thus we are attributing HT 409 to 1828-29, before the Hard Times era, without removing it from this reference book.

Given the extraordinary rarity of HT 409, it is entirely possible the survivors were no more than pattern pieces, never actually used. The unusual, intricate border on each side of the Goodyear token was symptomatic of the button-making industry and is called the "watchcase button" border.

Goodyear & Brothers had an outlet at 16 Exchange Place in New York City in 1830.

SAMUEL & JOSEPH HARVEY

BRASS, 28MM, REEDED EDGE

HT #	Rarity	Year	VG	F	VF	Unc
410	R4	(1837)	20.00	25.00	75.00	400.

SAMUEL & JOSEPH HARVEY / 195 / MARKET / STREET / * PHILADELPHIA *. Rev: .IMPORTERS & DEALERS. / HARDWARE / & / CUTLERY / IN FOREIGN & DOMESTIC (Wright 1445)

COPPER, 27MM, REEDED EDGE

410A	R4	(1837)	20.00	25.00	80.00	400.

The reverse is similar to that of Hooper Martin & Smith of Philadelphia, Pa. 204. The firm appears at this address in the directories only in 1837.

The hardware firm of Samuel & Joseph Harvey must have issued its tokens in 1836-37, as they appear at 195 High (Market) Street only in the 1837 directory.

Samuel Harvey & Sons, hardware merchants, were at 62 No. Front Street 1832-33. Joseph was one son, Samuel Harvey Jr. the other. In the 1844 directory Samuel Harvey (Jr. ?) was a stonecutter at Marlboro below Bedford, while Joseph Harvey had an office at 139 High Street.

HT 410 also known in gilt brass, AU $150.

HOOPER MARTIN & SMITH

BRASS, 27MM, REEDED EDGE

HT #	Rarity	Year	VG	F	VF	EF
411	R4	(1837)	35.00	80.00	150.	300.

HOOPER MARTIN & SMITH / 113 MARKET ST. Rv: IMPORTERS & DEALERS. / HARDWARE / & / CUTLERY / IN FOREIGN & DOMESTIC. Plain edge. (Wright 1459)

John Hooper, merchant, is listed at 10th St. above Chestnut in the 1833 directory.

Also in the 1833 directory appeared the firm of Martin, Craven & Smith, merchants, at 113 High St., the same address on Low 385. The obvious conclusion is that the Hooper and MC&S firms merged sometime in the 1833-37 period.

John Hooper, alone, is listed as a merchant at 113 High St. in the 1844 directory.

JUSTICE

HT #	Rarity	Year	Metal	Size	VG	F	VF	EF
920	R8	(1844)	Silver	27mm	—	—	—	150.

JUSTICE in relief in serif capital letters within toothed rect. depression ctsp on U.S. 1805 Bust quarter. (PCAC June 16, 2001 sale, lot 36)

Joseph J. Justice was a Philadelphia silversmith working 1844-1848.

Gregory Brunk attributes this hallmark to Swan Justice, silversmith in Richmond, Va. circa 1818-1819. Swan Justice's recorded mark differs.

W. LEVIS

HT #	Rarity	Year	Metal	Size	VG	F	VF	EF
903	R7	(1836)	Copper	29mm	75.00	—	—	125.

W. LEVIS in relief within curving ribbon-shaped depression ctsp on U.S. Large cent. Dates examined: 1817, 1819, 1827, 1833, 1836. Only 7 known. (Brunk 24380; Hallenbeck 12.504; Rulau-E Pa 70)

904	R9	(1830's)	Copper	28mm	—	125.	—	—

Similar ctsp on Spanish-American quarter-real (cuartilla), probably Mexico Mint. Apprarently unique. (Donald Partrick coll.)

HT #	Rarity	Year	Metal	Size	VG	F	VF	EF
905	R7	(1830)	Silver	27mm	75.00	—	—	150.

Similar ctsp on Spanish-American 2-reales. Dates examined: 1773-Mo-FM, 1779, 1781-Mo, 1790, 1795-LME, 1796, 1796-LME, 1802. There are 8 known. (Chester Krause coll.; Duffield 1365)

A905	R9	(1830)	Silver	27mm	—	—	300.	—

Similar ctsp (ribbon-like) on U.S. 1825 Capped Bust quarter. (Hayden Dec. 2000 sale, lot 464, fetched $300)

The auction price realized in 2000 may have been an aberration, or a portent of coming price increases among Early American tokens of consequence.

906	R7	(1830)	Silver	32.5mm	100.	—	—	200.

Similar ctsp on U.S. Capped Bust half dollar. Examined: 1807, 1818, 1826. Only 4 known. (Larry Johnson coll.; Duffield 1410)

907	R7	(1836-37)	Copper	29mm	75.00	—	—	125.

W. LEVIS in relief within rectangular depression ctsp on U.S. Large cent. Dates examined: 1816, 1819, 1827, 1833, 1836. Only 9 known. (Rich Hartzog coll.; Rulau-E Pa 80; Henry Christensen Oct. 1987 sale)

908	R7	(1836-37)	Silver	19mm	75.00	—	125.	—

Similar ctsp on U.S. Capped Bust dime. Dates examined: 1830, 1835, 1836. Only 4 known. (Van Ormer sale 2731; Rulau-E Pa 81)

HT #	Rarity	Year	Metal	Size	VG	F	VF	EF
909	R9	(1836-37)	Silver	27mm	—	—	150.	—

Similar ctsp on Spanish-American 1786-Mo-FM 2-reales, KM 88.2. (John Ilgenfritz coll., Gladwine, Pa.; Rulau-E Pa 82)

HT 909 was found 1998 with a metal detector on the site of a farm which is now a public park in Gladwine, Pa. Treasure hunter Ilgenfritz says he has dug up many coins, but this was his first counterstamped piece.

William Levis has long been a man of mystery. In 1796-97 an apparently earlier William Levis is listed as a paper maker at 6 No. 8th St.

Then William Levis, born 1785, fails to appear in the Philadelphia directories for 1816, 1819 and 1823. Despite the absence of listings in 1816-23 directories, he functioned as a silversmith and applied his ribbon-like hallmark to coins about 1819. The same man (or a son?) appears in directories in 1832-33 as a currier at 292 Filbert. We meet him next in 1836-37 at 228 No. 3rd St., where he is listed as an oil and leather merchant. (His home in 1836-37 was at 242 Filbert.) Levis died in 1842.

The Levis stamps are quite important, and research into their provenance continues.

Q. David Bowers reported in 2001 that he owned a Levis stamp of HT 908 type (straight) on a U.S. 1877 Indian cent. If this is verified, Levis' punch must have fallen into someone's hands as the business ceased about 1842.

Old hallmarks often were used as trademarks by silver makers. Levis' mark could have been so used by a successor.

- 0 - 0 - 0 - 0 - 0 - 0 -

What follows may be pure coincidence, but through the Mormon Genealogical Library's Internet services, we may have located our mysterious W. Levis. In any event, the dates seem to match the realities of those facts stated above:

William Levis was born Jan. 15, 1785 in Kennet, Chester County, Pa. His parents resided in nearby Pennsbury, Chester Co. and they were William Levis and Mary Lownes Levis. At age 20, on Jan. 17, 1805, Levis married Rebecca Brinton at Birmingham, also in Chester Co. One of their children, also named William Levis, had a short life but could have been his father's assistant.

The younger Levis was born Dec. 22, 1822 and died July 27, 1842, each event taking place in Chester County.

The elder Levis, possibly the issuer of all the above counterstamped coins, died Feb. 9, 1849. Chester County is west of Philadelphia.

J. MENDENHALL

HT #	Rarity	Year	Metal	Size	VG	F	VF	EF
A411	R9	(1845)	Copper	29mm	—	—	150.	—

J. MENDENHALL in relief within rect. depression ctsp on U.S. 1845 Large cent. (B&M Taylor sale, March 1987, lot 1289; Brunk 27395)

This piece realized $154 in the Taylor sale.

John Mendenhall was a silversmith active in Philadelphia beginning 1841. He apparently descended from a Pennsylvania family of silversmiths, of whom Thomas Mendenhall of Lancaster, circa 1772, was one. More research is needed on this issuer.

E. C. O.
(E. C. Oertelt)

HT #	Rarity	Year	Metal	Size	VG	F	VF	EF
B411	R9	(1833)	Silver	27mm	—	40.00	—	—

E. C. O. in relief within rect. depression ctsp on Spanish-American 1776 2-reales. (Kirtley May 1993 sale, lot 1054)

The attribution is very tentative. The reported specimen realized $35 in Kirtley's 1993 Greater New York sale.

Oertelt apparently was part of a family of silversmiths. Charles E. Oertelt operated ca 1828-1850 in Philadelphia; the directories misspelled his name as O'Ertell and Ortelet. A Charles G. Oertelt was active 1847-1849.

J. NICOLLS

Philadelphia, Pa. ?

HT #	Rarity	Year	Metal	Size	VG	F	VF	EF
E411	R9	(?)	Brass	18mm	—	—	2000.	—

J. NICOLLS / G / 6 1/4. Rv: Blank, but intaglio of obverse. Thin planchet. (Bill Miller coll.)

This piece, first reported in Sept., 1998, bears an uncanny resemblance to the rare S. Feather tokens of Norristown, Pa. and may have been executed by the same maker. The mysterious "G" at center continues to defy translation.

There is no exact name-match in the Pennsylvania census records of 1830, 1840 and 1850, though one James A. Nicholl (or James Nicols) appears in Philadelphia in the 1830 and 1850 reports. (Research courtesy Lawrence Dziubek)

PHILADELPHIA CORPORATION

HT #	Rarity	Year	Metal	Size	F	VF	EF	Unc
412	R8	(1835-36) One Shilling	GS	26.4mm	—	—	—	20,000.

HT #	Rarity	Year	Metal	Size	F	VF	EF	Unc
413	R7	(1835-36) 50 Cents F.S.	GS	26.4mm	2000.	5500.	6500.	7500.

The "Corporation of Philadelphia" here refers to the city government of Philadelphia. Both 412 and 413 use the same obverse. Only 2 known of HT 412.

An HT 413, VF with scratches, appeared as lot 2274 in the B&M Nov. 1996 Vlack sale. It has not been discovered what the "F.S." stands for.

An HT 413 in F-VF realized $2750 in PCAC Nov. 1999 sale, lot 45. There are 10 pcs. Known of HT 413.

W. D. RAPP

HT #	Rarity	Year	Metal	Size	VG	F	VF	EF
414	R6	(1835-40)	Copper	29mm	90.00	—	175.	—

W D. RAPP in relief within rectangular depression ctsp on U.S. Large cent. Dates examined: 1808, 1810, 1816, 1819, 1821, 1822, 1825, 1827, 1828, 1829, 1835. There are at least 14 pieces known. No period after W. (Brunk 33530; Rulau-E Pa 422; J. Henderson coll.; Bowers coll.)

HT #	Rarity	Year	Metal	Size	VG	F	VF	EF
414A	R7	(1835-40)	Copper	23mm	90.00	—	175	—

W D. RAPP in relief within toothed rect. depression ctsp on U.S. Half cent. Dates examined: 1804, 1807, 1809, 1819, 1821, 1826, 1828, 1829, 1832. At least 11 pieces known. (Rulau-E Pa 420 and 421; Hartzog 538; Bowers coll.)

HT #	Rarity	Year	Metal	Size	VG	F	VF	EF
414E	R9	(1835-40)	Silver	27mm	—	—	200.	—

Ctsp similar to that on HT 414 on Spanish-American 1774 2-reales. (Rulau-E Pa 423)

HT #	Rarity	Year	Metal	Size	VG	F	VF	EF
414G	R9	(1835-40)	Silver	32.5mm	—	—	250.	—

Similar ctsp on U.S. Bust half dollar of 1834-36 type, date worn.

HT #	Rarity	Year	Metal	Size	VG	F	VF	EF
414J	R9	(?)	Copper	29mm	—	—	175	—

W. D. RAPP / W. A. RAPP in relief within two separate rect. depressions ctsp on U.S. 1816 Large cent. Although the W. A. Rapp hallmark is obviously that of another silversmith, we can find no reference to such a craftsman. He may have been an unrecorded successor. (Q. D. Bowers coll.)

William D. Rapp was a Philadelphia silversmith from about 1828 until 1850. The marks are those of his standard hallmarks. There are two varieties of the mark on HT 414, thick and thin letters. The thick letters are well cut; there is no period after W. Thin letters are poorly cut; there is no period after D. There may be other minor variations.

Rapp advertised in the 1837 Philadelphia city directory at 256 Race Street.

The Q. David Bowers collection contains six specimens of HT 414 and one of HT 414A in March, 2001, he revealed.

H. REES

NOTE: The letters in the H. Rees punches are distinctive – wide serif-type capitals. The same lettering is on the related stamps, H. LANDIS, HEISSER, R. NYE and PHILa. HT 415N is an exception, carrying a second stamp of the hallmark type.

HT #	Rarity	Year	Metal	Size	VG	F	VF	EF
415	R7	(1837)	Copper	29mm	—	80.00	—	200.

H. REES (straight) ctsp incuse on U.S. Large cent. Examined: 1817, 1825, 1827, 1832. (Hallenbeck 18.502: Brunk 33770; Rulau Pa-Ph 343)

HT #	Rarity	Year	Metal	Size	VG	F	VF	EF
415M	R9	(?)	Copper	29mm	—	—	100.	—

H. REES (straight) / HEISSER ctsp incuse on U.S. 1837 Large cent. (Hartzog 541)

HT #	Rarity	Year	Metal	Size	VG	F	VF	EF
415N	R9	(?)	Copper	29mm	—	—	100.	—

H. REES (straight) / R. NYE ctsp incuse on U.S. Large cent. (Brunk 33770/29985)

HT #	Rarity	Year	Metal	Size	VG	F	VF	EF
415B	R4	(1838)	Copper	29mm	—	50.00	—	80.00

H. REES (curved in upward arc) ctsp incuse on U.S. Large cent. Examined: 1793, 1794, 1799, 1800, 1802, 1803, 1807, 1808, 1811, 1813, 1816, 1817, 1818, 1819, 1820, 1821, 1822, 1823, 1825, 1826, 1827, 1828, 1829, 1830, 1831, 1833, 1836, 1837, 1838, unknown or worn dates. At least 76 pieces reported. (Brunk 33770; Rulau Pa-Ph 344)

HT #	Rarity	Year	Metal	Size	VG	F	VF	EF
415C	R9	(1838)	Silver	32.5mm	—	—	225.	—

Similar ctsp on U.S. 1825 Bust half dollar.

HT #	Rarity	Year		VG	F	VF	EF

SILVER, 32.5MM

HT #	Rarity	Year		VG	F	VF	EF
416	R8	(1833)		—	—	400.	—

S & D in relief within large toothed rectangular depression ctsp on U.S. 1806 or 1814 Bust half dollar. (Duffield 1442; Brunk 35433)

SILVER, 40MM

| 416A | R9 | (1833) | | — | — | 400. | — |

Similar ctsp on U.S. 1801 Bust silver dollar.

Shaw & Dunlevy were silversmiths in Philadelphia about 1833. Edward G. Shaw had started the firm about 1825; Robert Dunlevy Jr. was admitted about 1831. In 1833 they were located at 7 Lodge Road (Alley).

A sea captain named Robert Dunlevy appears in the 1819 directory at Bird's Alley. In the 1823 volume he is located at Federal near 2nd St. This may be the father of the silversmith.

The 1833 directory lists Robert Dunlevy Jr., silversmith, at Lodge Alley. The 1837 directory places him at 7 Lodge Alley.

SCHIVELY

HT #	Rarity	Year	Metal	Size	VG	F	VF	EF
B416	R9	(?)	Copper	28mm	—	125.	—	—

SCHI / VELY neatly ctsp on obverse of U.S. 1787 Fugio cent, Newman type 17-S1. Rv: Same ctsp on reverse of coin. Both stamps are carefully applied in small letters at center of coin. (B&M Hoke Green 1985 sale, lot 2398; Brunk 35780; Rulau-E Mav. 40)

HT #	Rarity	Year	Metal	Size	VG	F	VF	EF
C416	R9	(?)	Silver	27mm	—	—	125	—

Similar ctsp on Spanish-American LME monogram (Lima Mint) 2-reales. (Koppenhaver Feb. 25, 1998 sale, lot 250)

| D416 | R9 | (?) | Copper | 29mm | — | — | 75.00 | — |

SCHIVELY in small logotype ctsp incuse on U.S. 1826 Large cent. (Bowers coll.)

Schively family members appear in Philadelphia census records for 1820, 1830, 1840 and 1850. Henry Schively is a possibility.

Schively is an unusual name. It appears in U.S. census records in Ohio 1790-1890 and in Pennsylvania 1772-1890, only a few times.

Though it may have no connection: One John Schively appears in Pa. census records circa 1840, married to Ruth Ann Haucke, and a further Pa. listing shows one Lydia Schively was born June 28, 1876, dying in 1914. Lydia Schively married twice, to Francis Steiner and bore Luella Mae, Carrie Edith and Francis Steiner. Then she married Peter T. Lora and gave birth to a "living" (2001) Lora.

W. H. SCOTT

Philadelphia, Pa. ?

HT #	Rarity	Year	Metal	Size	VG	F	VF	EF
E464	R7	(ca 1838)	Copper	29mm	75.00	—	100.	—

W. H. SCOTT ctsp on U.S. Large cent. Examined: 1807, 1823, 1826, 1829, 1837, unknown dates. There are 7 pieces known. (Brunk 35920)

| E464A | R7 | (ca 1838) | Copper | 23mm | 75.00 | — | 100. | — |

Similar ctsp on U.S. Half cent. Examined: 1826, 1828, 1834. There are 5 pieces reported. (Ganter sale 1093)

William H. Scott, dry goods merchant, was located at 15 North 3rd Street in Philadelphia from 1825 to 1845. This location was just off the corner of Market and 3rd and within one block of the hardware store of the Buehlers and dry goods establishment of Joseph I. Sharpless.

Scott also sold brass buttons with his backmark W. H. SCOTT / .+. PHILADELPHIA .+., though he did not manufacture buttons. Thus far there is no proof that William Scott was responsible for these counterstamps, but it is a realistic possibility.

SMITH & GEMRIG

Philadelphia, Pa.

HT #	Rarity	Year	Metal	Size	VG	F	VF	EF
535	R9	(1839-)	Copper	29mm	—	—	60.00	—

SMITH & / GEMRIG ctsp on U.S. Large cent. (Brunk 36905)

HT #	Rarity	Year	Metal	Size	VG	F	VF	EF
536	R9	(1839-)	Silver	15.5mm	—	—	100.	—

Similar ctsp on U.S. 1838 S.L. half dime. (Koppenhaver June 1979 sale, lot 730)

| 537 | R9 | (1839-) | Silver | 18mm | — | — | 100. | — |

Similar ctsp on U.S. Seated Liberty dime.

Gemrig is a very unusual name, not appearing once in the computerized 80 million-plus phone book names in America. Rich Hartzog says the mark's style is that of a watchmaker or silversmith firm, which has escaped listing in silversmith/jewelry reference works.

While there are no Gemrigs traceable today, one has been located in the early 19th century. Jacob Henry Gemrig of Philadelphia, married to Maria (nee Widmer), fathered a daughter in Philadelphia Oct. 22, 1842, Anne Maria Gemrig. (Ref: Mormon church genealogical records.)

The surname Gemrig probably originated in Wurttemberg in South Germany. The name Gemrig has never appeared in any federal census 1790-1880, but may have been misspelled by a census taker in, for example, 1840. Penmanship in early census records is often careless and spelling execrable.

The Smith & Gemrig partnership has not been traced, but we feel comfortable in locating it in Philadelphia tentatively.

J. H. Gemrig, surgical and dental instruments maker, 1851, was at 43 So. 8th St.

| 415D | R9 | (1838) | Silver | 27mm | — | 175. | — | — |

Similar ctsp on Spanish-American 1801-NG-M 2-reales.

| 415E | R9 | (1838) | Silver | 21mm | — | 125. | — | — |

Similar ctsp on Spanish-American 1795 1-real. Only 1 pc. reported over many years.

| 415G | R7 | (1838) | Copper | 29mm | — | 100. | — | 150. |

H. REES (curved) / PHILa (straight) ctsp incuse on U.S. Large cent. Examined: 1797, 1814, 1817, 1818, 1823, 1830, 1831, 1832, worn dates. Only 11 pcs. known. (Hallenbeck 18.503; Brunk 33780; Rulau Pa-Ph 345; Bowers coll.)

| 415J | R9 | (?) | Copper | 29mm | — | — | 100. | — |

H. REES (curved) / H. LANDIS (straight) ctsp incuse on U.S. 1820 Large cent. (Hartzog report; Brunk 33770/23800; Rulau Pa-Ph 344A)

| 415R | R9 | (?) | Copper | 29mm | — | — | 175. | — |

H. REES (curved, incuse) / B. RAPP (relief, in toothed rect. depression) ctsp on U.S. 1798 Large cent. The Rapp stamp was applied later. (Brunk 33770/33520)

| 415P | R9 | (?) | Copper | 29mm | — | — | 85.00 | — |

H. REES (curved) / (two 6-pointed stars) ctsp incuse on U.S. 1831 Large cent. (Bowers coll.)

| 415Q | R9 | (?) | Copper | 29mm | — | — | 85.00 | — |

H. REES (curved) / 5 ctsp incuse on U.S. Large cent, worn. (Bowers coll.)

A blacksmith advertised himself as H. Rees, Arch near Broad, in the 1837 Philadelphia directory. He was a contemporary of W. D. Rapp the silversmith (1828-50). Neither Landis nor Nye have been traced, but Nye's stamp also appears on an 1842 Large cent, so it likely was stamped later on the Rees piece.

Q. David Bowers reports the existence of ironware bearing the H. Rees mark.

We withheld the Rees attribution to the Hard Times era from our catalog for some eight years until 1992, waiting to see whether any Rees stamp appeared on a post-1838 host coin. In those years — years of intense scrutiny by hundreds of collectors into counterstamped coins — no host coin has surfaced dated later than 1838, though some 82 Rees pieces have now been identified.

Rees must be one of the more prolific counterstampers of the Hard Times era, rivaling Houck's Panacea of Baltimore. Many more pieces are probably awaiting discovery.

Henry Rees appears in the federal census in Philadelphia 1810, 1820, 1830, 1840 and 1850. He does not appear in 1860. It cannot be certain this is the counterstamp issuer, but it seems likely.

A Henry Rees also appears in the first federal census in Philadelphia in 1790, possibly an ancestor.

B. Rapp is apparently a Philadelphia issuer circa 1840. The 1840 census shows Bastian Rapp and Benjamin Rapp in that year.

The Q. David Bowers collection contains 33 Rees counterstamps, primarily HT 415B, in March, 2001.

ROGERS BROS. & CO.

Philadelphia, Pa.

HT #	Rarity	Year	Metal	Size	VG	F	VF	EF
589	R9	(1832-46)	Copper	29mm	—	—	75.00	—

MADE FOR / ROGERS BROS. & Co. / No 52 MARKET St. / PHILAd in four separate one-line punches ctsp incuse on U.S. 1832 Large cent. (Van Ormer April 1985 sale, ex-Ray Byrne; Brunk 34860)

John Rogers founded this gunsmith firm in Philadelphia 1805, operating under his own name, and also operated Valley Forge Gun Factory in Valley Forge, Pa. The Valley Forge firm later came under his nephew, Charles H. Rogers.

About 1830 John, Charles and Evan Rogers constituted Rogers Bros. & Co. in Philadelphia, supplying flintlock pistols marked ROGERS & BROTHERS / WARRANTED. One of their addresses was 52 High (later Market) Street. The firm became hardware merchants, dealers in firearms and munitions, and ceased business in 1846.

S & D
(Shaw & Dunlevy)

J. H. GEMRIG,
MANUFACTURER OF
SURGICAL AND DENTAL
INSTRUMENTS,
ELASTIC
Trusses & Bandages,
No. 43 South Eighth Street,
PHILADELPHIA.

Jacob Henry Gemrig is listed in the 1851 *Thomson's Mercantile and Professional Directory* as a manufacturer of surgical and dental instruments, at 43 South 8th Street, Philadelphia.

SMITH & BROTHERS

BRASS, 27MM, REEDED EDGE

HT #	Rarity	Year	VG	F	VF	Unc
417	R4	(1837)	25.00	45.00	115.	350.

Anvil at center, 188 on it. MARKET above. STREET below. All within roped central circle. Outside circle: SMITH & BROTHERS / * PHILADELPHIA *. Rv: .IMPORTERS & DEALERS. / HARDWARE / AND (on saw blade) / CUTLERY / IN FOREIGN & DOMESTIC. Plain edge. (Wright 996)

SILVERED BRASS, 27MM

417A	R5	(1837)	30.00	75.00	125.	350.

GILT BRASS, REEDED EDGE

417B	R8	(1837)	—	—	150.	—

(Hayden 666)

Clifford and Cornelius Smith appear at 188 High (Market) 1836-44.
In 1832-33 Clifford Smith, merchant, was at 19 No. Front St. and Cornelius S. Smith, merchant, at Spruce above 12th. During 1844 Cornelius S. Smith left the partnership and became a bookseller at 3rd and Mulberry.
A double struck 417A is known in EF, valued at $400.

SNYDER & SHANKLAND

COPPER, 33MM, PLAIN EDGE

HT #	Rarity	Year		VG	F	VF	Unc
A417	R7	(1840-44)		200.	450.	1000.	3400.

Standing Cupid drawing his bow right, at upper center, SNYDER & SHANKLAND above. Below: DRAPERS & TAILORS / 102 SOUTH FIFTH STREET / CORNER OF POWELL ST. / PHILADA. Rv: CONSTANTLY ON HAND / AN / ASSORTMENT / OF / FASHIONABLE CLOTH / CASSIMERES VESTINGS / &C. / WHICH WILL BE MADE / TO ORDER ON / REASONABLE / TERMS. (Miller Pa 483)

BRASS, 33MM, PLAIN EDGE

HT #	Rarity	Year		VG	F	EF	Unc
B417	R7	(1840-44)		100.	300.	500.	1000.

As last. (Miller Pa 484)

WHITE METAL, 33MM, PLAIN EDGE

C417	R8	(1840-44)	—	1400.	2000.	3000.

As last. (Wright 1013; Miller Pa 485)

George A. Snyder and John R. Shankland were in business only 1840 to 1844. Thus these are Hard Times tokens and were removed from our *U.S. Merchant Tokens 1845-1860* volume. These attributions are due to the inquiries of H. Joseph Levine.
The Snyder & Shankland pieces have enjoyed some excellent auction records in recent years. The copper specimen in EF fetched a remarkable $3,190 in the PCAC Middendorf sale (lot 117) in Dec. 1990.
Three white metal specimens enjoyed mixed results recently. An EF in the PCAC Landmark II sale in June 1990 (lot 35) realized $1,900, yet in the 1989 Gil Steinberg sale another in EF (lot 575) fetched only $110. More recently another EF made $1,700 in the PCAC Gold Medal sale of Dec. 1991 (lot 032).

SPAYD & BELL

HT #	Rarity	Year	Metal	Size	VG	F	VF	EF
E417	R9	(1830's)	Silver	41mm	—	—	800.	—

SPAYD & BELL / PHILADA in relief in two separate rect. depressions with crenellated edges, ctsp on Spanish-American counterfeit 1790 8-reales. (Van Ormer sale 2845; Brunk 37615)
Spayd & Bell manufactured wooden planes in the 1830's, according to *American Wooden Planes and Their Marks* by Emil and Marty Pollak, pg. 269. Q. David Bowers also located a teaspoon shank with the same impression as above, indicating that the firm may also have been distributors of silverware made by others. This piece realized $120 in the Van Ormer sale, before it was attributed; as an HT piece it assumes greater significance.
Robert Merchant believes Spayd & Bell were retailers who stamped all the goods they sold.

SPERING, MIXSELL & INNES

HT #	Rarity	Year	Metal	Size	VG	F	VF	Unc
418	R4	(1838-40)	Brass	28mm	40.00	50.00	150.	400.

HT #	Rarity	Year	Metal	Size	VG	F	VF	Unc
418A	R5	(1838-40)	S/Brass	28mm	50.00	60.00	200.	400.

This is the same address as Spering Good & Co. Directory evidence is lacking to pinpoint dates on this issuer, but there is room for deduction. In the 1837 Philadelphia directory there appear these two listings:
Spering (William), Innes (Francis) & Co., 138 Market St.
Mixsell (E.B.), Wilson & Co., 206 Market St.
Apparently the two firms merged in the 1838-1840 period. Spering, Mixsell & Co. were in business as early as 1832. Known with reeded edges.

LOW NUMBERS

For veteran collectors still using the century-old "Low" numbering system, there is a conversion chart of the "HT" numbers in the Introduction to this reference.

SPERING, GOOD & CO.

BRASS, 32.3MM

HT #	Rarity	Year	VG	F	VF	Unc
419	R6	(1841-43) Plain edge	125.	225.	500.	900.

SILVERED BRASS, 33MM

HT #	Rarity	Year	VG	F	VF	Unc
419A	R5	(1841-43) Crudely reeded edge	—	80.00	125.	250.

Spering, Good & Co. appear in the directories from 1841 on, to at least 1848. William Spering was the senior partner. This firm evidently succeeded Spering, Mixsell & Innes about 1841. HT 419 was Wright 1026. HT 419 in VF-EF fetched $527.50 in PCAC 1999 Hard times sale.

THIBAULT & BROS.

HT #	Rarity	Year	Metal	Size	VG	F	VF	EF
420	R8	(1829-36)	Copper	29mm	—	—	1500.	

THIBAULT & / PHILADA. / BROTHERS in relief within large oval depression ctsp on U.S. Large cent. Examined: 1814, 1816, 1817. 3 pcs. known. (Brunk 39713, ex-Rudduck; Kirtley 1991; Bowers coll.; Duffield 1423)

Thibault & Brothers were wholesale and retail jewelers and silversmiths on the southeast corner of Fifth and Chestnut Streets 1825-1836 only. The oval depression measures 15 by 6.5 millimeters.

These pieces are considered among the most desirable counterstamped coins of the Hard Times period, with a long provenance.

Enlargement

These were Francis Thibault (active at least 1780-1807), Felix Thibault (1807-1837) and Frederick Thibault (1807-1833). The firm had been Thibault & Co. from 1797, then Thibault & Brothers from 1810 on.

In 1832-33 the firm was located at 150 Chestnut St. The firm had disappeared when the 1844 Philadelphia directory was published.

JOHN THORNE

HT #	Rarity	Year	Metal	Size	VG	VF	EF	Unc
A420	R9	(1837-41)	GS	19mm	—	2500.	—	—

Eagle displayed, head right, JO THORNE (recent article in Bowers & Merena Rare Coin Review)

HT #	Rarity	Year	Metal	Size	VG	VF	EF	Unc
B420	R9	(1837-41)	GS	19mm	—	2500.	—	—

JOHN THORNE (Maverick Z95 in Rulau's *U.S. Merchant Tokens 1845-1860*)

G.W.

HT #	Rarity	Year	Metal	Size	VG	VF	EF	Unc
E420	R7	(ca 1842)	GS	18mm	—	300.	700.	—

Plow right, initials G W above, eagle displayed with head turned right at top. Around all is ornate border. Rv: Blank. (Garrett 1905; Baker T-505; ex-W. W. C. Wilson sale; Krause coll.)

HT E420 had long been thought to be associated with George Washington. Steve Tanenbaum believes the piece is reposing in a more suitable venue in this time period.

F. A. VACHÉ
Philadelphia, Pa.

HT #	Rarity	Year	Metal	Size	VG	F	VF	EF
C420	R7	(ca 1842)	Copper	29mm	50.00	—	75.00	—

F. A. VACHé ctsp on U.S. Large cent. Examined: 1796, 1803, 1817, 1819, 1826, 1841, 1847. (Brunk 40990; Hallenbeck 22.500)

HT #	Rarity	Year	Metal	Size	VG	F	VF	EF
C420A	R8	(ca 1842)	Silver	18.5mm	65.00	—	100.	—

Similar ctsp on U.S. Bust dime. Examined: 1833, 1835.

HT #	Rarity	Year	Metal	Size	VG	F	VF	EF
C420C	R8	(ca 1842)	Silver	27mm	65.00	—	100.	—

Similar ctsp on Spanish-American 2-reales. Examined: 1777, 1782.

Francis A. Vaché appears in the 1824 Philadelphia city directory as a gunsmith. In the 1845 directory he is listed as a machinist, at 155 North 10th Street. He was apparently of French ancestry.

WARD

HT #	Rarity	Date	Metal	Size	VG	F	VF	EF
G420	R8	(1838-39)	Copper	29mm	60.00	—	90.00	—

WARD ctsp on U.S. 1816 or 1838 Large cent. (Larry Laevens coll.)

HT #	Rarity	Date	Metal	Size	VG	F	VF	EF
H420	R9	(1838-39)	Silver	39mm	—	—	150.	—

Similar ctsp on Spanish-American 1799 8-reales.

HT #	Rarity	Date	Metal	Size	VG	F	VF	EF
J420	R9	(1838-39)	Copper	29mm	—	—	150.	—

WARD / 67 MARKET ST. ctsp on U.S. 1807 Large cent.

John Ward was a silversmith located at 67 Market St. 1803 to 1839.

JAMES WATSON

BRASS, 27MM, REEDED EDGE

HT #	Rarity	Year	VG	F	VF	Unc
421	R4	(1835)	30.00	45.00	75.00	300.

Anvil at center, numeral 11 on it. * NORTH FOURTH * above, STREET below. All within beaded circle. Outside circle: JAMES WATSON / (leaf) PHILADELPHIA (leaf). Rv: * IMPORTERS & DEALERS * / HARDWARE / AND (on saw) / CUTLERY / IN FOREIGN & DOMESTIC. Plain edge. (Wright 1208; Miller coll.)

GILT BRASS, 27MM, REEDED EDGE

HT #	Rarity	Year	VG	F	VF	Unc
421A	R5	(1835)	—	50.00	100.	350.

As 421.

GILT BRASS, 27MM, REEDED EDGE

422	R5	(1835)	—	55.00	90.00	350.

Similar to 421, but from different die.

Scovill Mfg. Co., Waterbury, Conn., received an order for "gilt counters" from James Watson on March 2, 1835. HT 421 and 421A were struck in response to this order. HT 422 may have been struck somewhat later.

The firm was in business until 1839.

There are two die varieties of 421. Stars flank anvil (as shown), and dots flank anvil. It is not known if either is more scarce.

W. H. WHITE & CO.

Philadelphia, Pa.

HT #	Rarity	Year	Metal	Size	VG	F	VF	Unc
423	R6	(1835-37)	Copper	26mm	50.00	150.	300.	750.

Watch within a circle. Around: IMPORTERS OF WATCHES, JEWELRY, & C. Rv: W. H. WHITE & CO. / 129 / MARKET ST. / PHILADA / W. H. WHITE - J. M. HARPER. (Wright 1725; Miller Pa 574)

William H. White was active as a silversmith, jeweler and importer in Philadelphia 1822-1838. William H. White succeeded H. White & Son (1818-22) in the latter year. In 1835 he admitted Benjamin H. Smith as a partner and the firm became W. H. White & Co.

In 1838 the firm became B. H. Smith & Co. (Benjamin H. Smith, William K. Smith and William H. White). The Smith firm seems to have disappeared after 1838. It cannot be traced in the 1844 directory.

W. H. White died in 1859.

This very rare early store card is now admitted as a legitimate Hard Times token and is removed from our *U.S. Merchant Tokens 1845-1860*.

R. & W. WILSON

Philadelphia, Pa.

HT #	Rarity	Year	Metal	Size	VG	F	VF	EF
539	R9	(1834-35)	Copper	29mm	—	—	200.	—

R & W. WILSON in relief serif letters within rect. depression ctsp on U.S. 1802 Large cent. (R. Merchant coll.)

Robert and William Wilson were silversmiths, jewelers, clockmakers and makers of silverplated ware in Philadelphia 1825-1846. Advertisements in 1827 proclaimed they manufactured silver to these standards:

"Crown" – "the finest silver manufactured in the United States"
"5 Francs" – "the next finest"
"Spanish Dollar"
"Standard"

Robert Wilson appears in New York City directories 1803-1810, then in Philadelphia 1814 on. He died 1846.

The stamp above is one of six hallmarks illustrated in Belden for the R. & W. Wilson firm. Robert Merchant, a specialist, notes "their surviving silverware is very common, yet this is their only known counterstamped coin."

E. GILLIAM

Pittsburgh, Pa.

HT #	Rarity	Year	Metal	Size	VG	F	VF	EF
424	R9	(1836-40)	Copper	29mm	—	—	50.00	—

E. GILLIAM ctsp on U.S. 1836 Large cent. (Brunk 16147)

According to Britten (see Bibliography), Gilliam was a clockmaker in Pittsburgh in the 1830's. This needs verification through other sources.

W. SCOTT

Pittsburgh, Pa.

HT #	Rarity	Year	Metal	Size	VG	F	VF	EF
530	R9	(1839)	Silver	31mm	200.	—	300.	—

W. SCOTT in relief within oblong serrated (toothed) depression ctsp on U.S. Seated Liberty half dollar. (Gould 55; Brunk 35905; Rulau Ky 103)

531	R9	(1839)	Silver	32.5mm	—	—	300.	—

Similar ctsp on U.S. 1812 Bust half dollar. (Rulau Ky 103A)

532	R8	(1839)	Silver	27mm	—	—	200.	—

Similar ctsp on Spanish-American 2-reales. Examined: 1801, 1820-LME.

533	R9	(1839)	Copper	28mm	—	—	150.	—

Similar ctsp on Canada token. (Rulau Ky 103G)

These tokens were issued by William Scott, one of the earliest plane-makers in Pittsburgh. The mark matches that illustrated in Pollack's "Makers of American Wooden Planes."

In 1812 Scott purchased property. He worked first in "Pittsburg City" and then across the river in "Allegheny Town" (now Pittsburgh's north side). He appeared in directories 1813-1839. Since the Seated Liberty half dollar was first struck 1839, we must assume 1839 as the date of stamping, making these pieces Hard Times tokens.

Previously they had been attributed to William D. Scott, a Louisville, Ky. silversmith active circa 1841-49. Gregory Brunk reattributed these recently and we are assigning them new HT numbers and removing them from the USMT section.

RHODE ISLAND

G. G. CLARK
Providence, R.I.

HT #	Rarity	Year	Metal	Size	VG	F	VF	EF
A424	R8	(1833-37)	Copper	29mm	175.	—	300.	—

G. G. CLARK in relief within rectangular depression ctsp on U.S. Large cent. Dates examined: 1803, 1832. (Rulau/USMT Z4J; Brunk 7980)

| B424 | R9 | 1854 | Copper | 29mm | — | — | 75.00 | — |

Geo. Clark in relief within rect. depression ctsp on U.S. 1854 Large cent. Placed here to keep the Clark pieces together; this was his final year of work. (Bowers coll.)

George G. Clark began trade as a silversmith with Jabez Gorham 1813-18. Together with Lorenzo D. Anthony, he organized Clark & Anthony, listed in directories 1824-32 and 1836-37. Clark is listed alone 1844-68.

The stamp on the Large cents is an exact match with the teaspoon hallmark given in Louise Belden's *Marks of American Silversmiths*, page 108.

We now place these pieces squarely in the Hard Times period, standing alone from their time frame of issuance, and also as the token precursors of the Clark & Anthony HTT issues. Previously they were cataloged as mavericks in our *U.S. Merchants Tokens 1845-1860*.

CLARK & ANTHONY

HT #	Rarity	Year	Metal	Size	VG	F	VF	Unc
425	R1	1835	Copper	28.5mm	5.00	10.00	15.00	170.

HT #	Rarity	Year	Metal	Size	VG	F	VF	EF
426	R9	(1824-33)	Copper	29mm	—	—	200.	—

Six different silversmiths' hallmarks impressed on U.S. 1803 Large cent, viz: (Donald Partrick coll.)
CLARK & ANTHONY (relief, in rect. depression)
P. MILLER (relief, in rect. depression)
F. RICHMOND (relief, in rect. depression)
E.W. MAXCY (relief, in rect. depression)
G.G. CLARK (relief, in rect. depression)
F. MILLER / PURE COIN (relief, in rect. depression)

Clark & Anthony were manufacturing jewelers in Providence, 1824-1837 or later. They issued HT 425. (In 1790 Anthony had been located in New York City).
Pardon Miller was a Philadelphia silversmith ca. 1824-52.
Franklin Richmond was a Providence silversmith 1824-52.
E.W. Maxcy has not yet been identified.
George G. Clark was a Providence silversmith ca. 1813-1868.
The F. Miller has not been identified.
The "crossover" date of all these hallmarks seems to be about 1824-33, but the coin has been included with the HTT period because of the Clark & Anthony connection.

W.A. HANDY

HT #	Rarity	Year	Metal	Size	F	VF	EF	Unc
427	R1	1834	Copper	28.5mm	10.00	45.00	80.00	250.

EPHRAIM A. HATHAWAY

HT #	Rarity	Year	Metal	Size	F	VF	EF	Unc
428	R1	1833	Copper	28.5mm	10.00	20.00	50.00	200.
428A	R3	1833	S/Cop	28.5mm	—	25.00	60.00	250.

HT #	Rarity	Year	Metal	Size	F	VF	EF	Unc
428B	R8	1833	Copper	28.5mm	—	—	250.	

Counterstamped with fireplace shovel on one side and spoon on other side. There are 3 pieces known.

P. MILLER
Providence, R.I.

HT #	Rarity	Year	Metal	Size	VG	F	VF	EF
429	R9	(?)	Copper	29mm	—	—	150.	—

P. MILLER in relief within rect. depression ctsp on U.S. 1803 Large cent. (Brunk 27850)

| 429A | R9 | (?) | Copper | 29mm | — | — | 200. | — |

Similar ctsp on 1794 Talbot Allum & Lee cent.
Pardon Miller was a Providence silversmith circa 1824-1852, according to Louise Belden. Also see HT number 426 under Clark & Anthony above.

Miller may have been an Early American rather than a Hard Times issuer, possibly in the 1824-33 period.

SOUTH CAROLINA

R.L. BAKER
Charleston, S.C.

HT #	Rarity	Year	Metal	Size	VG	F	EF	AU
430	R7	1837	GS	19mm	900.	2000.	4600.	6000.
430A	R9	1837	Copper	19mm	—	—	—	Rare

An AU specimen of HT 430 fetched $3630 in the 1989 Gil Steinberg sale. A VF specimen fetched $4620 in the PCAC Oct. 2000 sale, lot 38.

Only 7 pieces of HT 430 are in public hands.

F. MICHEL

HT #	Rarity	Year	Metal	Size	VG	F	VF	EF
585	R9	(1830-44)	Copper	29mm	—	—	60.00	

F. MICHEL in relief within rect. depression ctsp on U.S. 1826 Large cent. (Bowers coll.)

Although F. Michel has not been traced, the Michel silversmith family was active in Charleston. Lewis C. Michel (1822), John E. Michel (1819-44) and Adrian L. Michel (1820-58) were probably all relatives in the trade.

Tentative attribution.

M. MILLER
Charleston, S.C.

HT #	Rarity	Year	Metal	Size	VG	F	VF	EF
542	R8	(1835-51)	Copper	29mm	—	—	80.00	—

M. MILLER in relief within rectangular depression ctsp on U.S. Large cent. Examined: 1835, 1851. (Brunk 27838)

For an additional Miller counterstamp, see under G. S. Gelston in New York City in this Hard Times section.

The 1851 cent carries two additional ctsps: date 1822 and numeral 26.

Possible connection: Matthew Miller married Rose Ann May on March 21, 1805, at Independent Congregational Church, Charleston.

SLAVE TAGS
Charleston, S.C.
With Blank Reverses

HT #	Rarity	Occupation on Badge	Fine	EF
500	R5	SERVANT 1802-1865	2500.	3500.
		(auction record in EF dated 1811 to $8259)		
501	R6	PORTER 1815-1863	2500.	3750.
502	R8	CARPENTER	8500.	
503	R7	MECHANIC 1842-1864	4000.	7500.
		(auction record in VF to $12,100)		
503A	R9	MECHANICK (sic!) 1837	—	6500.
504	R8	FRUITERER 1821	7000.	9000.
		(auction record in EF to $10,450)		
505	R9	FISHER 1817	6000.	8000.
505A	R9	FISHERMAN	Rare	
506	R9	Cook	Rare	
507	—	MERCHANT	Not verified	
508	—	B C (Bread Carter)	None now known	
A508	—	C C (Dog Trainer)	None now known	
509	—	DRAYMAN 1813	Only piece bogus!	
510	R9	SEAMSTRESS	Rare	

The only known HT 500 dated 1865 also bears the date 1863, a wartime expedient. It was dug by "BM" and bears the number 13.

In addition, occupations such as BLACKSMITH, BOATMAN, BRICKLAYER, WAGONEER and SPINSTER are reported to have been authorized by Charleston ordinances, though no tags bearing these duty descriptions are known.

CIRCULATION AS MONEY

In the 1837-1842 period, almost 26% of the Large cent-sized pieces in circulation in the United States were Hard Times tokens, the balance being perhaps 3% foreign coppers of about 29mm size, and just 71% U.S. Mint cents.

Charleston Neck, S.C.
With Blank Reverses

HT #	Rarity	Occupation on Badge	Fine	EF
515	R8	SERVANT 1849-1850	8000.	—
A515	R9	FRUITERER	Rare	

Only three pieces are known of HT 515: Lot 1427 in June 1917 Elder sale; Kirtley Summer 1993 price list; ANS collection. Numbers known: 105, 115, 117. (A reported number 177 was an auction cataloging error in 1917)

The sole A515, dug, was cut in half with the date and number missing.

Charleston, S.C.
With Maker Hallmarks on Reverse

John Joseph Lafar

HT #	Rarity	Occupation on Badge	Fine	EF
513	R6	SERVANT 1811-1834	3000.	4500.
		(*auction record in VF dated 1816 to $7150*)		
513A	R7	FISHER 1810-1819	6000.	7500.
513B	R8	PORTER 1820-1829	3500.	5000.
513C	R8	FRUITERER 1814-1817	6000.	7500.
513D	R9	CARPENTER 1813	Rare	
513E	R9	MECHANIC 1824	—	Rare

HT 513 to 513E bear hallmark on reverse: LAFAR in relief within rectangular depression. A few pieces bear the hallmark on obverse. John Joseph Lafar, silversmith, Charleston, working 1805-1849.

Ralph Atmar Jr.

HT #	Rarity	Occupation on Badge	Fine	EF
512	R8	HOUSE SERVANT 1800	7000.	8500.
512A	R9	MECHANIC 1800	7500.	9000.

HT 512 and 512A bear a hallmark on reverse: ATMAR in relief within rectangular depression. Known numbers: House servant no. 88, 170. Mechanic no. 349. Ralph Atmar Jr., silversmith, Charleston, working 1793-1803.

Ralph Atmar Jr. married Elizabeth Arnold on June 4, 1792 in the Independent Congregational Church in Charleston. His parents were Ralph Atmar Sr. and Elizabeth Freer, who also bore Ann Eliza Atmar, christened Jan. 2, 1795 in the same Charleston church, and Robert Atmar, born Oct. 22, 1797 in Sumter, S.C.

The only other traceable Atmar of this family is Mary Elizabeth Atmar, born Feb. 20, 1835 in Sumter, S.C. and married May 24, 1854 in Crockett, Texas. Her father was, apparently, Robert Atmar.

With J. J. LAFAR Hallmark

HT #	Rarity	Occupation on Badge	Fine	EF
513G	R9	? 1827	Not verified	

John Joseph Lafar was christened Nov. 25, 1781 at St. Philips Church in Charleston. His mother's name is listed as Catherine Lafar, but no father's name was recorded on the christening record.

A son, John Joseph Lafar Jr. was born Dec. 17, 1823 at Charleston, and this son married Ann Caroline Cobia on March 4, 1847 in St. John's Lutheran Church, Charleston; their son John Francis Lafar was born Aug. 20, 1848 in Charleston.

John Joseph Lafar III was born Jan. 19, 1871 to John Francis Lafar and his bride, Margaret Will Seyle, also in Charleston.

FREE BLACK TAGS

Charleston, S.C.

HT #	Rarity	Year	Metal	Size	VG	VF
517	R8	(1790)	Copper	Oval 36x42mm	—	7500.

Liberty cap on pole, large word FREE on cap. Around, in scroll: CITY OF CHARLESTON. The word No and a numeral are punched in flanking the pole. Rv: Blank. (ANS coll.; B&R Garrett IV sale, lot 1993, ex-W. Eliot Woodward sale of Oct. 13-18, 1884, lot 1237; Charleston Museum coll.)

The badges are diestruck. There is no indication of date of manufacture, but these do not seem to have been used after the earliest part of the 19th century. In the 1981 Garrett sale, the VF specimen fetched a then-incredible $4000.

Only three specimens are verified, bearing the numerals 33, 156 and 341. A fourth specimen appeared in a 2001 Internet auction, but its authenticity has not been established.

NOTE: Dates given following the occupation in the catalog above are date ranges of known specimens in public or private collections. Prices above $4000 are based upon actual auction or private treaty sales results.

Though most slave tags have blank reverses, there are a few exceptions. The hallmarks ATMAR, LAFAR and C. PRINCE are listed above. Also a few badges bear stamps 1862 or 1863 on reverse, with the earlier date on obverse being defaced; this was a wartime expedient.

Slave tags cover the EAT, HTT and USMT periods, but for convenience are grouped together here under the Hard Times section.

Charleston was the principal slave mart in the South prior to the Civil War. Metal tags worn by slaves hired out by their owners to perform outside work for other employers are typically similar to the illustrations shown. Most tags are diamond-shaped, though round, octagonal, square, irregular or crescent shapes are known.

Charleston city officials ordered slave artisans to wear badges in 1751 and extended the requirement to slave vendors of fruits and vegetables in 1783. Free blacks were also required to wear a badge at all times. These practices were ended in 1790. However, **no badges dated 1751-1790 are known** today!

A Charleston ordinance of 1800 reinstituted the practice of requiring the wear of slave hire badges. Such badges had to be purchased annually. The fee schedule for 1800 was as follows: Handicraft or tradesman $3; carter, drayman, porter or day laborer, $2; fisherman, house servant or washerman, $1; fruit vendor $6.

By 1843 the fee schedule was: Handicraft or tradesman $7; carter, drayman, porter, day laborer or fisherman $4; house servant or washerman $2, and fruit vendor $5.

The highest control number known on a slave tag is 5081, dated 1821, in the South Carolina State Museum. Badges are known in collections from 1800 through 1865, the latter not verified by laboratory analysis.

Each badge required relief stamps labeled CHARLESTON (always in an upper arc); the date; occupation, and a control number, the latter either stamped in or engraved. The introduction No. is sometimes presented in relief before the control number was added by the city treasurer. Unnumbered badges are known.

It is estimated Charleston had 15,354 urban slaves in 1830 and 14,673 in 1840. From 12 to 30 percent of Charleston's urban slave population may have been engaged in slavery for hire at any one time. Badge numbers apparently were issued sequentially each year.

Only somewhere about 300 genuine slave tags are known to have survived – about 60 in museums and the balance in private hands. The Charleston Museum has 36, the ANS has 7, and a few are in the Winterthur, Smithsonian and South Carolina State museums. A good number of those in private hands have been excavated in the past six years as interest has soared.

Until about 1990 these pieces sold for $1000-$1200 in Fine through $2000-$3000 in EF. But the 14-piece John J. Ford collection sold by Stack's Inc. on Sept. 9, 1993 cracked this structure. The Ford pieces commanded prices (including buyer's fee) of $2310 (1836 Porter, VF) to $12,100 (1850 Mechanic, about VF), with a surprising $10,450 (1817 Fruiterer, EF) and $8259 (1811 Servant, EF). This sale, massively advertised and competently cataloged, probably exceeded actual resale value in 1993, though pricing on such rarities is always affected by recent public auctions.

In June, 1999 Rich Hartzog offered five slave tags at public auction. These prices helped stabilize the breakthrough levels attained in the Stack's-Ford sale. The results in the 1999 sale were: (all diamond shaped specimens)

1816 Servant, 284, LAFAR hallmark, about VF	$5460
1845 Mechanic, 239, VG-F dug	$2900
1849 Porter, 105, VG-F bowed	$2487
1850 Servant, 1266, VF-EF	$2950
1861 Servant, 2022, F-VF	$2475

An HT 500 slave tag (127/SERVANT/1856) in corroded VF condition, possibly grading only Very Good overall, fetched $2090 in the PCAC June 1996 sale, lot 340.

The Bowers & Merena March, 2001 LaRiviere sale offered seven slave tags at public auction, again with massive advance advertising. Five of these seven pieces had been purchased in the June, 1999 Hartzog sale and thus revealed how some tags had fared in just 21 months.

C. Prince

HT #	Rarity	Occupation on Badge	Fine	EF
514	R8	SERVANT 1801-1807	4500.	6500.
514A	R9	MECHANIC 1801	Ex. Rare	
514B	R9	CARPENTER 1804	Ex. Rare	
514C	R9	PORTER 1803	Rare	
514D	R9	HUCKSTER 1803	Unique	

There are ten known specimens of the 514 varieties: 1801 no. 181; 1801 no. 437; 1802 no. 73; 1803 no. 689; 1807 octagonal no. 39; 1807 no. 159.

The only known specimen of 514A is 1801, number not reported, a report by "J. H." Presence of the C. PRINCE hallmark is not verified.

The only known copy of 514B is octagonal, number not reported, hallmark not verified. The sole specimen of 514C known, round, bears number 265, and the only reported 514D, round, is numbered 25.

HT 514 varieties bear hallmark on reverse: C. PRINCE in relief within rectangular depression. Prince has not been identified through silversmith sources, despite intense research in the Charleston area. Rich Hartzog, an expert on slave tags, opines this might signify wealthy landowner Clement Lampriere Prince of Mt. Pleasant, S.C., who also operated Prince's Ferry across Cooper River to Charleston ca 1804, and was active in Christ Church, Charleston, ca 1804-1810.

Clement Lempriere Prince was christened March 23, 1794 at St. Philips Church, Charleston. His father, Clement Prince, married Mary Prince at St. Philips Church Dec. 21, 1792. Note spelling difference in the baby's middle name; the church record could be in error.

LOW NUMBERS

For veteran collectors still using the century-old "Low" numbering system, there is a conversion chart of the "HT" numbers in the Introduction to this reference.

The 1816 Servant tag, LAFAR hallmark, about VF, advanced from $5460 in 1999 to a floor offer of $7150 before being removed back to the book by a reserve of $10,000. The 1845 Mechanic tag, 239, VG-F, advanced from $2900 to $3080. The other three tags remained in the "ballpark" pricewise.

Two never-before-published tags appeared in the B&M 2001 sale, which deserve special mention. An 1837 MECHANICK (sic!) tag, numbererd 87, diamond shaped 60.3mm vertically, EF condition, realized $6050. An 1823 SERVANT tag, diamond shaped 66.5mm vertically, number 1785 with LAFAR hallmark on obverse, fetched $3080.

Two apparently genuine slave tags appeared in a recent catalog of "black collectibles," both diamond shaped Charleston servant pieces, 1820 no. 1592 and 1862 no. 550. The 1820 is 68mm tall and the 1862 48mm.

Several Recent Slave Tag Sales (October, 2001)

(all photos courtesy Rich Hartzog)

HT 501, PORTER, 1857 in rectangle, 896, VF with two large indentations 50x50mm across flats. $4350.

Fake and Fantasy Slave Tags

The high prices being obtained by genuine tags have, for at least the past decade, aroused the cupidity of forgers and fantasy-makers and tempted the greed of collectors to ignore the multiple warnings the numismatic hobby has placed against "bargain-priced" slave tags, "distress sales" and, worst of all, the sale of multiple specimens at flea markets, antique and gun shows and over Internet auctions. The latter, we believe, is most dangerous of all since eBay (for example) will not assist buyers in recapturing their purchase price of phony merchandise.

Most fake and fantasy tags are easy enough to spot. No tag reputed to have been issued in Mississippi, Alabama, Georgia or Virginia is genuine. None of these states ever authorized the issuance of metal slave tags as Charleston did. It is true that Savannah, New Orleans, Mobile and Norfolk had badge laws in the 19th century, but no metal artifact from any of these venues has ever been verified.

All genuine tags have the majority of their legends in relief within recessed depressions. No tag which is entirely incused from punches or engraved by hand is genuine! A great many all-incused fantasy tags are appearing on the market, usually selling at $50 to $600, frequently with accompanying documents which are themselves forgeries on artificially aged paper.

Rich Hartzog has compiled a listing of known forgeries which are more dangerous and difficult to spot except by experts. This is updated frequently and may be accessed without charge on the Internet thru this address: http://www.exonumia.com/Fakes/fslave.htm.

About 1998 a crook had quite good bar-punches made up to duplicate those on genuine tags. He also had the good sense to use only copper blanks (a great many lead and copper-coated lead fakes had appeared). Two of these excellent forgeries are:

1856 Charleston SERVANT with green patina over all, and often offered with a fantasy bill of sale with the very same punched number (533) on it!

1862 Charleston SERVANT, very dangerous fake. Sometimes offered on lead instead of copper! Some other fantasies being sold:

1804 Kemp Plantation, MISSISSIPPI.
1826 Campfield Plantation, MISSISSIPPI.
1862 WASHWOMAN on trapezoid-shaped flan.
1861 R.R. MISS. PORTER.
1836 HOUSE ALA 384 on 42x55mm flan. Heavily patinated.
1842 Virginia SERVANT 38, flaky patina.

The best source for authentic information on slave tags is the 25-page illustrated article by Theresa A. Singleton of the South Carolina State Museum staff entitled "The Slave Tag: An Artifact of Urban Slavery." This appeared in the 1984 volume, South Carolina Antiquities; the Second Decade, part of the *Journal of the Archaeological Society of South Carolina*, Columbia, S.C.

HT 500, SERVANT, 1832 in ornate cartouche, Nr 194, choice EF (never dug; obtained from original family), 68x69mm across flats. Possibly one of the finest known, and larger than usual for such tags. $7500.

HT 500, SERVANT, 1811 in toothed rectangle, 1499, about Fine, 62x64mm across flats. $3150.

Credit for research on the slave tags is due to Rich Hartzog, Michael Hodder, Larry Johnson, Stack's Inc., American Numismatic Society and the staff of the Charleston Museum.

Fake 1813 Drayman tag

Background of Slavery in Charleston

The excellent book by Robert Rosen, "A Short History of Charleston," reveals that the first African slave arrived in Charles Town (as the city was known until 1783) in 1670. The city was new then, a walled fortress.

During 1772-1773, 65 vessels brought more than 10,000 Africans to the city to work in the homes of wealthy rice planters and to work in the fields that produced that wealth.

The buying and selling of slaves was conducted in the streets, at the docks or in the Old Slave Market on Chalmers Street.

Slaves in the city, Rosen says, "were coopers, engineers, mechanics, carpenters and every other sort of skilled worker. Charleston's many historic buildings, so much on display today, are monuments to their skill." Male slaves "were the backbone of the city's industrial force. The institution of slavery shaped and defined Charleston as much as, if not more than, any other force in its history."

Rosen added, "The economy and the great wealth of the city rested on slave labor, and Charleston was more committed to the institution than any other Southern city." South Carolina was the first to secede (Dec. 20, 1860), the first to fire shots (at Fort Sumter in Charleston harbor on April 12, 1861), and the last state to surrender (in Feb., 1865 after a 19-month siege).

Charleston even for a while had its own "Ellis Island" to quarantine newly arrived African slaves, Sullivans Island, in the late 1700's. During the year 2000, the Charleston Museum, repository of the largest number of genuine slave tags, had a public exhibit titled "City Under Siege: Charleston in the War Between the States." The exhibit was to have closed Sept. 4, 2000.

The white population of Charleston before the American Revolution was very cosmopolitan, including a large colony of French Huguenots and the largest Jewish community in the American colonies.

One contemporary account of Charleston slave tags by a black man has been uncovered. John Andrew Jackson, a plantation slave, received a Christmas furlough in Charleston, worked there for wages, and eventually escaped. He made his way to London, where he published, in 1862, *The Experience of a Slave in South Carolina.* Jackson wrote:

"It is the custom there for the masters to send their slaves out in the morning to earn as much money as they can, how they like. So I joined a gang of Negroes working on the wharfs and received a dollar-and-a-quarter per day, without arousing any suspicion. Those Negroes . . . have to pay their masters two-and-a-half dollars per week out of this . . . if they fail they receive a severe castigation with a cat-o'-nine-tails."

He continued, "Every Negro is expected to have a badge with his master's name and address inscribed on it. Every Negro unable to produce such badge when asked is liable to be put in jail."

This contemporary first-hand account shows Charleston slaves could net $5 per week, but it also shows Jackson misunderstood the slave hire badge system, as none has ever been discovered with a person's name or address on it. Jackson as a newcomer – and escapee – probably thought the tag number was identification, and he implies that he had no slave tag. The Jackson reference was discovered by B&M researchers for the March, 2001 auction.

TENNESSEE

TEXAS

The Kohn Daron & Co. token, HT 431, formerly listed under Memphis, has been repositioned under New Orleans, La. due to 1996 research.

BERSON
Franklin, Tenn. (or) Brownsville, Tenn.

Illustration enlarged

HT #	Rarity	Date	Metal	Size	VG	F	VF	EF
560	R9	(1834-38)	Silver	19.5mm	—	—	200.	—

Berson in serif letters in relief within toothed rect. depression, ctsp on U.S. 1820 Bust dime. (Arvid Johnson coll.)

Silversmith's hallmark, possibly that of William Berson, active in Franklin,Tennessee 1834-1838. Another possibility is that it was applied by silversmith Solomon Berson, active in Brownsville, Tenn. 1834-1858.

Silversmith references apparently have never pictured a Berson hallmark. The illustration above may thus represent a first in the antique as well as numismatic fields.

Franklin is in Williamson County, near Nashville, while Brownsville is near the Mississippi River. Both men could be related, however. Few precious metal craftsmen operated in Tennessee this early.

The attribution, while tentative, seems on good footing.

2 BITS TEXAS

SILVER, 27MM

HT #	Rarity	Year	VG	F	VF	EF
F432	—	1842	—	—	10.00	—

2 / BITS / TEXAS ctsp on reverse of Mexico Republic 2-reales of 1830's, date worn off. 1842 ctsp on obverse of coin. (R. Byron White coll.)

This is a fantasy concoction made to sell to collectors. It was made by a different hand than the two concoctions listed by Dr. Gregory Brunk which read, respectively: TEXAS / 4 BITS and TEXAS / 8 BITS. Brunk opines that these latter and the similar LOUISIANA concoctions were made as early as 1930 to gull unsuspecting collectors.

White's 1842-dated concoction may have been produced earlier.

The same punches used for this fantasy were used on the Union Mine (Oregon) fantasies.

ONE BIT OF TEXAS

SILVER, 21MM

HT #	Rarity	Year	VG	F	VF	EF
G432	—	1841	—	15.00	—	—

ONE / BIT OF / T TEXAS / 1841 ctsp on Spanish-American 1-real, very worn. GUESS / 1936 / ONCE ctsp on opposite side of coin. (PCAC July 1998 sale, lot 953; realized $16.50)

We have not examined G432, but feel comfortable in condemning it as a fantasy. The 1998 cataloger suggested it might have been issued for Texas' 1936 centennial exposition; no counterstamps have ever been reported for that expo.

VERMONT

GUSTIN & BLAKE

Chelsea, Vt.

HT #	Rarity	Year	Metal	Size	G	VG	F	VF
433	R5	1835	Copper	28.5mm	100.	350.	800.	1500.

HT #	Rarity	Year	Metal	Size	G	VG	F	VF
434	R5	1835 Retouched Rev			100.	350.	800.	1200.
434A	R7	1835 Silvered Copper			—	—	1500.	2000.

Gustin & Blake comprised Sebre Gustin, born in Chelsea, Vermont, Jan. 18, 1808 and Amos S. Blake, born in Brookfield, Vermont, Jan. 18, 1812. They were not associated long in business, Blake removing to Waterbury, Conn. to manufacture percussion caps for the government, among other things. Blake was considered wealthy when he retired.

Gustin continued the Chelsea hardware business for several years, later becoming a dentist and remaining in that practice until his death, Sept. 7, 1883. Sarah Gustin, his daughter, lived in the old family mansion before 1905 when Low interviewed her; she had in her possession the dies from which these tokens were struck.

C.C. CLARK

Windsor, Vermont

COPPER, 29MM, PLAIN EDGE

HT #	Rarity	Year	VG	F	VF	Unc
435	R9	1841 Ctsp on 1788 Mass. cent	—	—	400.	—

The countermark on a 1788 Massachusetts cent reads: C.C. CLARK 1841. (Duffield 1395; Brunk 7900)

HT #	Rarity	Year	VG	F	VF	Unc
436	R6	(1842) Ctsp on Starbuck token. (Brunk 7820)	—	250.	—	—

The countermark on Low 284 reads: CLARK.

| 436A | R9 | (1842) Ctsp on U.S. 1828 half cent | — | — | 250. | — |

The counterstamp reads: CLARK.

| 437 | R8 | (1842) Ctsp on U.S. 1825 or 1842 Large cent | — | 250. | — | — |

The countermark reads: C.C. CLARK.

SILVER, 32MM, CORDED EDGE

HT #	Rarity	Year	VG	F	VF	Unc
437A	R9	(1842) Ctsp on Bolivia 1830 4-Sueldos	—	—	300.	—

The countermark reads: C.C. CLARK. (Robert Leonard collection; Brunk 7890)

| 437B | R9 | (1842) Ctsp on German thaler | — | 400. | — | — |

(Tanenbaum coll.)

Carlos C. Clark was a maker of flintlock and percussion rifles at Windsor, Vermont from 1832 to 1846. A number of New England gunsmiths countermarked coins for use as advertising tokens, but most did this later, in the era between the Hard Times period and the Civil War, or after the Civil War.

Clark's counterstamping, probably for advertising purposes, continued long after the Hard Times period. Dated counterstamps of his are known as late as 1879, and these will appear in *U.S. Merchant Tokens 1845-1860*.

According to A. Merwin Carey, *American Firearms Makers*, (1953), Clark was a self-employed gunsmith who made flintlock and percussion rifles 1832-46. It is possible '1832' is in error in Carey and 1841 is his actual starting date in business. From 1846 to 1856 he was employed by Robbins & Lawrence, gunmakers. Then 1856-59 he again was self-employed.

In 1859 he moved from Windsor, Vt. to Nashua, N.H., and in 1863 to Manchester, N.H., but he kept a branch business in Windsor, Vt. until 1868. He was in business at least until 1879.

The date '1841' on HT 435 could possibly refer to 'Model 1841,' a rifle Clark made for the U.S. government as an employee of R&L in 1849, but since Clark dated many later counterstamps with dates such as 1842, 1859, 1864 and 1879 for commemorative purposes, we believe that 1841 was the issue date.

VIRGINIA

J. A. KLEIN
Leesburg, Va.

HT #	Rarity	Year	Metal	Size	VG	F	VF	EF
439	R9	(1833-37)	Copper	29mm	—	—	1000.	—

J. A. KLEIN / LEESBURG in relief within two parallel toothed rectangular depressions ctsp on U.S. 1826 Large cent. (Brunk 23118)

John A. Klein was a silversmith in business in Leesburg during the 1833-1837 period, according to references on American silversmiths. Not much of his work is known, but a surviving silver sauce ladle bears his signature and the date 1835. Leesburg is a small town in Loudon County, Virginia.

This Hard Times discovery piece was first reported in the June 1989 issue of *TAMS Journal* (page 103) by David E. Schenkman, who cited "The Silversmiths of Loudon County, Virginia" by Robert A. Green, appearing in the July 1970 issue of *Silver-Rama*.

S.N. BOTSFORD
Norfolk, Va.

HT #	Rarity	Year	Metal	Size	VG	F	VF	Unc
440	R4	(1839-42)	Copper	27.5mm	25.00	60.00	175.	450.
440A	R5	(1839-42)	Brass	27.5mm	25.00	100.	300.	500.

Samuel N. also issued tokens in the Merchant Token era from Bristol, Conn. See Miller Conn 2 and 3 from the 1840's period in *U.S. Merchant Tokens 1845-1860*.

Botsford advertised watches and clocks in Norfolk at least May, 1839 to Oct., 1842. Botsford appears in the 1840 Norfolk census but not in 1850.

FREEMAN & POLLARD
Norfolk, Va.

HT#	Rarity	Year	Metal	Size	VG	F	VF	EF
A440	R9	(1832-34)	Copper	29mm	—	—	275.	—

FREEMAN & POLLARD in relief within rect. depression ctsp on U.S. 1822 Large cent. (Brunk 15060)

Joseph M. Freeman and Lewis R. Pollard were jewelers, watchmakers and silversmiths in the 1832-1834 period. Freeman continued alone in the business until 1856 or later. (Belden report)

BECK'S PUBLIC BATHS
Richmond, Va.

HT #	Rarity	Year	Metal	Size	VG	F	VF	Unc
441	R3	(1832-44)	Copper	28.5mm	50.00	90.00	325.	500.
441A	R8	(1832-44)	WM	28mm	—	—	750.	1500.
441B	R8	(1832-44)	GS	28mm	—	—	750.	1500.

On this intriguing early token a nude female is seated, testing the bath waters. The copper piece was listed by Dr. Wright as number 72. Plain edge.

Charles Beck is recorded in the October 1832 Richmond City Deed Book as a confectioner who operated a public bath on the south side of Main Street, between 13th and 14th Streets. Local tax records reveal Beck operated the baths through the year 1844.

Most of the copper tokens found have seen a good deal of wear, indicating either their circulation as cents, or their use as admission checks for the public baths. The nude female was definitely a risque design in the second quarter of the 19th century Southland. Unc. copper tokens, and all tokens in white metal or German silver, are rare.

This token was discussed by David Schenkman in *The Numismatist* for May 1980.

Researcher Wesley Cox has shown by die links that Beck's tokens were struck in New York by James Bale and his associates (1999 die study).

WISCONSIN

Milwaukee, Wis.

HT #	Rarity	Year	Metal	Size	VG	F	VF	EF
543	R8	(1840-46)	Copper	29mm	—	—	55.00	—

MILWAUKEE ctsp incuse on U.S. Large cents. Examined: 1802, 1833, 1838. (Brunk 27975; Thoele coll.)

Placing the Milwaukee counterstamps under the Hard Times era is a stretch, but settlers displaced the fur traders in the Milwaukee bay and river area in 1835 and the city was incorporated in 1846. Wisconsin had achieved territorial status in 1836 and statehood in 1848.

Solomon Juneau, a French-Canadian fur trader who arrived in 1818, was elected first mayor in 1846. By 1850 immigrants had made Milwaukee's population 64% foreign-born, mostly German but also Irish and English.

German culture (singing societies, dramatic groups and the turnvereins – gymnastic unions) had Milwaukee nicknamed "Deutsch Athen" (German Athens). German-owned breweries abounded; there were more than 24 by 1856.

A. B. C. *

HT #	Rarity	Year	Metal	Size	VG	F	VF	EF
447	R8	(?)	Copper	28.5mm	15.00	—	25.00	—

A. B. C. * ctsp on various Hard Times tokens. 4 pieces known. (Brunk 35; Zaffern coll.)

| 447A | R9 | (?) | | | 15.00 | — | 25.00 | — |

Similar ctsp on Germanic coin, no description available.

C. AGNER

HT #	Rarity	Year	Metal	Size	VG	F	VF	EF
450	—	(?)	Silver	32.5mm	—	—	100.	—

C. AGNER (script) in relief within rect. depression ctsp on U.S. 1836 Capped Bust half dollar. (Van Ormer sale 2503; Brunk 420)

P. B.

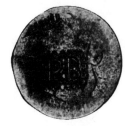

HT #	Rarity	Year	Metal	Size	VG	F	VF	EF
544	R9	(?)	Copper	29mm	—	—	30.00	—

Large non-serif P . B in relief within toothed square depression ctsp on U.S. 1807 Large cent.

T. D. B.

HT #	Rarity	Year	Metal	Size	VG	F	VF	EF
448	R9	1839	Copper	29mm	—	—	150.	—

T D B / 1839 (indiv. letter punches) ctsp on an 1833 Hard Times token, HT 70. (Kirtley June 18, 1996 sale, lot AD 11, where it realized an incredible $500; formerly HT B99)

This is a maverick. In the 6th edition of *Hard Times Tokens* (1996), it had erroneously been attributed to Thomas Danforth Boardman, the famous Hartford, Conn. pewterer active 1805-50, but that attribution was made before the piece was actually examined. The above marking matches no known Boardman "touch," though it is still possible that he is responsible.

BAINBRIDGE

HT #	Rarity	Year	Metal	Size	VG	F	VF	Unc
A448	R9	(?)	Copper	18mm *	—	Very Rare		

Eagle surrounded by 15 stars. BAINBRIDGE. (Groh 1860, lot 489)

* The size is an estimate.

This token is unknown except for the Groh sale catalog of Feb. 28-29, 1860, conducted by Bangs Merwin & Co. of New York, a linear predecessor of today's Sotheby's. It must have been issued 1859 or earlier, quite likely in the Hard Times era because of its style. This piece was called Very Rare in 1860.

D. BALL

HT #	Rarity	Year	Metal	Size	VG	F	VF	EF
449	R9	(?)	Copper	28mm	—	—	75.00	—

D. BALL ctsp on Henry Clay 1840 Hard Times token, HT 79. (Kirtley June 18, 1996 sale, lot AD3, where it realized $66)

| 449A | R8 | (?) | Copper | 29mm | — | — | 65.00 | — |

Similar ctsp on U.S. Large cent. Examined: 1822, 1838. (Bowers coll.)

| 449B | R9 | (?) | Copper | 28mm | — | — | 65.00 | — |

Similar ctsp on Canada token, type not specified.

| 449C | R8 | (?) | Copper | 23mm | — | — | 75.00 | — |

Similar ctsp on U.S. Half cent. Examined: 1805, 1809.

| 449D | R9 | (?) | Silver | 32.5mm | — | — | 125. | — |

Similar ctsp on Spanish-American 1781 4-reales.

| 449E | R9 | (?) | Silver | 32.5mm | — | — | 150. | — |

Similar ctsp on U.S. 1830 Bust half dollar.

| 449F | R9 | (?) | Silver | 40mm | — | — | 200. | — |

Similar ctsp on U.S. 1800 silver dollar. (Brunk report)

HT 449 is the first reported counterstamp on HT 79, the 1840 Clay token.

By the number of pieces reported, D. Ball was an important issuer of stamped coinage.

W. BASSETT

HT #	Rarity	Year	Metal	Size	VG	F	VF	EF
550	R9	(?)	Copper	29mm	—	—	35.00	—

W. BASSETT in relief within rect. depression ctsp on U.S. 1827 Large cent. (Merchant coll.)

A. BENEDICT

HT #	Rarity	Year	Metal	Size	VG	F	VF	EF
562	R9	(1827-36)	Copper	29mm	—	50.00	—	—

A. BENEDICT ctsp on Spanish-American 1796 2-reales. (Koppenhaver July 1997 sale, lot 540)

Not examined. If a hallmark, possibly silversmith A. Benedict, active circa 1835 in Syracuse, N.Y.

T. BOYNTON

HT #	Rarity	Year	Metal	Size	VG	F	VF	EF
A450	R9	(?)	Copper	29mm	—	—	45.00	—

T. BOYNTON in relief within toothed rectangular depression across coin, ctsp on U.S. 1828 Large cent.

A. BRIGHAM

HT #	Rarity	Year	Metal	Size	VG	F	VF	EF
451	—	(?)	Copper	29mm	—	—	50.00	—

A. BRIGHAM in relief within rect. depression ctsp on U.S. 1837 Large cent. (Kovacs coll.; Brunk 5196)

C. L. BUTLER

HT #	Rarity	Year	Metal	Size	VG	F	VF	EF
452	—	(?)	Silver	32.5mm	—	—	100.	—

C. L. BUTLER ctsp on reverse of U.S. 1831 half dollar. (Krause coll.; Brunk 6285)

J. BYRON

HT #	Rarity	Year	Metal	Size	VG	F	VF	EF
551	R9	(?)	Silver	32.5mm	—	—	40.00	—

J. BYRON in large serif-letters punch ctsp incuse on U.S. 1826 Bust half dollar. (Brunk 6349; Thoele coll.)

COLLINS

HT #	Rarity	Year	Metal	Size	VG	F	VF	EF
108	R8	(1830s)	Copper	29mm	—	—	100.	—

COLLINS in relief within toothed rect. depression ctsp on U.S Large cent. Examined: 1817, 1835. (Brunk 8870)

HT 108 ctsp is not related to Samuel Collins & Co. of Hartford, Conn. and is removed to the Maverick section. It is a plane maker marking, probably used by one of four different issuers.

H.A. CORLISS

HT #	Rarity	Year	Metal	Size	VG	F	VF	EF
453	R8	(?)	Copper	29mm	—	—	50.00	—

H.A. CORLISS ctsp on obverse of U.S. 1832 Large cent. Same ctsp on reverse of the coin. Rarity 8. (Rulau coll.; Brunk 9620)

Possibly Horation A. Corliss, Boston, Mass. printer circa 1859.

DOUBLE GILT NO. 2

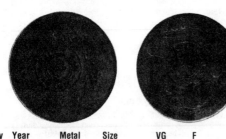

HT #	Rarity	Year	Metal	Size	VG	F	VF	EF
577	R9	(1830's)	Copper	29mm	—	—	65.00	—

DOUBLE GILT / * No 2 * in circle enclosing a sphere, ctsp on reverse of U.S. 1806 Large cent. Rv: Retrograde version of obverse punch ctsp on coin's obverse.

A buttonmaker's backmark. Connecticut?

J. M. DUBOIS

HT #	Rarity	Year	Metal	Size	VG	F	VF	EF
552	R9	(1841-44)	Copper	29mm	—	—	45.00	—

J. M. DUBOIS in relief within rect. depression ctsp on reverse of U.S. 1838 Large cent, the ctsp neatly placed between ONE and CENT. (Eagle) in relief within oval depression ctsp on coin's obverse. (Robert Merchant coll.)

A silversmith mark, not identified. Probably from the large family of Dubois silversmiths of Philadelphia founded by Abraham Dubois, working 1777-1807 (died 1807). Possibility: John Dubois, active 1831-33 or a successor such as Peter Dubois using an old punch 1841-43.

There were also Dubois silversmiths in New York in this time frame, but no smith called J. M. Dubois has as yet been identified.

L. DUDLEY

HT #	Rarity	Year	Metal	Size	VG	F	VF	EF
559	R9	(?)	Copper	29mm	—	—	125.	—

L. DUDLEY / CAST STEEL ctsp incuse on reverse of U.S. 183. Large cent. (Brunk 12340; World Exonumia June 1999 sale, lot 379; R. Merchant coll.)

Probably a toolmaker after 1830 when steel was substituted for iron in axes and other tools. It is possible this issuer was a predecessor of Dudley Lock Co. of Chicago, padlock maker reported by Arnall (without giving a first initial).

H. H. EASTON

HT #	Rarity	Year	Metal	Size	VG	F	VF	EF
553	R9	(?)	Silver	32.5mm	—	—	65.00	—
553A	R9	(?)	Silver	31mm	—	—	60.00	—
553B	R9	(?)	Silver	25mm	—	—	60.00	—

H. H. EASTON in serif punch ctsp incuse on U.S. Bust half dollar. Examined: 1809. (Brunk 12870)

Similar ctsp on U.S. Bust half dollar of reduced weight and diameter. Examined: 1837. (Van Ormer 2630; Thoele coll.)

Similar ctsp on U.S. Bust quarter of 1836.

F.

HT #	Rarity	Year	Metal	Size	VG	F	VF	EF
G453	—	(?)	Copper	28mm	—	—	15.00	—

Large serif-type capital F ctsp on 1841 Hard Times token, WEBSTER CREDIT CURRENT, Low 58. (Rulau coll.)

N.F.

HT #	Rarity	Year	Metal	Size	VG	F	VF	EF
454	R8	(?)	Copper	29mm	—	—	25.00	—

N F (large) in relief within toothed rect. depression ctsp on U.S. 1833 Large cent. (PCAC Dec. 1990 sale, lot 641)

P. FANAN

HT #	Rarity	Year	Metal	Size	VG	F	VF	EF
455	R9	(?)	Silver	32.5mm	—	—	40.00	—

P. FANAN / TEQ ctsp on U.S. 1830 Bust half dollar. TEQ ctsp on reverse of the coin. (Frank Kovacs coll.; Brunk 13770)

G. FARRAR

HT #	Rarity	Year		VG	F	VF	Unc
456	R8	(1835) Ctsp on 1835 Cent.				85.00	—

The countermark shows G. FARRAR above a Liberty head, a rooster to left, hog running to right, and eagle on head — all on an 1835 U.S. cent. (Duffield 1399; Brunk 13835; Bowers coll.)

A.G.

HT #	Rarity	Year	Metal	Size	VG	F	VF	EF
A458	R9	ND	Copper	29mm	—	—	50.00	—

Large A G (relief), in wide-toothed rectangular depression ctsp on U.S. 1807 Large cent. (Dr. Sol Taylor coll.)

This is not a mark of silversmith, pewterer or gunsmith. Pewterer Ashbil Griswold used an AG mark of totally different style.

E. E. G.

HT #	Rarity	Year	Metal	Size	VG	F	VF	EF
B458	R9	(?)	Silver	21mm	—	—	40.00	—

E. E. G. in relief within scroll-shaped depression ctsp on Spanish-American 1782 (?) 1-real, very worn. (Hayden Nov. 1998 sale, lot 533)

The punch is likely that of an early metalsmith, but we can find no match in silversmith, pewterer etc. references. Most counterstamps of this type were applied from 1834 on, when large numbers of worn Spanish silver became available on the marketplace.

H. H.

HT #	Rarity	Year	Metal	Size	VG	F	VF	EF
E458	R7	(?)	Copper	23mm	—	—	—	35.00

Serif capitals H . H ctsp incuse from a prepared punch on U.S. Half cent. Examined: 1805, 1828, 1832, 1833, 1835. (Henderson coll.)

The five reported ctsp pieces, all in the James Henderson collection in North Carolina, are all from the same distinctive punch.

It may be coincidental, but some flintlock Kentucky rifles of the 1840's bear similar initials, their maker not known.

J. H.

Illustration double normal size!

HT #	Rarity	Year	Metal	Size	VG	F	VF	EF
572	R9	(?)	Brass	19mm	—	—	—	200.

Arc of seven 6-pointed stars above eagle displayed, head turned right, U.S. shield on its breast. Large serif J at left, H at right, 12 1/2 below. Rv: Blank. Thin (.5mm) planchet. Reeded edge! (Donald Miller coll.)

This unpublished rarity, possibly unique, is early in fabric. It may date as far back as 1820, but more likely is from the Hard Times era. It is less crude than the S. Feather tokens, but probably emanates from the same time period. (Lawrence Dziubek photo)

J.B. HARDY

HT #	Rarity	Year		F	VF	EF	Unc
457	R8	1838 Ctsp. U.S. Cent		—	—	100.	—

The countermark on a U.S. 1818 Large cent reads: J.B. HARDY 1838. (Hallenbeck 8.503; Brunk 18205)

A. B. HARRINGTON

HT #	Rarity	Year	Metal	Size	VG	F	VF	EF
K458	R9	(?)	Silver	32.5mm	—	—	—	65.00

A. B. HARRINGTON in neat incuse punch ctsp on U.S. 1832 Capped Bust half dollar, which was AU when struck and still has some mint luster. (Thoele coll.; Brunk 18357)

The 1840 census records show these possibilities: A. B. Harrington, Palermo, N.Y.; Alexander B. Harrington, Camden, Maine, and Amaziah B. Harrington, Bombay, N.Y. The 1830 census adds Abel B. Harrington, West Newbury, Mass. Occupations of these men have not yet been determined.

BEN T. HEALD

HT #	Rarity	Year	Metal	Size	VG	F	VF	EF
C458	R9	1837	Silver	40mm	—	—	600.	—

BEN T. HEALD, MARCH 25TH 1837 (star) ctsp. on U.S. 1799 silver dollar. (Brunk 18960; Krause coll., ex-Vlack)

An attribution to Philadelphia is uncertain. Heald is thought to have been a businessman, but the use of this large piece as a store card is doubtful. This was lot 81 in the H. Joseph Levine sale of May 30, 1981, bringing $425. It was last sold in Oct., 1993.

HEWET PATENT

HT #	Rarity	Year	Metal	Size	VG	F	VF	EF
D458	R9	1840	Copper	29mm	—	75.00	—	—

HEWET / PATENT / 1840 / 1840 / PATENT / PATENT ctsp on U.S. 1826 Large cent.

G. HORR

HT #	Rarity	Year	Metal	Size	VG	F	VF	EF
583	R8	(1830's)	Copper	29mm	—	—	35.00	—

G. HORR in logotype ctsp incuse on U.S. Large cents. Examined: 1831, 1833, worn date. (Brunk 20095)

Also see under Albany, N.Y., HT 582.

W. J.

HT #	Rarity	Year	Metal	Size	VG	F	VF	EF
593	R9	(?)	Brass	27mm	—	—	60.00	

W. J / W . J ctsp incuse on 1834 Hard Times token of Seward, HT 26.

S. C. KINGMAN

HT #	Rarity	Year	Metal	Size	VG	F	VF	EF
G458	R9	(?)	Copper	28.5mm	—	—	—	75.00

S. C. Kingman in tiny script lettering ctsp on 1837 Hard Times token, HT 34. (Hayden March 1997 sale, lot 514)

HT #	Rarity	Year	Metal	Size	VG	F	VF	EF
H458	R9	(?)	Silver	24.3mm	—	—	1500.	—

Similar ctsp on Massachusetts 1652 Pine Tree shilling of type Noe 16. Host coin is F/VF. (Arvid O. Johnson coll.)

Pine Tree shillings, small planchet, though dated 1652, were struck 1675-1682. The host coin, if unmarked, would be worth about $2,000.

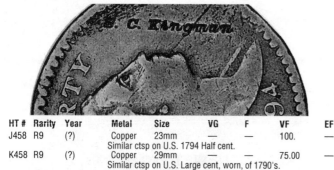

HT #	Rarity	Year	Metal	Size	VG	F	VF	EF
J458	R9	(?)	Copper	23mm	—	—	100.	—

Similar ctsp on U.S. 1794 Half cent.

HT #	Rarity	Year	Metal	Size	VG	F	VF	EF
K458	R9	(?)	Copper	29mm	—	—	75.00	—

Similar ctsp on U.S. Large cent, worn, of 1790's.

Collector Johnson advances the theory that Kingman may have been an early numismatist who marked his specimens. Was there such a collector?

The Kingman counterstamps, all appearing on collector-type coins, are one of America's numismatic mysteries. Was there a collector named S. C. Kingman who stamped his coins, as some 19th century folks did before realizing it might destroy their value?

Samuel Clayton Kingman is a possibility if it can be proven that he was a collector. Born May 15, 1830 at Wakefield, Mass., the son of Samuel and Sarah R. Kingman, he married Emily Eustis Brooks about 1857 and appears in the 1860 census at Bridgeport, Conn. (Another genealogical source has him born in Bridgeport "about 1834," parents not named.)

Gregory Brunk states that the punch is of hardened steel of the type used on watchcases, medical instruments, jewelry, etc. at a later period (1875-95). Our belief is that a steel stamp could have been prepared before the Civil War. Before the American Numismatic Society was organized in 1858, there is very little information recorded about America's earliest collectors.

There are other possibilities: Steven Cunard Kingman, born Aug. 25, 1849 in Lincoln Township, Morrow County, Ohio, died March 18, 1926 in Mount Gilead, Ohio. He was the son of Orman Kingman and Mary Charlotte Cunard, who had been married July 16, 1845 in Delaware, Ohio. Steven Cunard Kingman married Ada Eudora Coe on Feb. 14, 1877 by whom he sired two daughters. Later he married Mary Alexandra Ireland, by whom he had two daughters and a son, Cunard Maxwell Kingman.

Another possibilty is Shane Chandler Kingman, son of Kenneth Leroy Kingman and Virginia Lee Carriger (dates not available).

W. KNOX

HT #	Rarity	Year	Metal	Size	VG	F	VF	EF
554	R7	(ca 1842-44)	Copper	29mm	—	25.00	40.00	—

W. KNOX ctsp incuse on U.S. Large cent. Examined: 1816, 1827, 1833, 1835, 1838, 1841, 1845, worn date. 8 pcs. reported. (Brunk 23360; Thoele coll.)

In more than 25 years, this ctsp has not appeared on a coin dated later than 1845, so we feel safe in assigning it to the Hard Times period.

C.L.

HT #	Rarity	Year	Metal	Size	VG	F	VF	EF
458	R7	(?)	Copper	23.5mm	—	—	25.00	—

C.L. in relief within large serrated, rectangular recessed cartouche, ctsp on U.S. 1803, 1805, 1825, 1826, 1828 or 1834 Half cent. (Hallenbeck 3.003; Krause coll.)

This mark may well be that of silversmith Charles Leach of Boston, Mass. (1765-1814), whose career began about 1787. Half cents dated 1803 and 1828 bear the mark, the latter well after Leach's death in 1814. However, the C . L mark could have been used by a successor. Both Nathaniel Leach and John Leach practiced their craft in Boston.

C.P.L.

HT #	Rarity	Year	Metal	Size	VG	F	VF	EF
E458	R7	1837	Copper	29mm	—	—	20.00	—

C.P.L. ctsp. on obverse of an 1837-dated HT political token. (Stanley L. Steinberg 1981 sale.)

J. LYNE

HT #	Rarity	Year	Metal	Size	VG	F	VF	EF
459	R8	(?)	Copper	23mm	15.00	—	25.00	—

J. LYNE ctsp on U.S. 1828, worn 1795-97 or 1832 Half cent. (Brunk 25410)

HT #	Rarity	Year	Metal	Size	VG	F	VF	EF
459A	R9	(?)	Copper	29mm	15.00	—	25.00	—

Similar ctsp on U.S. 1829 Large cent.

BRASS, 25MM, REEDED EDGE

459B	R9	(?)			25.00	—	40.00	—

Similar ctsp on Andrew Jackson 1828 campaign medalet, DeWitt AJACK 1824-1, Rulau-E Med 1.

BRASS, —MM

459C	R9	(?)			15.00	—	25.00	—

Similar ctsp on Nuremberg, Germany New Year jeton, NEUE LHRE NEUES GLUCK / IETTON (blundered legend). (Brunk 25410)

With five host pieces from the late 1820's or earlier, it seems likely J. Lyne was active in the 1830's or 1840's. Tentative attribution.

UNCIRCULATED

As used in this reference, the "Unc" equates approximately to Uncirculated Mint State 63 in the U.S. coin series. Unc prices are based upon the desire of Hard Times token collectors to obtain part red, no problem specimens.

D. McWAIN

HT #	Rarity	Year	Metal	Size	VG	F	VF	EF
547	R9	(1839?)	Copper	29mm	—	—	60.00	—

D. McWAIN ctsp on U.S. 1838 Large cent. (Brunk 27220)

| 548 | R9 | (1839?) | Silver | 27mm | — | — | 200. | — |

Similar ctsp on U.S. 1836 Bust quarter. (Coin Galleries Nov. 1989 sale, lot 3009)

| 549 | R9 | (1839?) | Silver | 32.5mm | — | — | 300. | — |

Similar ctsp on U.S. 1808 Bust half dollar.

The evidence is thin that these are Hard Times pieces.

Possibility: DeLong McWain, Sacketts Harbor (Jefferson County), N.Y., 1840 census.

R. METCALF

HT #	Rarity	Year	Metal	Size	VG	F	VF	EF
B459	R9	1833	Silver	39mm	—	—	175.	—

ADAMS / 1833 / R. METCALF (curved) / (Eagle) / WARRANTED (curved) ctsp on France silver ecu, Craig 42. Examined: 1732-BB. (Brunk 27490)

The stamp gives every indication of a gunsmith, cutler or similar trade, but attribution has not as yet been made.

N.Y. BAKERY

HT #	Rarity	Year	Metal	Size	VG	F	EF	Unc
540	R8	(?)	Silver	32mm	200.	—	300.	—

N.Y. BAKERY ctsp on 1808 or 1829 Bust Half dollar. (Brunk 2010; Rulau Z65). Probably a Hard Times-era issue.

I.E. NEWALL

HT #	Rarity	Year	Metal	Size	VG	F	VF	EF
A459	R9	1838	Copper	29mm	—	35.00	—	—

I. E. NEWALL / 1838 ctsp on U.S. 1838 Large cent. (PCAC Gold Medal sale, Dec. 1991; lot 535, where it fetched $28.) Tentative attribution.

The only known specimen was worn before stamping, so date 1838 may be commemorative rather than contemporary.

Possibility: Increase Newall, Poasttown (Butler County), Ohio, 1850-51. Trade not known.

G. NEWCOMB

HT #	Rarity	Date	Metal	Size	VG	F	VF	EF
C459	R8	(?)	Copper	29mm	—	—	15.00	—

G. NEWCOMB ctsp three times on U.S. 1838 Large cent. (PCAC Dec. 1990 sale, lot 641; Brunk 29463)

M. A. NOTT

HT #	Rarity	Year	Metal	Size	VG	F	VF	EF
G459	R9	(?)	Silver	39.3mm	—	—	—	85.00

M. A NOTT ctsp on Spanish-American 1801-Mo-FM 8-reales, Mexico KM-109. (Joseph Zaffern coll.; Brunk N/L)

Zaffern has attributed this 1996 discovery to Newburyport, Mass., but we have as yet been unable to verify this. A valuation of about $135 would be justified if attributable.

O. & G.

HT #	Rarity	Year	Metal	Size	VG	F	VF	EF
545	R5	(1837-38)	Copper	28mm	—	60.00	110.	135.

* / O & G / ** (in circle of dots) ctsp on U.S. 1835 Half cent.

There are 46 known. (Duffield 1579; Brunk 29995; Ganter 1042; Rulau Z67)

| 546 | R8 | (?) | Copper | 29mm | — | 35.00 | — | 80.00 |

Similar ctsp on plain copper flan of 29mm (U.S. Large cent size). (Duffield 1579)

| 546A | R7 | (?) | Copper | 23mm | — | 50.00 | — | 80.00 |

Similar ctsp on U.S. Half cent other than 1835. Examined: 1824, 1825, 1827, 1828, 1832, 1833, 1834, 1837. There are 13 known. (Van Ormer 2773)

| 546B | R8 | (?) | Copper | 29mm | — | 50.00 | — | 80.00 |

Similar ctsp on U.S. 1827, 1837 or worn date Large cent. (Ganter 1043)

The illustrated specimen is the Al Oravec collection piece. The half cent was EF before overstriking.

The bulk of these pieces were new or near-new 1835 Half cents before counterstamping. No satisfactory explanation for O & G has ever been advanced.

The opinion that they were transport pieces for an "Ohio & Georgia" railroad is pure conjecture.

They are shifted from the USMT to the HTT period, since in 19 years of exposure no host coin dated after 1837 has been reported.

B. O'NEILL

HT #	Rarity	Year	Metal	Size	VG	F	VF	EF
460	—	(?)	Copper	28.5mm	—	50.00	—	—

B. O'NEILL ctsp on reverse of Jackson / Donkey Hard Times token, Low 51 (1833). (Krause coll.; Brunk 30250)

LOW NUMBERS

For veteran collectors still using the century-old "Low" numbering system, there is a conversion chart of the "HT" numbers in the Introduction to this reference.

M.P.

HT #	Rarity	Year	Metal	Size	VG	F	VF	EF
461	R6	(?)	GS	25mm	500.	1500.	3000.	3500.

MP monogram in relief within oval depression ctsp on reverse of an 1837 German silver 3-cent token of Dr. Lewis Feuchtwanger (HT 263). The ctsp is at top center (12 o'clock) or right center at 3 o'clock of the wreath, (B&M 1985 Kosoff sale, lot 4080; B&M Leidman sale 1986, lot 4550; PCAC Nov. 16, 1996 sale, lot 012). About 14 pieces known. (Brunk 25505; Miller 242A)

Illustration enlarged!

HT #	Rarity	Year	Metal	Size	VG	F	VF	EF
461C	R9	(?)	GS	18.5mm	—	—	800.	

Similar ctsp, at 11 o'clock position, on 1837 Feuchtwanger 1-cent token, HT 268. (Kirtley Feb. 10, 1998 sale, lot J018; this is the first reported instance of this mark on anything but Feuchtwanger 3-cent pieces)

The stamp appears to be the hallmark of a silversmith, but the hallmark has not been published. The MP monogram is distinctive, the capital letters being sans serif and with one common leg - that being the right leg of the M and upright of the P (This is said to be "ligate").

Three examples of HT 461 in VF to AU condition appeared as lots 1169-1171 in the B & M Fred auction, Nov. 13-14, 1995. They realized only $786.50 in EF, $786.50 in VF, and $665.50 in VF.

The only MP hallmark appearing in the Kovel reference is MP (not ligate) within rectangle, belonging to New York City silversmith Matthew Petit, who is known to have been working about 1811. This is a possibility, but probably is too early to be considered. We think New York is the likeliest location, since Feuchtwanger's 3-cent pieces were made and circulated there.

One possibility:

Maltby Pelletreau, who worked 1815-40, of Erie Canal medal fame (Pelletreau, Bennett & Cooke, 1826).

C. C. PAIGE

This has been determined to be under Boston, Mass. circa 1861 (USMT)

DOCTOR A. PERRET

HT #	Rarity	Year	Metal	Size	VG	F	VF	EF
563	R9	(?)	**	32.5mm	—	—	35.00	—

** Silvered, lead-based alloy?

DOCTOR / A. PERRET ctsp on counterfeit U.S. 1833 Bust half dollar. (Photo by Ken Hill; Koppenhaver May 25, 1998 sale, lot 226)

The good doctor certainly didn't use this as an advertising medium! More likely a pocket piece.

It seems likely this bogus half did not circulate long, so we tentatively assign the ctsp to the Hard Times period. This piece's existence is proof that half dollars were once worth counterfeiting.

PHOENIX HOUSE, B & H

HT #	Rarity	Year	Metal	Size	VG	F	VF	EF
462	R7	(1840's ?)	GS	14.4mm	—	—	400.	750.

* / PHOENIX / HOUSE / B & H / *. Rv: (Arc of 10 stars) / 5 / CENTS. Plain edge. (Rich Hartzog coll.; PCAC Nov. 1999 sale, lot 75)

This piece has every appearance of belonging in the late Hard Times era. It could be earlier.

An EF specimen fetched $770 in the 1999 auction.

W. POND

HT #	Rarity	Year	Metal	Size	F	VF	EF	Unc
463A	R9	1837	Copper	28mm	—	—	300.	

W. POND (relief, in rect. depression) ctsp on 1837 NOT ONE CENT Hard Times token. (Brunk 32 395)

Possibly William Pond, watchmaker, Boston, 1861. In business 1840?

RICH GILT

HT #	Rarity	Year	Metal	Size	VG	F	VF	EF
588	R9	(1830's ?)	Copper	29mm	—	—	40.00	—

RICH / * (Circular design) * / GILT ctsp on U.S. 1819 Large cent. (Bowers coll.)

Die trial for a button backmark, typical of the Connecticut designs of the 1830-1845 period.

J. ROTHERY

HT #	Rarity	Year	Metal	Size	VG	F	VF	EF
A464	R8	(1830's)	Copper	29mm	50.00	—	75.00	—

J. ROTHERY ctsp on U.S. 1832 and worn Large cents. (Brunk 35082)

| A464A | R9 | (1830's) | Silver | 18.5mm | 60.00 | — | 85.00 | — |

Similar ctsp on U.S. 1835 Capped Bust dime.

| A464C | R8 | (1830's) | Copper | 29mm | 50.00 | — | 75.00 | — |

CAST STEEL / J. ROTHERY ctsp on 1831 or worn U.S. Large cent. (Brunk 35083)

John Rothery was a maker of hammers in the middle 1830's, but his location has not been determined. (Barlow, 1991, page 78)

Possibilities: John Rothery, Fishkill, (Dutchess Co.), N.Y., 1840-60. Also John Rothery, North East Twsp., (Erie Co.), Pa., 1830 census.

RUHL (?)

Illustration enlarged

HT #	Rarity	Year	Metal	Size	VG	F	VF	EF
B464	R9	ND	GS	18mm	—	60.00	—	

(all incuse) NE. ... / (Eagle displayed, head turned left) / RUHL (last two letters uncertain). Plain Edge. (Dave Wilson coll.)

The upper legend might be NEW YORK. The only known specimen, first reported in Feb. 1992 is quite illegible due to erasure or wear.

In style, this piece is similar to the Wiman Coppersmith piece, Brunk 43840.

In 1830 there were Ruhle and Ruhlman families in Pa., plus one Ruhle in Baltimore. The name Ruhl appeared in the 1860 New York City census six times.

S. & C.

HT #	Rarity	Year	Metal	Size	VG	F	VF	EF
G464	R8	(?)	Silver	25mm	—	—	35.00	—

Large S & C in relief within oval depression ctsp on U.S. 1840-O Seated Liberty quarter. (Donald Miller coll.; L. Dziubek report)

The *description* matches one of the known hallmarks of Utica, N.Y. silversmith Storrs & Cooley, but we have not examined it to verify a match.

Charles Storrs and Oliver Blanchard Cooley were in business 1831-1839. A large firm, they had partners: Horace P. Bradley, David S. Rowland and Erastus C. Starin. The partnership dissolved 1839, but Cooley continued in business until 1844, so the stamp could have been used by him.

S.S.B.

HT #	Rarity	Year	Metal	Size	VG	VF	EF	Unc
464	R6	1837	Brass	19.6mm	500.	1900.	2500.	3500.
464A	R9	1837 Ctsp YK			—	2400.	—	—

In the B&M Zeddies Brand 1990 sale, an HT 464 in VF realized $2200. Another VF with digs appeared in the PCAC June 3, 2000 sale, lot 20, ex-Chester Krause coll.

HT 464 in VF-EF fetched $1870 in PCAC Nov. 1999 sale, lot 43. In Fine, a PCAC June 2000 piece brought $1320.

Weight 2.5 grams.

It has been suggested, without evidence, that S.S.B. could stand for "Scovill's Superfine Buttons." The die work and size seem to clearly indicate some connection with the button-making industry.

J A S Monogram

HT #	Rarity	Year	Metal	Size	VG	F	VF	EF
D464	R9	(?)	Copper	23mm	—	—	—	100.

Script monogram J A S in relief within rect. depression with squared-off corners, ctsp on U.S. 1835 Half cent, near-new when stamped. (Kirtley Dec. 9, 1997 sale, lot W048; realized $102.30)

The late-1997 price realized indicates the high regard in which such relief-initial counterstamps on early coins are held, even though unattributed.

J.S.

HT #	Rarity	Year	Metal	Size	VG	F	VF	EF
C464	R9	(?)	Copper	29mm	—	35.00	—	—

J . S . incuse within oval outline, ctsp on U.S. 1816 Large cent. (Kenneth Hallenbeck coll.; HT 416)

This stamp was reported to be a hallmark of Joseph Shoemaker earlier. Comparison with known Shoemaker hallmarks makes this doubtful. Shoemaker was active as a silversmith in Philadelphia from about 1793 until his death in Sept. 1829 at age 65.

Thus it is being relocated from Pennsylvania to the uncertain locale section.

W. H. SCOTT

See these ctsps under Philadelphia in HTT section.

SEE DEUTERONOMY 23: 1.2!

NOTE: This whole series probably belongs in the 1850s, but will not be removed as yet.

COPPER, 23MM

HT #	Rarity	Year	VG	F	VF	EF
465	R8	(1834-38)	—	50.00	—	80.00

SEE DEUTERO- / NOMY 23: 1.2! ctsp on U.S. Half cent. Dates examined: 1834. (Van Ormer sale 2618; Brunk 11490)

COPPER, 29MM

466	R7	(1834-38)	—	50.00	—	80.00

Similar ctsp on U.S. Large cent. Dates examined: 1831, 1833, 1843, 1851.

SILVER, 32.5MM

467	R8	(1834-38)	—	60.00	—	90.00

Similar ctsp on U.S. Capped Bust half dollar. Dates examined: 1832, 1834.

SILVER, 21MM

HT #	Rarity	Year	VG	F	VF	EF
467A	R9	(1834-38)	—	50.00	—	80.00

Similar ctsp on Spanish-American 1-real, date worn. (PCAC Dec. 1990 sale, lot 1164)

467B	R8	(1834-38)	Silver	27mm	—	60.00	—	90.00

Similar ctsp on Spanish-American 2-reales. Examined: 1778, 1794-NG. (Krueger Apr. 1991 sale, lot 1680)

The counterstamp is deep and clear and has been incused with a single punch. The Book of Deuteronomy, the fifth book of the Old Testament, sets forth the extensive laws for the Jews composed from the word of God by Moses. The passage cited is one of the Bible's less delicate — and less charitable — commandments. The standard King James version of the Bible states:

"He that is wounded in the stones, or hath his privy member cut off, shall not enter into the congregation of the Lord.

"A bastard shall not enter into the congregation of the Lord even to his tenth generation shall he not enter into the congregation of the Lord."

Just why this passage was chosen, and what viewpoint was being expressed by the counterstamper, may never be known at this distance, but we suspect shock value was a factor. The probability is that more of these counterstamped coins may be discovered and that some additional light may be shed.

The Rulau collection contains an 1831 cent with the Deuteronomy stamp, and an additional stamp in larger letters from a prepared punch: L. JEWELL. Taken alone, this might connect Jewell and the biblical passage, but the Jewell stamp alone has also been reported on cents of 1843 and 1851, proving that Mr. Jewell simply used cents for counterstamping without regard to what an earlier mutilater may have done.

The Deuteronomy citation may be connected with the religious fervor of the 1830's, which spawned among other things prohibition against alcoholic beverages — and sparked vitriolic responses from the wayward.

The oversize (32.5mm) half dollars were replaced in 1836 by smaller (31mm) half dollars containing less silver and the earlier pieces rapidly disappeared from circulation (though banks held them for many years afterward).

J.S. SIMMONS

HT #	Rarity	Year	Metal	Size	VG	F	VF	EF
468	R9	1844	Silver	25mm	—	—	45.00	—

Incused on planed-off obverse of a U.S. "no motto" quarter of about 1838-44 is: J.S. SIMMONS. / .-. / - AUG. / - 27. - / - 1844. - / * / * . 28 . * / * 72. *. Around rim is incused border of alternating dots and wavy dashes. Reeded edge. (Krause coll.)

D. TUNIS

HT #	Rarity	Year	Metal	Size	VG	F	VF	EF
555	R9	(?)	Silver	40mm	—	—	90.00	—

D. TUNIS ctsp on variety of Austrian Netherlands thaler of Vienna (A) Mint, type of 1792-97, KM 61.1, Craig 47.1. (Thoele coll.)

Possibility: Daniel Bishop Tunis, born Feb. 20, 1794, died April 24, 1865. Married Martha F. Searing on March 1, 1815. Born Morristown, N.J.

U. S. / B. / P.

HT #	Rarity	Year	Metal	Size	VG	F	VF	EF
473	R9	(?)	Copper	23mm	—	—	—	50.00

U S (incuse) / B (incuse) / P (in relief within toothed square depression) ctsp on obverse of U.S. 1835 Half cent. U S (incuse) ctsp on reverse of coin. (Henderson coll.)

U.S. government inspectors of guns, swords, etc. used similar markings. However, we are unable to pinpoint the inspector "P."

One possibility: Arms inspector N. W. Patch, active 1834-40, location uncertain.

U. S. / 20 / H.

HT #	Rarity	Year	Metal	Size	VG	F	VF	EF
474	R9	(?)	Copper	29mm			Rare	

US (in relief within oval depression)/ 20 (incuse) / H (incuse). Rv: US (in relief within oval depression) ctsp on U.S. 1803 Large cent. (J. T. Henderson coll.)

Probably an early arms inspector's stamp. The "US" marking was used in New England and elsewhere.

J. W.

HT #	Rarity	Year	Metal	Size	VG	F	VF	EF
556	R7	(?)	Copper	23mm	—	—	35.00	

Large serif J. W. in relief within dentilated oval cartouche depression, ctsp on U.S. Half cent. Examined: 1832, 1833, smoothed. 4 pcs. known. (Brunk 21330; Thoele coll.)

Hallmark of a metalsmith, not yet traced.

F. Z.

HT #	Rarity	Year	Metal	Size	VG	F	VF	EF
477	R7	(?)	Copper	23mm	—	—	65.00	

(Cross) / F. Z. ctsp on U.S. Half cent. Examined: 1809, 1825, 1832, 1834. 6 pcs. known. (PCAC July 1993 sale, lot 920; Brunk 13715)

(Eagle) (12 CTS in Shield)

HT #	Rarity	Year	Metal	Size	VG	F	VF	Unc
558	R8	(?)	xx	27mm	—	—	100.	—

xx German silver shell. Plain edge.

Shield bears: 12 / CTS. Eagle perched atop shield, head turned right. Around: 7 stars on left, 6 stars on right. Rv: Intaglio of obverse. Well made piece. (Charles Litman coll.)

It is possible this piece has a connection to Dr. Lewis Feuchtwanger.

Photo at 200%!

HT #	Rarity	Year	Metal	Size	VG	F	VF	EF
480	R8	(?)	Copper	28mm	—	75.00	—	125.

Numeral 20 ctsp above MINT on reverse of 1837 Hard Times token of 'Mint Drop' type, HT 61, Low 37. (PCAC Gold Medal sale, Dec. 1991, lot 005, where a part red AU specimen fetched $80.) 3 specimens reported.

The numeral 20 is deeply incused, with relief central parts. It must have some definite significance. In the Kirtley June 22, 1993 sale, lot L9, fetched $175.50 in Unc-MS-60!

16 in Shield

HT #	Rarity	Year	Metal	Size	VG	F	VF	EF
479	R7	(?)	Copper	23mm	—	25.00	—	45.00

Serif numeral 16 within shield-shaped cartouche ctsp incuse on U.S. Half cent. Examined: 1826, 1832, 1835 (2). Six pieces known. (James Henderson coll.)

The shield shape carries a crossbar separating the chief (top) from the base; the 16 appears in base. This has the appearance of a commercial logo.

Since three known specimens are in the Henderson collection, we assume more must exist.

1836

HT #	Rarity	Year	Metal	Size	VG	F	VF	EF
482	R9	1836	Silver	27mm	—	—	25.00	—

1836 ctsp on Spanish-American Ferdinand VII 2-reales of Mo Mint, from which rectangular cutout was taken. (Stanley Steinberg Sept. 1997 sale)

It is tempting to associate this piece with Texas' fight for independence, as Steinberg suggested, but there is no indication the stamping is American, or what the cutout indicates. This could be a Mexican piece.

(Dagger)

HT #	Rarity	Year	Metal	Size	VG	F	VF	EF
520	R9	(?)	Copper	28.5mm	—	—	35.00	—

Dagger-like device ctsp on obverse (Lafayette side) of Walsh's General Store token, HT 217. (L. B. Fauver coll.)

HT #	Rarity	Year	Metal	Size	VG	F	VF	EF
521	R9	(?)	Copper	28.5mm	—	—	35.00	—

Similar ctsp on obverse (plow side) of Walsh's General Store token, HT 216. (L. B. Fauver coll.)

(Wrapped scroll) and (Large leafy tulip)

HT #	Rarity	Year	Metal	Size	VG	F	VF	EF
519	R9	(?)	Copper	28mm	—	—	—	55.00

(Wrapped scroll) at left; (Large tulip with three leaves) at right, ctsp on 1837 Hard Times token, HT 56. (Phoenix, NO SUBSTITUTE type) obverse. (Thoele coll.)

(Leaf)

HT #	Rarity	Year	Metal	Size	VG	F	VF	EF
522	R9	(?)	Copper	28.5mm	—	—	25.00	—

Three small leaf-shaped marks ctsp on reverse (Jackson side) of Running Boar token, HT 9. (L. B. Fauver coll.)

APPENDIX I

MISCELLANEOUS TOKENS AND MEDALS

Included in this appendix are tokens which do not belong in the body of the catalog, but which resemble genuine Hard Times pieces, or on which there is some question. The listings for Eastern Railroad, Mullen, Peacock and some Doremus issues, were included in the body of the catalog in the earlier editions of this book and thus have a rightful claim to continued collector exposure.

AMERICAN INSTITUTE
New York, N.Y.

GOLD, 28MM

HT #	Rarity	Year	F	VF	EF	Unc
M1	R5	(1833-60) LOVETT	—	300.	400.	600.

M1 was awarded to Fisher & Norris for the best anvils, 1850, while M1a was awarded to Utica Screw Co. for superior wood-screws, 1847. Latter in James Henderson coll.

"Lovett" may be George Hampden Lovett rather than Robert Lovett Jr. G. H. Lovett signed the larger American Institute silver award medals.

M2	R7	(1833-38) FURST	—	—	500.	750.

Designed by Moritz Furst or G.H. Lovett, , whose signatures FURST or LOVETT are in exergue on obverse, this is the award medal which served as a model for the Robinson and Robinson-Jones cards of Attleboro, Mass. The first specimen, awarded in 1850, appeared in the 1981 NASCA sale of Hard Times tokens and related items. Weight is 16.63 grams.

HT #	Rarity	Year	Metal	Size	VG	F	VF	Unc
M3	R9	(1853-60)	Copper	28.3mm	—	—	—	1100.

As M1 (Lovett), uninscribed, struck over U.S. 1853 Large cent.
(B&M March 2000 Lindesmith sale, lot 1163)
Unpublished, and unique. In Unc. MS-63 the piece fetched $1124.13 in the 2000 sale.

E.R.R.
Boston, Mass.

BRASS, 22MM, PLAIN EDGE

HT #	Rarity	Year	VG	F	VF	EF
M9	R6	(1845-52) Check	100.	150.	200.	300.

BRASS, 22MM, OCTAGONAL

M10	R6	(1845-52) Up. Check	125.	200.	300.	500.

WHITE METAL, 24MM

M11	R8	(1845-52) Blank Rev.	—	—	—	Rare

NOTE: M11 may not exist.
Probably issued 1845-1852 period.

WM. J. MULLEN
New York, N.Y.

COPPER, 32.8MM

HT #	Rarity	Year	F	VF	EF	Unc
M17	R4	1835 Medallic	40.00	50.00	130.	300.

Bushnell in 1858 stated the dies for this piece were "cut by Lander in 1837." Later research has shown that Louisa Lander cut the dies in 1847 and the piece was struck by Charles Cushing Wright.

The latest of the three dates on the piece is 1835. The report by Miller of NY 616A, using the Mullen obverse portrait combined with a differing reverse date 1862 adds to the conclusion that this is not a Hard Times piece at all.

(See "The William J. Mullen Store Card" by R.J. Lindesmith, in the *Journal of the Token and Medal Society* for Dec. 1968.)

Louisa Lander is unknown as a medalist except for M17. She had a solid reputation as a sculptor and left a large body of work. She had studied under Thomas Crawford. She was 21 when she executed the Mullen medal.

C.D. PEACOCK
Chicago, Il.

COPPER, 31MM, PLAIN EDGE

HT #	Rarity	Year	F	VF	EF	Unc
M19	R2	1837 Peacock Hd Rt, date inside circle	—	—	20.00	75.00
M20	R7	1837 Same, Silver	—	—	—	300.

HT #	Rarity	Year	F	VF	EF	Unc
M21	R2	1837 Head Rt, date in exergue	—	—	30.00	80.00
M22	R7	1837 Same, Silver	—	—	—	300.

Specific gravity of M22 is 9.04.

HT #	Rarity	Year	F	VF	EF	Unc
M23	R2	1837 Peacock Hd Lft	—	—	20.00	75.00

HT #	Rarity	Year	F	VF	EF	Unc
M24	R9	1837 Same, Silver	—	—	—	750.

NOTE: These are not Hard Times tokens, but were struck 1900-1906.

Cards M19-20 were issued by jeweler Charles Daniel Peacock with the date 1837, in the size and style of Hard Times tokens. Peacock's Jewelers (still in 1992 one of Chicago's foremost jewelry firms) was founded by Elijah Peacock (died 1889) in 1837 and C.D. Peacock, his son, died in 1903. C.D. Peacock Jr. became the firm's head on his father's death in 1903.

Numbers M19-20 were struck by Gorham Mfg. Co. in 1900 (for the Diamond Jubilee of the firm in 1897). 10,000 in copper, only 4 in silver.

Numbers M21-22 were struck by Gorham in 1902, 7,500 in copper and 4 in silver. All the Peacock tokens measure 31mm.

Number M23 was struck by Gorham with a new obverse die in 1906, in 10,000 specimens. One copy was struck in silver proof for the firm's president in 1906. Illustration of the silver piece by Joseph Schmidt. Silver piece is marked STERLING on edge and is 4mm thick!

None of the Peacock tokens are HT issues, but they cannot easily be separated from that series by collectors. C.D. Peacock had a numismatist's desire for nostalgia.

JEREH. SMITH
Rye, England

HT #	Rarity	Year	Metal	Size	VG	F	VF	Unc
M30	R6	1835	Lead	20mm	—	35.00	—	—

Five-petaled flower above date 1835, all within central circle. Around: JEREH SMITH. Rv: Large numeral 12. (Formerly HT 469)
Jereh = Jeremiah.

This piece is now de-listed as an American token. It has been determined to be a hop picker's chit of Jeremiah Smith (1795-1864), of Rye, Kent, England. In the years 1845-52 he is said to have been the largest hop grower in the country, farming 1,000 acres. At his death, however, he was bankrupt.

Interestingly, this specific 12-bushel chit is not cataloged in the standard reference on this subject, *Hop Tokens of Kent and Sussex & Their Issuers* by Alan C. Henderson, London, 1990.

LUKE CLARKSON
Boston, England

HT #	Rarity	Year	Metal	Size	VG	F	VF	EF
M33	R8	(1830's)	Copper	34mm	—	45.00	65.00	—

LUKE / CLARKSON / BOSTON in relief within three separate toothed rect. depressions ctsp on England 1797 Cartwheel penny, KM-618. Rv: R. JACKSON ctsp incuse on reverse of the coin. (Robert Merchant coll., ex-James Curto)

Issued by Luke Clarkson of Boston, Lincolnshire, England who was married in 1822 and again in 1831. The late James Curto had considered this a Boston, Mass. stamp.

It is not known what Clarkson's trade may have been, though the marks resemble plane maker markings. Sir Charles Jackson (1921) lists only a few Lincolnshire smiths from 1155 through 1726; he states that hallmark registers are not known to exist, though Lincoln was a town authorized in 1423 to "have divers touches." Many Lincoln gold and silversmiths are thought to have gone to London to work from the 14th century onwards.

Clarkson does not appear as a watchmaker in Britten nor a pewterer in Cotterell, nor does Jackson mention him under London goldsmiths.

WHITE HOUSE HOTEL
Hulme, England
(now Manchester)

HT #	Rarity	Year	Metal	Size	VG	F	VF	EF
M35	R8	(1833)	Copper	28.4mm	50.00	100.	200.	275.

Small wood pigeon flying left above crossed halfstock sporting rifles. Around all is a thick circular laurel wreath border. Rv: WHITE HOUSE / HOTEL / HULME / (crossed laurel sprays). Plain edge. (Bangs Merwin Jan. 1863 Haines sale, lot 1571; B&M Nov. 1999 Lindesmith sale, lot 3154, ex-Cliff Edwards; Davis & Waters 123; Bell pg. 45; Jim Noble, Australia sale Aug. 1999, lot 775, ex-Baldwin 1992; *Numismatic News* for June 15, 1999, pg. 22 and for Nov. 16, 1999, pgs. 22-24; Batty 1877 catalog; Rulau Z46K; Bullowa Aug. 2000 sale, lot 307)

HT #	Rarity	Year	Metal	Size	VG	F	VF	EF
M35A	R8	(1833)	Brass	28.4mm	—	100.	200.	275.

As last, in Brass. (D&W 124; Jim Noble Aug. 1999 sale, lot 775, ex-L. Bennett 1987)

HT #	Rarity	Year	Metal	Size	VG	F	VF	EF
M36	R7	(1833)	Copper	23mm	—	—	150.	Rare

Swan in water left. Rv: WHITE HOUSE HOTEL / HULME / *. Plain edge. (Bell Lancashire 14 and 80; Batty 301C; D&W 125; Noble Aug. 1999 sale, lot 775, ex-Baldwin 1989)

The copper halfpenny (D&W 123) realized $253 on the Nov. 13, 1999 B&M sale. The three pieces (D&W 123-125) fetched A$132.25 as a single lot in the Noble Australia sale of Aug. 3-4, 1999, or a mere US$28.65 per token! Catherine Bullowa estimated her VF offering at $350 in Aug. 2000.

Batty (1877) lists a variety of the swan farthing without * as his number 130; R. C. Bell says this may not exist. Bell never saw any of the Hulme tokens listed above, copying his data from Batty, as apparently did Davis & Waters. All are rare!

Hulme does not appear as such on any atlas of Great Britain we have examined back to 1890. Batty in 1877 placed it in Lancashire. British specialist John Farquharson told the author in February, 2000, exactly why Hulme appears on no maps since 1838, and these facts were unknown to Waters, Davis and Bell, though Batty probably knew them as he was a Lancashire man.

Hulme was a sub-manor of Manchester as early as 1320, when it had 30 people. By 1838 (five years after the token issue) it had just under 1,000 population; it was incorporated into Manchester Municipal Borough 1838, and by 1870 it had become a southern slum of Manchester with about 86,267 people. The White House Hotel was built about the time the token was issued, and was demolished about 1970, and another White House Hotel built on its site near the corner of Erskine and Ely Streets (Erskine Street has since been renamed Shawheath Close). The hotel stood next to St. Gabriels Anglican Church (on the corner), and as a young man Farquharson often imbibed at "The House" as it was called; the church itself was demolished 1970.

Hulme was known as Holme in the Saxton 1579 and Speed 1610 maps of Lancashire, located then a mile southwest of Manchester. It may have been a Danish Viking settlement called Holmr (holmr being a dry island in a marsh area). Quite by coincidence, Farquharson, a Roman and Byzantine specialist, resides in Cheadle Hulme in Cheshire, which never had a hotel called White House.

D&W (pg. 60) stated, "Sharp says these were struck in 1833." Thomas Sharp was the cataloger of the Chetwynd collection.

The copper halfpenny was listed erroneously by Bangs Merwin in 1863 as American, and we repeated this attribution (with reservation) in the 2nd and 3rd editions of this reference (1997 and 1999).

FLORA GARDENS

HT #	Rarity	Year	Metal	Size	VG	F	VF	EF
M38	?	1822	Copper	22mm			Rare	

Bull's head. Rv: FLORA GARDENS / HULME / 1822. (Bell pg. 3; Batty 128; D&W 120)

R. C. Bell notes the 1822 may refer to the founding date of the gardens. The resemblance to the White House Hotel pieces of 1833 is obvious. Bell never saw this farthing token.

Davis & Waters describe the token's obverse as "A crest, leopard's head." Possibly different pieces are meant, but both authors may have been listing from inaccurate auction descriptions. Leopard and bull heads are not easily mistaken for each other.

POMOMA GARDENS

HT #	Rarity	Year	Metal	Size	VG	F	VF	EF
M40	?	ND	Copper	26mm			Rare	

Group of fruit. Around: POMOMA / GARDENS. Rv: W. & J. BEARDSLEY / POMOMA / GARDENS / CORNBROOK / HULME. (D&W 121)

HT #	Rarity	Year	Metal	Size	VG	F	VF	EF
M40A	R8	ND	White Metal 26mm				Rare	

As last, in White Metal. (D&W 122)

Probably struck 1830's. At 26mm, these were store cards only, too small for halfpenny and too large for farthing in exchange.

Special Bibliography for Hulme (Lancashire) Tokens:

Batty, D. T., "Catalogue of the Copper Coinage of Great Britain, Ireland, The British Isles and Colonies." Vol.I. (Manchester, 1868). Vol. II. (London, 1877)

Bell, R. C., "Unofficial Farthings 1820-1870." (London, 1975)

Davis, W. J. and Waters, A. W., "Tickets and Passes of Great Britain and Ireland." (London, 1922; reprinted London 1974)

Sharp, Thomas, "The Chetwynd Collection."

HARD TIMES TOKEN MAKERS & DESIGNERS

With the assistance of a good number of the world's finest numismatists, we are attempting with the following chart to attribute every Hard Times token of which we have a record to its maker. The process is fraught with opposing opinion and some admitted guesswork, but we have the advantage of complete freedom to use the eight-volume unpublished manuscript of Wesley S. Cox Sr. of Columbia, Missouri. Cox has spent years with die-evidence study backed up by enlarged photographs of letter-punches, design punches and other scientific visual aids to come to his conclusions.

Many of the same men who fashioned Hard Times tokens were buttonmakers and we are indebted to Warren K. Tice and his encyclopedic treatment of America's military buttons, their genesis and manufacture in the 18th and 19th centuries.

Other contributors to whom we owe debts of gratitude include H. Joseph Levine, Michael Hodder, George J. Fuld, Steve Hayden, Denton V. Curtis and others too numerous to mention.

So there can be no complaint about the outcome(s), in every case the final determination, after examining all the facts and opinions, has been your author's (Russ Rulau). If it's wrong, blame me, not my collaborators in this first-ever pioneering effort.

Unless specified otherwise, all token makers are located in the United States of America. The heading "Verified by Cox?" means the 8-volume Cox manuscript agrees completely with the attribution.

Only struck tokens are included in this compilation. For obvious reasons, counterstamped pieces are beyond the scope of this analysis.

HT Number	Token Designer	Token Maker	Verified by Cox?	Remarks
1-1A		Wright & Bale	Y	
2-2A		W&B	Y	
3-3A		W&B	Y	
4				
5-5A				
6-6B				
7-7A				
8				
9	E. Hulseman	Robinson's Jones	Y	
10-10A	Hulseman	RJ	Y	
11-11A	Hulseman	RJ	Y	
12-12A	Hulseman	RJ	Y	
13	Hulseman	RJ	Y	
13R				Replica
14		R. Lovett Sr.	Y	
14A		Lovett		
14B		Lovett		
14C		Lovett		
15		Bale	Y	
15B		Bale	Y	
15C		Bale	Y	
15D		Bale	Y	
15E		Bale	Y	
16	Eaves	Scovill Mfg. Co.	Y	
16A	Eaves	Scovill	Y	
17	Eaves	Scovill	Y	
18	Eaves	Scovill	Y	
19	Eaves	Scovill	Y	
20-20C	Hulseman			NYC
21	Hulseman			NYC
22-22A	Hulseman			NYC
23	Eaves	Scovill	Y	
24	J. Gibbs	Belleville Mint	Y	
25-25B	Hulseman	RJ	Y	
26-26A		Belleville	Y	
27-27A		Belleville	Y	
28-28A		Belleville	Y	
29-29A		Belleville	Y	
30-30B		Belleville	Y	
31-31B		Belleville	Y	
32		Belleville	Y	
33	Hulseman			
33A	Hulseman			NYC

HT Number	Token Designer	Token Maker	Verified by Cox?	Remarks
A33				
34-34C	Hulseman			NYC
35				
36				
37		Belleville	Y	
38				Bushnell
39				Bushnell
39A				Bushnell
40				Bushnell
40A				Bushnell
40B				Bushnell
41				Bushnell
41A				Bushnell
42		Belleville	Y	
43		Belleville	Y	
44		J. Moffet	Y	
45	Eaves	Scovill	Y	
46	Eaves	Scovill	Y	
46R	Eaves	Scovill	Y	
47	Eaves	Scovill	Y	
48	Eaves	Scovill	Y	
48A	Eaves	Scovill	Y	
49	Eaves	Scovill	Y	
50	Eaves	Scovill	Y	
51	Eaves	Scovill	Y	
52	Eaves	Scovill	Y	
53				Bushnell
53A				Bushnell
54				Bushnell
54A				Bushnell
55				Bushnell
55A				Bushnell
56	Eaves	Scovill	Y	
57	Eaves	Scovill	Y	
58-58B	Eaves	Scovill	Y	
59				Bushnell
59A				Bushnell
60				Bushnell
60A				Bushnell
61	Eaves	Scovill	Y	
62	Eaves	Scovill	Y	
63		Belleville	Y	
63A		Belleville	Y	
64	Eaves	Scovill	Y	
65	Eaves	Scovill	Y	
66	Eaves	Scovill	Y	
66A	Eaves	Scovill	Y	
67	Eaves	Scovill	Y	
67F		B. True	N	Contemp. countfeit
68	Eaves	Scovill	Y	
69	Hulseman			NYC
70	Hulseman	RJ	Y	
70A	Hulseman	RJ	Y	
71	Hulseman			NYC
72		Belleville	Y	

HT Number	Token Designer	Token Maker	Verified by Cox?	Remarks
73	Hulseman		Y	NYC
73F				Contemp. countfeit
74	Hulseman		N	Feuchtwanger
75		J. F. Thomas	Y	
75A		Thomas	Y	
75B		Thomas	Y	
76				
77-77B				
78-78A				
79	J. Gardiner		Y	
79A	Gardiner		Y	
79B	Gardiner		Y	
81		Belleville	Y	A.A.S.S.
81A		Belleville		A.A.S.S.
81B		Belleville		A.A.S.S.
81E		Belleville	Y	A.A.S.S.
81G		Belleville	Y	A.A.S.S.
82		Belleville	Y	A.A.S.S.
83		Scovill	Y	
83A		Scovill	Y	
A83		(England)		
98		Scovill	N	HuntPyn
99	Eaves	Scovill	Y	Stickney
101	Eaves	Scovill	Y	Davenport
102	Eaves	Scovill	Y	Fobes
104		Benedict	Y	B & B
105	Eaves	Scovill	Y	Scovill
106		Scovill	Y	Scovill
107	Eaves	Scovill	Y	Scovill
107A		Scovill	Y	Scovill
110		W&B	Y	Gilbert
110A		W&B	Y	Gilbert
111		W&B	Y	Morrison
115				Daquin
115A				Daquin
116				Daquin
117		B&S	Y	Folger
118	Eaves	Scovill	Y	Gasquet
119				Henderson
199A				Henderson
120		Bale	Y	HenWalt
121		Bale	Y	HW&W
121A		Bale	Y	HW&W
122	Eaves	Scovill	Y	Merle
123		Bale	Y	PuechBein
127				Valeton
128		Bale	Y	Walton
129		B&S	Y	WaltonWlr
129A		B&S	Y	WaltonWlr
132				Chapman
133				Chapman
134				Chapman
135 (note 1)		Bale	Y	Cole
135A		Bale	Y	Cole
139				Herring
147				Randall

HT Number	Token Designer	Token Maker	Verified by Cox?	Remarks
147A				Randall
148				Randall
150	Hulseman	RJ	Y	Richards
151	Hulseman	RJ	Y	Richards
152	Hulseman	RJ	Y	RJ
153	Hulseman	RJ	Y	RJ
154	Hulseman	RJ	Y	Robinson
155	Hulseman	RJ	Y	Robinson
155A	Hulseman	RJ	Y	Robinson
156	Hulseman	RJ	Y	Robinson
157	Hulseman	RJ	Y	Schenck
157C	Hulseman	RJ	Y	Schenck
158	Hulseman	RJ	Y	Schenck
158A	Hulseman	RJ	Y	Schenck
159	Hulseman	RJ	Y	Schenck
160	Hulseman	RJ	Y	Schenck
162		W&B	Y	Farnsworth
163	W. Jones	RJ		Milton
163A	W. Jones	RJ	Y	Milton
164 obv.	Hulseman	Jones Co.		Milton
164 rev.	W. Jones	Jones Co.		Milton
164A	W. Jones	Jones Co.	N	Milton
165	Hulseman	RJ	Y	Milton
166	Hulseman	RJ	Y	Milton
167	Hulseman	RJ	Y	Peck
168	Hulseman	RJ	Y	Peck
169	Hulseman		Y	Roxbury
169A	Hulseman			Roxbury
170				Rutter
171	Hulseman		Y	Willard
171A	Hulseman		Y	Willard
A171		Mitchell	N	Bunker
B171		Mitchell	N	Bunker
172	Hulseman		Y	EastBost
172A	Hulseman		Y	EastBost
174	Hulseman	RJ	Y	Wilkins
175-175A	W. Jones	RJ		Brigham
176-176A	W. Jones	RJ		Brigham
181-181B	W. Jones	Jones Co.		J. Adams
182-182A	W. Jones	Jones Co.		Crocker
187-187A		B&S	Y	HB&J
187B		B&S	Y	HB&J
188-188A		B&S	Y	B&J
192	Hulseman	RJ	Y	Haselton
193	Hulseman	RJ	Y	Smith
194	Hulseman	RJ	Y	March
195	Hulseman	RJ	Y	Sise
200		Belleville	N	Howell
201-201A		Belleville	N	Howell
202	J. Gibbs	Belleville	Y	J. Gibbs
203	J. Gibbs	Belleville	Y	I. Gibbs
204		Belleville	Y	Duseaman
204A		Belleville	Y	Duseaman
204B	J. Gibbs	Belleville	Y	Seaman
C204				Elder
205-205X				Bergen

HT Number	Token Designer	Token Maker	Verified by Cox?	Remarks
206-A206				Bergen
207		W&B	Y	Bragaw
207A		W&B	Y	Bragaw
207B		W&B	Y	Bragaw
210-210A	Bale		Y	Safford
211				Cochran
212	Eaves	Scovill	Y	Patterson
212A	Eaves	Scovill	Y	Patterson
213				Thomson
214				Thomson
215-215C				Robinson
216	Hulseman	RJ	Y	Walsh
217	Hulseman	RJ	Y	Walsh
218	Hulseman	RJ	Y	Walsh
218 adds				Elder
219	Eaves	Scovill	Y	Anderson
220		B&S	Y	Atwood
221		B&S	Y	Atwood
222-222A		B&S	Y	Atwood
223-223A		B&S	Y	Atwood
224-224A		B&S	Y	Atwood
226-226A				Bailly
227-227A		B&S	Y	B&S
228-228A		B&S	Y	B&S
229	Bale		Y	Bale
230		W&B	Y	Barker
235-235A		W&B	Y	Brewster
236-236A		Bale	Y	Brewster
239	Eaves	Scovill	Y	Centre
240	Eaves	Scovill	Y	Centre
240A				Centre
A240-B240				Clinton
241		Lovett	N	Collins
243		Moffet	Y	Crossman
244		Moffet	Y	Crossman
245-245A				Crumbie
247-247A		B&S	N	DayNewl
248		B&S	N	DayNewl
249	J. Gibbs	Belleville	Y	Dayton
250	Eaves	Scovill	Y	Deveau
251	Eaves	Scovill	Y	Deveau
252	Eaves	Scovill	Y	Deveau
253		W&B	Y	Doremus
254		W&B	Y	Doremus
254A		W&B	Y	Doremus
254B		W&B	Y	Doremus
255		W&B	Y	Doremus
256		W&B	Y	Doremus
257		W&B	Y	Doremus
A258		W&B	Y	Doremus
258		B&S	Y	Doremus
258A		B&S	Y	Doremus
258B		B&S	Y	Doremus
259-259A				Doremus
260		B&S	Y	Feuchtwngr
261		B&S	Y	Feuchtwngr

HT Number	Token Designer	Token Maker	Verified by Cox?	Remarks
262-262A		B&S	N	Feuchtwngr
263-264				Feuchtwngr
265-267A				Feuchtwngr
268-2A	**	B&S	N	F 1-cent
268-3E	**	B&S	N	F 1-cent
268-6G	**	B&S	N	F 1-cent
268-6I	**	B&S	N	F 1-cent
268 (other varieties; more study needed)				
269		W&B	Y	Field
270		W&B	Y	Field
271				FifthWrd
272	J. Gibbs	Belleville	Y	W. Gibbs
275	Eaves	Scovill	Y	Hallock
276	Eaves	Scovill	Y	Hallock
277	Eaves	Scovill	Y	HD&B
278	Bale			Hewett
279	Bale			Hewett
280-280B				Hooks
281-281B				Hooks
282	Bale	B&S	Y	Pease
282A		B&S	Y	Pease
A282		B&S	Y	Pease
283	Eaves	Scovill	Y	Jarvis
284	Eaves	Scovill	Y	Jarvis
285-285A		B&S	N	Jones
286	J. Gibbs	Belleville	Y	Law
287-287A	W. Jones	RJ		Leverett
288		Lovett	Y	Lovett
289		Moffet	Y	Maycock
290		Moffet	Y	Maycock
291	Eaves	Scovill	Y	MerchExch
292	Eaves	Scovill	Y	MerchExch
293	Eaves	Scovill	Y	MerchExch
294	Hulseman		Y	MerchExch
295		Moffet	Y	Moffet
295A		Moffet	Y	Moffet
297		Moffet	Y	Moffet
298-300		B&S	Y	NY RR
A300				NY RR
302				Parmele
303-303A				Peale
304	Eaves	Scovill	Y	Phalon
304A	Eaves	Scovill	Y	Phalon
305	Eaves	Scovill	Y	Riker
306	Eaves	Scovill	Y	Riker
307		W&B	Y	Ruggles
307A		W&B	Y	Ruggles
307B		W&B	Y	Ruggles
307D		W&B	Y	Ruggles
308		Bale	Y	Ruggles
308A		Bale	Y	Ruggles
308B		Bale	Y	Ruggles
308E		Bale	Y	Ruggles
309		B&S	N	Russell
310-310E				SansSou
311	Eaves	Scovill	Y	Smith

HT Number	Token Designer	Token Maker	Verified by Cox?	Remarks
312	Eaves	Scovill	Y	Smith
313	Eaves	Scovill	Y	Smith
314	Eaves	Scovill	Y	Smith
315	Eaves	Scovill	Y	Smith
316		Scovill	Y	Smith
317	Eaves	Scovill	Y	Smith
318-323		Bale	N	Squire
324 varieties		Bale	Y	Squire
332		Bale	Y	Suydam
332A		Bale	Y	Suydam
333-333A		B&S	Y	Suydam
334-335		Scovill	N	Sweet
336		B&S	Y	VanNostr
337		Bale	Y	Webb
337A		Bale	Y	Webb
338		Bale	Y	Webb
339		Bale	Y	Williams
340		W&B	Y	Wright/Bale
340A		W&B	Y	Wright/Bale
341		W&B	Y	Wright/Bale
342		W&B	Y	Wright/Bale
342A		W&B	Y	Wright/Bale
344-344A		W&B	Y	Henderson
345		B&S	Y	Judson
346		B&S	Y	Judson
347-347B		True	Y	Boutwell
348		Bale	Y	Bucklin
349		True	Y	Bucklin
350		True	Y	Bucklin
351		True	Y	Bucklin
352		True	Y	Bucklin
353		True	Y	Bucklin
354		True	Y	Bucklin
355		True	Y	Bucklin
356		True	Y	Bucklin
357		True	Y	Bucklin
357A		True	Y	Bucklin
357B		True	Y	Bucklin
358		True	Y	Bucklin
359		True	Y	Carpenter
360		True	Y	Carpenter
361	Hulseman	RJ	Y	Haskins
362	Hulseman	RJ	Y	Haskins
363		True	Y	Peck
364		True	Y	Peck
365		True	Y	Peck
366		True	Y	Starbuck
367		True	Y	Starbuck
368		True	Y	Starbuck
369		True	Y	Starbuck
370		True	Y	Starbuck
371		True	Y	Starbuck
372				Sibley
375		W&B	Y	Evens
375A		W&B	Y	Evens
375B		W&B	Y	Evens

HT Number	Token Designer	Token Maker	Verified by Cox?	Remarks
376		Bale	Y	Evens
376A		Bale	Y	Evens
376B		Bale	Y	Evens
376C		Bale	Y	Evens
377-379C				Loomis
380-381C				Loomis
385	Eaves	Scovill	Y	Barton
385A	Eaves	Scovill	Y	Barton
386-396		?		
399				Bender
399A				Bender
401R-401V				Bolivar
402	Eaves	Scovill	Y	Buehler
402A	Eaves	Scovill	Y	Buehler
402B	Eaves	Scovill	Y	Buehler
403-407		?		Catch
408				Feather
A408				Feather
409		R. Trested	Y	Goodyear
410	Eaves	Scovill	Y	Harvey
410A	Eaves	Scovill	Y	Harvey
411	Eaves	Scovill	Y	Harvey
E411				Nicolls
412		B&S	N	Philada
413		B&S	N	Philada
417	Eaves	Scovill	Y	SmithBro
417A	Eaves	Scovill	Y	SmithBro
A417		R. Lovett	Y	Snyder
B417		R. Lovett	Y	Snyder
C417		R. Lovett	Y	Snyder
418	Eaves	Scovill	Y	Spering
419	Hayden	Scovill	Y	SperGood
A420-B420				Thorne
E420				G.W.
421	Eaves	Scovill	Y	Watson
421A	Eaves	Scovill	Y	Watson
422	Eaves	Scovill	Y	Watson
423		Bale?	N	White
425	Hulseman	RJ	Y	Clark
427	Hulseman	RJ	Y	Handy
428	Hulseman	RJ	Y	Hathaway
428A	Husleman	RJ	Y	Hathaway
430-430A				Baker
431	Eaves	Scovill	Y	KohnDarn
433-434				Gustin
440	Eaves	Scovill	Y	Botsford
440A		Scovill	N	Botsford
441		Bale	Y	Beck
441A		Bale	Y	Beck
441B		Bale	Y	Beck
A448				Bainbrig
461-461C		Pelletreau ?		M. P.
462				Phoenix
464-464A		Scovill ?	N	S.S.B.
485-488		B&S ?		Dickson
500-510		?		SlaveTag

HT Number	Token Designer	Token Maker	Verified by Cox?	Remarks
512		R. Atmar	N	SlaveTag
512A		Atmar	N	SlaveTag
513		J. Lafar	N	SlaveTag
513A		Lafar	N	SlaveTag
513B-513G		Lafar	N	SlaveTag
514		C. PrinceN		SlaveTag
514A		C. Prince	N	SlaveTag
514B		C. Prince	N	SlaveTag
514C		C. Prince	N	SlaveTag
514D		C. Prince	N	SlaveTag
515-A515				SlaveTag
517				FreeTag
558				Eagle12
567				Ettenheim
571				Disston
577				DblGilt
580	Eaves	Scovill	Y	CW&S
580A	Eaves	Scovill	Y	CW&S
580B	Eaves	Scovill	Y	CW&S
581	Eaves	Scovill	Y	CW&S
800		J. F. Thomas		
801-801A				
802		W. M. Wagner		
803				
804		Thomas		
805				
806				
807				
808				
810-810C				
811		J. Gardiner		
811A		Gardiner		
812		Gardiner		
814		E. E. Pritchard	N	
814A		Pritchard	N	
815-815A				
817		Belleville	Y	
818	Hulseman		Y	NYC
819				
820		B&S	Y	
901-901A		W&B	Y	Doremus
902-902B		W&B	Y	Doremus
905				Astor
K1				
K2				
K3		J. Thomas	N	
K3A		Thomas	N	
K10		Thomas	N	
K11		Thomas	N	
K12				
K13				
K14				
K25	Stimpson		N	
K27				
K28	James Bale	B&S	N	
K29	James Bale	B&S	N	

HT Number	Token Designer	Token Maker	Verified by Cox?	Remarks
M1		G. H. Lovett		AmInst
M2		M. Furst		AmInst
M3		G. H. Lovett		AmInst
M9-M11				E.R.R.
M17	L. Lander	C. C. Wright		Mullen
M19-M24		Gorham		Peacock
M30		(England)		Smith
M35-M40A		(England)		Hulme

Note 1: Discovery of the original maker of the James Cole cards of Baltimore was made by Wesley Cox, working with ANS photo enlargements supplied by ANS staff. The "mintmark" is the rosette within sprays inherited by Bale's associates from Richard Trested. Trested used the device on Rulau-E NY 923 and Bale and associates on HT 135, 258 and 441. It has not previously been published.

Note 2: Lyman H. Low ascribed all the following tokens as being struck by H. M. & E. I. Richards of Attleboro, Mass.: 150, 151, 152, 153, 154, 155, 156, 157, 158, 174, 194, 195, 216, 217, 218, 361 and 425. Cox' die-study indicates all were actually struck by the Robinson's Jones or R. & W. Robinson firms of Attleboro, though the Richards firm must have distributed many of them through their jewelry outlet network. This would explain the Low (and Robert Lindesmith) findings of correspondece on sale of these tokens as late as 1839.

** Q. David Bowers does not agree with this attribution, saying he sees too little resemblance to Bale punches.

Special Abbreviations used in Hard Times Token Tables

A. A. S. S.	American Anti-Slavery Society, New York
Atmar	Ralph Atmar Jr., Charleston, S.C.
B & B	Benedict & Burnham, Waterbury, Conn.
B & S	Bale & Smith, New York
Bale	James Bale, New York
Conradt	Conradt, Philadelphia, contract diecutter to Scovill Autumn 1828-Jan. 1829
Croft	James Croft, Scovill diecutter 1821-1822
Eaves	William Eaves, Scovill diecutter Jan. 1835-Jan. 1841
Gardner	Joseph B. Gardner, Scovill diecutter ? to May 1841
Gardiner	John B. Gardiner
Hayden	Hiram Washington Hayden, Scovill diecutter 1829-1838 and 1841-1853
Hulseman	Edward Hulseman, Attleboro, Mass.
	Edward Hulseman, New York
Jones Co.	W. H. Jones & Co.
W. Jones	W. H. Jones
Lafar	John Joseph Lafar, Charleston, S.C.
Lovett	Robert Lovett Sr., New York
Moffet	James G. Moffet, New York
Pritchard	Elizur Edwin Pritchard, Waterbury, Conn. 1820-50
Prince	C. Prince, Charleston, S.C. (?)
R. J.	Robinson's Jones & Co., Attleboro, Mass.
Robinson	R. & W. Robinson, Attleboro, Mass.
Thomas	Joseph F. Thomas, Newark, N.J.
True	Benjamin C. True, Albany, N.Y.
W & B	Wright and Bale, New York
Wagner	William M. Wagner, Pa.
Wright	Charles Cushing Wright, New York

Die evidence study compiled by our colleague Wesley S. Cox suggests that we may now definitively assign most known Hard times token to a specific maker.

W. H. Jones & Co. 1835-1840

William Henry Jones, apprenticed as a diecutter in England, joined the Robinson brothers in Attleboro, Mass. in 1828, and the firm became Robinson's Jones & Co. 1828-1834. On Nov. 24, 1834 Jones sold out to his partners and formed his own button-making enterprise in Waterbury, Conn., W. H. Jones & Co.

Jones' "green shop" was located on Great Brook in Waterbury. The site had been the clockmaking factory of David Prichard, and David's son Elizur E. Prichard continued making political and sporting buttons at the site. Merrit Lane, founder of Lane Mfg. Co., was associated with Jones & Co.

W. H. Jones & Co. went bankrupt in 1840, one of many Hard Times-era firms to do so, and the factory site was taken over by George Beecher and W. H. Merriman.

Jones moved to Philadelphia in 1840, later returning to Waterbury to set up a daguerreotype studio.

Die link evidence shows William H. Jones cut the dies for many HTT's.

The Belleville Mint

The establishment known as the "Belleville Mint" in Belleville, New Jersey was in reality a combination of two separate diesinking, engraving and minting firms located together and with common goals, primarily the production of tokens, political medalets and minor coinage. The output seems confined to copper, brass and similar alloys.

The minting entity manufactured and rolled sheet brass for buttons also, but no backmarks identify them as buttonmakers. Still, they may have produced buttons for the backmarks of other distribution firms.

Minor coinage was produced at the Belleville Mint for Liberia, Brazil and San Domingo (later Dominican Republic). Tokens were made in good quantities for Canada, especially in the so-called "Bouquet Sou" series.

Gibbs, Gardner & Company and Stevens, Thomas & Fuller were the two firms involved. John Gibbs was the senior partner and primary diesinker of his firm. The other firm had at least two skilled diesinkers, J. F. Thomas of Newark (about 3 miles from Belleville) and Stevens (an Englishman who learned his trade in Birmingham in Great Britain).

John Gibbs' partner was Joseph B. Gardner.

Thomas was listed in New York City directories as a wood engraver 1832-1846, located across the river in Newark. In the *Newark Daily Advertiser* for Jan. 2, 1835 he announced: "J. F. Thomas, Die Sinker, Letter Cutter and Engraver, Mechanic St., near Broad. Dies cut for coins, medals, etc."

Joseph Conradt

There apparently were two medalists named Conradt working in Philadelphia at the same time. From Scovill Manufacturing Co., Waterbury, Conn. correspondence, we know that Godfrey Conradt did work for Scovill in the 1828-1832 period, seemingly via long distance. He did not remove to Waterbury.

Joseph Conradt is known to have distributed two of the most famous early George Washington medals. In an advertisement appearing in the *United States Gazette* for December 28, 1805, he offered the CCAUS medal in silver at $5 each and in gold at $50 each.

The CCAUS medal (Commander in Chief, Armies of the United States) is listed as Baker 57, the dies being cut by John Reich of the U.S. Mint on the order of Joseph Sansom. The 1805 advertisement gives Conradt's first name as John and occupation as a bookseller, but my colleague Dr. George Fuld recently concluded this was the same person.

Much later, Fuld states that Joseph Conradt of 170 North 4th Street, Philadelphia, engraved the 1832 Cordwainers' medal for Washington's centennial of birth. At least, the signature below the Washington bust reads: CONRADT, 170 N. FOURTH S. Cordwainer is an obsolete term for one who works in cordwainer leather, now called cordovan leather.

In the 2nd edition of *Medallic Portraits of Washington* by Dr. Fuld and your author, the engraver of the cordwainer piece, Baker 162, is given as Godfrey Conradt of the same address, who appears as an engraver in the Philadelphia directories for 1831 through 1848.

The logical conclusion to all this is that Joseph Conradt operated as a medal distributor 1805-1832 and Godfrey Conradt as an engraver 1831-1848, both from the same address. They could have been father and son, brothers or otherwise related. More research is needed, but only in the Hard Times sense because our colleague Wesley S. Cox uncovered the fact that one "Conradt" of Philadelphia engraved tokens for Scovill in that era.

James Croft

The English immigrant James Croft (1774-1837) was associated with the Scovills for a brief period, and then became employed by Benedict & Burnham, designing buttons and other metallic products for B&B until his death June 10, 1837.

In 1820 an agent of a firm in Naugatuck, Conn. was introduced in Philadelphia to Croft, who professed to have come recently from England and claimed to be able to secure the "orange tint" so much desired by American makers of brass buttons. He said he'd been employed by a Birmingham firm whose products were held in the highest rank in the American marketplace.

The agent passed this information to one of the Scovill partners, but the partner resisted the approach, saying, "We've tried English workmen enough." Croft traveled to Waterbury, Conn. anyway and the Scovills employed him. He convinced Leavenworth, Hayden & Scovill that their machinery was inferior to the British, and he was sent to England to secure these better machines and a British toolmaker. He came back with both.

Croft stayed only a year with Scovill and was lured by Aaron Benedict, LH&S' principal Waterbury competitor. Seven times Benedict sent Croft to England for tools and workmen, enabling Benedict to compete with the older Scovill enterprise (dating from 1802). In 1829 Croft was rewarded by being made a partner in the new Benedict & Coe firm.

Benedict & Coe was organized Feb. 2, 1829, capitalized at $20,000, and its partners were Aaron Benedict, Israel Coe, Bennet Bronson, Alfred Platt, Benjamin DeForest and James Croft. This firm became Benedict & Burnham, issuer of HT 104, in 1834; Waterbury Button Co. in 1849, and Waterbury Companies Inc. in 1944.

James Croft, B&B's principal designer, was born at Little Whitby, Worcestershire, England, Jan. 28, 1774. It is believed he came to America about 1818. Croft married Polly Carter and they had two children, Edward and Margaret. Edward Croft married Martha M. Packard and this union produced two sons and three daughters. (Edward Croft died Jan. 31, 1885)

William Eaves

Early in 1829, the Scovills in Waterbury, Conn. felt the need for a skilled English diecutter and they hired William Eaves of Birmingham to create dies for their button-making enterprises. He soon was creating token dies for them also. In January, 1835 they renewed the immigrant's contract for six years. Eaves left Scovill's on his contract expiration in January, 1841.

In 1842 Eaves opened his own button factory at Wolcotville, Conn. under the style William Eaves & Sons. This firm lasted until 1848.

It is now known that Eaves prepared many of the Hard Times token dies for the Scovill firm. Wesley Cox has assembled photo-evidence data to show this, some of which is included in this catalog. Eaves' style was distinctive and, usually, excellent.

Gardner

Theodore F. Marburg authored a series of articles in the 1946 issues of the *National Button Bulletin* entitled "Brass Button Making, 1802-1852, The Early History of Scovill Enterprise, Chapter 1." Marburg stated:

"In May, 1839 one Gardner, a die sinker but not a tool maker, was hired for two years at $1,000 per year." (Letter from J. M. L. Scovill to W. H. Scovill on May 8, 1839.) He agreed to come only on condition that the arrangement was agreeable to William Eaves and that there should not be any jealousy on his part. (J. M. L. Scovill to W. H. Scovill letter on May 1, 1839.)

Eaves, the British master diecutter, served the Scovills 1829-1841 at Waterbury, Conn.

This Gardner was the same Joseph B. Gardner associated with John Gibbs in the Belleville Mint in New Jersey.

There is also some confusion between Gardner and the John B. Gardiner who used the signature initials I. B. G., and who has sometimes has been erroneously referred to as Joseph B. Gardiner.

Hiram W. Hayden

We have assigned HT 419, the James Watson hardware store card of Philadelphia, to the 1841-1843 time period. This would be just before or after William Eaves left the Scovills in January, 1841.

Only the numerals on HT 419 are the Scovill style of the 1830's. The letter style of 419 is similar to that used by the Scovills on some of their tokens in the 1840's and early 1850's (for example USMT numbers NY 144, NY 572, NY 1018).

None of the ornamental devices of HT 419 appear on Scovill tokens of the 1830's. Perhaps some of these devices appear on Scovill tokens of the 1840's.

We suspect the die work of HT 419 is that of Hiram Washington Hayden. Hayden left the Scovills in 1838 to work with William H. Jones in Waterbury (the same Jones of Robinson's Jones & Co.). Hayden wanted to learn diecutting and he returned to Scovill's in 1841, probably when Eaves decided not to renew his contract with Scovill's.

Perhaps HT 419 is the first of many token dies cut by Hayden for Scovill from 1842 to 1853.

Hiram W. Hayden (1820-1904) was a long-time resident of Waterbury, Conn. and a master diesinker, embosser, inventor and daguerrian. He patented many inventions including one that revolutionized brass and copper kettlemaking, a breech loading rifle, breech loading cannon and a magazine rifle.

He also held patents and designs for buttons, medals, kerosene oil lamps and one of the first daguerreotypes put onto paper. Hayden also designed dies for a daguerreotype case with a bas relief copy of Sir Thomas Lawrence's "The Calmady Children."

Edward Hulseman

Attleboro, Mass. and New York, N.Y.

Hulseman worked as a card engraver in Attleboro, Mass. from 1833 through 1836, working for Robinson's Jones & Co., the button-makers. His and their first tokens came in the fall of 1833 — HT 70 among the politicals and HT 428 (Hathaway) and 152 and 153 (Robinson's Jones) among the store cards. Hulseman also did some work for H. M. & E. I. Richards, notably the Lafayette Standing dies (HT 150, etc.), beginning in 1834.

From 1837 through 1841 he worked as an independent card engraver at 80 Nassau Street, New York City. He also executed Hard Times tokens from the New York location, notably HT 31, 32, 73 and 81.

His 'H' signature appears under the safe on obverse of HT 69, 69A, 70, 71, 71A and 70A. The 'H' signature also appears on the Standing Lafayette type (the initial is at the right side of the ground under Lafayette's feet) used on the cards of W. P. Haskins, H. M. & E. I. Richards, Walsh's General Store and S. L. Wilkins. This Lafayette type token is said by both Low and Lindesmith to have been struck by the Richards firm, manufacturing jewelers in Attleboro, Mass., but this view is now in dispute. The Richards firm may have been merely distributors.

The standing figure of Marquis de Lafayette is from an engraving after Ary Scheffer's celebrated painting, and attained great popularity in the United States. Lafayette made a triumphant visit to America in 1825.

All Hulseman's tokens with the 'H' signature were cut in 1833-1834. After 1834 he stopped signing his token products. In 1838 the U.S. government started cracking down on manufacturers of cent-sized tokens, who were said to be impinging on the sovereign right of coinage.

Alexander C. Morin

This craftsman plied his trade as "die sinker and chaser" in Philadelphia from 1821 to 1860, making him one of America's earlier medalists and token-makers. He prepared a number of political campaign medals in the 1840's.

Anthony C. Morin, probably his son, first appears in Philadelphia directories in 1852, at the same address as Alexander. (Research courtesy H. Joseph Levine, who corrected the long-accepted views of J. Doyle DeWitt in July, 1998)

Dr. Feuchtwanger
and a Brief History of German Silver

Despite his claims to have patent rights to German silver, Dr. Lewis Feuchtwanger did not invent the alloy, but he was the first to popularize it in America.

Feuchtwanger was a German Jew, brilliant and persevering. His prolific writings do not teach us how he pronounced his own surname, but in our lengthy numismatic career (now more than 62 years) we've heard it mispronounced so badly that we digress here to point out that the careless American rendering of

FOOSHT WANG' GER cannot be the correct one. He was an educated man, and in Hochdeutsch (High German) it would be rendered more as FOIKT' VONG ER. We have no reason to suspect a separate Yiddish rendering. And if all this is too difficult to swallow, perhaps just a courteous "Doctor F" would simplify our hobby's pronunciation struggles.

The name itself has an interesting, possibly medieval, derivation. In German, feuchtwanger means "moist cheeks."

Argentine (or Argentina) was the name first applied to a newly-invented European alloy of tin and antimony, originally intended as a cheaper substitute than silver for plating base metal tableware.

Credit for the metal's development belongs to W. Hutton & Sons of Sheffield, England, the first firm to manufacture spoons and forks from Argentine, in 1833.

William Hutton (1774-1842) established his firm of silversmiths, cutlers and electroplaters in Birmingham in 1800, moving his operations to Sheffield in 1832. William Carr Hutton succeeded his father, and the business continued under several name changes until William Hutton & Sons Ltd. was absorbed by James Dixon & Sons Ltd., (founded 1806) in 1930. The latter is still in business, though reorganized in receiverships in 1976 and 1982, and now under the holding company Betashire Ltd.

The British Argentine of 1833 was not the same as that which Feuchtwanger named "American silver" in 1831 in his attempts to introduce the alloy. The British did have a similar alloy in 1833, argentan, manufactured by James C. Booth.

The metal the German doctor introduced was a silvery white alloy of copper, zinc and nickel. Names of its variations include German silver, nickel silver, "British plate," Craig silver, argentan and packfong (the latter in China). In America it was called Feuchtwanger's composition beginning in 1837 because of its promoter's monetary uses of it. It is believed he either developed, or adopted, the specific alloy of 53% copper, 29% zinc and 18% nickel.

In 1831 he opened his druggist business at 377 Broadway, where he remained until 1836. He was awarded the silver medal of the American Insitute for his new alloy in 1834, 1835 and 1836; he displayed more than 100 articles made of the silvery metal.

His claims to have invented the alloy, however, were patently false. The firm of Henninger in Berlin in the Kingdom of Prussia is believed to have been his supplier when, in1831, he imported a quantity of the alloy, being forced to pay Customs duties on it as silver since the Customs inspectors could not tell the difference.

Packfong (sometimes rendered as paktong) had been known in China for years before the 1830's. In central Germany the alloy (minus zinc) had been known for nearly 80 years before Feuchtwanger's 1831 importation, or since about 1755, called "Luhler weiss kupfer" (white copper).

Credit for the invention of German silver as the metallic alloy known in the 1830's properly belongs to Dr. E. A. Geitner, who first introduced it in use in 1812 at Hildberghasuen, Germany. Ernst August Geitner was born in 1783 at Gera, in Gera district in the principality of Reuss.

The year 1824 was, perhaps, the most important in the development of German silver, and Lewis Feuchtwanger the student was merely an observer. Geitner began to manufacture his metallic alloy, which he was then calling argentan. That same year Brandes in Berlin, capital of Prussia, began manufacturing paktong under the name "German silver."

The Henninger Brothers in Berlin began their manufacture of a variation of the alloy which they called "nickel silver," and which was recognized around the world as the best, most durable version of this copper-zinc-nickel alloy which so resembled silver.

Another German, Von Gerstdorf, was the first to produce metallic nickel industrially for use in these various alloys, though in 1824 the problem of producing nickel free of cobalt still remained.

In 1837 Dr. Feuchtwanger had plenty of competition in the preparation and sale of German silver. In the same issue of the *Evening Journal* (May 22) in which he advertised his new alloy. William Chandless, manufacturer, of 6 Clarkson Street, New York, offered German silver forks, spoons, ladles, etc., saying he'd been established in the city nearly five years and was awarded "first premium by the American Institute at their late Fair."

At the time the *New York Journal of Commerce* noted that a Middletown, Conn. firm was flourishing in the manufacture of Argentina for locks, knobs, etc. which would supersede the use of brass and prove to be "a cheap and elegant substitute for silver." (This was quoted in the July 22, 1837 issue of *Niles' Weekly Register*.)

During World War I the name German silver fell from favor for a time in favor of the more neutral "nickel silver." In numismatics the name German silver is preferred, and persists despite efforts of some world mints to suppress the term.

An advertisement of Dr. Feuchtwanger in the May 22, 1837 issue of New York's *Evening Chronicle* is very instructive:

DUE BILLS. As these are becoming generally in circulation, the subscriber will, in order to prevent counterfeiting, contract to furnish "Coins of his American Silver Composition," of the value of one shilling and upwards, or any specific value desired, to any establishment that may be disposed to contract for the same, **Dr. Lewis Feuchtwanger, 2 Courtland St.**

The "due bills" referred to were the shinplasters, worthless paper notes of small denominations such as 6 1/4 or 12 1/2 cents. Cortlandt Street was either misspelled or had its name evolve over the years.

In a May 24 followup ad in the same paper Feuchtwanger offered to "redeem them at fair value." Presumably this offer did not include the reeded edge 1-cent and 3-cent 1837-dated tokens, HT 268, 262 and 263, yet since they circulated widely, they must have possessed redemption value at some point.

The full May 24 followup ad follows:

NOTICE: To Rail Road and Steamboat Companies, Hotels, and other public establishments. The subscriber is prepared to make contracts for furnishing any establishment with Cards, representing a due bill of any value and to any amount, in his American Silver Composition, and he will engage not only to put them on very reasonable terms, but to redeem them at fair value. **Apply to Dr. Lewis Feuchtwanger, 2 Courtlandt St.**

In the ad just above, notice that Dr. F promises to redeem at "fair value" – not face value.

The only known tokens of German silver of the value of "one shilling or upwards" are HT 74, 412 and 413, respectively Feuchtwanger's 25-cent American silver pattern, Philadelphia Corporation shilling and the same entity's 50-cent piece bearing the enigmatic initials "F. S." All are of great rarity. (It has been suggested that F.S. could stand for Feuchtwanger's sample, without any evidence.)

At least some transportation companies used German silver tokens at this time, for example HT 169, 1837 Roxbury Coaches in Massachusetts; HT 172, 1837 Maverick Coaches in Massachusetts; New York & Harlaem Railroad Co. of New York City (signed by Bale & Smith).

In his as-yet-unpublished book, "A Cabinet of Fifty Numismatic Pearls," (copyright 2001), Q. David Bowers estimated that by late summer, 1837, more than one million of his German silver 1-cent tokens and a few thousand 3-cent pieces were in circulation!

Feuchtwanger petitioned Congress Sept. 13, 1837 to adapt his German silver composition for the legal U.S. cent. Sen. Thomas Hart Benton distributed cent pieces to his fellow legislators. Mint director Robert M. Patterson rejected the planned "silver penny" scheme on Jan. 4, 1838, and thereafter Feuchtwanger kept on producing more of his cent pieces for unofficial trade. There is no doubt the cents and 3-cent pieces circulated as they can be found well worn from the handling of commerce.

Bowers further opines that Dr. Feuchtwanger prepared all the cent and 3-cent blanks himself as he had rolling and blanking equipment – and that he may have actually struck the pieces himself!

While we do not support Bowers' view on the striking of tokens or preparation of dies, we do not dismiss it either. My colleague Dave Bowers has the happy facility of being right more often than being wrong about innovative numismatic ideas. New York City had a plentiful number of excellent diesinkers in 1837, and the associates of James Bale are known to have prepared Feuchtwanger's store cards (HT 260 and 261), the Evens cards of Cincinnati (HT 375 to 376C), Day Newell & Day (HT 247 and 248), and other Hard Times cards in GS.

What of Lewis Feuchtwanger, the man? He was born in Furth, Mittelfranken, Kingdom of Bavaria, of a prominent Jewish family. His mother's maiden name was Wolf. He married Augusta Levy in a ceremony in Philadelphia on August 26, 1835. Augusta Levy was older than Lewis, the daugher of Solomon Levy and Rebecca Eve Hendricks, and she had been born in New York City in 1801. Their eldest son, Oscar Uriah Feuchtwanger, was born in New York July 1, 1836. Rebecca Feuchtwanger was born in New York May 16, 1838, and then Joseph Washington Feuchtwanger, same city, Sept. 12, 1840. In Nov. 1842 Emma Feuchtwanger was born to the union, and finally Charles Feuchtwanger, on Oct. 29, 1847, when his mother was 46.

His distant kinsman, Lion Feuchtwanger, born July 7, 1884 in Munich, Germany, became a noted German novelist and playwright, who fled the Nazis in 1933 and eventually came to America. He died in 1958.

Lewis Feuchtwanger attended Heidelberg University, where he attained his doctorate in chemistry in the 1820's. In his student days he was noted as a duellist with rapier, having successfully overcome nine opponents with only one serious wound. It is not known exactly when he immigrated to New York City, but it was probably about 1829 and 1830.

It is reported that Feuchtwanger's one serious wound was inflicted by a German prince so infuriated by his opponent's ease in disposing of him that he struck as Feuchtwanger's guard was down, thus disgracing himself in those days of the "code duello." Lewis Feuchtwanger & Son did business at 42 Cedar Street in 1861, as the federal government was issuing its own copper-nickel cent coins – but of 88% copper and 12% nickel and of a yellowish cast of color, from 1857 to 1864. It is interesting to note that the 88-12 alloy adopted by the Mint was nearly the same as the "Luhler weiss kupfer" of which Director Patterson had cited Keferstein's analysis in 1837 to reject the Feuchtwanger proposal. (Keferstein found that white copper averaged 88% copper, 8.7% nickel, 1.7% iron and .6% sulphur. It was almost impossible to eliminate the trace elements in those days.)

Feuchtwanger tried once more to interest the U.S. in his German silver 3-cent piece, and caused to be struck both 1837 and 1864-dated patterns from new and sharp dies (HT 265 and 267). He submitted his proposal to the U.S. Mint on March 28, 1865. On March 30 Director James Pollock gave an instant rejection as being too expensive.

That same year, 1865, the Mint contracted with James Wharton to supply nickel for its new 75% copper 25% nickel 3-cent coins, and in 1866 a 5-cent coin of the same composition.

Thus, Dr. F "won the war of ideas but lost every battle with the Mint. There were no reparations." The quote is my own. Lewis Feuchtwanger died June 25, 1876, aged 69.

Feuchtwanger's daughters, Rebecca and Emma, then in their late Thirties, carried part of the family gem and mineral collection to Paris after their father's death, where it was stolen. About 1900 the women donated the remainder to the Society of Ethical Culture in New York City.

In the June, 1913 issue of *The Nusmismatist*, the noted token authority Edgar H. Adams wrote a six-page perspective on the life, times and achievements of this great chemist, gemologist and writer on scientific matters, who was far ahead of his times in the coinage sphere. Adams missed a great many details, but he lacked access to 21st century computers and numismatic research.

The firm of L. Feuchtwanger & Co. was still in business in 1913, at 54 Fulton St., under the direction of Albert U. Todd. The R. G. Dun directory for September, 1918 lists L. Feuchtwanger & Co. Inc. in Manhattan and with a branch at Little Ferry, N.J. The firm had disappeared well before World War II.

In Theodore Marburg's 1945 thesis on button production (see Bibliography), the Scovill entry into token-making is examined. Marburg's writings are little known in the numismiatc field, as they were never published and only some typed copies are possessed by collectors in our field.

He wrote, "The Scovill venture in the production of tokens, or counters, is of interest as showing how the enterprise adopted production to whatever the demand might call for. As early as 1829 the Scovills were supplying business houses with inscribed medals, bearing the name of the business house and some slogan ("label") that were stamped with a die and lacquered. (They) may have served this function and were made already in 1829."

To prove the 1829 date, Marburg quotes from a letter from James Carrington to J. M. L. and W. H. Scovill dated July 22, 1829.

He added, "These passed at first primarily as business cards or political campaign (items) or as souvenirs, and their use increased in the early 1830's." (R. Mattison & Co. letter to Scovill, Nov. 12, 1834).

"With respect to cost, we observe in a letter of Curtis & Hand to Scovill, June 16, 1836, that a customer 'is to allow for the cost of the die, say $15, and pay at the rate of $25 per thousand for the counters.' The fact that they were in especial demand for use in the West suggests, however, that they may have passed as currency at some points as early as 1834."

Marburg notes there was a great amount of currency passed which was of dubious value and in 1830 the use of paper notes was general, even for denominations less than $5. In the 1830's specie started selling at a pemium and the smaller metallic currency which was in existence was hoarded or melted down because of the value of the metal in the coins exceeding face value – Gresham's Law in full effect.

Mid-1830's Token Production and Use as Currency

With Gresham's Law (Bad money drives the good from circulation) and hoarding begun, well before the Panic of 1837, subsidiary small coins became scarce and the only currency passed consisted of depreciated notes and the so-called "shin plasters" for denominations such as 6 1/4 and 12 1/2 cents.

Marburg said, "It was in a situation of this sort, during the later 1830's, that the Scovill medals came to circulate as money and the concern manufactured considerable quantities of these for sale (J. Chamberlin letter to Scovill, Oct. 2, 1837), or else minted to order for others (Curtis & Hand letter to Scovill, June 16, 1836). Some patriotic inscriptions and the words NOT ONE CENT FOR TRIBUTE appeared on them (Thompson letter to Scovill, Oct. 3, 1838).

"Because of their use as coins, the Scovills got into trouble. Toward the end of 1837 J. M. L. Scovill reported that the brokers handling such tokens might be prosecuted by a (federal) district attorney and he advised, "You might as well hold on for a few days and see what the turn will take."

In a letter from J. M. L. to W. H. Scovill discovered by Marburg, dated Nov. 27, 1837, the partner wrote in part: "I find all the small papers are not against the better paper currency and are asking the district attorney for Wall Street to make an example of some of the brokers. I think all we have on hand will sell in a few days. On the whole, I have concluded you might as well hold on for a few days and see what happens. I will stay here un-til Wednesday morning and will arrange to deliver whatever may come by tomorrow's boat."

One week later the Scovill still in New York wrote that "the government officials are (threatening) dealers in copper counters." As a consequence of the fear that developed in the beginning of December, 1837, the price of the counters fell and the agent reported that he has "been offered them at 50 cents per 100" (J. Chamberlin letter to Scovill, Dec. 3, 1837). Chamberlin evidently thought this price so low that Scovill's might wish to buy back some of the tokens (or "counters" as he called them).

In 1839, the grand jury of the United States district court for Connecticut issued a bill against Scovill's for issuing such tokens, which it claimed was tantamount to the issuance of a currency.

The history of counter manufacture is interestingly presented in an article by E. H. Davis in the *Scovill Bulletin* for Oct., 1926, pages 13-14. In William James' paper "History of Waterbury and the Naugatuck Valley" (1912, vol. 1, page 106) the date of 1842 is given as the time when "issue was halted by the government."

Contemporary Comments

Newspaper editors at this time and even for years afterward found this subject of tokens passing as coins an interesting subject for editorial comment, especially as the Scovills were known to be Whigs while the personnel of the courts were adherents of the radical wing of the party of Andrew Jackson .

Amusing, balanced editorials are preserved in the *Litchfield Enquirer* for Oct. 25, 1837, and the *Waterbury American* for April 25, 1846.

Nothing stopped the Scovill token production in the 1830's. In 1839, J. M. L. Scovill observed that "a competitor was stamping Canada Nova Scotia tokens and Southern coins at 35 cents a pound" (J. M. L. to W. H. Scovill letter, April 4, 1839).

As a consequence the contract with a diesinker, hired that year, was drawn to provide that Scovill's receive the "profits of such medals as he made in his spare time." The manufacture of such medals as "business cards" did, of course, also continue. It is interesting to note that such tokens were made by Scovill's for their New York City store after 1846.

In the 1850's tokens were produced for business firms and some were minted with Spanish inscriptions, counters for export to Central or South America (J. M. L. Scovill to Mallory letter, March 26, 1851).

Scovill-struck tokens are known for Cuba, Mexico, Costa Rica, Colombia, Guatemala (see *Latin American Tokens*, Iola, Wis., 2000).

Late in the 1840's the Scovill's were careful to refuse to mint tokens with a human head on one side and an eagle on the other. This self-imposed limitation was a result of legal advice they received. But their manufacture of daguerreotype plates caused them to throw caution to the wind and starting about 1848-50 they were turning out thousands of Coronet Liberty-and-Eagle Displayed imitations of U.S. $10 and $5 gold pieces, even gilding them to make them appear more like the real thing. Large buyers of their daguerreotype plates evidently received the tokens at minimum cost, if any, with the distributors' business names carefully added in place of the government legends.

Marburg Did His Research Well

Wesley S. Cox, who unearthed the 1945 Marburg thesis, on which he'd begun work in 1942, summed up some of the thesis' conclusions.

Cox writes, "I find it more than coincidential that the first Scovill correspondence cited by Marburg related to tokens as being in July, 1829, the same month the master diesinker William Eaves arrived in Waterbury from England. The Scovill's did not know they had secured Eaves' services as a diesinker until his arrival."

I suspect the Scovill's did not 'push' tokens and medalets until they knew they had a full-time engraver, and probably entered the token-making business simply to have more work than just cutting button dies. This would keep a full-time diesinker always occupied.

"I also find interesting that the letter of July, 1829 was from James Carrington. Is he a forerunner of the Carrington of Co. of New York City which issued Miller number NY 144 to 147A tokens that state "established 1851"? My study of the Carrington & Co. tokens suggests NY 144 was the work of one of the Lovetts, but it's not impossible that the earlier Carringon had a token struck which is now unrecognized as such, or that he distributed tokens for others.

"Had it not been for the massive fire in the spring of 1830 at the Scovill Waterbury works, there probably would be more tokens prepared by Scovill's in the 1830's. As it turned out, Scovill's lost what token business there was in the early 1830's to the Wright & Bale group in New York and the Kettle factory in England. The 1834 correspondence suggest some of the "West" tokens of New Orleans and Alabama were being bid upon in 1834-35 – at least letters were being written.

"The letters found by Marburg also suggest that the Scovill button agents in New York and Philadelphia were involved in the sale of tokens during the Hard Times period.

"This was a normal Scovill procedure with a new product, whether it be tokens, gilt buttons, sheet brass, butt hinges or daguerreotype plates. The button agents handled the first sales, took care of complaints and sent recommendations to remedy problems, along with customer wants and comments. Afterward, separate agents and dealers were established for each product.

"The Connecticut grand jury information is the same as that found by Eric P. Newman, except that Theodore F. Marburg located it 60 years ago. The 'competitor' mentioned by Lamson Scovill in 1839 sounds like John Gibbs and the 'Belleville boys.'

"I gather from studying the manuscript that Marburg knew little to nothing of merchant or satirical tokens, many of which had a human face and an eagle. The self-imposed Scovill device rule must have been abandoned about 1848."

From an "academic history" page in his thesis, we learn a little about the man. Theodore Francis Marburg was born in New York City on Jan. 12, 1914. He received his BA degree from Antioch College in 1936 and his MA degree from Clark University in 1937.

He was an instructor at Worcester Polytechnich Institute in 1939 and then at the University of Nebraska 1939-42. In 1942 he was on leave from the University of Nebraska for the duration of the war but did not go into uniform, instead being with the U.S. Bureau of Labor Statistics. Marburg's doctoral thesis was defended and accepted in 1942 and he copyrighted it in 1945.

Marburg died April 21, 1989 at Portland, Oregon.

The Scovill Lineage

Using all sources, your author (Russ Rulau) has outlined the Scovill lineage and antecedents. We are especially grateful to Warren K. Tice and Wesley S. Cox for their input. Scovill's undoubtedly produced the largest quantities of Hard Times tokens and campaign medalets.

Grilley Brothers (1800-1802). Silas, Henry and Samuel Grilley, of French Huguenot extraction, were among the first buttonmakers in Waterbury, Conn. They produced hard white pewter buttons finished by lathe in 1800.

Abel Porter & Co. (1802-1811). Partnership of Abel Porter, Levi Porter, Daniel Clark and Silas Grilley produced stamped brass as well as pewter buttons. David Hayden of Attleboro, Mass. joined in 1808, but Silas Grilley withdrew in 1809.

Lamson & Scovill (1810-1820). William King Lamson and James Scovill Jr. produced woolens in the War of 1812 and began manufacturing metal buttons for the army in 1813. Lamson withdrew and moved to Berwick, Pa. in 1820.

Leavenworth, Hayden & Scovill (1811-1827). James Mitchell Lamson Scovill partnered with David Hayden (of the Abel Porter firm) and Frederick Leavenworth. J. M. L. Scovill, son of James Scovill of the Lamson & Scovill firm, was always known as "Lamson Scovill" and served as sergeant major of the 26th regiment of Connecticut militia in the War of 1812. James Croft of England was hired in 1821. This firm was able to compete for metal button business with British firms on an equal footing and was the real precursor of the Scovill hegemony over the American brass industry.

J. M. L. & W. H. Scovill (1827-1840). James Mitchell Lamson Scovill and William Henry Scovill, brothers, each owned a half interest in this firm which succeeded LH&S. They hired the best talent they could find, such as Hiram Washington Hayden, William Eaves, Gardner and others, and added token and medalet production to their buttonmaking about July, 1829.

Scovills & Co. (1840-1850). Brass hardware was added to the Scovill line in 1840 as the brothers brought in their brother-in-law John Buckingham, who had been a militia captain in the War of 1812. Added as partners where their sister's Elizabeth's son Scovill Merrill Buckingham and the wealthy Abram Ives. By 1845 Scovill's were producing most of the daguerreotype plates made in America. The Scovill's invested heavily in Michigan copper mines to assure a source of the metal.

Scovill Manufacturing Co. (1850-ca1970). A corporate structure was adopted in 1850. Millions of brass buttons and small cent-sized tokens were produced during the Civil War, as well as the casings for Gault's patent encased postage stamps. In both World Wars Scovill's supplied blanks for the U.S. government, and they struck some coinage and tokens for foreign governments and Latin American plantations. The brass works were closed about 1970 and the sprawling Waterbury complex itself was razed in 1995 to make room for a shopping center.

APPENDIX III

THE COX SYSTEM OF DIE EVIDENCE

In the following pages the users of this reference may examine the methodology devised by Wesley S. Cox, Sr. to determine the makers of Hard Times tokens.

Starting with a plentiful supply of <u>signed</u> or otherwise origin-known tokens, he used photographic enlargements to study and catalog each letter, numeral and device appearing on these pieces. Then he matched these features against those used on unsigned and previously-undetermined products of various diesinkers.

Since many of the token-makers were also manufacturers of metal buttons fashionable in that era, he was able to use comparisons in the button field with its multiplicity of "backmark" signatures.

In the process, Cox uncovered much new data on who cut dies, who struck tokens, when pieces were made, and some background on the craftsmen involved. He showed that many long-held theories on origins were wrong.

His work is contained in eight thick three-ring binders in possession of your author, but for obvious reasons of space we can illustrate only a tiny sample of Cox' investigative efforts.

HT 1 OBVERSE

HT 1 (LOW 1)
METAL: COPPER
DIAMETER: 27.0mm
       Diagonally reeded
MASS: 5.727 grams
DIE AXIS: 12:00 (Medal alignment)

7X SIZE
ANS IMAGE
 # 0000.999.30374

HT 1 REVERSE

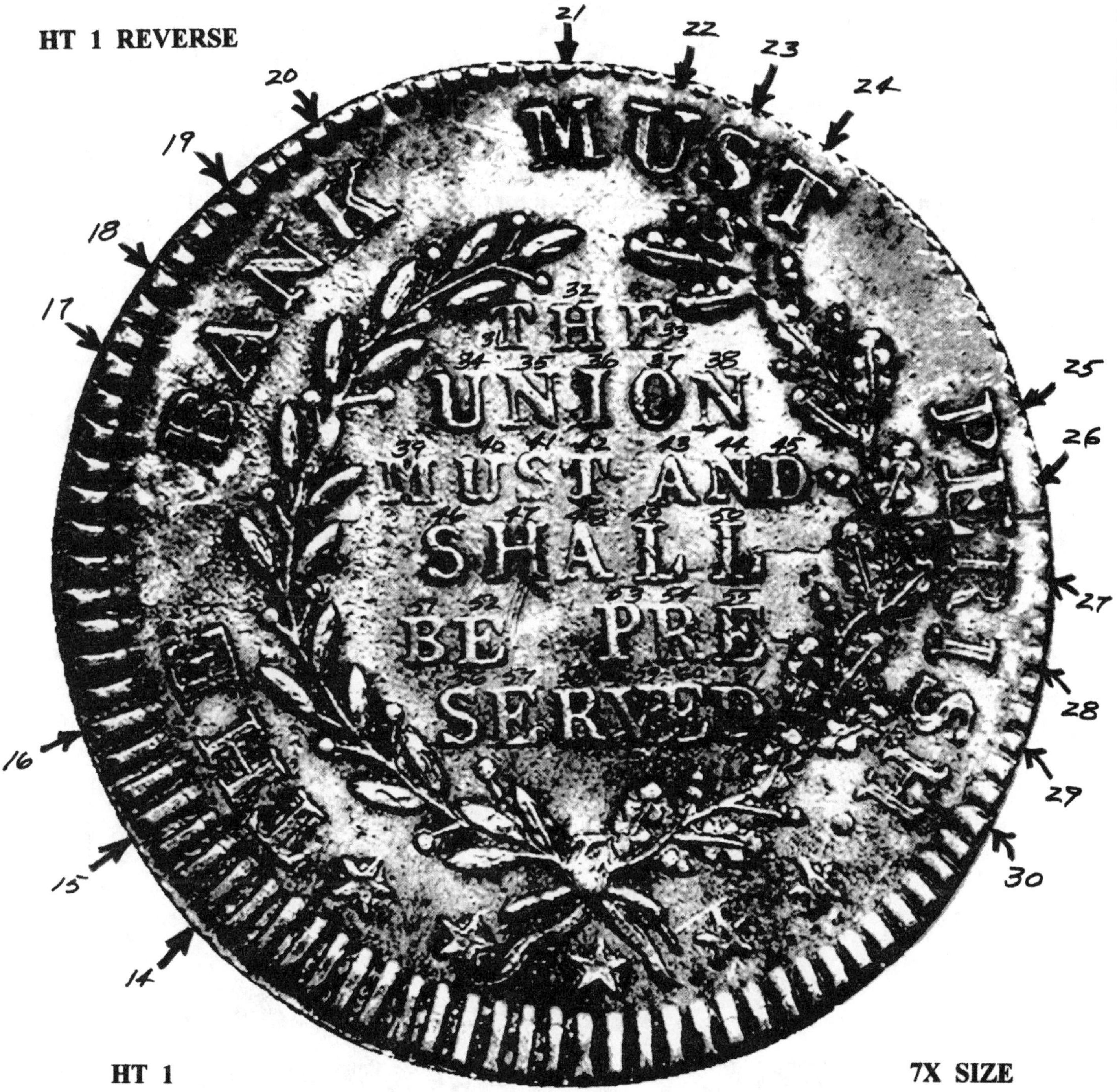

HT 1

7X SIZE

ANS NOTES

HT.1, 0000.999.30374, copper, 5.727.27.0 diagonally reeded (the reeds point to 11:00 and 5:00, when the edge is viewed head-on with the coin horizontal), no collar. This token is the Society's only specimen of HT.1, and it is sharper than the following token, which is our only specimen of HT.2 an our only other example of this type.

HT.2, 0000.999.30381, copper, 5.438, 26.8, diagonally reeded (the reeds point to 11:00 and 5:00, when the edge is viewed head-on with the coin horizontal), no collar.

BALE DEVICE "E"

Wright and Bale used this leaf punch on the Washington obverse of HT 344 (Rulau-E NY 1017). They also used this leaf on the reverse die of HT 1 thru 3A. Raised center vein is a second, separate punch.

COMPARISON OF DIE DEVICES OF HT 344 AND HT 1

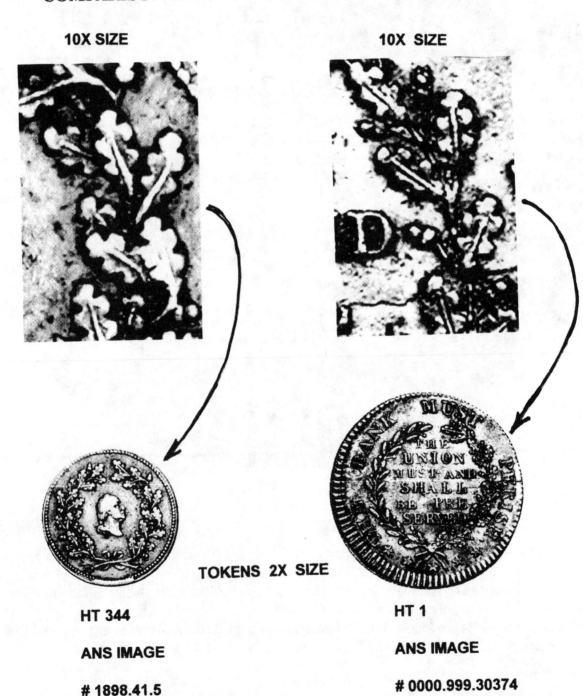

10X SIZE   10X SIZE

TOKENS 2X SIZE

HT 344   HT 1

ANS IMAGE   ANS IMAGE

1898.41.5   # 0000.999.30374

SCOVILL E PLURIBUS UNUM SCROLLS (OBVERSE)

ALL IMAGES 10X SIZE

HT 23

HT 284

HT 45

HT 45 OBVERSE DIE'S ORDER OF USE
(determined by left asterisk deterioration)

HT 23
HT 284
HT 45

HT 23

HT 284

HT 45

ALL IMAGES 10X SIZE
EXCEPT TOKEN 2X

HT 73 (Low 49)   **7X SIZE**

Diesinker: Edward Hulseman

Metal: Copper

Mass: 5.24 grams   **Specific gravity: 8.71**

Coin alignment

Mass of U.S.A. half cent coin (1800-57): 5.44 grams

HT 73 Reverse　　　　　　　　　　**7X SIZE**

HT 73 OBVERSE AND REVERSE LETTERS 10X SIZE

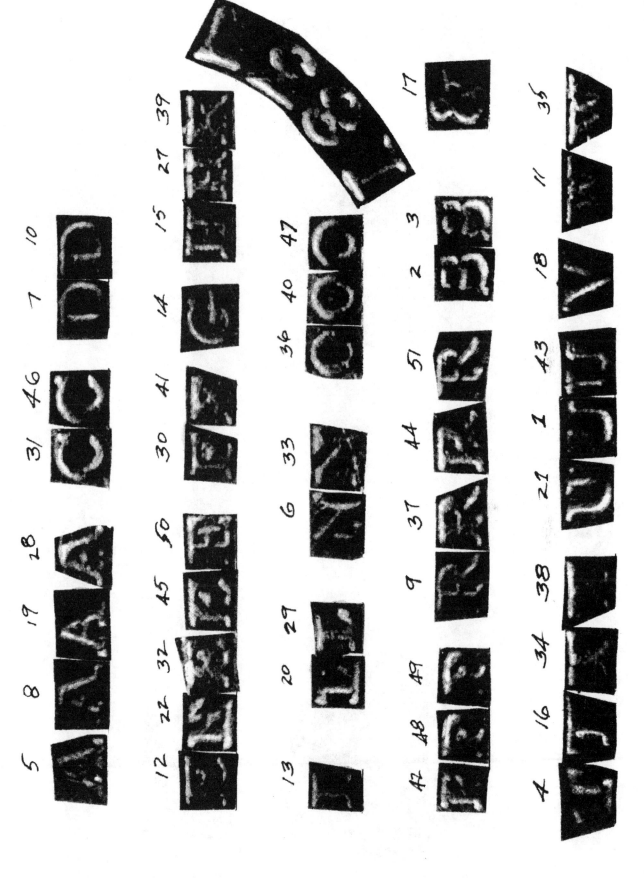

HT 99 AND 99A DEVICES

HT 99

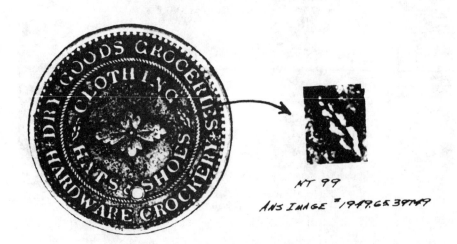

HT 99

HT 135   **7X SIZE**

Diesinker: James Bale   **ANS Image # 1891.3.6**

Metal: Copper   **Diameter: 23.5mm**
Mass: 4.429 grams   **Axis: 12:00, Medal alignment**
**ANS description: Thin piece, edge smooth except for crack in
    fabric in plane of the specimen, as if perhaps it were
    struck on a laminated flan.**

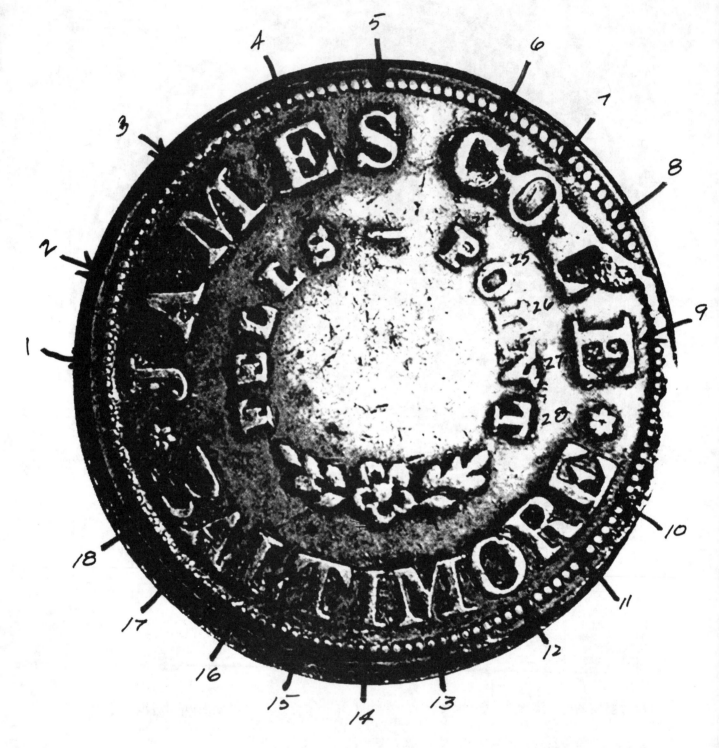

HT 135

Diesinker: James Bale

7X SIZE

ANS Image # 1891.3.6

HT 260

ANS Image # 1898.45

Wright & Bale

Same Reverse Die

HT 261

ANS Image # 1898.46

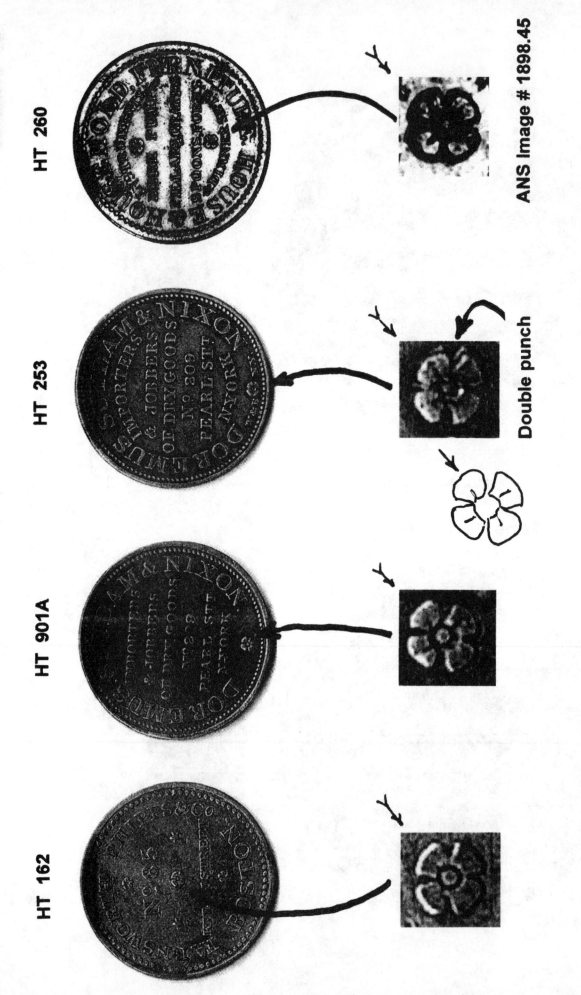

HT 260

HT 253

HT 901A

HT 162

ANS Image # 1898.45

Double punch

Token images 2X size
Bale rosette device "C" images 10X size
Small arrows denote device orientation
Device "C" also appears on HT 901, HT 111, HT 117
Dies of HT 901 similar yet differing from HT 901A dies

L. G. IRVING / J. S. PEASE TOKEN OF
NEW YORK AND ST. LOUIS

HT 282

ANS IMAGE

1898.47

IMAGES 3X SIZE

METAL: Brass

DIAMETER: 27.3mm

Plain edge, no collar

MASS: 6.791 grams

DIE AXIS: 12:00 (medal alignment)

MOFFETT EAGLE HEADS

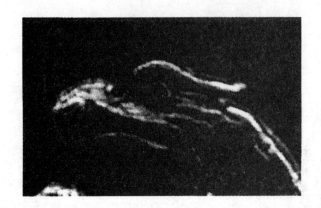

HT 244 HENRY CROSSMAN

HT 295 JAMES G. MOFFET

HT 297 JAMES G. MOFFET

ALL IMAGES 10X SIZE

HT 295

7X SIZE

METAL: Copper

Medal alignment

DIAMETER: 29.0mm

MASS: 9.75 grams

Plain edge

SPECIFIC GRAVITY: 8.85

HT 295   **7X SIZE**

HT 295 OBVERSE AND REVERSE LETTERS

10X SIZE

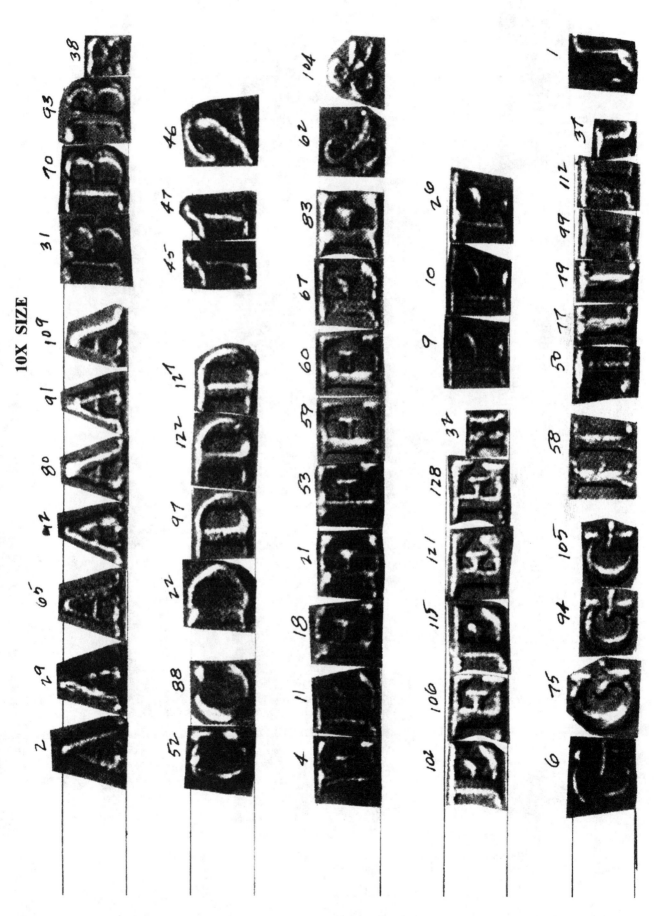

HT 295 LETTERING CONTINUED

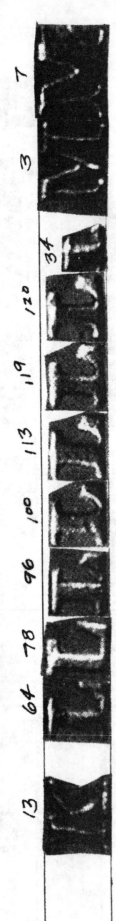

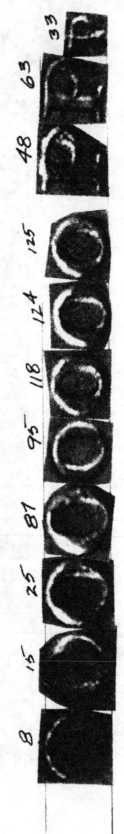

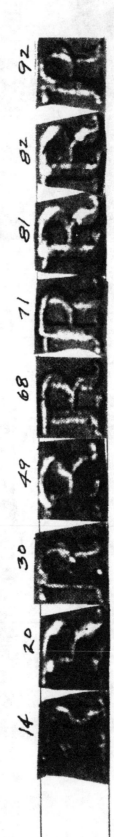

10X SIZE

HT 295   OBVERSE & REVERSE LETTERING AND DEVICES
SYMPTOMATIC OF MOFFET DIESINKING

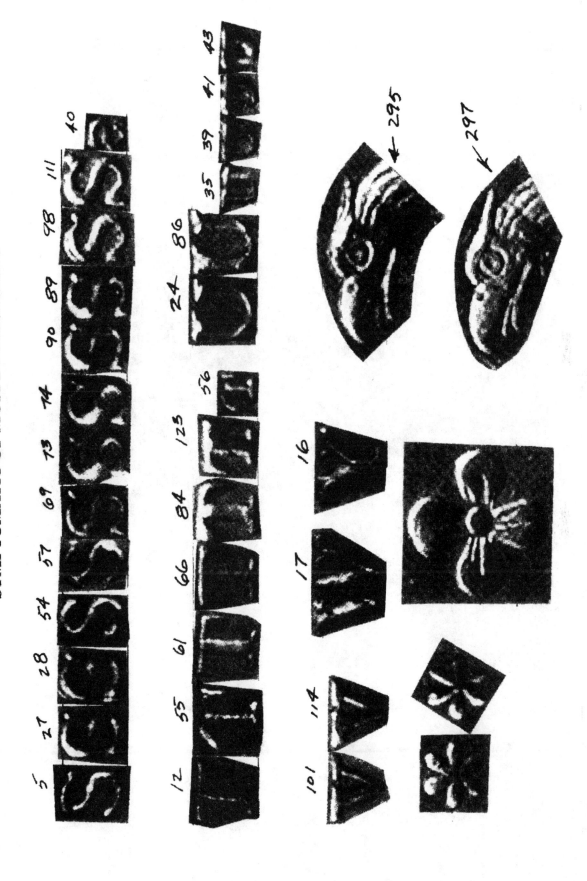

HT 295 AND 297 E PLURIBUS UNUM SCROLL CLOSE-UPS

10X SIZE

Was there another letter first
punched under the "B's" ?

Funny looking "E's" almost "H's" or "M's"

HT 295

HT 297

More like an "I" than an "L". HT 296 PLUBIBUS may exist!

ALL IMAGES 10X SIZE

HT 811 OBVERSE

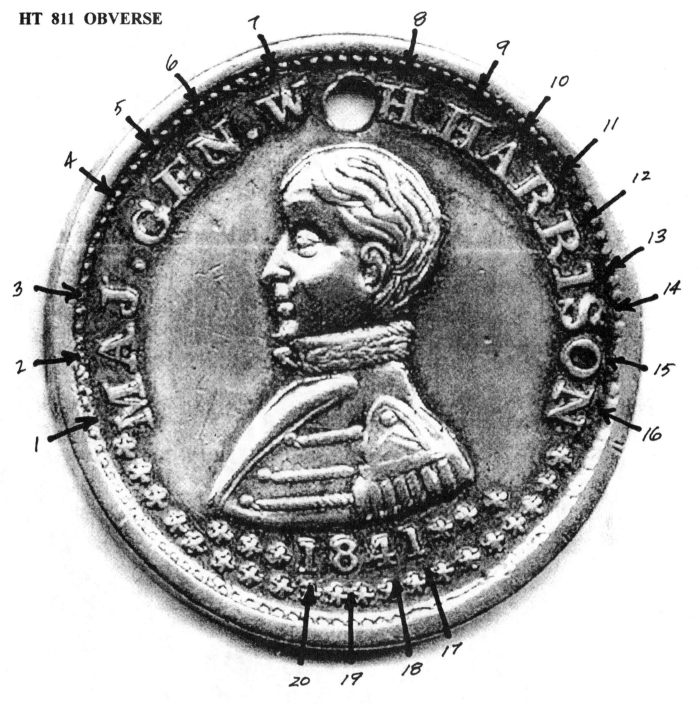

HT 811 (WHH 1840-28)　　　　　**7X SIZE**

METAL: GILT COPPER

DIAMETER: 25.6mm

SPECIFIC GRAVITY: 8.74

Medal alignment

HT 811 REVERSE

HT 811

7X SIZE

HT 811 Obverse and Reverse Letters, 10X SIZE

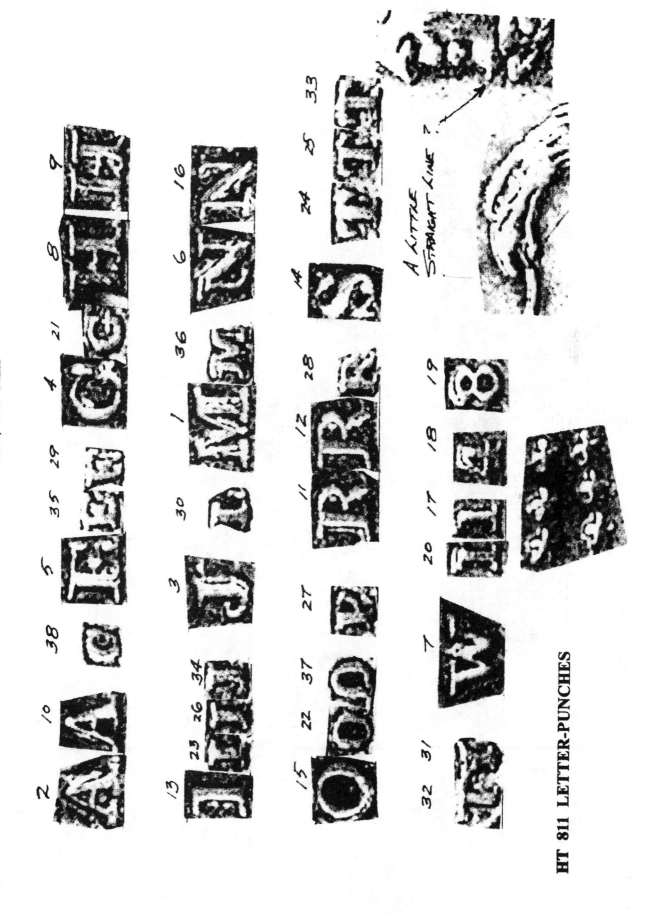

A LITTLE STRAIGHT LINE?

HT 811 LETTER-PUNCHES

HT 811 AND HT 79 LETTERS 10X SIZE

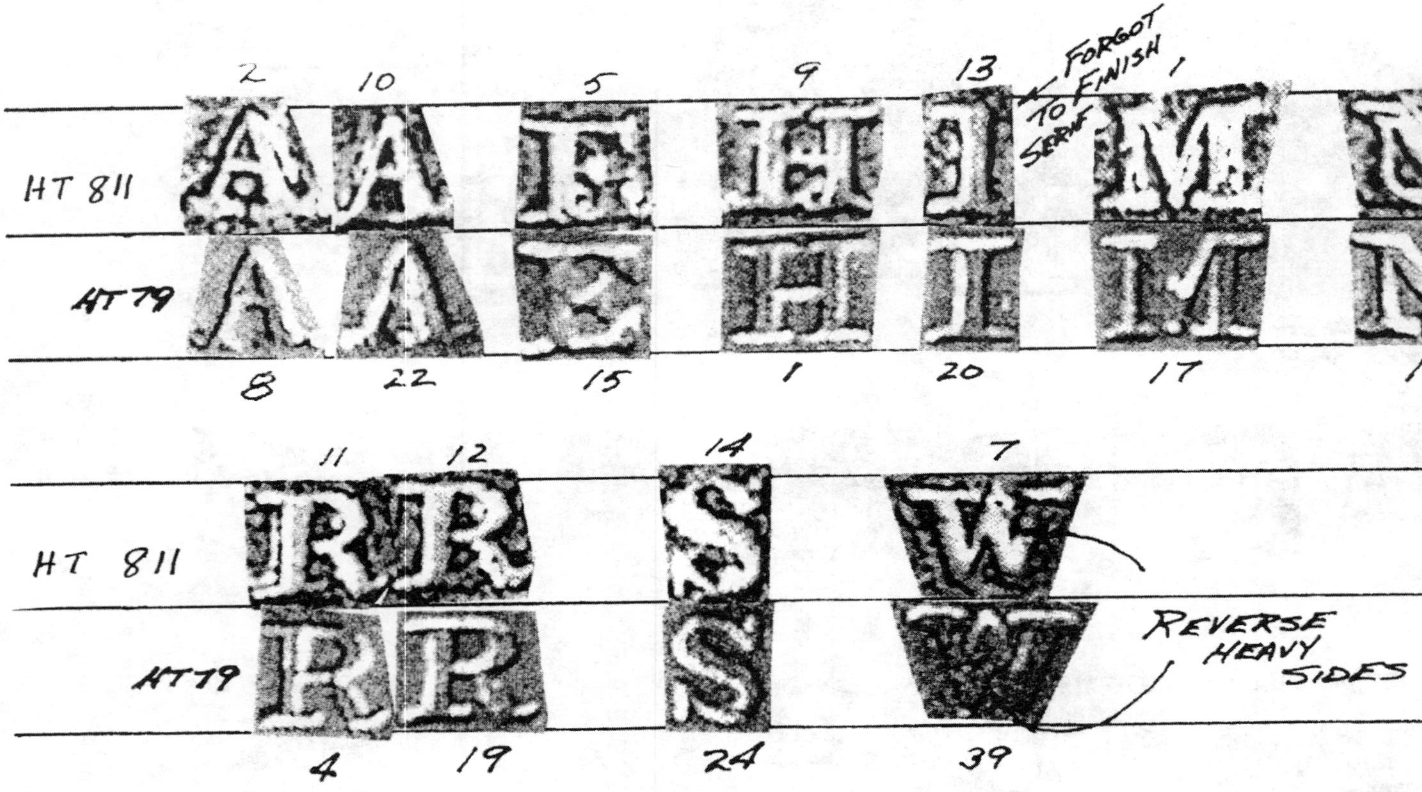
2
10
5
9
13
FORGOT TO FINISH SERIF
1
6
16
HT 811
HT 79
8
22
15
1
20
17
11
23
11
12
14
7
HT 811
HT 79
REVERSE HEAVY SIDES
4
19
24
39

HT 811 LETTER-PUNCHES CONTINUED

HT 818 OBVERSE

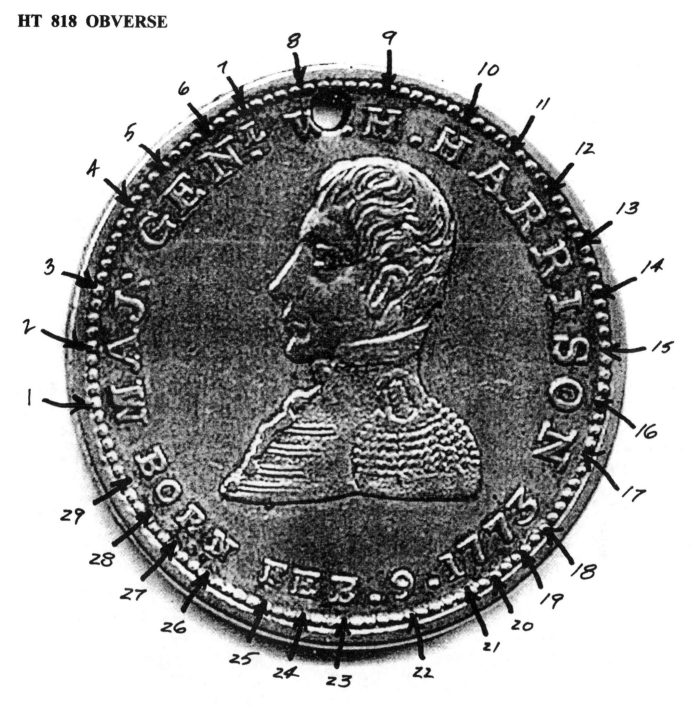

HT 818

7X SIZE

METAL: GILT BRASS

DIAMETER: 23.1mm
          Plain edge

MASS: 4.45 grams

SPECIFIC GRAVITY: 8.59

Medal alignment

HT 818 REVERSE

HT 818   7X SIZE

HT 818 LETTER-PUNCHES

HT 818 (WHH 1840-55) Obverse and Reverse Letters 10X SIZE

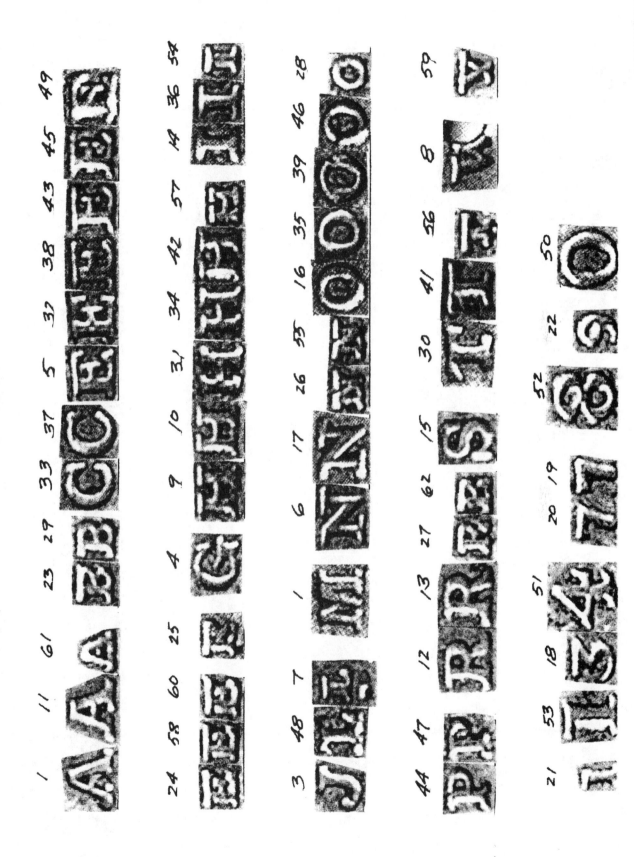

FIRST DIE STATE OF SCOVILL (WATERBURY, CONN.)
LIBERTY HEADS USED ON HARD TIMES TOKENS
AND STORE CARDS

In the following pages, 7-times enlargements (mislabeled 10X) show the first die states discovered by Wesley S. Cox for Liberty Head obverses used by the Scovill manufactory in Waterbury, Connecticut. Progressive die wear produced variations in each case, such as the famous HT 46R which appears to result in the date "1857" instead of "1837."

While the Cox manuscript illustrates many facets of die wear, up to eight states in one case, we felt we could not devote space in this reference to more than a sampling of his photographic enlargements, preferring the first (and "best") die states so that students of the series may understand the nuances of differences Cox determined in various dies.

We are grateful to the American Numismatic Society's digital imaging processes for several of these illustrations for our own enlargement purposes.

HT 23   10X SIZE

SCOVILL FIRST DIE STATE

DIE USED ON HT 23, HT 45, HT 284

HT 47   10X SIZE

SCOVILL FIRST DIE STATE

DIE USED ON HT 47, HT 48, HT 240, HT 283

HT 62

10X SIZE

SCOVILL FIRST DIE STATE

DIE USED ON HT 49, HT 50, HT 51, HT 52, HT 61, HT 62, HT 65, HT 239

HT 68   10X SIZE

SCOVILL FIRST DIE STATE

DIE USED ON HT 58, HT 64, HT 68

HT 46R **10X SIZE**

SCOVILL LATE DIE STATE

This is a very late state of the HT 46 obverse die. The "M" of
UNUM has become a mere blob, the second "U" of UNUM
almost unrecognizable, the "E" misshapen and the "L" also
misshapen. Most important, the "3" o ̧f the date has filled to
the point where it appears to be 1857. Census shows this HT
46R is much more common than at first thought.

HT 47 REVERSE   **10X SIZE**

SCOVILL FIRST DIE STATE

Apparent order of die usage:

HT 47, HT 17, HT 46, HT 46R, HT 291, HT 49, HT 50

APPENDIX IV

SOME OUTSIZE CAMPAIGN MEDALS

(MVB)

HT #	Rarity	Year	Metal	Size	VG	F	VF	EF
K1	R6	1841	WM	38mm	—	100.	150.	200.

Bust left. Around: ***** MARTIN VAN BUREN **** / & DEMOC-RACY. Rv: Flying eagle carries balance scales in its beak. Scale at left bears FEDERAL(ISM) and at right has DEMOC(RACY) out-weighing that at left. Between the scales: MARCH 4 / 1841. Around: OUR PRINCIPLES ARE JUSTICE / *** & EQUALITY ***. Plain edge. (DeWitt MVB 1840-1; Satterlee 49; Hayden 1038)

March 4, 1841 would have been Van Buren's inaugural date had he been reelected.

HT #	Rarity	Year	Metal	Size	VG	F	VF	EF
K2	R6	(1836)	WM	36.6mm	—	—	400.	600.

Similar to HT 78A, in larger (dollar) size, and struck in finer detail. Eagle perches atop Temple of Liberty. Plain edge. (DeWitt MVB 1836-1; Satterlee 48; Bushnell 12; Kirtley Oct. 1989 sale, lot 1100; McSorley 10)

A holed AU specimen in the 1998 McSorley sale made $1210!

HT #	Rarity	Year	Metal	Size	F	VF	EF	AU
K3	R6	(1840)	WM	37mm	—	—	525.	615.

Bust left. Around: MARTIN VAN BUREN / ***** & DEMOCRACY ****. Rv: Eagle perched atop cage-like Temple of Liberty. Around: A UNIFORM & SOUND CURRENCY / THE SUB / *** TREASURY ***. Plain edge. (DeWitt MVB 1840-2; Satterlee 50; PCAC March 1999 sale, lot 295, fetched $517 in holed AU; McSorley 31 fetched $605 in holed AU)

HT #	Rarity	Year	Metal	Size				
K3A	R5	(1840)	Brass	37mm				

As last, but struck in Brass.

Struck by Joseph F. Thomas, Newark, N.J.

H. Joseph Levine posits that early catalogers describe the reverse as an eagle escaping a cage, even though the "cage" is labeled LIBERTY. A Paul Revere woodcut depicts an eagle and empty cage.

(WHH)

The Temple of Liberty on HT K2 is unlabeled and clearly shows a temple, with statue inside its four support posts.

HT #	Rarity	Year	Metal	Size	VG	F	VF	EF
K10	R6	(1840)	WM	37mm	—	—	—	200.

Military bust left, tiny I. F. T. on base of bust. Around: MAJ. GEN. W.H. HARRISON / BORN FEB 9 1773. Rv: Log cabin, cider barrel and tree at left, flag flying right atop. Around: THE . PEOPLES . CHOICE / THE HERO / OF / TIPPECANOE. Plain edge. (DeWitt WHH 1840-13; Satterlee 75; PCAC Emrich sale of Dec. 1977; Kirtley Oct. 21, 1989 sale, lot 1101)

HT #	Rarity	Year	Metal	Size	VG	F	VF	EF
K11	R6	(1840)	WM	37mm	—	—	—	200.

Similar to preceding, but flag flies to left and a smoking chimney has been added. (WHH 1840-14; Kirtley Oct. 1989 sale, lot 1102)

Joseph F. Thomas (I. F. T.) struck the last two tokens in Newark, N.J. The University of Hartford, Conn. collection contains a bronzed example of WHH 1840-14.

These tokens, as well as HT 801 of Martin Van Buren, were much too large to circulate as cents, which measured 29mm in the 1836-40 period, but could have passed as dollars (38.1mm). Anecdotal evidence that they did is not available, but these pieces are known well circulated.

HT #	Rarity	Year	Metal	Size	VG	F	VF	EF
K12	R6	(1840)	WM	37.2mm	—	—	—	300.

Large military bust left. Around: MAJ. GEN. W. H. HARRISON / (semicircle of 26 stars). Rv: Edge-on view of log cabin; file of nine soldiers at left. Around: THE PEOPLES CHOICE / THE / HERO OF TIPPECANOE. Plain edge. (DeWitt WHH 1840-18; Satterlee 76 1/2; McSorley 21 fetched $286 in holed AU)

HT #	Rarity	Year	Metal	Size	VG	F	VF	EF
K13	R6	(1840)	WM	37mm	—	—	—	200.

Smaller bust left, inscription similar. Rv: As last, but file of six soldiers at left. In exergue: THE HERO / OF / TIPPECANOE. Plain edge. (DeWitt WHH 1840-19; Satterlee 77; McSorley 22 in holed AU realized $173.80)

HT #	Rarity	Year	Metal	Size	VG	F	VF	EF
K14	R6	(1840)	WM	34.8mm	—	—	—	275.

Similar to last, but differing even smaller bust, and stars are replaced by: BORN. FEB. 9. 1778 (sic!). Rv: Similar to last, but file of four soldiers at left. Plain edge. (DeWitt WHH 1840-20; Bushnell 25; McSorley 23 in holed AU fetched $264; Zaffern coll.)

The 1778 date on the last medal above should have been 1773. Comparison of letter punches reveals that the last three medals were designed by the same person, but that craftsman's identity is not known.

HT #	Rarity	Year	Metal	Size	F	VF	EF	Unc
K14A	?	(1840)	Pewter	34.8mm	—	—	Scarce	—

As K14, but struck in Pewter rather than White Metal. Probably silvered before striking. Plain edge. (Zaffern coll.)

HT #	Rarity	Year	Metal	Size	F	VF	EF	Unc
K25	R6	(1860)	CN	39mm	—	—	55.00	—

Small, ugly civil bust right. Around: HONOR WHERE HONOR'S DUE / GEN WILLIAM H. HARRISON / TO THE HERO OF TIPPECANOE. Rv: Bunker Hill obelisk. Around: BUNKER. HILL. / A NATION'S GRATITUDE. Plain edge. (DeWitt WHH 1840-7; Satterlee 77 1/2; Kirtley Sept. 3, 1994 sale, lot 2627, fetched $45.10 in cleaned AU)

Originals were struck in 1840 from dies cut by Stimpson, for the Bunker Hill Fair of Sept. 8 that year. The originals were in White Metal. (Also see HT A171 and B171 under Charlestown, Mass.)

In 1860 the dies were used to make the following restrikes: 11 in silver, 26 in copper, 36 in cupronickel, 11 in brass and 26 in white metal. Blank reverse restrikes are also known.

The Battle of Tippecanoe

With infinite care and patience the Shawnee Indian chief Tecumseh (1768-1813) wove together a great confederacy of Indian tribes stretching from the Great Lakes to Georgia, including much of today's Midwest, with the goal of creating an Indian nation to prevent the Americans from expanding westward. By 1811 his confederacy was in being in the Northwest. In the autumn of 1811 he traveled south to enroll the Creeks and other tribes of the southeast.

William Henry Harrison, military governor of Indiana Territory, had been provoking the confederated Indians to battle, and during Tecumseh's absence he attacked Tecumseh's "capital", Prophetstown (50 miles south of Chicago). The Battle of Tippecanoe Creek took place Nov. 8, 1811 between Harrison's 1,000 regulars and militia and the Indians under Tenskwatawa ("The Prophet"), Tecumseh's brother.

The Americans suffered 61 killed and 127 wounded against 36 Indians killed and 70 wounded, but the Indians lost their nerve and abandoned their base. When Tecumseh returned in early 1812, he found all cohesion had gone out of his movement and he allied himself with the British, bringing his Indian force of 2,000 braves to Detroit.

(H C)

HT #	Rarity	Year	Metal	Size	VG	F	VF	EF
K27	(?)	1844	Copper	26mm	—	—	60.00	—

Toga-clad bust left, HENRY at left, CLAY at right, all within circle of 26 stars, with border of small pellets near edge. Rv: Arc of 13 stars above shield bearing fouled anchor with HOPE in upper gap of the circular wreath. (DeWitt HC 1844-28)

This token, most likely struck 10 years or more after 1844, also is known in silver, brass, white metal and lead. The reverse was the obverse of a 12-design series of tokens depicting hunting scenes called "Rhode Island tokens."

Despite its date, it could not have served as a currency piece in 1844.

HT #	Rarity	Year	Metal	Size	VG	F	VF	EF
K28	R8	1845	WM	21.5m	—	—	—	525.

Small bust right within oak wreath. Around: PRESIDENT HENRY CLAY / 1845. Rv: UNITED / WE STAND / (clasped hands) / DIVIDED / WE FALL. amid flourishes. Plain edge. (DeWitt HC 1844-41; Satterlee 164; Bushnell 42; McSorley 53)

Excessively rare token, missing from most of the great collections. The McSorley specimen, in holed prooflike AU, realized $533.50 in 1998.

Charles McSorley ascribed the diesinking on this piece to James Bale of New York City. Though bearing the 1845 date, these were struck in 1844 for Whig operatives who hoped to see Clay inaugurated the next year.

This medalet and its fellows which follow would be too small to serve even as Half cents in change. The need for small change also had dissipated by 1844.

HT #	Rarity	Year	Metal	Size	VG	F	VF	EF
K29	R7	1845	WM	21.5mm	—	—	50.00	—

Obverse as last. Rv: Eagle displayed with U.S. shield on its breast, radiant. Foul anchor below. Around: UNITED STATES OF AMERICA. Plain edge. (DeWitt HC 1844-39; Satterlee 162; Bushnell 41)

A variation of the above medalet, DeWitt HC 1844-40, with larger bust (McSorley 52) fetched $49.50 in holed VF in the 1998 sale. Dies were cut for both varieties by James Bale.

NOTES WITH TIES TO TOKENS

CENTRE MARKET
New York, N.Y.

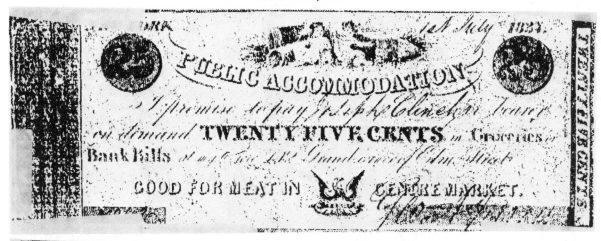

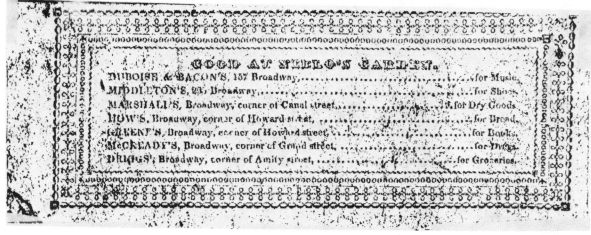

HT #	Date	Denomination	Size	VF
N1	July 1, 1837	25 Cents	158x60mm	300.

Only one specimen known.

NEW YORK JOINT STOCK EXCHANGE COMPANY
New York, N.Y.

HT #	Date	Denomination	Size	VG
N3	1837	12-1/2 Cents	158x75mm	500.

N4	1837	25 Cents	167x75mm	650.

HT #	Date	Denomination	Size	VG
N4A	1837	50 Cents	—	750.

HT N4 fetched $651.25 in Stack's March 2001 auction, lot 2306.

VALENTINE
New York, N.Y.

HT #	Date	Denomination	Size	EF
N AA4	1837	12-1/2 Cents	84x42mm	50.00

Black print on thin white watermarked paper. Uniface. (Peter Mayer coll.)

HT #	Date	Denomination	Size	EF
N A4	1837	50 Cents	86x43mm	50.00

"Sold at Valentines 50 John St". Black print on thin white watermarked paper, with blank reverse. This is one of the notes referred to in the introduction to the Hard Times section under TOKEN DESIGNS, first recorded by Lyman Low in the 1880's. Unissued remainders, such as that shown, are quoted in price; issued notes, completed in ink, would command higher prices. (Dave Wilson coll.)

HT #	Date	Denomination	Size	EF
N B4	1837	75 Cents	97x61mm	50.00

Black print on thin white watermarked paper. Uniface. (Peter Mayer coll.)

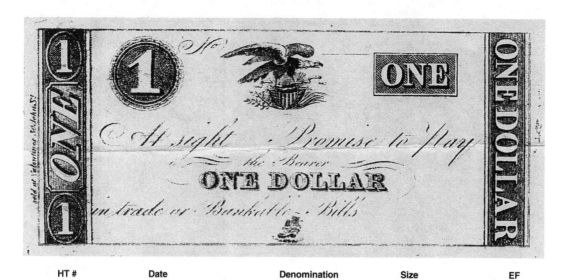

HT #	Date	Denomination	Size	EF
N C4	ND	$1	138x69mm	130.

Black print on thin white paper. Uniface. (Peter Mayer coll.)

Only a single specimen of N C4 has been reported.

WINSLOW Stock Scrip

New York, N.Y.

HT #	Date	Denomination	Size	VF-EF
F4	(1837)	6 1/4 Cents	—	70.00

No description available. (R. M. Smythe March 2, 2001 sale, lot 2347)

HT #	Date	Denomination	Size	VF-EF
N G4	(1837)	12 1/2 Cents	—	70.00

(Smythe 2347)

HT #	Date	Denomination	Size	VF-EF
N H4	(1837)	37 1/2 Cents	—	85.00

Two seated females amid scenes of manufacturing and agriculture. At either side, large: 37 1/2 / Cents. Below: THIRTY SEVEN & HALF CENTS / in Current Bank Notes. Imprint: Winslow, 6 Little Creek. Unissued remainder. Rarity 7. (Smythe March 2001 sale, lot 2347)

These mockeries of currency had fancy printing, and were sold to anyone who wanted them. Issued (signed) notes, if any survive, would be worth more than quoted valuations, which are based on the 2001 paper money auction.

HOWELL WORKS CO.

Allaire, N.J.

HT #	Date	Denomination	Size	EF
N5	18—	6-1/4 Cents	—	75.00

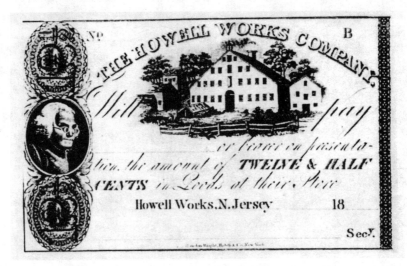

HT #	Date	Denomination	Size	EF
N5A	18—	12-1/2 Cents	100x62mm	75.00
N5B	18—	25 Cents	—	100.
N5C	18—	50 Cents	—	100.
N6	18—	$1	—	100.

N6A	18—	$2	154x66mm	125.
N6B	18—	$3	—	125.
N6C	18—	$5	—	150.

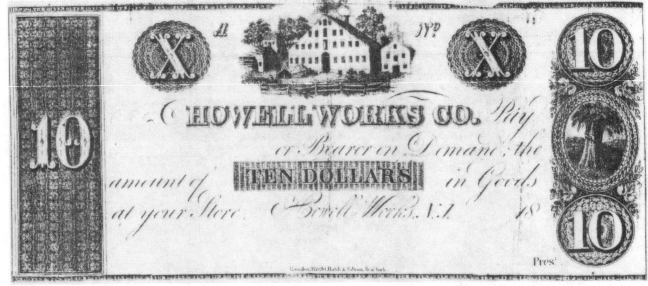

N6D	18—	$10	174x73mm	150.

HT #	Date	Denomination	Size	EF
N6E	18—	Sheet of 4 notes	3-3-5-10	800.
N6F	18—	Sheet of 8 notes	—	2000.

N6E fetched $2,000 in the Feb. 4, 1993 William Christensen sale.

The depiction of buildings on the Howell Works Company notes is, presumably, that of the manufacturing facility itself. Depictions of Benjamin Franklin, sheaf of wheat and numeral guilloches are from the extensive stock devices of the printers, Rawdon, Wright, Hatch & Edson of New York.

CAUTION! Some of these notes have been reprinted, seemingly from original plates, thus holding down their price for many years. Actual signed, dated issued notes would command a premium over values quoted here.

BERGEN IRON WORKS
Lakewood, N.J.

HT #	Date	Denomination	Size	VF
N7	February, 1840	25 Cents	165x71mm	600.
N7A	(believed to exist)	50 Cents	—	—
N7B	(believed to exist)	$1	—	—

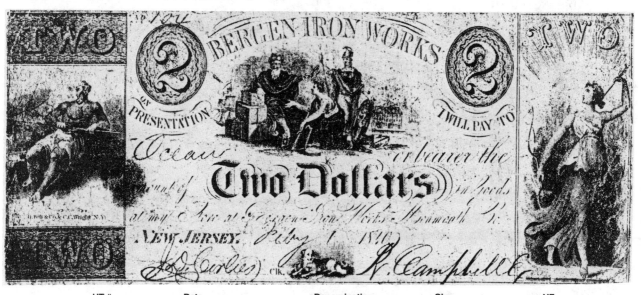

HT #	Date	Denomination	Size	VF
N7C	February, 1840	$2	171x71mm	600.

A beautiful series of Bergen Iron Works notes was printed by Danforth, Bald & Co. of New York and Philadelphia, bearing the printed date March 1, 1851. These obligations were drawn on The Ocean Bank of Ocean County, N.J. Central devices include a sailor, rolling mill scene, ships near harbor, and ships-and-shells. These notes, even as unissued remainders, are quite rare but not included here as they postdate the Hard Times period by seven years. Known notes are in $1, $2, $5 and $10 denominations.

CITY OF NEW ORLEANS
Municipality No. One

NOTE: All Louisiana notes, N8 thru N8Q, are snown at 75% normal size!

HT #	Date	Denomination	Size	UNC
N 8	1838	$4	—	90.00

Full length Washington statue at left. Man seated on grain at center. (Criswell C450)

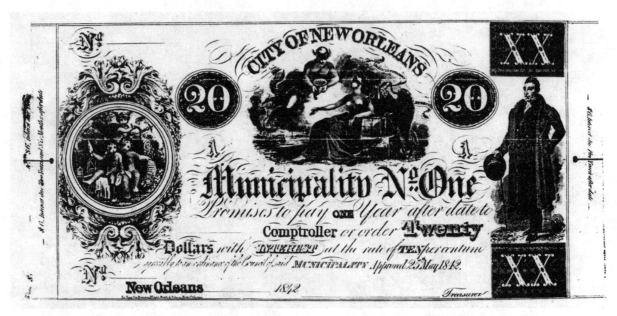

N 8A	May 25, 1842	$20	210x115mm	60.00

Black print on face. Three cherubs at left, Mercury and female at center, Lafayette standing at right. Bright orange reverse. Engraved by Rawdon Wright Hatch & Edson, New Orleans. (Criswell C-468; Rulau coll.)

N8A was a promissory note to pay principal plus 10% interest per annum.

A specimen of HT N8A in EF appeared in the Smythe June 16, 2000 sale in lot 1191, where it was estimated at $37 to $64.

The Lafayette portrait by Ary Scheffer used on many Hard Times tokens is seen in full on N8A.

N 8B	October 30, 1837	$50	228x99mm	60.00

Black and brown print on face. Female at either side, huge 4-story building at center. Light blue and brown reverse. Engraved by Jno. V. Childs, New Orleans. (Criswell C-483; Rulau coll.)

N 8C	May 25, 1842	$50	—	50.00

Similar to 8B, but Indian in canoe at center. (Criswell C-478)

N8B carried 6% annual interest, while N8C promised 10% per annum. Both notes, and others in this series, are known stamped PAID in used condition. These are generally valued at about the Unc. prices given above, as almost all Unc. pieces are unissued remainders. An issued note, not stamped PAID, carries a 10% or more premium.

HT #	Date	Denomination	Size	UNC
N 8E	October 30, 1837	$100	214x100mm	55.00

Black and light brown printing on face. Washington statue at left, horseman lassooing steer at center, female and eagle at right. Engraved by Curtiul & Curley (?). Green reverse. (Criswell C-496; Rulau coll.)

| N 8F | 1843 | $100 | — | 60.00 |

Similar to 8E. Engraved by Rawdon Wright Hatch & Edson, New Orleans. (Criswell C-508)

| N 8G | October 30, 1837 | $200 | — | 125. |

Female at left, City Square in center, Napoleon-like statue at right. Brick red reverse. Engraved by J.V. Childs, New Orleans.   (Criswell C-521)

CITY OF NEW ORLEANS

Municipality No. Two

HT #	Date	Denomination	Size	VF
N 8J	Dec. 21, 1829	12 1/2 Cents	—	70.00

Paddlewheeler steamships at either side of large ornate 12 1/2 circle. (Criswell C-581)

| N 8K | Dec. 2, 1839 | 50 Cents | — | 70.00 |

Horse. (Smythe 1911 in G-VG, estimated at $50)

| N 8L | — | $3 | — | 70.00 |

Series C. (Smythe 1911 in VG repaired, estimated at $40)

| N 8LA | Due 1847 | $100 | — | 85.00 |

(Smythe 1191 in AU stained, holed, estimated at $60)

June, 2000 Smythe sale of lot 1191 exceeded expectations. Municipality No. 2 notes are avidly sought by collectors.

| N 8M | August 26, 1842 | $3333.33 | 208x91mm | 400. |

Black printing. Paddlewheeler steamship amid large floreate guilloche at left, pelican feeding its young at center. "Issued under resolution of 20 March 1838." Blank reverse is endorsed twice. Printed by Greene's Lithography, 53 Magazine St., New Orleans. Ex. rare. (Rulau coll.)

Numbered New Orleans Municipalities

The terms "Municipality No. 1" and "Municipality No. 2" on the New Orleans notes of the Hard Times period require explanation.

By 1840 New Orleans had become the fourth largest city in the United States, and it rivaled and in some aspects surpassed New York City as the nation's busiest port.

In 1836 the city was divided into three separately governed municipalities (numbers 1, 2 and 3), each with the power to issue obligations to fund its governmental functions. This division of municipal responsibility came about due to the conflicts which arose in the period after 1803 when the U.S. purchased Louisiana Territory from France, and immigrants from England, Germany, Ireland and other nations, plus a flood of Americans from the east, dramatically changed the demographics of the old French and Spanish city.

The Creoles, the old French aristocracy and other French and Spanish settlers, welcomed the influx of money but resented the brash newcomers who brought it. The city officially reunited in 1852. (The reunion didn't end the squabbling, but at least it made for a better-governed city corporation.)

EXCHANGE AND BANKING HOUSE
Jas. Robb & Geo. K. Lee
New Orleans, La.

HT #	Date	Denomination	Size	VF
N 8Q	April 5, 1847	$115.58	195x91mm	40.00

Black printing. Classic female head left in oval at center. Second of exchange, signed by James Robb Co. Reverse blank. Endorsed across face of this bill of exchange. (Rulau coll.)

New Orleans was hit particularly hard in the financial crises of 1837, 1839 and 1841, as many of the "cotton banks" which failed were located there.

Bills of exchange were normally issued in triplicate, the first copy retained by the shipper, the second accompanying the merchandise being the principal (paid) copy, and the third of exchange retained by the recipient. Occasionally a third of exchange is found as the paid copy. New Orleans was a major import-export center for Europe, South America and the eastern United States.

The Bank of James Robb in 1857-1859 issued $5, $10, $20, $50 and $100 notes printed by Rawdon Wright Hatch & Edson. In 1859 the bank became the (2nd) Merchants' Bank, which closed in 1879.

D. FELT & CO. STOCK DESIGN BILL OF EXCHANGE
New Orleans, La.

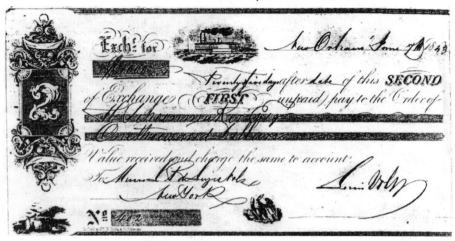

Photo reduced!

HT #	Date	Denomination	Size	VF
N 8R	1843	$1,000	220x112mm	125.

Black printing on thin high-grade white paper.

Paddlewheel steamer under way left in top center vignette. Floreate large numeral 2 within ornate cartouche at left. Dated at New Orleans June 7, 1843, payable 25 days after date, a Second of Exchange to H. Schounma Ker, Esq. and drawn on a New York entity. Imprint reads: D. Felt & Co N. York & N. Orleans. (Ronnir P. Talbot coll.)

This is a typical example of the stock-design bills of exchange used in New Orleans during the Hard Times period. The city had largely recovered from its depressionary period by the summer of 1843.

The payer need only enter in ink the date, term of payment, amount, payee, on whom drawn, number of the note, and his signature. In the note illustrated above, the Second of Exchange is the paid copy, the First unpaid. (No Third of Exchange is mentioned).

ABM. BELL & CO.
New York, N.Y.

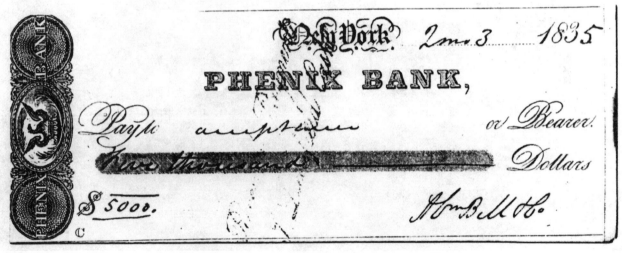

HT #	Date	Denomination	Size	VF
N A8	1835	$5,000	165x64mm	125.

Check printed in very light greyish-tan on rough white paper stock. The printed portions read: PHENIX (phoenix rising from flames) BANK vertically in left-end guilloche / New York (Gothic script) (space) 183 / PHENIX BANK (large shaded letters) / Pay to (space) or Bearer / (shaded wide oval) Dollars / $ (space) / C (open letter, perhaps a series letter or a form of imprint).

The ink-script portion reads: 2mo 3 183 (printed) 5 / acceptances / Five thousand _____ / $ (printed) 5000. (signature) Abm Bell $& Co. An almost illegible two-line endorsement is handwritten in ink across the face of the check diagonally right, the last word of line 1 being Payment and the last word of line 2 being Cashr. Rv: Blank. (Rulau coll.)

HT #	Date	Denomination	Size	VF
N A8B	1835	$5,098.75	165x64mm	85.00

Check very similar to N A8 except date is 2mo 12 1835, denomination changes, and item is both cut-canceled and cancelled by large wide light red ink cross across face. (Rulau coll.)

Whatever Bell's business was, checks in the Rulau collection show they changed bankers to City Bank 1849-1851 and Nassau Bank 1853. Throughout Bell's check-writing career, he used the odd "5mo 16 1849", "6mo 27 1850" etc. to indicate 5th month (May) connected to the date of the month.

The style became Abraham Bell & Son 1849-53 and in the latter year his address is given as 25 Park Row.

"Pay to acceptances or Bearer" in fact constituted a negotiable instrument. Included in this section to add some financial details of the HT era.

KITCHEN CABINET BANK

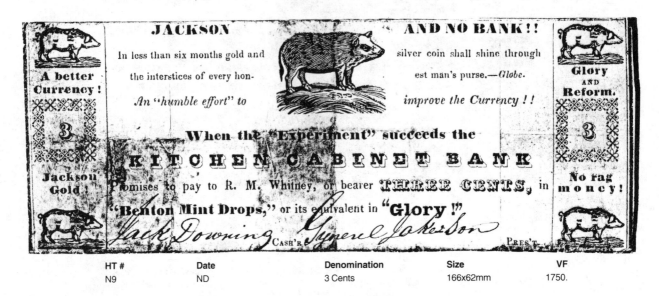

HT #	Date	Denomination	Size	VF
N9	ND	3 Cents	166x62mm	1750.

SULPHUR PUMP, DROVERS' AND HOG BANKING INSTITUTION
Baltimore, Md.

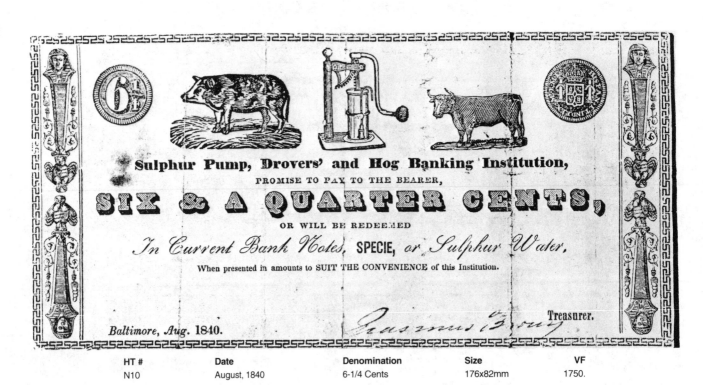

HT #	Date	Denomination	Size	VF
N10	August, 1840	6-1/4 Cents	176x82mm	1750.

THE ELTONIAN KOMICK BANK
New York, N.Y.

HT #	Date	Denomination	Size	VF
N11	1837	6 Cents	189x95mm	300.

Product of Oliver, printer, 28 Cribstone (?) St., N.Y. References on note are to Elton's Comic Almanac for 1838, and addresses 134 Division St. and 68 Chatham St. (Smithsonian Institution collection)

RAG BANK OF THE UNITED STATES
Philadelphia, Pa.

HT #	Date	Denomination	Size	VG
N12	May 10, 1834	$5	185x61mm	1750.

This note satirizes the Tories of the 1770's, the flow of U.S. silver to Europeans (Jews) to pay interest, Henry Clay, John C. Calhoun, Nicholas Biddle and the Whig Party. It is a reminder of the "Anti-Masonic Party" movement of that period, according to Dr. Alan York, a specialist in the satirical scrip of the Jacksonian period.

Branch Lexington is Lexington, Ky, American System refers to Henry Clay, perennial unsuccessful candidate for the presidency.

THE GLORY BANK
Washington, D.C.

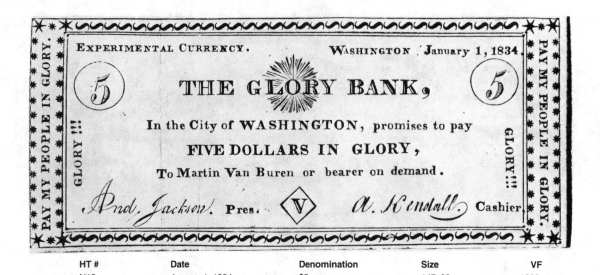

HT #	Date	Denomination	Size	VF
N13	January 1, 1834	$5	147x62mm	1300.

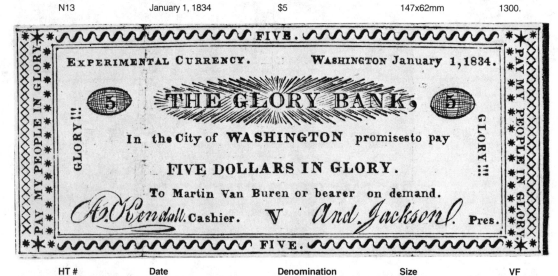

HT #	Date	Denomination	Size	VF
N14	January 1, 1834	$5	146x61mm	1300.

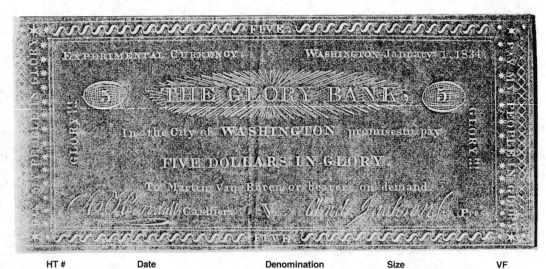

HT #	Date	Denomination	Size	VF
N15	January 1, 1834	$5	143x62mm	1300.

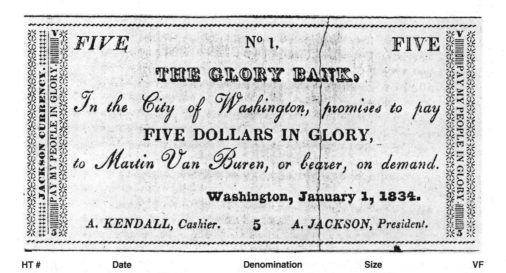

HT #	Date	Denomination	Size	VF
N16	January 1, 1834	$5	122x62mm	500.

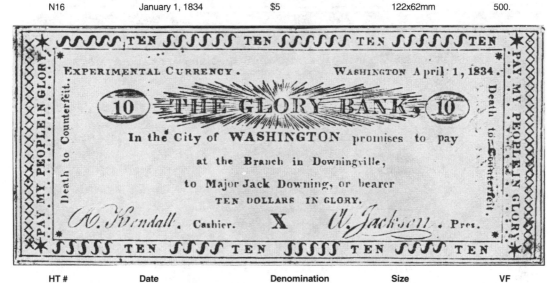

HT #	Date	Denomination	Size	VF
N16A	April 1, 1834	$10	144x62mm	1500.

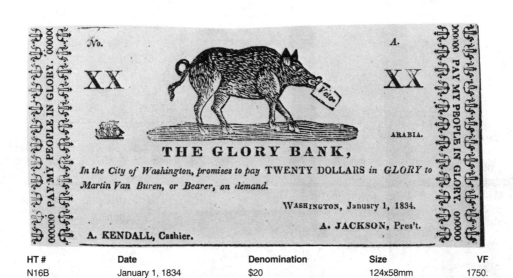

HT #	Date	Denomination	Size	VF
N16B	January 1, 1834	$20	124x58mm	1750.

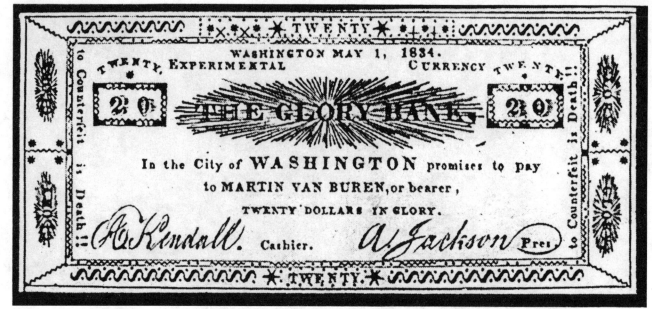

HT #	Date	Denomination	Size	VF
N 16M	May 1, 1834	$20	144x62mm ?	500.

(R. M. Smythe June 16, 2000 Memphis, Tenn. sale, lot 2180, estimated in about VF at $250-$500.
The cataloger was evidently unaware that this **unpublished** satirical note was part of the rarities listed in this Hard Times section.)

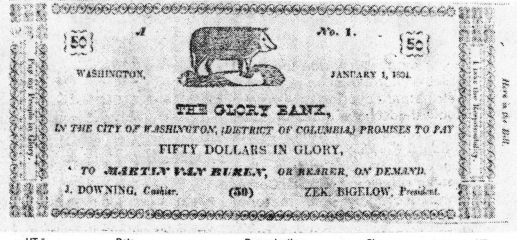

HT #	Date	Denomination	Size	VF
N16C	January 1, 1834	$50	140x57mm	200.

HUMBUG GLORY BANK

HT #	Date	Denomination	Size	VF
N17	1834	5 Cents	141x57mm	1600.

HT #	Date	Denomination	Size	VF
N18	August 21, 1837	6 Cents	162x70mm	1800.

Product of H.L. Winslow, New York. A surviving specimen has in ink on its blank reverse: "To Franky dear —to get a nipper with —"

9 Specimens known, on either white or yellow paper.

N18 has sales records to $1,000 in VF. In 1995 a torn & repaired Good specimen, trimmed, fetched $500!

B&M March 2000 Lindesmith sale, lot 1166 in VG, ex-ANA 1956, realized $1454.75.

HT #	Date	Denomination	Size	VF
N18A	1834	6 Cents	159x70mm	1500.

As 18, but imprint line at bottom, beginning 'Entered according to Act of Congress.' is missing from the printing plate. (Bill Noyes collection)

HT #	Date	Denomination	Size	F
N19	1834	10 Cents	142x58mm	1750.

NATIONAL CURRENCY
Washington, D.C.

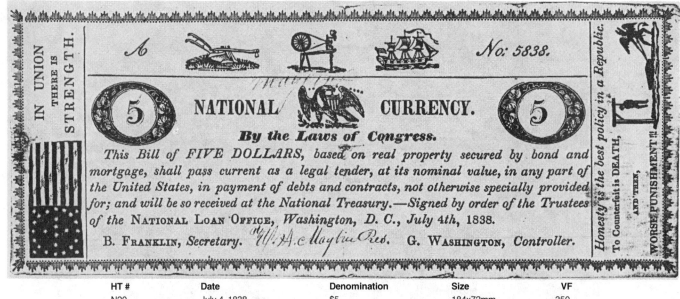

HT #	Date	Denomination	Size	VF
N20	July 4, 1838	$5	184x72mm	350.

This note actually appeared in 1834. Eric P. Newman has discovered that this note is not satirical at all, but a genuine proposal for a national currency in paper form. Its prototype was pasted into a pamphlet entitled "An Entire New Plan for a National Currency Suited to the Demands of this Great, Improving, Agricultural, Manufacturing & Commercial Republic," by Thomas Mendenhall (Philadelphia, 1834). A copy of the pamphlet is in the Newman collection. At least 4 known.

GREAT LOCOFOCO JUGGERNAUT

HT #	Date	Denomination	Size	VF
N21	ND	12-1/2 Cents	191x79mm	2500.

Note N21 — Great Locofoco Juggernaut — was designed and printed in 1837 by satirist/[artist David Claypool Johnston (1798-1865). Johnston engraved banknotes and stock certificates for Tanner Kearney & Tiebout of Philadelphia 1815-19 and New England Banknote Co. of Boston circa 1835. It is known he engraved the $100 and $500 notes of Ohio Exporting & Importing Co. of Cincinnati (1816-17) and the $1, $2, $3, and $5 notes of Oriental Bank of Boston (1835).

Johnston caricatured Andrew Jackson beginning with the 1824 presidential race, and Martin Van Buren during 1837-41, and Jefferson Davis in 1861. He taught art from about 1840 until 1861.

HT #	Date	Denomination	Size	VF
N21A	ND (1837)	12-1/2 Cents	198x84mm	2500.

As N21, but imprint line added bottom center: 'Eng'd by the Locofoco Shinplaster engraving Co'. Printed on flimsy onion-skin paper similar to banknote paper of the period, and on heavy stock white paper.

HT #	Date	Denomination	Size	VF
N21B	ND (1971)	12-1/2 Cents	198x84mm	200.

Reprint by Woodbury & Co., Worcester, Mass., from original copperplate engraving in collection of American Antiquarian Society of Worcester, Mass. A total of 1,950 specimens were printed on 8-1/2 x 11 inch sheets of high quality white bond paper, unwatermarked. Price of 21B includes the book with which issued; an auction price of $650 was recently achieved!

SHIN PLASTER

(Illustration greatly reduced)

HT #	Date	Denomination	Size	VF
N22	May 10, 1837	50 Cents	432x304mm	400.

Product of H. R. Robinson, 52 Cortlandt St., New York. This item was lot 2974 in the June 19, 1986 NASCA sale. At least three specimens known.

ROGO VILO DISHONESTO ASSOCIATO

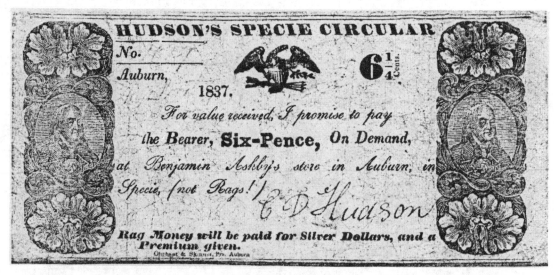

HT #	Date	Denomination	Size	VF
N23	1841	$5	165x62mm	750.

Product of H. Young, Passyunk Rd. and Shippen St. Only a single specimen reported, by Robert Vlack.

HT #	Date	Denomination	Size	VF
N23A	1842	$5	165x62?	800.

Similar to N23, but dated 1842, and the vignettes at right are altered. (Stack's Jan. 1999 sale, lot 866, described as Fine, realized $776.25)

HUDSON'S SPECIE CIRCULAR
Auburn, N.Y.

HT #	Date	Denomination	Size	VF
NA23	1837	6-1/4 Cents	147x66mm	2000.

Satirical scrip for either 6-1/4 cents or 6 pence sterling, the latter a reference to English bankers holding a large share of control over Biddle's Bank of the United States. (Dr. Alan York coll.)

CORPORATION LOAN

Philadelphia, Pa. with satirical overprint on reverse

HT #	Date	Denomination	Size	VF
N24	May 20, 1837	10 Cents	145x58 mm	1500.

Overprinted on reverse with faces and hogs to resemble Jackson and Van Buren. "In a pig's ass" is meant.

HICKORY DOLLARS

Philadelphia, Pa.

HT #	Date	Denomination	Size	VF
NB24	May, 1837	$3	124x60mm	2000.

Andrew Jackson was known as "Old Hickory" and James K. Polk as "Young Hickory."

SUCKER INSTITUTION
Guard Wall, Pa.

HT #	Date	Denomination	Size	VF
N25	July 22, 1837	10 Cents	145x56mm	2200.

Only reported specimen was in the Robert J. Lindesmith collection, Dayton Wash., ex-Stack 1956 ANA. No explanation for "Guard Wall" has been advanced.

B&M March 2000 Lindesmith sale, lot 1167, in VF realized $2,777.25. The same note fetched $2,185. in the March, 2001 Stack's Americana sale.

All wording and signatures have a subtle warning effect against worthless shinplaster notes.

OYSTER HOUSE
Pine Ward, Philadelphia, Pa.

HT #	Date	Denomination	Size	VF
NA26	(ca 1837)	6-1/4 Cents	135x65mm	300.

HT #	Date	Denomination	Size	VF
N26	May 16, 1837	10 Cents	146x63mm	1300.

NOTE: 102 Spruce Street was the back entrance to the Bank of America in Philadelphia.

Illustrated above is a specimen of HT N26, similar in every respect to the note illustrated just before it, except that this note is in finer state of preservation, hand-numbered 191 in ink, on which has been written (below word QUAKERS at left center): Chapman Bros. It must be presumed this was appended by S. H. & H. Chapman of Philadelphia in the 1880's or later. The note was valued at $1,000-plus in the Kirtley March 10-14, 1998 sale, lot 1098.

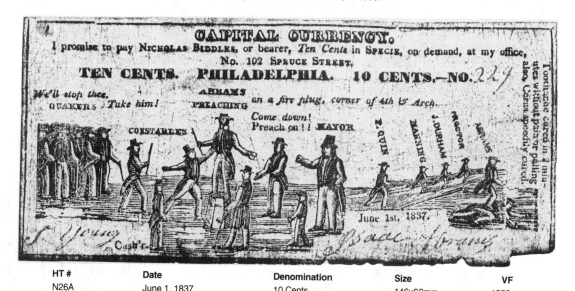

HT #	Date	Denomination	Size	VF
N26A	June 1, 1837	10 Cents	146x63mm	1550.

Similar to N26, but CAPITAL CURRENCY at top center, and different issue date. (Dr. Alan York coll.)

HT #	Date	Denomination	Size	VF
N26B	May 15, 1837	10 Cents	141x67mm	1550.

Similar to 26, but 'I promise to pay A. B. or order' in place of 'I promise to pay Nicholas Biddles, or bearer' at top left.

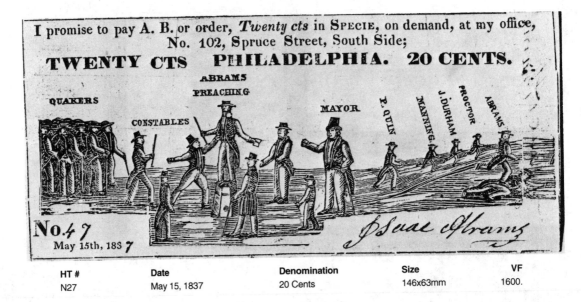

HT #	Date	Denomination	Size	VF
N27	May 15, 1837	20 Cents	146x63mm	1600.

DR. FAUSTUS
Philadelphia, Pa.

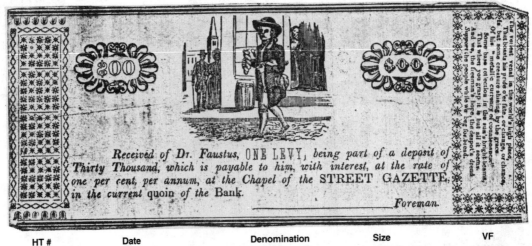

HT #	Date	Denomination	Size	VF
N28	(ca 1837)	1 Levy	140x59mm	1600.

This is a Hard Times period satirical note with anti-Semitic connotations issued by an association of printers. The vignette is of a penniless Benjamin Franklin arriving in Philadelphia.

The note compares not so subtly a Jew to the devil, as those who control hard currency. The reference to "chapel" is both to the organization of printers and a Jewish place of worship, and the word "levy" as both a tax and Jewish name.

The word "quoin" refers both to a printer's typelock and is a play on the name Cohen. The unravelling of the anti-Semitic references is courtesy of Dr. Alan York, East Hampton, N.Y., who discovered this note.

PRINTERS BANK
Philadelphia, Pa.

HT#	Date	Denomination	Size	VF
N28C	(ca 1837)	1 Dime	—	400.

Similar to N28 with Franklin vignette. Oval vignette at left depicts jugate Guttenburg, Fust and Shoeffer. Printers Bank.

JOBSTOWN, NEW JERSEY

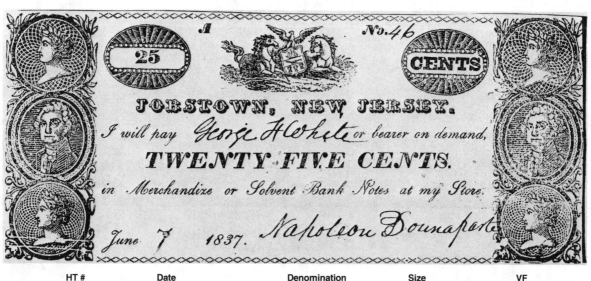

HT #	Date	Denomination	Size	VF
N29	June 7, 1837	25 Cents	159x66mm	1100.

HARD TIMES AND PLENTY OF MONEY
Texas

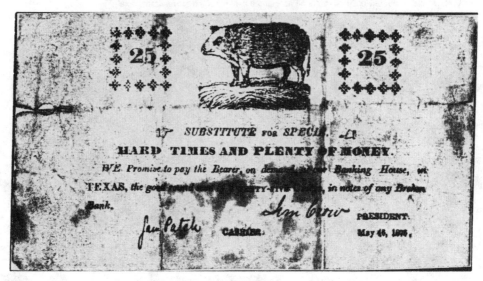

HT #	Date	Denomination	Size	VF
N30	May 16, 1876	25 Cents	125x69mm	500.

Though dated 1876, this is clearly an 1837 product. In 1837 Texas was independent, not part of the United States or Mexico. It seems that the signatories, 'Jam Patch' and 'Jim Crow,' would pay off this note only in faraway Texas 39 years after issuance! All part of the satirical nature of the scrip. (Smithsonian Institution collection)

"Jam Patch" may refer humorously to "Dan Patch," the most famous race horse of the period.

CUSTIS' BAR
Vicksburg, Mississippi

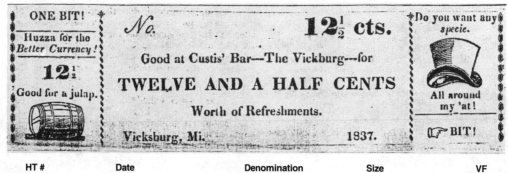

HT #	Date	Denomination	Size	VF
NA31	1837	12-1/2 Cents	138x40mm	1750.

One Bit = 1/8 Spanish dollar = 12-1/2 Cents. Julap = Julep.

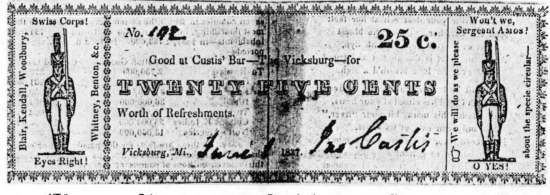

HT #	Date	Denomination	Size	VF
N31	June 1, 1837	25 Cents	147x48mm	1250.

HT #	Date	Denomination	Size	VF
N32	1837	25 Cents	138x50mm	950.

"Sergeant Amos" is Amos Kendall. The reference "Swiss Corps" is to the Pope's Swiss Guard, satirizing U.S. Army and state militia uniforms of the day. (Dr. Alan York coll.)

BANK OF SPECIE PAYMENTS IN GRAND TARTARY
Constantinople

HT #	Date	Denomination	Size	VF
N42	1839	10 Cents	?	1450.

Engraved note. Though lacking imprint, it is believed printed by Manly and Orr of Philadelphia. The cataloger reasoned that "Grand Tartary" and "Constantinople" harkened back to the Barbary Pirates naval actions of 1801-05, but there is doubt on this point. "Tartary" referred to Russia, not North Africa. In any event, solving the mystery of this puzzling satire should prove interesting,

MANSION HOUSE
Vicksburg, Mississippi

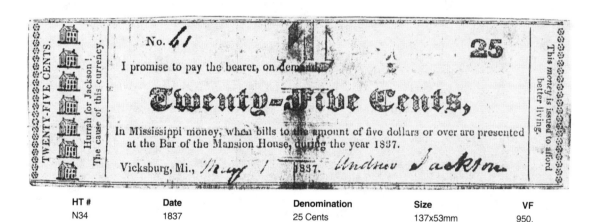

HT #	Date	Denomination	Size	VF
N34	1837	25 Cents	137x53mm	950.

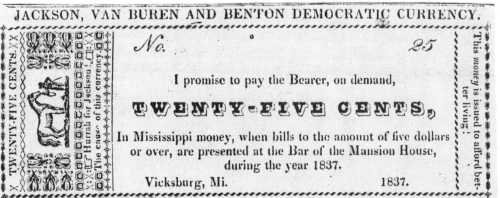

HT #	Date	Denomination	Size	VF
N35	May 1, 1837	25 Cents	148x46mm	2000.

"Mississippi Money" is paper money of state (not federal) banks. N34 was lot 622 in the Nov. 1979 NASCA Brookdale sale.

BAR OF THE SHAKSPEARE
Vicksburg, Mississippi

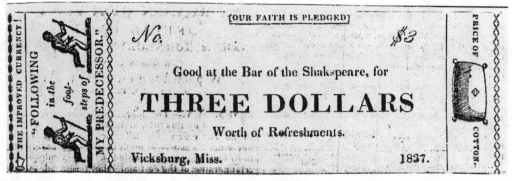

HT #	Date	Denomination	Size	VF
N37	1837	$3	138x46mm	1750.

Runaway slaves at left, cotton bale at right. See HT tokens 31-33 for a motto similar to that on this note near the slaves.

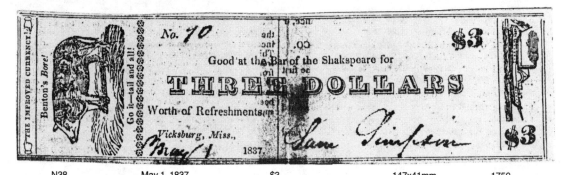

N38	May 1, 1837	$3	147x41mm	1750.

"Benton's Bore" (boar) refers to Thomas Hart Benton at left. This note was lot 623 in the Nov. 1979 NASCA Brookdale sale. (Dr. Alan York coll.)

PORT CARBON SAFETY FUND SOCIETY
Port Carbon, Pa. with satirical overprint on reverse

HT #	Date	Denomination	Size	VG
N39	Sept. 7, 1837	5 Cents	149x64mm	250.

Regular 5-cent note overprinted on blank rev. with two striding hobos labeled VAN BUREN, and hobo astride a milk cow labeled VAN BUREN RIDING HIS COW. The only known specimen, in Chester Krause coll., ex-Neil Shafer, is unsuitable for photography.

BLUE CLAY BANKING CO.
Bath, N.Y.

HT #	Date	Denomination	Size	VF
N40	April 1, 1830	$10	158x65mm	1100.

"Blue Clay" was one of the many pejorative appellations applied to wildcat bank notes, others being Red Dog, Blue Pup, Rag-Tag, Brindle Pup and Stump Tail. "Dangerous Fund" refers to the newly established safety fund of the New York State banking department (1829-1866), which became the safest banking system in the country. "Tan-Town" refers to areas inhabited by newly emancipated slaves in New York State.

The cashier's name, Obadiah Sopps, was an old monicker for bribe-takers. (Dr. Alan York coll.)

KNOWN ENGRAVERS / PRINTERS OF SATIRICAL NOTES

E. W. Clay	?	?
David C. Johnston	Boston (1825-61)	NA21
Oliphant & Skinner	Auburn, NY (1837)	NA23
Oliver	New York (1837)	N11
H. R. Robinson	New York (1837)	N22
H. L. Winslow	New York (1837)	N18
H.Young	Philadelphia (1841)	N23

Bibliography

Adams, Edgar H., "Benedict & Burnham." In *The Numismatist* for Nov. 1912.

Adams, Edgar H., "United States Store Cards." New York, 1920.

Adams, Edgar H., "J. M. L. & W. H. Scovill." In *The Numismatist* for July 1912.

B&M. Bowers & Merena sale catalogs, various. Wolfeboro, N.H.

B&M95. Bowers & Merena Galleries sale of April 28, 1995. (Small select group of HTT's at fixed prices)

Barrett, Walter, "The Old Merchants of New York." New York, 1862 (Reprinted 1885)

Belden, Louise Conway, "Marks of American Silversmiths in the Ineson-Bissell Collection." Winterthur, Del., 1980.

Britten, F. J., "Old Clocks and their Makers." 4th edition, London, 1919.

Brunk, Gregory G., "American and Canadian Countermarked Coins." Rockford, Ill., 1987. (Also copyrighted, unpublished revisions, 1993 and 2001)

Clain-Stefanelli, Elvira and Vladimir, "Two Centuries of American Banking." (Washington, D.C., 1975)

Coin World for Jan. 11, 1989, pg. 36. (B&M NASC auction)

Coombe, Philip W., "The Howell Works Company Scrip and Tokens." In *The Numismatist* for May 1991.

Cotterell, Howard H., "Old Pewter, Its Makers and Marks." London, 1929.

Cox, Wesley S., unpublished manuscript on Hard Times token die variations, die-link studies and history of HT makers, in eight notebooks, 1997-2001.

DeWitt, J. Doyle, "A Century of Campaign Buttons 1789-1889." Hartford, Conn., 1959.

Dillistin, William H., "Bank Note Reporters and Counterfeit Detectors." New York, 1949.

Doty, Richard G., editor, "The Token: America's Other Money." American Numismatic Society, New York, 1995.

Duffield, Frank, "A Trial List of Countermarked Modern Coins of the World." In *The Numismatist* for 1919-1922 (with supplements)

Forrer, Leonard, "Biographical Dictionary of Medallists." London, 1904-1930.

Fred. Bowers & Merena Fred/Ward auction of Nov. 13-14, 1995. (Offered 144 Feuchtwanger 1 and 3-cent tokens)

Fuld, Melvin and George, "Anti-Slavery Tokens." In *The Numismatist* for 1957.

Fuld, Melvin and George, "The Token Collectors Page." Articles in *The Numismatist* beginning Jan. 1951.

Garrett. Bowers & Ruddy Galleries sale of the Johns Hopkins University's John Work Garrett collection, Part 2. Los Angeles, 1980.

Gold Medal. Presidential Coin & Antique Co. sale of the Gold Medal collection, Lanham, Md., Dec. 14, 1991.

Hard Times. Auction sale of the Gregory Heim, Chester Krause and "Hoosier" collections of Hard Times tokens, by Presidential Coin & Antique Co., March 20, 1999 at Baltimore, Md.

Hartzog. World Exonumia Sale of June 29-30, 1999. Rockford, Ill.

Hayden, Steve. Mail bid sale of May 26, 2001, Mauldin, S.C. Civil War, Hard Times, Pan-American Expo items in 1067 lots.

Hayward, John, "The New England Gazetteer." Boston, 1839.

Jacobs, Carl, "Guide to American Pewter." New York, 1957.

Jenkins, Stephen, "The Greatest Street in the World, Broadway." New York, 1911.

Johnson, Malcolm, "Great Locofoco Juggernaut." Barre, Mass., 1971.

Kagin, Donald, "Hard Times Tokens and their Significance." In *Journal of Economic History* ca. 1984.

Kenney, Richard D., "Early American Medalists and Die-Sinkers." New York, 1954.

Kirtley, Charles E. Various exonumia sale catalogs 1986-2001. Elizabeth City, N.C.

Korin-Ford. Sale catalog of Harold Korin and John J. Ford Jr. collections by Stack's Inc., New York, Sept. 8-9, 1993. (Included 14 South Carolina slave tags)

Kovel, R.M. & T.H., "A Directory of American Silver, Pewter and Silver Plate." New York, 1989.

Krueger, Kurt R. Sale catalog of 6125 lots, Iola, Wis., April 16, 1991.

Lindesmith, Robert J., "Edward Hulseman, Hard Times Token Engraver." In *TAMS Journal* for Dec. 1968.

Lindesmith. Bowers & Merena sale of the Linde-smith-LaRiviere collections, Nov. 11-13, 1999. Baltimore, Md.

Low, Lyman H., "Hard Times Tokens." New York, 1899. (Supplement 1906). Reprints 1955, 1977, Adams' prints 1980.

Marburg, Theodore F., doctoral thesis on button and token making in America, copyrighted 1945 in Nebraska but unpublished.

Mayer, Werner G., "Riley's Fifth Ward Museum Hotel." In *TAMS Journal* for June 1978.

McSorley. Charles McSorley collection of political campaign tokens, sold by Presidential Coin & Antique Co., July 10-11, 1998 at Newark, Del.

Middendorf. Presidential Coin & Antique Co. auction of the J. W. Middendorf collection. Lanham, Md., Dec. 8, 1990.

Miller, Donald M., "A Catalogue of U.S. Store Cards or Merchant Tokens." Indiana, Pa., 1962.

Moore, Waldo C., "A. Loomis and his Store Cards." In *The Numismatist* for Feb.1913.

Newman, Eric P., "The Promotion and Suppression of Hard Times Tokens." Festschrift for Catholic University of Louvain, Belgium, 1988; published in full in ANS' COAC 1994 (see Doty above).

Rainwater, D.T. and Redfield, J., "Encyclopedia of American Silver Manufacturers." 4th edition, Atglen, Pa., 1998.

Raymond, Wayte, "List of New York City Store Cards Struck in the Hard Times Period." In *The Numismatist* for Dec. 1928.

Rulau, Russell, "Additions to Hard Times Merchant Cards." In *TAMS Journal* for 1961 and 1963-64.

Rulau, Russell, "Coin Dealer Used Tokens for Commentary." In *Numismatic News* for July 18, 2000. (Elder Hard Times imitations)

Rulau, Russell, "The Coppersmith Directory." Unpublished manuscript, 2001.

Rulau, Russell, "The Clockmakers Directory." Unpublished manuscript, 2001.

Rulau, Russell, "Standard Catalog of United States Tokens 1700-1900." 3rd edition, Iola, Wis., 1999.

Satterlee, Alfred H., "An Arrangement of Medals and Tokens Struck in Honor of the Presidents of the United States, and of the Presidential Candidates from the Administration of John Adams to that of Abraham Lincoln." 1862.

Schweich, Thomas, "Hard Times Tokens, Relics of Jacksonian America." In *The Numismatist* for Feb. 1981.

Sellers, Frank M., "American Gunsmiths." Highland Park, N.J., 1983.

Singleton, Theresa A., "The Slave Tag: An Artifact of Urban Slavery." In *Journal of Archaeological Society of South Carolina* for 1984.

Smythe. Memphis, Tenn. auction of paper money, 2949 lots, by R. M. Smythe & Co. of New York, June 16, 2000.

Sotheby's. Auction sale of the Captain Zabriskie collection of early tokens by Sotheby's, June 25-26, 1999 at New York City.

Steinberg. Stack's Inc. auction of the Gil Steinberg collection, New York, Oct. 17, 1989.

Tainter, John S., "History of United States Bank Notes, 1782-1865 Era." In *Numismatic Scrapbook Magazine* for 1968-69;

Tice, Warren K., "Uniform Buttons of the United States 1776-1865" Gettysburg, Pa., 1997.

Ulex. Adolph Hess Successors auction of the Georg F. Ulex-Hamburg collection. Frankfurt am Main, 1908. (Reprint Richardson, Texas, 1981)

Van Ormer. Auction of the Roy Van Ormer collection by Bowers & Merena Galleries, Wolfeboro, N.H., 1985.

Vattemare, Alexandre, "Numismatique des Etats-Unis d'Amerique. Pieces Taractiques." In *Revue Numismatique* for 1864, pgs. 59-68, Paris, France.

Wright, Benjamin P., "The American Store or Business Cards." In *The Numismatist* for 1899-1901. (Reprints 1963 et seq.)

Wurtzbach, Carl, "New Varieties of Hard Times Tokens." In *The Numismatist* for March 1910.

NOTE: There are also many references cited in this catalog itself, which should prove helpful to the user. These references often pertain to a single token or series.

INDEX

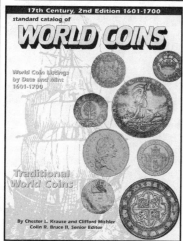

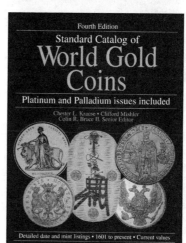

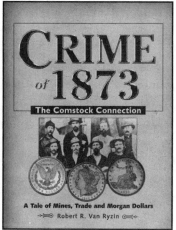
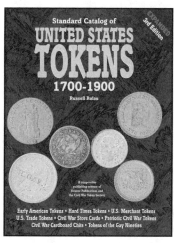

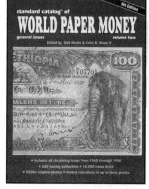
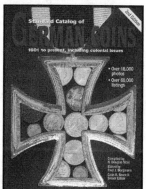